STAGING THE NORTH

TWELVE CANADIAN PLAYS

Edited by

**SHERRILL GRACE, EVE D'AETH,
and LISA CHALYKOFF**

Staging the North: 12 Canadian Plays © Sherrill Grace, Eve D'Aeth and
Lisa Chalykoff Copyright 1999.
Each play in this collection is copyrighted in the name of the author whose
name appears on the appropriate play.
"Degrees of North: An Introduction" © Sherrill Grace,1999.
Introduction to each play is the property of the author/editor of the piece.

Playwrights Canada Press
54 Wolseley St., 2nd fl. Toronto, Ontario CANADA M5T 1A5
Tel: (416) 703-0201 Fax: (416) 703-0059
e-mail: cdplays@interlog.com   http://www.puc.ca

**We acknowledge the support of The Canada Council for the Arts
for our publishing programme,
and the Ontario Arts Council.**

Cover art by Armand Tagoona.
Cover design: Jodi Armstrong

Canadian Cataloguing in Publication Data

Main entry under title:

Staging the North: 12 Canadian plays

ISBN 0-88754-564-5
I. Canadian drama (English) - 20th century.* 2. Canada, Northern – Drama.
I. Grace, Sherrill E., 1944-   II. D'Aeth, Eve. III. Chalykoff, Lisa

PS8309.N67S72 1999   C812'.5408032719   C98-931304-2
PR9196.7.N67S72 1999

First edition: May, 1999.
Printed and bound by Hignell Printing at Winnipeg, Manitoba, Canada.

FOR

RICHARD, MATT, and JOHN

iv

TABLE OF CONTENTS

Acknowledgments

The editors would like to thank the playwrights for permission to include their plays in *Staging the North* and for their enthusiastic interest in this project. We would also like to thank the Tagoona family for permission to use Armand Tagoona's drawing on the cover, Actors' Equity, and the actors and photographers who gave permission for the inclusion of production photographs. Every effort has been made to contact copyright holders, and the editors and publisher will be pleased to correct any errors or omissions in a reprint of the volume. Special thanks go to Kathy Chung, Louise Forsyth, Amanda Graham, Aron Senkpiel, and Jerry Wasserman for their advice and suggestions on drafts of the introductions, to the Northern Research Institute for financial support, and to Jodi Armstrong for designing a handsome book. This volume would not exist without the support of Angela Rebeiro, who believed in it from the start, and of the Social Sciences and Humanities Research Council of Canada. To Angela and Playwrights Canada Press and the Council, our sincerest thanks. We believe this is a volume of which we can all be proud.

COVER ART & PRODUCTION SHOTS

Cover:

"Drum Dancing" (1975). Drawing by Armand Tagoona, reprinted from *Shadows*, and reproduced with permission. Copyright: Mary Tagoona.

Production Photographs:

Esker Mike & His Wife, Agiluk, with Alexander Diakun as William (left) and David Petersen as Esker Mike (right). Troupe production, Vancouver, February 1972. Photograph: Cheryl Sourkes.

Inuk and the Sun, with Felix Mirbt's puppeteers. Third Stage production, Stratford, August 1973. Photograph: Henry Beissel.

The Victory Point Record, quoted in *Terror and Erebus*.

Ditch, with Greg Kramer as Whitbread (left) and Jonathan Tanner as Hennesey (right). Inkenstink production, Toronto, August 1993. Photograph: Greg Tjepkeme.

Who Look In Stove with Gary Reineke as Jack, Dan Lett as Harold, and Glyn Thomas as Edgar. Alberta Theatre Projects, Calgary, February 1994. Photograph. Trudie Lee

Free's Point, with Philip Adams as Mick. Nakai Theatre production, Whitehorse, February 1996. Photograph: Les Osland.

The Occupation of Heather Rose, with Tamsin Kelsey as Heather Rose. Dinamo Theatre production, Vancouver, September 1989. Photograph: Glen Erikson.

Trickster Visits the Old Folks Home, with Jackie Williams as Anna. Nakai Theatre production, Whitehorse, April 1996. Photograph: Philip Adams.

Colonial Tongues, with Kent Allen as Butch Barnett. 25th Street Theatre production, Saskatoon, September 1993. Photograph: Grant Kernan.

Sixty Below, with Lorne Cardinal as Johnny (left), Kennetch Charlette as Henry (centre), and Gilbert Clements as Big Joe (right). Native Earth Performing Arts production, Toronto, April 1997. Photograph: Vision Quest.

DEGREES OF NORTH: AN INTRODUCTION

Sherrill Grace

When Herman Voaden published *Six Canadian Plays* in 1930 and "dedicated [it] to the north" (xviii), he wanted to encourage the writing of Canadian plays about Canadian subjects and places. He wanted to foster a *Canadian* theatre, and he believed that such a theatre would spring from a desire to dramatize "the north." Voaden did not ask what "the north" meant or where it was because he identified it with the country north of Lake Superior, the country painted by the Group of Seven; it was up and out there; it was, ultimately, for Voaden, synonymous with Canada. Voaden's Canadian theatre would be naturally (he thought) a northern theatre, whether as realist exploration of human relations and social issues, historical romance and adventure recreating actual events, or an experimental "art" theatre with symbolic or expressionist qualities and strong links with music and the other arts (*Six Canadian Plays*, xx-xxiv).

Much has changed since 1930. We now have Canadian theatre with all the types of plays that Voaden envisioned, and many others besides. We have several anthologies of Canadian drama, many presses that publish Canadian plays, and we can see our playwrights' work performed on all the main stages of the country and reviewed in the newspapers. Canadian drama is taught in our schools and universities, studied by scholars, and analysed in an ever-growing secondary literature. So the publication of a new collection of Canadian plays should not be a surprise.

What may come as a surprise is that, sixty-nine years after Voaden's *Six Canadian Plays*, a new volume appears that is "dedicated to the north." But much has changed on this score as well. It is no longer possible to assume that there is a *North* that can be the subject of a Canadian theatre or that can be *staged*. In fact, a number of fundamental questions and assumptions about North and about staging inform and surround this collection, and these must be posed and exposed before I can talk about the plays themselves. To claim that one can put the North on stage is immediately to ask: Whose North? What stage? And these questions open out to reveal others: Which playwrights? Staging for whom? The "true North," like the "we" who guard it in the Canadian national anthem, is a complex, changing, and problematic term.

There are, in fact, almost as many Norths in this volume as in the country, and Armand Tagoona's cover drawing of drum-dancing reminds us of their power. These Norths come to life for us — readers, listeners, audience — in the voices and movements of the story-tellers. Indeed, it is this visual concentration of the basic elements of staging the North that makes Tagoona's image such an apt metaphor for the volume. What

Tagoona shows us is less a staging of the North than the North as a stage on which we can dance, sing, and communicate with each other across time, space, and cultural difference. Tagoona's story-telling-drum dancer is a figure of the playwrights and the characters who take to the stage in this volume and before whom we sit spellbound.

Before saying anything further about this volume, however, I must return to those questions and assumptions because considering the questions and teasing out the assumptions, which underlie any attempt to write plays *about* or *set in* the North, prepares the stage for the plays themselves, highlights what they have in common, underscores the many ways in which they differ, and reminds us of where we have come from since 1930.

* * *

Over the past century and a half, Canadians have consistently thought of themselves as a northern nation. As early as 1869, R.G. Haliburton, lawyer, man of letters, and founding member of the Canada First Movement, lectured publicly on what he saw as *our naturally* northern identity and superiority; his lecture, *The Men of the North and their Place in History*, was reviewed and excerpted in the major papers of the day and published in pamphlet form. Haliburton's ideas of North and Canadian identity were not original, but they were influential, and they can be traced from the 1860s to the present (see Grace, "Re-inventing Franklin"). Haliburton's North of white racial purity, romantic idealism, spiritual inspiration, and masculinist adventure is fundamentally the North of Lawren Harris and the Group of Seven, of Herman Voaden, Grey Owl, and Stephen Leacock, and of more recent thinkers and artists such as W.L. Morton, Glenn Gould, R. Murray Schafer, Margaret Atwood, Aritha van Herk, and Judith Thompson.[1] Above all, this North is a southern construction that has little to do with what James Lotz calls "Northern Realities" or Louis-Edmond Hamelin defines, in precise geographical indices, as Canadian nordicity.

There have always been other Norths, of course. Quebec has a long cultural and literary tradition of North as *le pays d'en haut* (see Warwick); W.L. Morton, taking his cue from Harold Innis's study of the fur trade, was the first Canadian historian to put a wider concept of North (which included the northwest and the territories north of sixty), and, thus, of Canada, on our historiographic map; and the Norths of the Klondike Gold Rush, of oil and mineral exploration along the Mackenzie to the Beaufort Sea, and of "Eskimo" art from Baffin Island have steadily expanded the parameters and the images of where and what *North* is and means. Repeatedly, in what I call the discursive formation of North, the dominant culture produces images of North that are creations of a southern imaginary and that serve and legitimize southern needs and interests. What are those billboard ads for beer and mutual funds selling us with their majestic Inukshuks and pristine lakes surrounded by mysterious, untouched pines? And who is *us*? The answers were quite clear in the 1995-96 retrospective exhibition of the Group of Seven, which opened in Ottawa at the National Gallery and travelled to Montreal, Toronto, and Vancouver: according to the sub-title, it was *Art for a Nation, L'Émergence d'un art national* (see Hill). The *us* was southern Canadians, especially those in the national capital and the three major cities strung along the country's southern border, who buy beer and mutual funds or visit galleries. The *what* was national history, pride, identity, and unity as represented by a selection of powerful icons of that identity, the great majority of which depict Canada as North and North as northern Ontario.

The problem, if problem it be, is not that southern Canadians have imagined North in particular ways, usually without having ventured any further north than Algonquin Park or the West Edmonton Mall. As the 1998 ice storm reminded sophisticated, southern, urban Canadians, we are northerners by virtue of our geographical location and meterological reality. There is nothing wrong with these representations: the ads are very clever because they touch us subliminally; the Group of Seven exhibition was expertly mounted and the art shown was excellent. Moreover, these icons of cultural identity, using powerful images of a deeply felt nordicity, contribute directly to the construction of what it means to be Canadian. They function as patriotic reminders to Canadians who have been here for generations and they train newer Canadians to recognize where they are (see Brand). What is sometimes forgotten is that they are *representations* of North and that they do crucial ideological work. As representations, they have great power over our imaginations; we repeat them unconsciously and come to believe in them. As representations, however, they change over time, while maintaining a central core of meaning, and that meaning will work, will be put to work, as long as it resonates in some notion of a shared, public mind.[2]

For many southern Canadians, North has come to signify a place of adventure, and of physical and moral challenge. Wally Mclean, the narrator/philosopher in Glenn Gould's *The Idea of North*, put it very well when he said that the North was "the moral equivalent of war" (liner notes). It is also viewed as a place of spiritual beauty, silence, even transcendence, and of terror — a place of isolation, madness, and death. To the southern mind, the North is a paradox: it is at once empty — with nothing but lakes, rivers, forests, muskeg, taiga, tundra, and ice — and full — full of exotic peoples, caribou, mineral riches, unsolved mysteries, and ghosts. Many southern Canadians fear and dread it, running to the beaches of more southern climes at every opportunity, and yet they cannot live without it because, whether as *terra incognita* or as a hinterland playground for summer holidays, it is there . . . and here.

But North has never been solely the preserve of southern Canada. The Inuit, Dene, Inu, northern Cree, and many other First Nations have occupied the provincial Norths, the territories, and the high Arctic for millennia. Slowly, southern Canadians have come to understand that their imaginary North is not *north* but *home* to these peoples as well as to those Canadians, of many ethnic backgrounds, who have gone north, settled there, and stayed. How that understanding has grown is a story too long for this essay. It reaches back to the 17th century and to a colonial history of exploration and trade, and it is an understanding that is still growing. Northern constructions of North are both older and newer than southern ones, older insofar as they spring from the oral traditions and cultures of indigenous northern peoples and newer insofar as they are now being articulated in ways that make them more accessible south of sixty. Northerners represent their Norths in stories about a way of life, in myths about an ancestral homeland, or in images familiar in the South from sculpture, prints, and other arts. Increasingly, they are representing themselves in magazines like *Up Here*, in radio and television programs made by and for northerners, and in political developments, the most important of which is Nunavut. Northern historians have called for and begun to write a northern history from a northern perspective (see Coates and Morrison). And while this realization may come as a shock, northerners construct representations of the South and of the *us* targetted by those beer ads and national exhibitions (see Freeman, Ipellie, and Highway).

Within the broad distinction between southern and northern representations of North, there are many further distinctions, refinements, and complexities, some of which emerge from the plays themselves. The key point is that North is not a monolithic concept or fixed set of images; Canadians living south or north of sixty, from whatever ethnic and cultural background, imagine a variety of Norths in widely differing geographical areas. Wherever North is located and however it is represented, it is a cultural construction. Being North, going North, imagining North, like staging North, are human activities, and to some degree they contribute to a collective understanding of who Canadians are. The more inclusive and diverse the Norths we construct, the richer will be our image of Canada as *"our* home and native land."

* * *

In his 1977 essay, "Is There a Canadian Drama?" Brian Parker argues that a key reason for the slow development of Canadian theatre is our lack of an appropriate myth. According to Parker, Canada's frontier myth of the North is "antidramatic" (155), and while he accepts the centrality of the North for Canadian identity and recognizes the capacity of poets, novelists, and painters to represent the North, he cannot conceive of a dramatic art that can put such a resistant, non-human landscape on stage. He dismisses early attempts by Voaden, Merrill Denison, and Gwen Ringwood to stage the North or to represent, on stage, the experiences of living in and with such a landscape. But Parker misses the point: North can be and has been staged. The challenge is not the myth, which is highly dramatic, but the audience for which a play is written and the stage upon which it is played.

As Voaden knew, plays about the North can take many forms to enact many different kinds of stories; the subjects are not limited by a northern landscape but embedded in it. What matters is how the drama is presented and where it is situated, whether within the social interaction of individuals, within a historical context, or within a single human mind. To be sure, trying to transplant a detailed forest set or a live dog-sled team to the stage can have disastrous or comic results, but good theatre has never been hobbled by such reductive literalism. More importantly, different stagings create different Norths, and different concepts of acting and production styles necessarily produce different stagings. What may have slowed the development of Canadian theatre is not something inherently antidramatic in the landscape or the myth of North, or in the stories that arise from that mythology, but the inhibiting influence of such demographic and economic factors as theatre spaces, audience size and demand, and the costs of production. Despite these obstacles, however, Canadian drama has flourished over the past sixty years, and a tradition of plays about the North is a component of that growth.

The strongest tradition of northern plays is still one grounded in southern Canada, and its genealogy, to which I will return, begins with Voaden and continues into the 1990s with Thompson's *Sled.* There are alternatives to this version of Canadian theatre history, of course, and they come from theatre companies based in the North. To date, very few of the plays written and produced in the North have been published *down south,* and few of these plays have been produced south of sixty. Over the past fifteen years, the Playwrights Union of Canada has published working scripts of some of these plays. In 1992 two publications appeared that introduced southern readers to northern plays by northern playwrights: *Canadian Theatre Review*'s special issue on the Arctic called *Beast of the Land* (see Cowan and Rewa) and *Writing North: An Anthology of Contemporary Yukon Writers* (see Friis-Baastad and Robertson). In addition to valuable commentary on northern theatre and many splendid production photographs, *CTR* includes scripts by Inuit writers and *Hornby* by Yellowknife playwright Bruce Valpy; *Writing North* includes scripts by Philip Adams, Patti Flather and Leonard Linklater, and Leslie Hamson.

The emergence of a northern tradition is very recent. Nevertheless, there are lessons to learn about Canadian theatre, generally, and about northern theatre, in particular, from comparing the experiences of theatre groups like Nakai in Whitehorse and the Northern Arts and Cultural Centre

(NACC) in Yellowknife. If success is to be measured in productivity and longevity, then Nakai is the northern theatre success story. It began in 1978 as a bottom-up adventure with community and Native roots outside and independent of Whitehorse. From the beginning, it developed a vital tradition of workshopping scripts, training local talent, and sponsoring writing competitions and story-telling festivals. It does not rely on imported plays for its main season or privilege plays by southern Canadian, American, or British playwrights. Moreover, the subjects of Nakai's plays are of local, regional relevance and interest. By big city standards, this philosophy should be the kiss of death, leading audiences and reviewers to sneer: regionalism, parochialism! But on this point NACC's history provides an interesting contrast.

The Yellowknife experiment has faltered and failed. NACC started in 1984 with a great deal of money, a new theatre, and enthusiastic volunteers. However, it soon lost sight of its original stress on local talent and its close ties with the Dene community. It failed to workshop and train. And it put money, time, and effort into mounting imported plays by playwrights with an international reputation (see Francis Thompson, 48-49). NACC tried to create theatre in the North from the top down, and the absence of a play from Yellowknife in this collection suggests that northern Canadian theatre, like Canadian theatre generally, must be home-grown. Among other northern theatre groups, Tunooniq Theatre from Pond Inlet now survives through David Qamaniq, who continues to create community-based scripts about social issues of immediate concern to the Inuit. The Native Theatre Group in Yellowknife and the Igloolik Dance and Drama Group have been less active in recent years, although both are represented in *Beast of the Land.*

* * *

The context for staging the North is complex and multi-faceted. Moreover, it cannot be confined to the theatre. Popular representations of the North, and of Canada-as-North, can be traced well back into the 19th century, but even in this century the genealogy is extensive. Early films used the North as their subject and setting; three examples that come to mind are Nell Shipman's *Back to God's Country* (1919), Robert Flaherty's *Nanook of the North* (1922), and W.S. Van Dyke's *Rose Marie* (1936). As Pierre Berton has told us, this was but the tip of a celluloid iceberg because Hollywood mass-produced hundreds of films about the North or the RCMP.[3]

Radio drama was not far behind film. From the mid-thirties to the late forties, Canadian children were entertained by shows such as *Renfrew of the Mounted*, the all-Canadian *Men in Scarlet*, and the popular *Sergeant Preston of the Yukon*; to the sound of howling blizzards and cries of "Mush," the valiant Sergeant, with his noble dog and horse, pursued his man over the frozen air waves.   By the fifties, Preston had moved to television, where he still performs in Saturday afternoon re-runs.   In 1959, weary of the American bowdlerization of the national symbol,   the CBC introduced a highly popular series called *R.C.M.P.* starring Gilles Pelletier, and *North of Sixty* has had a very successful run through the 1990s (see Warley).   From the early forties, Canadian children have enjoyed northern comic book heroes such as Nelvana of the Northern Lights and North Guard.

None of this material could have influenced the boyhood of Voaden or Denison, of course, but what about later artists and writers?   Did the young Glenn Gould thrill to Sergeant Preston?   Was it radio drama and films, as much as the Group of Seven and maps of Canada's North, that inspired his life-long passion for the North?   And what about R. Murray Schafer, with his *Music in the cold* and *North/White*, in which he brings a snowmobile on stage years before Judith Thompson's *Sled*?   By the time Gould and Schafer were adults, younger generations of southern Canadians had many sources of inspiration about the North in fiction, non-fiction, poetry, National Film Board documentaries, and in real-life dramas about mad trappers, bush pilots, drowned artists (Tom Thomson being the mythic figure) and exhumed corpses on Beechey Island (see Grace, "'Franklin Lives'").   Canadian feature-length films continue to represent Canada-as-North, either by setting their stories in the Arctic (*Never Cry Wolf*, 1983, *Shadow of the Wolf*, 1992, and *Map of the Human Heart*, 1993), or by exploiting northern imagery (*Thirty-two Short Films about Glenn Gould*, 1993).   Judging by our popular culture, novels, and documentaries (see Grace, *Representing North*), Canadians are obsessed with the North, and nothing testifies to that obsession more clearly than our annual search for Sir John Franklin and his missing ships, *Terror* and *Erebus* — a subject explored by two of the plays in this volume.

The historical context for a southern tradition of plays about the Canadian North begins with Voaden in the late 20s and early 30s.   His initial efforts, such as *Northern Song* (1930) and *Wilderness* (1931), were followed by more complex pieces with a stronger plot line (*Hill-Land*, 1934, and *Murder Pattern*, 1936), but all his plays call for the staging of an idealized northern landscape that attracts but overwhelms human beings (see *A Vision of Canada*).   In putting *his* North on stage, Voaden took inspiration from paintings by the Group of Seven, especially those by Lawren Harris and Tom Thomson, and he created sets with stylized rocks, hills, and trees flooded with silver-grey or blue light.   But Voaden was not working in a theatrical vacuum. While the positive influences on his plays included the Group and his own love of wilderness, the negative spur to his art came from Denison, who had published a volume of plays called *The Unheroic North* in 1923.   Denison's characters are crude country yokels or defeated northern Ontario farmers. In *Brothers in Arms*, for example, any remnant of romantic charm associated with a "hunting camp in the backwoods" (*Unheroic North*, 9), where the action takes place, is stripped away to expose it as a "God-forsaken hole" (*Unheroic North*, 10). And yet, when Denison turned his attention to Canadian history, he was drawn by the excitement of northern adventure and the heroics of exploration; his radio dramas on Henry Hudson and Alexander Mackenzie were historical romances such as Voaden called for in *Six Canadian Plays*.

Gwen Pharis Ringwood also wrote plays with northern settings: her classic *Still Stands the House* (1939) is a psychological drama that is inseparable from the northern blizzard that dominates and destroys her isolated, prairie family, and *The Road Runs North* (1967), with music by Art Rosoman, is a celebration of Billy Barker and the 1860s Cariboo Gold Rush in British Columbia. By going as far northwest as the Cariboo or Hudson Bay, Ringwood and Denison moved the parameters for a southern representation of North well beyond Voaden's boundaries. The only subject matter left to explore — or so it must have seemed at the time — was the exotic world of the Inuit, whose culture was introduced to southern audiences and consumers through James Houston's *discovery* and development of "Eskimo" sculpture and print-making in the 50s.

During the late 50s and early 60s, the Inuit and their arctic world were put on stage in some striking ways that, by contemporary standards, seem painfully inept. The most problematic attempt was David Gardner's 1961-62 production of *King Lear* with the Canadian Players. In his desire to promote a national theatre, Gardner sought a primitive Canadian setting for the play and decided to mount an arctic *Lear*, complete with harpoons, mukluks, snow-goggles, arctic sets, and a Fool re-cast as "part seal, part penguin [sic], and part wise, old owl" (Garebian, 152). *The Great Hunger* (1958), by Leonard Peterson, is a white southern Canadian's attempt to dramatize an Inuit family caught between a traditional life-style and Christian teachings, which make little sense in their world. The result is a conventional tragedy interspersed with bits of Inuit myth, legend, and story. Robertson Davies took an entirely different approach to representing the Inuit and the Arctic in *Question Time* (1975), a complex, satiric allegory of Canadian spiritual and political life starring an Inuk Shaman who convinces a Canadian Prime Minister that life is worth living and Canada worth serving, as long as we remember the importance of the North.

A northern tradition of plays about the North may be much younger, but it is no less varied than the southern one. Oddly enough, this tradition, at least as it has emerged in theatre companies like Nakai, has usually heeded Brian Parker's warning about trying to put a northern landscape on stage. A brief comparison of two plays not included in this collection will suggest one reason why northerners often resist this temptation. In *Sled*, Judith Thompson goes to great lengths to specify a number of visual and aural details which, she hopes, will represent North to her southern audience; these include birch trees, the Northern Lights, the semblance of snow, wolf howls and snowy owl hoots, and, of course, the omnipresent "sled" (a snowmobile), suggested, in the production I saw, by simulated headlights and raked "trails." By contrast, Leslie Hamson calls for the simplest of stylized sets, using a scrim and lighting to evoke a feeling of the Yukon bush in *Land(e)scapes* and *Last Rites*. In *Land(e)scapes*, the main set is a cabin, and the sound effects are created by members of the cast using natural objects of wood or stone. Thompson's more elaborate set derives, I suspect, from her need to create an image of an exotic northern locale that her southern, urban audience will recognize as *northern*; Hamson, however, can assume that her northern audience will have no trouble imagining what is all too real in the outdoor world around them.[4]

First Nations and Inuit plays, and here Tunooniq is a fine example, also treat the North as a given. Their primary purpose is education, not entertainment, and the dramaturgy resembles aspects of Brechtian epic theatre. Mimetic representation, as such, is not a concern in a theatre that draws heavily on oral traditions, story-telling, and the physical enactment — or performance — of the story in mime, dance, and song. So deeply is the northern landscape a part of the story being told and of the experiences of the characters/story-tellers, that it demands little representation on stage. As in Tagoona's drawing, the North *is* the stage. *Trickster Visits the Old Folks Home* and the two Tunooniq plays must be read in this light, whereas *Sixty Below*, which combines native myth and story-telling techniques with western dramaturgy, offers a rich and fascinating hybrid theatre experience. In a sense, the southern and northern traditions I have outlined meet and complement each other in *Sixty Below*.

* * *

So far I have focussed on what North can mean, where it can be located, and how a context and tradition for northern drama can be described. But this particular volume exists as a result of many decisions made in the process of understanding how the North might be staged. It results, as well, from the editors' and publisher's shared conviction that the end of the century, with the inauguration of Nunavut, marks a significant moment in the history of the nation, a moment for reflection on the past and an ideal point for contemplating the future. The North is very much on the political, social, and cultural agenda in Canada. A major, state supported exhibition like *Art for a Nation* is part of that agenda. Books about the North — fiction, autobiography, memoir, and history — are as popular as ever, and the centenary of the Yukon Gold Rush has contributed to this renewed interest. Theatre, as this volume demonstrates, also makes an important contribution to this literary, artistic, cultural, political, and constitutional activity.

Inevitably, many worthy plays do not appear in this collection. In addition to earlier plays already mentioned and to plays about the Canadian North by non-Canadians, such as Wilkie Collins' and Charles Dickens' *The Frozen Deep* (1857), there are others we have not included: new scripts by Miche Genest ("The Fasting Girl"), Cristina Pekarik ("Cloudberry"); historical plays, such as Bruce Valpy's *Hornby*, Betty Lambert's play for children about the Cariboo Gold Rush called *The Song of the Serpent*, Edmonton New Heart Company of Artists' script "In the Teeth of the Shore," about the Franklin expedition, and Gerald St. Maur's scripts about Henry Hudson ("Abacuck," and "The Solstice Mutiny"); and musical pieces like *The Shooting of Dan McGrew*, a parodic re-writing of Service's famous poem, with text by John Bertram and music by Jim Betts, or more topical plays like *Running on Frozen Air* about the Yukon Quest dog-sled race, with text by Gordon McCall and music by Cathy Elliott. One of the few Quebecois plays about the far North is Jacques Languirand's *Klondyke*, a lengthy, mock-epic piece with music by Gabriel Charpentier, and there is an older francophone tradition of *pays d'en haut* plays about *coureurs de bois* and historical events, which, like the early anglophone plays, now seem anachronistic (see Dufresne, Ferron, Roux, Savard, and Thériault).

Among works by contemporary Quebecois playwrights, however, there are some powerful plays that might have been included if a quality translation existed. For example, Marie Laberge's *Ils étaient venus pour . . .*, set in the ghost-town of Val-Jalbert in the Saguenay area, is deeply rooted in regional history and language. Françoise Loranger's téléthéâtre piece, *Un cri qui vient de loin*, while visually stunning, is neither meant for the stage nor translated, and Franco-Ontarian Jean Marc Dalpé's award-winning *Le Chien* (translated by the playwright) is set in northern Ontario and has much in common with *Colonial Tongues*. By and large, however, contemporary Quebecois playwrights either do not write about a North or, when they do, that region is abstracted and reduced to the backdrop for a family drama of psychological violence, incest, and artistic rivalry — as in the work of Jeanne-Mance Delisle. For example, the father in Delisle's *Un reel ben beau, ben triste* vents his rage and frustration in a monologue about escaping North, like the voyageurs, while, in Laberge's hands, the North of exploitation and internal colonization, represented by "une ville fantôme" (128), becomes an image of Quebec. Despite their differences, the common ground shared by the *pays d'en haut* and contemporary plays is the construction of a symbolic North as a place for violent, masculine adventure and escape or of bitterness, betrayal, and defeat. This tradition constitutes a subject worthy of another study and another collection.[5]

The plays included in *Staging the North* have been chosen with definite criteria in mind. Each play, we believe, reads well on the page and has had at least one well-received production. Each play has something interesting to say about the theatre — about how to use the theatre and why, about production, dramaturgy, and dramatic subjects. Each play, of course, *stages* a North, and in doing so tells its audience or readers something new about what it is to be northerners — and Canadians.

These plays are about social problems, historical events, and personal conflicts. They offer vehicles for single actors, for two characters, or for a group, and the theatrical styles range from savage social satire in *Esker Mike & His Wife, Agiluk* to poetic lyricism in *Terror and Erebus*. The expressionistic mode of *Free's Point* is ideal for its subject — a man driven mad by his inner demons and the northern bush — and the symbolic, mythic qualities of *Inuk and the Sun* make an Everyman of its hero. There are realist plays here as well, even if they do resist the temptation to recreate a northern landscape on stage — plays about the loss of national identity that are rooted in political and family disintegration (*Colonial Tongues*), or psychological realism that confronts the reader/audience with bitter truths about southern ignorance and indifference (*The Occupation of Heather Rose*), or about hypocrisy in extremity and the necessity of love (*Ditch*). Realism is stripped to its minimalist bones in *Who Look In Stove*, a historical play about the Hornby disaster so understated that it seems to exist, finally, in gesture and silence. Along with *Colonial Tongues*, *Sixty Below* is the most complex and ambitious of the plays collected here. This complexity arises not only from the inter-relations of its characters, but also from the hybridity of its sources, style, and presentation; it is a play that tries to live in two worlds and does a remarkably successful job of it. *Changes, In Search of a Friend*, and *Trickster Visits the Old Folks Home* present southern and northern Canadians with another perspective on North and on theatre; to stage the North in these plays is to tell stories about daily life in the north by enacting them. These are overtly didactic plays in ways that none of the others, not even *Esker Mike* or *Colonial Tongues*, attempts to be.

And yet, despite these differences, a common view of North emerges from these plays with great clarity. North, they tell us, is a topos rich in imagery, story, history, living myth, legends, and ghosts. In fact, of all the possible subjects that I might single out as common to these plays, the one that insists on taking precedence is ghosts: the ghosts of madmen, explorers, past selves, vanished towns, dead fathers and brothers, and unappeased spirits stalk these plays, haunt the living, and dance in the Northern Lights. North is perceived and dramatized as a place of purity and freedom, even when — as is so often the case — purity and freedom collapse into violence, greed, and madness. And it is represented, time and again, as both stunningly beautiful and staggeringly dangerous. It is a landscape of challenge to western concepts of masculinity, and, more broadly, to notions of civilization, truth, and to life itself.

As staged in these plays, North is a landscape of extremity that resists the human need to capture it in words. A significant aspect of such extremity is the challenge it poses to the theatre itself, to language, and to representation. Each of these plays asks fundamental human questions about how we can say what we mean, or make sense of existence *in words* when faced with that extremity, and about how we can represent and embody the distillation of that experience on stage. All the plays gathered here draw upon cultural and social sources to help them in this task, whether from literary intertexts, other plays, myth, music, or political and historical allusions, but in the final analysis, when the lights come up, it is the body, through gesture and voice, that must register and convey the experience, that must remain silent or speak. It is the embodied voice that counts — the words which the dying men in *Ditch* struggle to say aloud, which Edgar in *Who Look In Stove* just barely manages to sound and write, and that Heather throws directly at us in *The Occupation of Heather Rose*. Several of the plays in *Staging the North* use a minimalist style to convey the extremity of the North; *Terror and Erebus*, *Changes*, *Ditch*, and *Who Look In Stove* are the clearest examples of the simplicity and stripped-down quality that I associate with minimalism in the arts. Paradoxically, but fittingly, the less *of* the North they put on the stage, the more they represent — through embodying in performance — that phenomenon, place, or idea an audience can recognize as North.

Cindy Cowan, a southerner who has lived in the North, suggests that the land determines how northerners see themselves (Cowan, 3). If this is so, then staging the North will involve an attempt, at least, to *re*present who we think we are. But *who* is represented in these plays, or, to put the question differently, what is Canadian about them? Perhaps an answer lies in the spare, taut, simplicity of the action, themes, and language, in the emphatic absence of traditional heroes, in the obsession with death and ghosts, in the fascination with history, genealogy, identity, and document, or the rich sub-stratum of myth that comes to the surface in *Inuk and the Sun*, *In Search of a Friend*, and *Sixty Below*. Or perhaps the answer lies in the stern social ethic that informs all of these plays and that couples the meaning of being human with a respect for the land and the people who are a part of it. It is the loss of this ethic that Hardin portrays in *Esker Mike*, that contributes to the failure of Franklin and Hornby, and that sabotages Mick in *Free's Point*.

To my mind, however, it is Butch Barnett, in *Colonial Tongues*, who articulates this ethic most forcefully by reminding us about the cost of forgetting where we are. "We gave it away," he cries:

> This place. The north. We had everything we needed. We could have built a home. But we volunteered to build our own coffins instead. . . . We turned this place into a colony of a colony. (385)

If there is an answer to my question, of course, it will lie in the plays themselves and in the eye of the reader or theatre-goer. Canada is certainly a northern nation, but it also contains many norths. Insofar as the North determines how we define ourselves, then in these plays it is a stage upon which Canadians perform a complex, multiple identity.

---

[1] Atwood, van Herk, and Thompson, as well as Rudy Wiebe and Robert Kroetsch, critique aspects of this myth; however, by reacting to the dominant discourse of North, which they have inherited, they reproduce, while modifying, its semiotics (see Grace, "Gendering Northern Narrative").

[2] The concept and trope of North has been used deliberately to shape a shared, public mind. In the last century, and through much of this, that shaping has been racist, sexist, and exclusionary, but this collection demonstrates that the North can be shared, without excluding individuals or groups on the basis of race, ethnicity, class, or gender.

[3] According to Berton, between 1907 and 1956 Hollywood made 575 films set in Canada. Many were preposterous tales about the Mounties, and all represented Canada as an unspoiled wilderness of trees, ice, and snow (Berton, 51-56).

[4] In the 1994 Tamanhous production of *Land(e)scapes*, Vancouver audiences appeared to have difficulty imagining the northern bush home that Hamson and her characters took for granted. *Last Rites* has not yet been produced south of sixty, but the set for the 1992 Nakai production was a huge abstract mask beneath a semi-circle of branches. In the 1997 Touchstone production of *Sled*, the set was (in my view) a failure because it was too literal.

[5] Quebec plays in which northerness is generalized as winter or as the countryside include: Garneau's *Les Neiges*, Tremblay's *La Maison Suspendu*, where city and country become opposites and the country is associated with a mythic North, and Marie-Claire Blais' *Sommeil d'hiver* (1984), in which a desolate arctic landscape emerges behind transparent scrims to provide the visual metaphor of the play. In the introduction to his translation of Blais' chamber plays, Nigel Spencer notes that the "Nordic sensibility" of these plays is "strong in Quebec writing — though rarely discussed by critics" (10).

Works Cited

Atwood, Margaret. *Strange Things: The Malevolent North in Canadian Literature*. Oxford: Clarendon, 1995.

Bertram, John. *The Shooting of Dan McGrew*. Music by Jim Betts. Toronto: Playwrights Union of Canada, n.d.

Berton, Pierre. *Hollywood's Canada: The Americanization of our National Image*. Toronto: McClelland and Stewart, 1975.

Blais, Marie-Claire. *Wintersleep*. Trans. Nigel Spencer. Vancouver: Ronsdale, 1998.

Brand, Dionne. "Driving North, Driving Home." *Canadian Forum*. Oct. 1998: 30-32.

Brannan, Robert Louis, ed. *Under the Management of Mr Charles Dickens: His Production of* 'The Frozen Deep'. Ithaca, N.Y.: Cornell UP, 1966.

Coates, K.S. and W.R. Morrison. "Writing the North: A Survey of Contemporary Canadian Writing on Northern Regions." Grace. *Representing North*. 5-25.

Collins, Wilkie. See Brannan.

Cowan, Cindy. "Beast of the Land." Cowan and Rewa 3.

— . and Natalie Rewa, eds. *Beast of the Land*. Special Issue. *Canadian Theatre Review* 73 (Winter 1992).

Dalpé, Jean Marc. *Le Chien*. Ottawa: Éditions Prise de Parole, 1987.

Delisle, Jeanne-Mance. *Un reel ben beau, ben triste*. Ottawa: Les éditions de la pleine lune, 1980.

Davies, Robertson. *Question Time*. Toronto: Macmillan, 1975.

Denison, Merrill. *Henry Hudson and Other Plays*. Toronto: Ryerson, 1931.

— . *The Unheroic North: Four Canadian Plays*. Toronto: McClelland and Stewart, 1923.

Dufresne, Guy. *Les Traitants*. Ottawa: Leméac, 1969.

Ferron, Jacques. *Les Grands Soleils*. Montréal: Éditions d'Orphée, 1958.

Freeman, Minnie Aodla. *Life Among the Qallunaat*. Edmonton: Hurtig, 1978.

Friis-Baastad, Erling and Patricia Robertson. *Writing North: An Anthology of Yukon Writers*. Whitehorse: Beluga, 1992.

Garebian, Keith. *William Hutt: A Theatre Portrait*. Oakville, Ont.: Mosaic, 1988.

Garneau, Michel. *Les Neiges*. Montréal: VLB Éditeur, 1984.

Gould, Glenn. *The Idea of North*. 1967. *Glenn Gould's Solitude Trilogy: Three Sound Documentaries*. CBC 2003-3, 1992.

Grace, Sherrill. "'Franklin Lives': More Atwood Ghosts." *Various Atwoods: Essays on the Later Poems, Short Fiction, and Novels*. Ed Lorraine York. Toronto: Anansi, 1995. 146-66.

— . "Gendering Northern Narrative." *Echoing Silence: Essays on Northern Narrative*. Ed John Moss. Ottawa: U of Ottawa P, 1997. 163-81.

— . "Going North on Judith Thompson's *Sled*." *Essays on Canadian Theatre* 16.2 (1998): 153-64.

— . "Re-inventing Franklin." *Canadian Review of Comparative Literature* 22. 3-4 (1995): 707-25.

— , ed. *Representing North*. Special Issue. *Essays on Canadian Writing* 59 (Fall 1996).

Haliburton, R.G. *The Men of the North and their Place in History*. Montreal: John Lovell, 1869.

Hamelin, Louis-Edmond. *Canadian Nordicity: It's Your North Too*. Trans. William Barr. Montreal: Harvest, 1978.

Hamson, Leslie. "Land(e)scapes." Unpublished script. 1997.

— . "Last Rites." *Canadian Theatre Review* 75 (Summer 1993): 55-71.

Highway, Thomson. *Kiss of the Fur Queen*. Toronto: Doubleday, 1998.

Hill, Charles C. *The Group of Seven: Art for a Nation.* Ottawa and
Toronto: National Gallery of Canada and McClelland & Stewart, 1995.

Innis, Harold. *The Fur Trade in Canada: An Introduction to Canadian
Economic History.* 1956. Rev. ed. Toronto: U of Toronto P, 1970.

Ipellie, Alootook. "Ice Box." Cartoon. *Inuit Monthly*, Jan. 1974-Feb. 1975.
Inuit Today, Feb. 1975-Spring 1982.

Kroetsch, Robert. *The Man from the Creeks.* Toronto: Random House,
1998.

Laberge, Marie. *Ils étaient venus pour* . . . . Montréal Boréal, 1997.

Lambert, Betty. *The Song of the Serpent. Boneman: An Anthology of
Canadian Plays.* Ed. Gordon Ralph. St John's, NFLD: Jesperson, 1995.
178-225.

Languirand, Jacques. *Klondyke.* Musique de Gabriel Charpentier. Montréal:
Cercle du livre de France, 1971.

Loranger, Françoise. *Encore cinq minutes et Un cri qui vient de loin.*
Ottawa: Le Cercle du Livre de France, 1967.

Lotz, James. *Northern Realities: The Future of Northern Development in
Canada.* Toronto: New P, 1970.

McCall, Gordon. *Running On Frozen Air.* Music by Cathy Elliott.
Toronto: Playwrights Union of Canada, n.d.

Morton, W.L. *The Canadian Identity.* 1961. 2nd ed. Madison, WI: U of
Wisconsin P, 1972.

Parker, Brian. "Is There a Canadian Drama?" *The Canadian Imagination:
Dimensions of a Literary Culture.* Ed David Staines. Cambridge, Mass:
Harvard UP, 1977. 152-87.

Peterson, Leonard. *The Great Hunger.* Agincourt, Ont: Book Society of
Canada, 1967.

Ringwood, Gwen Pharis. *Still Stands the House.* New York: Samuel
French, 1939.

— . "The Road Runs North." Music by Art Rosoman. Unpublished script
and music, 1967. Ringwood Papers. University of Calgary.

Roux, Jean-Louis. *Bois-Brulées: Reportage épique sur Louis Riel.* Montréal Éditions du Jour, 1968.

Savard, Félix-Antoine. *La Dalle-des-Morts.* Montréal: Fides, 1965.

Schafer, R. Murray. *Music in the cold.* Toronto: Coach House, 1977

— . *North/White.* Score. Toronto: Universal, 1982 .

Tagoona, Armand. *Shadows.* Toronto: Oberon, 1975.

Thériault, Yves. *Le Marcheur.* 1950. Ottawa: Leméac, 1968.

Thompson, Francis. "From Prestige Project to Simply Shell: The Short History of the Northern Arts and Cultural Centre." Cowan and Rewa 45-50.

Thompson, Judith. *Sled.* Toronto: Playwrights Canada, 1997

Tremblay, Michel. *La Maison Suspendue.* Trans. John Van Burek. Vancouver: Talon, 1991.

Valpy, Bruce *Hornby.* Ed. John Rafferty. Cowan and Rewa 60-76.

van Herk, Aritha. *Places Far From Ellesmere.* Red Deer, Alberta: Red Deer College P, 1990.

Voaden, Herman. *A Vision of Canada: Herman Voaden's Dramatic Works, 1928-1945.* Ed Anton Wagner. Toronto: Simon & Pierre, 1993.

— , ed. *Six Canadian Plays.* Toronto: Copp Clark, 1930.

Warley, Linda. "The Mountie and the Nurse: Cross-Cultural Relations North of 60." *Painting the Maple: Essays on Race, Gender, and the Construction of Canada.* Eds V. Strong-Boag, S. Grace, A. Eisenberg, and J. Anderson. Vancouver: University of British Columbia P, 1998. 309-33.

Warwick, Jack. *The Long Journey: Literary Themes of French Canada.* Toronto: U of Toronto P, 1968.

Wiebe, Rudy. *Playing Dead: A Contemplation Concerning the Arctic.* Edmonton: NeWest, 1989.

Esker Mike & His Wife, Agiluk

by

Herschel Hardin

Alexander Diakun as William (left) and
David Petersen as Esker Mike (right).

Herschel Hardin's *Esker Mike & His Wife, Agiluk* is a challenging play. Though it has moments of comic levity, its conclusion is deeply disturbing in its implied criticism of the liberal values non-indigenous Canadians have often relied upon to justify the colonization of Canada's far north by southern cultures and institutions. *Esker Mike* takes a hard look at the notion of a mutually productive dialogue between indigenous and non-indigenous cultures in Canada's North and declares this marriage, like Esker Mike's and Agiluk's, a sham.

There is another sense in which *Esker Mike* is a challenging play. The language Hardin uses to construct his story can leave new readers feeling lost in what seems initially to be a strangely flat linguistic and hermeneutic landscape. Much like the western Arctic's Mackenzie River Delta, where *Esker Mike* is set, this verbal landscape is without obvious distinguishing features to help the uninitiated find their way. But landmarks do appear as the interpretive eye gains familiarity with the surroundings. Careful readers will be rewarded amply by entering into Hardin's quirky, strangely poetic world, a world that is rich in metaphoric nuance, word-play, character-definition, and biting social satire.

Esker Mike was first published by Talonbooks in 1973. Reflecting on the play in 1998, Hardin is pleased about the success with which he was able to weave comic and tragic threads together. In a very real sense, these opposing elements are embodied in the characters of Esker Mike and Agiluk. Agiluk's story comprises the play's tragic component, a component which supports a feminist reading of the play. Agiluk is an Inuk woman who has mothered ten children, eight of whom have survived, and six of whom she has watched depart for Anglican and Catholic hostels in Inuvik. When the bottom falls out of the muskrat-hunting trade by which Esker Mike has attempted to support his family, Agiluk comes to a firm decision — no more sexual contact with Esker Mike until their children "can eat out of their own hands." It is not anger towards Esker Mike that inspires this decision; rather, it issues from the pain and humiliation Agiluk feels at finding herself alienated from the human products of her labours. As she tells her step-sister, "Nobody's to blame, but I can wait."

Esker Mike's response to Agiluk's decision constitutes the play's comic thread. Having lost command of both his means of subsistence and his lover, he reels from the blows to his manly pride. In attempting to recoup this pride, Esker Mike lurches from one potential solution to another — from marriage to Welfare-fraud to entrepreneurship to drunken oblivion, and finally, to rage. But to no avail. His actions garner little sympathy or respect from Agiluk. While the majority of Hardin's satiric ire is focused on the southerners who run Aklavik's religious, governmental and legal institutions, Esker Mike is the play's comic centre. Thus, although his story is poignant when considered objectively, the fact that it is mediated through comedy, and the fact that Esker Mike is unable to express his emotions sincerely, virtually dictate that our sympathies lie with Agiluk. Just as the emotional resonance of satiric comedy is no match for tragedy, so Esker Mike's energy and machismo are no match for Agiluk's strength, intensity and intelligence.

Yet this was not Hardin's original plan. He sat down to write with a plot and a sub-text firmly in place. The plot involved a commercial opportunist travelling north in search of vulnerable people to take advantage of. It was also to draw upon elements of George Buchner's *Woyzeck*, in which a Major from a visiting army wins the affections of the protagonist's mistress, causing Woyzeck to go mad, murder his wife, and drown himself. It was supposed to be Esker Mike's play. So what happened? In a word, Agiluk. Hardin says that she simply wrote herself into the centre of the play. As his emotional engagement with her character intensified, his critical engagement waned until the result surprised even him. "Setting the comic layer aside," Hardin reports, "the play is very close to Greek tragedy" (interview with author, 1 December 1998).

As a tragic hero, Agiluk's refusal to continue without her dignity constitutes her *hamartia*. This admirable conviction constitutes a tragic flaw because Agiluk's circumstances render it unattainable. As a woman living in a world (and a marriage) governed by patriarchal assumptions, and as an Inuk living in a place governed by colonial institutions, Agiluk can only attain this ideal through actions which place her outside of these systems of authority, and consequently, outside the rule of law. In the sense that Hardin sees North not only as a place, but as a metaphor for being on the outside, Agiluk's infanticide precipitates two reciprocal movements. Because this act constitutes an attempt on Agiluk's part to recover some sense of cultural authenticity, it instigates a metaphoric movement from South to North, from colonial to indigenous values. On the literal level, however, this act catalyses Agiluk's movement from North to South, from Aklavik to an Edmonton prison. If, as William predicts at the end of the play, "when the hot summer comes, she'll grow sick, and that will be the end," then Agiluk maintains her integrity, but at the price of her life.

Herschel Hardin has made an impressive and diverse contribution to Canadian culture. His career as a playwright began with *The Great Wave of Civilization* (Talonbooks, 1962). This was followed by *Esker Mike & His Wife, Agiluk* and *William Lyon Mackenzie*, Part I. Having little luck inspiring interest in his plays during a time when Canadian theatres were dominated by American and British works, Hardin turned to other pursuits. He has worked as a freelance broadcaster for CBC Radio and has enjoyed an accomplished career as a writer of non-fiction. Hardin recently returned to drama: in the early 1990s he wrote *The New World Order,* a play in which political figures from the afterworld return to discuss America's global agenda. His most recent publication is *Working Dollars. The VanCity Story* (1996).

L.C.

* * *

Esker Mike & His Wife, Agiluk was first performed at the Factory Lab Theatre in Toronto, Ontario, 4 June 1971.

Esker Mike	Booth Harding Savage
Agiluk	June M. Keevil
William	Russell Case
Oolik	Donna Farron
1st Woman	Jeanette Lourim
2nd Woman	Mary Fleming
Toomik	Ann de Villiers
Minister	William Garrett
Minister's Wife	Jacquelyn Jay
Administrator	Carl Gall
Priest	James Irving
Constable	David Friedman
Sergeant Green	Howard Cronis
Minister of Northern Affairs	Ashleigh Moorhouse
Albert Onchuk	Ashleigh Moorhouse

Directed by Maruti Achanta
Costumes by Shawn Kerwin
Lighting Design by Peter Ottenhoff

ESKER MIKE & HIS WIFE, AGILUK

CHARACTERS
Esker Mike
Agiluk
William
Oolik
1st Woman
2nd Woman
Toomik
Minister
Minister's Wife
Administrator
Priest
Constable
Sergeant Green
Minister of Northern Affairs
Albert Onchuk

In the Shack

A stove. ESKER MIKE and WILLIAM are drinking beer out of bottles. AGILUK is sewing. ESKER MIKE's grievance is real, and felt strongly, but the conversation is mostly comic exaggeration between friends.

ESKER MIKE   This is the truth, the whole truth and nothing but the truth, so help me God. I will now tell you a horrible story. Here I am, Esker Mike, that's fished more credit from the Hudson's Bay Company than any known trapper since A. Mackenzie himself. And Agiluk has decided to stop having children.

WILLIAM   There are other horrible stories, but that is horrible enough. Our race is going to the dogs.

ESKER MIKE   It's an old Eskimo law that women who won't bear children are left behind in a thick snowdrift. During a blizzard if possible. But she insists on staying in the shack.

WILLIAM   I would kick her a few times. I would kick those ideas from the south into the sky.

ESKER MIKE   You can kick her if you want. I can't get close
             enough to smell her, and that's far away. Do you see
             that store needle in her hand? Now look at this hole
             in my arm.

WILLIAM   It's round and deep like an air hole.

ESKER MIKE   The next time I try to jump on her, she is going to
             stick that needle into my neck. Harpooned like an old
             whale. The end of a man widely known in the Delta.

WILLIAM   A long time ago you could trade her in for another
             wife. Like that, she's worthless anyway.

ESKER MIKE   Worthless? Less than worthless. I couldn't get an
             old bitch of a wheel dog for her. I couldn't even sell
             her to the Bay for a pouch of tobacco.

WILLIAM   Problems. These are new problems, and we won't
             solve them. My mother and all her mothers were
             under ten feet of silt in the Delta before they came to
             this problem. Now our women live longer, but the
             men don't like it so much. An old sled wears well,
             but an old woman wears out.

ESKER MIKE   Her head is worn out, but that other part of her isn't.

WILLIAM   That other part must be good for something.

ESKER MIKE   That other part is good for nothing. The muskrats
             don't breed fast enough, she says, and if the muskrats
             don't breed fast, then we don't breed fast.

WILLIAM   That's true. You can rat all spring, until your hands
             are as raw as his underside, and all you get for it is
             another winter, and another child, if you happen to
             live with Agiluk.

ESKER MIKE   I've got enough seed for twenty or thirty myself.
             This country needs population.

WILLIAM   The barren lands. If the women are barren, the land is
             barren. And if the women are fertile, the children are
             barren children. They wander everywhere, and they
             can't do anything but play. Eight children from
             Agiluk, and it's no easier to keep alive now than it
             was after the first one.

ESKER MIKE   I don't let that bother me. I ship them off to Inuvik.
If I can ship the oldest four to Inuvik, why can't I
ship the next four?

WILLIAM   I don't know.

ESKER MIKE   The more the Anglicans get, the more the Catholics
want. And the more the Catholics get the more the
Anglicans want. The market for muskrat goes up and
down but the demand for children in Inuvik is stable.

WILLIAM   Eight Anglicans, just like that!

ESKER MIKE   Eight Anglicans? I wouldn't give all my trade to one
place. *(he empties a box of shells onto the table)*
These shells are my kids. Suzy, who came first, is in
the Anglican hostel. *(he places a shell on one side)*
John, number two, who came second, is going to be
a Catholic. *(he places a shell on the other side, etc.)*
Then Kinga will be Anglican. And Solomon, the
fourth, a Catholic. Or did Igtuk come fourth? Then
Solomon will be Anglican. Hmmmmmm . . . . . .
Maybe Igtuk was third. Do you remember the winter
that Jacob Jacob lost his foot? So Igtuk will be
Anglican, Kinga will be Catholic, Solomon,
Anglican, and Alice, Catholic. Or Alice, Anglican
and Solomon, Catholic. Anyway, the food is just as
good in one place as the other. Between a Catholic
omelette and an Anglican omelette there is no
difference at all.

WILLIAM   Inuvik!

ESKER MIKE   Did you know they heat even their garbage in Inuvik?
That's some place.

WILLIAM   I know that in the hostels the children get a free copy
of the Bible *and* a free picture of Jesus Christ.

ESKER MIKE   They smile at their teachers all day, but since my kids
are part white they don't smile all the time.

WILLIAM   Inuvik is Inuvik. Inuvik is not Aklavik. Aklavik is
sinking into the mud.

ESKER MIKE   Aklavik is a rotten hole. If Agiluk doesn't lie down
              for me tomorrow, I'm going to wreck this shack and
              move out. If that stove explodes again, I'm going to
              trade it in for a good Coleman.

WILLIAM   On a night like this we should go outside in the sun
              and talk about it. Everybody is outside. Why stay in
              here? *(they stand up)*

ESKER MIKE   Ten years ago she wouldn't be so stubborn. She used
              to chink her babies with moss. It holds piss like
              muskeg. You can't beat moss. Now the government
              has taught her how to use diapers. It's put ideas into
              her head.

WILLIAM   *(philosophically)* The only thing to do is to shoot
              her.

ESKER MIKE   If she doesn't change her mind, I'll just give her a
              good hard whack on the head with a two by four.
              Native spruce from the banks!

WILLIAM   A woman on the other side shot her husband. He
              didn't kill enough seals. Then she was very lonely.
              She found a new husband right away. But when there
              were no seals, he was afraid to go home, and camped
              by himself. *(they laugh)* The administrator told us
              that story.

ESKER MIKE   In the Delta, any woman who keeps her legs closed is
              asking for it.

WILLIAM   My grandfather would shoot her, and I would shoot
              her. The judge knows the difference between our law
              and outside law. He's a great man. There would be a
              big trial. I would see all my relatives and we would
              have a good time.

ESKER MIKE   Lucky for you, William, you're not a white man. I
              was born in Moosomin, Saskatchewan. They let me
              eat my blubber raw, but they wouldn't let me do a
              thing like that. They'd take me to Edmonton and
              hang me by the neck.

WILLIAM   I'd tell them the whole story.

ESKER MIKE   What's happening to her, that's what I'd like to know. An Eskimo is only supposed to think a day ahead. She's thinking ahead at least a year. You're not like that, are you?

WILLIAM   No, I only think up to the next boat, and in the winter, I don't think of anything at all.

ESKER MIKE   That's what I thought. *(aloud)* We're going outside to find a cure for your ailment. But I don't know if I'm going to come back.

Exit ESKER MIKE and WILLIAM.

In the Open

OOLIK and AGILUK.

OOLIK   Agiluk. Agiluk.

AGILUK   Oolik. Why are you whispering? It's a warm night and the sun is out.

OOLIK   I'm whispering so the men won't hear me. They said you were crazy. If they know I'm here, they'll say I'm crazy too.

AGILUK   Why should they say that to you, a young and healthy girl with good thighs and no relatives? A certain one wants your warmth. When the time comes, he won't say that.

OOLIK   I have *one* relative.

AGILUK   Yes, a poor step-sister who lets you live alone in a shack as big as a factor's outhouse. And how I became that step-sister only very old men can tell. Listen to me, Oolik. I know it's warm. Go home and try to sleep. If you can't sleep, come to my place and we'll talk. For a girl who's after a boy with a name, talk is the only thing.

OOLIK   You should know.

AGILUK   Why should I know?

OOLIK   If you don't know why, then ask somebody. You can ask the Reverend Smith's little boy and he'll tell you. Esker Mike! Esker Mike and three before him. And now you don't want any more. I won't do it like that.

AGILUK   I did it as I could. Four men and ten children. Eight are still living. I bore them all without so much as a bloodied hand from the father. And I'm bearing still. A woman's work! Esker Mike knows I'm a woman. But no more children. No more children from Agiluk until a man knows what he is. A seal that slips out of his hole and can't get back in!

OOLIK   Agiluk!

AGILUK   When Esker Mike can feed us, then that hole will open up again. Why should my children go to Inuvik? I want them to eat out of their own hands. Nobody's to blame, but I can wait.

OOLIK   You can wait. Crazy whore! Crazy whore!

AGILUK   Who said that?

OOLIK   Esker Mike said that. The men were laughing. They laugh like ghosts, but I can feel that laugh going right through my dress.

AGILUK   Let them say what they want. If the trapping's no good, they have to talk like that. And women are supposed to keep quiet. You live here and you die here and that's all. Aklavik is a man.

OOLIK   Aklavik is a white man.

AGILUK   I took the first one who wasn't afraid of me, and he was white. That's how it was.

OOLIK   Ooof! I pity your children.

AGILUK   *I* pity my children.

OOLIK   You're no mother!

AGILUK   *My* mother was no mother.

OOLIK   To bear a wolverine like you!

AGILUK	A wolverine! She was going to kill me. One girl too many in the camp was like excrement. A bad smell in the tent. But the mission said it was wrong. And after a few days it was impossible. I'm no mother like that. When the time comes, I'll know how to do it.
OOLIK	Stay there. You frighten me. I didn't know you were like that.
AGILUK	How am I like that?
OOLIK	Goodbye.
AGILUK	Then you're not coming to my place.
OOLIK	Esker Mike is coming to your place and I don't want to be there. I don't want to see what's going to happen.
AGILUK	You go home to sleep. What do you know about men, my little Oolik? They can't bring in enough furs. Or they can't get a good price. They go for welfare. On long days like this they like to do something and the women like to do it with them. It's an ordinary thing. But nothing's going to happen to Agiluk.
OOLIK	I won't be there anyway.
AGILUK	If someone decides the days are too long and takes you home from the hall, why bother waiting? There is only one Agiluk, and if she weakens, she will make herself pay for it.
OOLIK	I don't know what you mean. Why don't you talk like everybody else? *(exit OOLIK)*
AGILUK	No more children from Agiluk! *(she looks into the sun)* Esker Mike is somewhere and wide awake. Maybe I'll sleep and maybe I won't.

The Aklavik Fur Co-operative

Two Women sewing outside.

FIRST WOMAN It's a good thing they didn't wreck the churches and go away to Inuvik. Otherwise Esker Mike and Agiluk would be married in the bush.

SECOND WOMAN I was married in a bed of packed snow. It's all the same in the end.

FIRST WOMAN All the same? How can you say that? The Anglican Church in the summer has a nice mustiness. It's a real church smell. You don't get that in winter. All you get is the stink of fuel oil.

SECOND WOMAN When I married, the only stink I wanted to smell was my husband's.

FIRST WOMAN You must have smelled him all right.

SECOND WOMAN I did, and it was the heavy smell of a man. Even when he was out, I could lie under it.

FIRST WOMAN Yes, if you pressed that smell into a bag, it would fall through thick ice.

SECOND WOMAN A sod house kept smells. Living in a shack is different. There's more room, but it's lonelier.

They work silently.

FIRST WOMAN Esker Mike was going to beat her, but marriage is easier than beating Agiluk. There'll be a big crowd today to see what happens.

SECOND WOMAN Not as big as it could be. Summer is a poor season for the church.

FIRST WOMAN It's a good time for weddings. The bride doesn't have to wear leggings underneath her dress.

SECOND
WOMAN   All things considered, the winter is the best time for
                        Christianity. It's long and dark and bitter, and a man
                        is willing to listen to gloomy stories. In the
                        summer, the crucifixion makes me want to vomit.

FIRST WOMAN   *(looking around)* Shhhhh! If the Reverend Smith
                        hears you, he'll invite you to tea. You know what
                        that means.

SECOND
WOMAN   Winter! That's when Christianity comes in handy.
                        Why shouldn't I say it? If you're stuck in a tent
                        during a blizzard, you can sing hymns. It helps to
                        pass the time.

FIRST WOMAN   The flying Methodist from Texas always came in
                        summer.

SECOND
WOMAN   He was a fool. You can't convert an Eskimo in
                        summer. It's too light. A man isn't inclined to stay
                        put.

FIRST WOMAN   He converted Imluk last summer. They carried him
                        into the Great River and that was it. A Methodist!

SECOND
WOMAN   Old Imluk thought he was going to walk again!

FIRST WOMAN   He came out blue all over, but his legs were still
                        dead. He didn't have enough faith.

SECOND
WOMAN   He didn't make the grade.

FIRST WOMAN   It wasn't long before he was dead.

SECOND
WOMAN   Our only Methodist! And how many others are there
                        now in Aklavik? None. That's how we are. If the
                        man from Texas had stayed a winter, he would have
                        had much better results. Making a good convert is
                        like making a good carving. When the bone is hard,
                        you have to hack away for a long time.

                        Enter TOOMIK.

FIRST WOMAN   Hello, Toomik. Aren't you going to the wedding?
It's not every day the Anglican Church has something
on in summer.

TOOMIK   A church to bind Agiluk to Esker Mike? Pah!
There's no church like that! I'm going to meet the
boat.

FIRST WOMAN   The boat won't be here for a week at least. And the
wedding's today.

TOOMIK   I'm going to meet the boat. The Christianity will
come and go but the boat will arrive always. Have
you got a cigar?

FIRST WOMAN   What would we be doing with a cigar? ·

TOOMIK   If you had a cigar, I could tell you a thing or two
about Agiluk and her struggle with the spirits. That
struggle will come to a head . . . . . sometime.
Maybe today. Maybe tomorrow. It's too bad you
don't have a cigar.

Exit TOOMIK.

SECOND
WOMAN   *(singing)* You have lice. You have lice.

FIRST WOMAN   Be quiet!

SECOND
WOMAN   *(continuing)* Some so big you must kill them with a
rock.

She laughs.

FIRST WOMAN   Maybe today. Maybe tomorrow. What did she mean
by that?

SECOND
WOMAN   It was the first thing that came into her head. She
wants a cigar, that's all.

FIRST WOMAN   I wouldn't say that out loud. Anybody who speaks
against Toomik is headed for misfortune.

SECOND
WOMAN   *(as loud as she can)* Toomik steals cigars . . . . . .

FIRST WOMAN   Shhhh!

**SECOND
WOMAN**   . . . . . and sticks the butts in between her loose
floorboards.

FIRST WOMAN   *(shocked)* Sit down. You're lucky if she didn't hear
you. Imluk laughed at her, and the bear mangled his
legs. She could have given them life, but she didn't.

**SECOND
WOMAN**   She could have turned him into a goose with a stench
like that. She washes her hair in urine. It used to be
the style in her day.

FIRST WOMAN   Hold your tongue! Soon it won't be safe to sit with
you.

**SECOND
WOMAN:**   *(screaming)* The demons!

*She pricks the FIRST WOMAN in the behind
with her needle.*

FIRST WOMAN   *(jumping up)* Hooo! The demons!

*The SECOND WOMAN, choking with laughter,
holds up the needle.*

FIRST WOMAN   I wouldn't be surprised if Toomik had a curse on you
right now.

The laughter redoubles.

I don't think it's wise to go to the wedding after all.

The laughter continues.

Outside the Anglican Church

*Wooden folding chairs. Enter TOOMIK from
one side. Vigorous singing of "O God Our Help
In Ages Past" from the other side, offstage.
Then enter from that side ESKER MIKE and
AGILUK, and the congregation of REVEREND
SMITH, MRS. SMITH, SERGEANT GREEN,
the ADMINISTRATOR, FATHER ROGET,
OOLIK, WILLIAM and the SECOND WOMAN,
sprinkling confetti on the couple.*

ESKER MIKE	This is a fine wedding. A wedding as it should be, by God! Only suits and ties here.
MRS. SMITH	That was very nice, Mike. You did well. And you did *right*. A good example for some other squatters.
ESKER MIKE	You can't blame them. They think you're here just to convert Eskimos. They don't know any better.
MRS. SMITH	That's it. But marriage isn't an everyday affair. You do it once, and it's done. Now, Sergeant Green, will you take the photographs, please?
OTHERS	Photographs!
SGT. GREEN	(*good-naturedly*) When wasn't I church photographer? Compared to pulling out an abscessed molar in sub-zero weather, this is humiliating. But I do it just the same.
ESKER MIKE	Photographs? Good, I want this marriage to be absolutely legitimate.
MRS. SMITH	First the bride and groom.
REV. SMITH	After eight children! If you wait long enough in the North, something is bound to happen.

> *SERGEANT GREEN takes a photograph.*
> *Scattered applause.*

SGT. GREEN	One more.
MRS. SMITH	Beautiful! The fruits of isolation! There is nothing like an Anglican wedding on a warm summer day to make one love the North and hate the South.

> *Another photo. More applause.*

MRS. SMITH	Now with the best man and the bridesmaid.

> *WILLIAM and OOLIK arrange themselves.*
> *Photograph. Applause.*

Now everyone, please. Is that all right, Sergeant Green? Come along, Father Roget.

> *Photograph. Conviviality.*

ESKER MIKE	*(aloud to WILLIAM)* I'm glad that's over. Now Agiluk will have to sleep with me whether she likes it or not.
MRS. SMITH	Mike!
REV. SMITH	*(considerately)* That's the old North talking. We're trying to make a new North in the church.
ESKER MIKE	What? Holy and legal southern wedlock! You said it today and you said it yesterday.
FATHER ROGET	*(to the ADMINISTRATOR)* Anglican wedlock, in this case.
MRS. SMITH	He's got his nerve.
ESKER MIKE	Fortunately, today I *am* Anglican. Why else would I come to an Anglican Church? When I want a church it is always the Anglican Church I come to first, if it's open.

Murmurings from crowd.

ESKER MIKE	The marriage ceremony fixes it like a hook in a fish.

More reaction.

REV. SMITH	We can talk about this in the rectory.
ESKER MIKE	You can do your dirty work in the rectory. I'm going to kick my children out for the afternoon and show my wife what a man I am!
REV. SMITH	We're all men here. The great ones suffer the loneliness and the weak ones cannot. The fact that you have something between your legs will not impress her at all.
MRS. SMITH	Harold, what have you said?
REV. SMITH	Yes, I said it. And now I'm going to sit down.
ESKER MIKE	Look at that, William. The Anglican Church is sitting in a chair. I could knock it over with the back of my foot.
MRS. SMITH	You wouldn't dare.

ESKER MIKE	I wouldn't dirty my good pair of boots. The church is rotting anyway. You can see it with your own eyes.
REV. SMITH	You can leave the grounds right now.
ESKER MIKE	I'll leave when I want. There's no place in the Delta where a man can't stop if he wants to.

    SERGEANT GREEN signals negatively with his head.

    Well, I'll go in a minute. We still have to celebrate. Ten years with Agiluk and then I married her. For Aklavik, that's a record.

TOOMIK	A marriage that does everything undoes everything!
ESKER MIKE	Listen to that. The ties in a Christian marriage are stronger than the spring in a No. 8 trap.
AGILUK	I am not a Christian. *(she begins to undress)*
MRS. SMITH	What are you doing, woman?
AGILUK	I am taking off this dress. I wore it to please you but I don't want to wear it any more.

    She removes it. Underneath are her regular clothes.

    I am not a virgin, and I don't believe in them either. I can only believe in myself, which is nothing. So I don't believe in anything at all.

    MRS. SMITH snatches away the dress. Exit AGILUK.

TOOMIK	The marriage is dead, phttt, like an Arctic crocus. It should last longer, but it's gone before you know it.
ESKER MIKE	What's that?
TOOMIK	You have to be a Christian husband now, but Agiluk will be Agiluk. *(she chuckles)* Agiluk! Agiluk!
ESKER MIKE	*(to REVEREND SMITH)* You got me into this. Now you can get me out of it.
REV. SMITH	Go home. I can't do anything today.

ESKER MIKE	You wouldn't leave me married to a disbeliever. I'd go to hell, wouldn't I? You should give me an annulment.
REV. SMITH	Ten minutes after the wedding?
ESKER MIKE	An annulment is good anytime. I want one quick. On the grounds that my wife refuses to consume the marriage.
REV. SMITH	Not on those grounds. Not after all the children.
ESKER MIKE	If you can't give me an annulment, then Father Roget will give me an annulment.
ADMINISTRATOR	*(to himself)* The Anglicans bind and the Catholics cleave.
ESKER MIKE	These priests around here can do anything. Father McGeorge and his tug! Two blasts from his whistle and you knew that Christ was on his way with the Maple Leaf lard and the nails.
REV. SMITH	I won't compete. This is senseless.
FATHER ROGET	It would be out of place for me . . . . a guest . . . .
MRS. SMITH	Certainly out of place!
FATHER ROGET	I'm not in a position. This is Anglican territory. In Fort Simpson it would be different.

> *MRS. SMITH hisses quietly. The crowd is embarrassed.*

ESKER MIKE	That's a nice story. Do they give annulments in Fort Simpson? What's wrong with Aklavik?
FATHER ROGET	In the circumstances . . . . I can only tell you what possibilities the church offers. *(he starts out seriously, but grows progressively angry at himself as he becomes aware of how inappropriate and futile his speech is)* To begin with, if one spouse refuses to have children, then the other has certain grounds . . . . On the other hand, Agiluk has mothered eight children and has chosen abstinence, a

very Catholic measure. Catholic without knowing it. That's how Eskimos are. A wonderful people. Yes, that's true. On the other hand, all eight children are illegitimate, and two of them by other men. Then four are Anglican. Which should count in our considerations? All eight of them, illegitimate, the six by Esker Mike, the four Catholic children only, the three Catholic children by Esker Mike, or none of them. That is a question which the Rota of the Vatican must decide. On the other hand, a marriage outside the church can't be considered a marriage, so we might be applying for the annulment of a marriage which doesn't exist. *(bitterly)* Well, it's all useless! It doesn't fit! *(trying again calmly)* In any case, these things take time.

ESKER MIKE   How much time? The Bay sells traps across the counter. Why should I wait for an annulment? Annulments in the South, but crosses in the North! You can never get what you want without paying too high a price. Cabbage, sixty-one cents a pound!

MRS. SMITH   *(weeping)* This is terrible.

ESKER MIKE   I'm not a Christian anyway.

REV. SMITH   For the last time, get out.

ESKER MIKE   That church smells. You use too much disinfectant. The next time I want a church, I'll give Toomik a box of cigars.

Exit ESKER MIKE.

TOOMIK   *(calling)* Wait for me! Wait for old Toomik! *(she stumbles)* Ouch! Priests and hungry owls! Hey!

Exit TOOMIK, hobbling.

MRS. SMITH   This is terrible. I hate it! I hate all of this!

Exit MRS. SMITH.

Main Street

*The MINISTER of NORTHERN AFFAIRS and
the ADMINISTRATOR, followed in a straight
line by REVEREND SMITH, SERGEANT
GREEN and CONSTABLE MACINTYRE.
Also the Townspeople, including AGILUK,
somewhat apart.*

ADMINISTRATOR   *(sardonically)* I told him he should move to Inuvik,
and he began to weep.

MINISTER   My God! You've got to be damned careful with these
people.

ADMINISTRATOR   Free land, I said, and a 512 for four thousand dollars.
And all he did was sit there and look at me. In his
case, we can't even get the horse to water.

MINISTER   The same as two years ago. And seven years ago!
We're spending millions in the Delta! How do they
do it in Norilsk? The Danish ambassador told me he
can't make head nor tail of this place. All civilized
men, he said, and nothing's civilized. What a
contradiction! Greenland was never like this.

ADMINISTRATOR   *(skeptically)* The Danish ambassador? They say a
Greenlander will study the Bible, but an Inuk will
skin it. The Delta is its own civilization.

MINISTER   I didn't appreciate that. Stop talking in riddles. I
thought I could count on my own men, at least, to
explain the situation. There's something here I can't
quite grasp, some central fact which eludes all of us,
that if we could only seize upon . . . . .

ADMINISTRATOR   There's no solution. Why should there be?

MINISTER   I never thought of that. *(he reflects)* No. It's
impossible. It defies common sense. You gave me a
start.

They stroll on.

ADMINISTRATOR   What does H.B.C. stand for?

MINISTER   *(incredulous)* Hudson's Bay Company!

ADMINISTRATOR   Here Before Christ.

The Minister smiles and nods his head.

What time do you think it is?

MINISTER   *(looking at the sky)* I seem to have lost all
                  sense . . . . You can't tell on days like this, can you?

ADMINISTRATOR   No you can't. A day like any other.

MINISTER   There you go. Conundrums again!

ADMINISTRATOR   The sun stays out all day, so the words come out of
                  my mouth like flies out of a jar.

MINISTER   This is depressing. I've been depressed ever since
                  Tuktoyaktuk. They gave me a banquet of muktuk
                  and I had to eat the stuff. My metabolism's shot to
                  hell!

ADMINISTRATOR   The same thing happened to Canarvy and he ate
                  chocolate bars. He ended up trying to walk to
                  Whitehorse.

MINISTER   Are you pulling my leg? Listen, it sounds silly, but
                  the worst part is not knowing when to eat lunch.
                  How can I think about rot and poverty? I keep on
                  thinking about myself. *(he stops)* This is endemic,
                  isn't it? I'm not the only one?

ADMINISTRATOR   No. I keep on thinking that history never happened.
                  Julius Caesar was a muskrat! Or that the world is in
                  the shape of a skullcap. Step below the Circle and
                  you fall into space.

MINISTER   My God! What's that got to do with it?
                  (conscientiously) Capital investment! Transport!
                  Wage opportunities! Let's get down to earth. Can
                  we or can we not bring these things to the Delta?
                  The Russians are twenty years ahead! Let's at least
                  find out what the people feel!

                  He greets AGILUK.

                  Good morning.

ADMINISTRATOR   Agiluk. The Minister of Northern Affairs.

> *The other Townspeople come nearer. The MINISTER offers his hand. AGILUK stares. He bends forward as if to offer his nose. She impulsively bites it. He shrieks. CONSTABLE MACINTYRE seizes her.*

MINISTER   No! Let her go!

> *AGILUK is freed and leaves.*

Blood! What does it mean? Is this some kind of primitive ritual? Why didn't you warn me?

ADMINISTRATOR   Yes, why didn't I? Maybe I should have warned *her.*

MINISTER   I'm still bleeding. Thanks a lot. I've heard of rubbing noses, but biting noses . . . . It's not humiliating. It's saddening. Sad! Sad! *(he turns to the ADMINISTRATOR)* What was her name?

ADMINISTRATOR   Agiluk.

MINISTER   *(distracted)* Agiluk. Her eyes. Those were winter eyes and it's midsummer. My God! Our master plan for the District seems so far away now.

> *Exit the MINISTER and the ADMINISTRATOR, followed in a line by REVEREND SMITH, SERGEANT GREEN and CONSTABLE MACINTYRE.*

The Administrator's Office

WILLIAM and ESKER MIKE.

ESKER MIKE   Down at the mouth! Are you sure you weren't a whale once? If you look like that when he comes in, he'll grow suspicious and make me fill out forms.

WILLIAM   Maybe I should go home.

ESKER MIKE   Go home? A friend like you wouldn't go home.

WILLIAM   I'm sad today.

ESKER MIKE   You still can't go home. With you here, he might mistake me for a white-faced Eskimo. A bastard. It runs in the family.

WILLIAM   Bastards look like everybody else.

ESKER MIKE   They're not like everybody else, though. The
                 illegitimate kind are much better than the others when
                 it comes to welfare. My children get extra candy at
                 Inuvik. *(by way of explanation)* Bastards.

                 WILLIAM examines ESKER MIKE.

WILLIAM   You can't be an Eskimo. You have to shave every
                 day.

ESKER MIKE   It's the atmosphere. If he feels there are Eskimos
                 around, he won't be so mean. *(he rubs his chin)* It is
                 rough. Well, I'm not going to pluck them out.
                 There's a limit.

WILLIAM   If you *were* an Eskimo, you could make a good living
                 telling stories. Before, there were no storytellers.
                 Only people who told stories. Now we can sell them
                 like furs.

ESKER MIKE   That's a racket for you! I'm only going to borrow
                 some money from the government.

WILLIAM   Yes, I'm sad today, sadder than I've been for a long
                 while.

ESKER MIKE   Oh, you know how to be sad all the time.

WILLIAM   But now I'm weeping for Esker Mike, who will soon
                 be gone. Neytuna invented a cousin too. And the
                 Administrator killed him. Ah, Neytuna! He realized
                 he had done wrong! "I'm miserable," he used to cry.
                 "But now that I have this cousin, what can I do with
                 him?"

ESKER MIKE   He could have abandoned him to the weather.

WILLIAM   No, he couldn't. The Administrator wouldn't allow
                 it. He kept on giving Neytuna money for his cousin
                 until Neytuna died from misery. It was a punishment
                 that even Toomik couldn't have thought of. Slow,
                 like starvation, but with no hunger.

ESKER MIKE   What a story! The Administrator is as simple as
                 cold.

WILLIAM

(contemplatively) No. He can smell evil at five hundred yards, whichever way the wind is blowing.

ESKER MIKE

You're an underdeveloped native, William. He can't smell a dead char when it's five days old. A man who sits in a chair inside a heated house can't smell anything.

WILLIAM

I don't care about the char. He can smell evil inside an oil drum.

ESKER MIKE

Since I don't believe in your disgusting old demons, and since I'm a pioneer in good standing, I'm going to ask him for the money anyway. It's only the grubstake. The profit comes by itself. Esker Mike and Company and Sons Ltd. . . . that's about it. When Agiluk sees me holding a Chamber of Commerce in the Native Hall, she'll decide we can risk another offspring after all.

WILLIAM

This is worse than waiting for a vaccination.

ESKER MIKE

It will all be over in ten minutes. You just have to teach me how you do it.

WILLIAM

I stand in line.

ESKER MIKE

Is that all?

WILLIAM

And then he looks me in the eye, and I just stand there.

ESKER MIKE

You're no Eskimo. I can do better than that. You have to grin. Otherwise he thinks you're up to no good.

WILLIAM

I just stand in front of him, like this. *(he stands, a proud man beggared)*

ESKER MIKE

No, you have to grin. And pretend you're shy. It helps if your teeth are yellow.

He strikes a pose. Enter the
ADMINISTRATOR, who eventually looks up.

ADMINISTRATOR

Is that an abscessed bicuspid? In the old days Sergeant Green would have them all out in an afternoon.

Esker Mike points to the gaps in his teeth.

ESKER MIKE   As a matter of fact, this one is lying in Sergeant
              Green's cupboard, next to a killer bullet and other
              important souvenirs of his lifetime. This one was
              swallowed by my lead dog Mabel, who then began to
              slobber, and died from infection.

WILLIAM   These young constables who can't pull teeth aren't
              worth spitting at.

ESKER MIKE   This has nothing to do with welfare, but can I show
              William your molars?

              *The ADMINISTRATOR sits down and opens his
              mouth.*

              See. Perfect. I told you, William.

WILLIAM   I've seen better. How about Miss Reynolds, the
              teacher? *Her* teeth were perfect. Full of gold!
              Whenever she was hungry, she could get credit just
              by opening her mouth.

              The ADMINISTRATOR opens a file.

ADMINISTRATOR *(reading)* Esker Mike. *(he peruses the contents)*
              This is one of the best welfare portfolios I've worked
              out in my life, if not *the* best. Well-balanced security
              at all times and all seasons. I don't think the Prime
              Minister himself could manage to give you more
              money.

ESKER MIKE   Oh, the Prime Minister. He's not an Arctic linguist
              and scholar like you.

ADMINISTRATOR Neither is Sergeant Green. If I gave you the beaver
              off a nickel, I'd be in prison tomorrow.

ESKER MIKE   *(chastened)* Prison?

WILLIAM   How can the government send itself to prison?

ESKER MIKE   *(philosophically)* The government can do what it
              wants. They could put old Tulugak on a stick and
              roast him to a crisp.

WILLIAM   Nobody could do that to Tulugak. He'd turn into a
              grain of sand. He was a spirit!

ESKER MIKE A spirit? Don't give us that. Tulugak was a son-of-a-bitch. A raven who did it to women! You couldn't run a Sunday School with stories like that. The government would censor you into the ground.

ADMINISTRATOR Sodomy with huskies and young caribou is also discouraged.

ESKER MIKE *(uneasy)* I'm not a caribou man myself.

ADMINISTRATOR *(musing)* Entry from the rear. The South enters the North from the rear. Sodomy as it should be done, in Canada as it is in the U.S. *(he smiles at his own humour)* Opening up the territories! *(to ESKER MIKE)* When they open up the territories, where are you going to go? Any further north, and you'd soon be heading south. The Sisyphus of the Arctic wastes! Esker Mike versus the shape of the earth!

ESKER MIKE *(alarmed)* I don't know where I'd go! I'm North wherever I am!

ADMINISTRATOR *(cynically nodding his head)* The tragic archetype of the 67th parallel! *(he looks intently at ESKER MIKE)* What a discovery! I see the Ancient Mariner in his Stanfield thermal underwear, damned to float endlessly downstream astride a forty-gallon drum!

    ESKER MIKE first looks behind him.

ESKER MIKE *(puzzled)* He sounds hungry and cold. *(awkwardly)* He sounds almost as hungry as Agiluk's cousin, who is so desperate that a mere look from her good eye could melt a frozen dog from your door and turn him into mock muktuk.

ADMINISTRATOR *(cunningly)* Agiluk's cousin? Where did she come from?

ESKER MIKE She's from one of the ten lost tribes.

ADMINISTRATOR Ten lost tribes? Biblical fairy tales! Mediterranean scum!

ESKER MIKE I mean, she just came from nowhere, from some tent somewhere out there. From out of the great space!

ADMINISTRATOR   (*amused*) And you intended to let her starve. That's why you didn't come to me. Otherwise you would have come to me.

ESKER MIKE   But . . .

ADMINISTRATOR   The strong dispose of the feeble. A fine tradition revived. Only these days it happens to be murder!

ESKER MIKE   But . . . . I mean . . . . She doesn't exist! I just made her up!

ADMINISTRATOR   (*severely*) Let's have the truth. You would look her in the face until that face couldn't look back!

ESKER MIKE   No! It wasn't me! It was Agiluk! She's a primitive one, you know. The spitting image of her great, great grandmother, who still comes to see her, in the shape of a dog or a lynx. Do you want to hear that story?

> *The ADMINISTRATOR looks at him, then opens a drawer with a key.*

ADMINISTRATOR   Here's forty dollars for this month. But I don't want to see how she looks at you. Keep her healthy, but keep her out of my sight.

> *ESKER MIKE and WILLIAM rise.*

ESKER MIKE   Oh, you won't see her. I'll take care of that. You don't have to worry about that.

> *Exit ESKER MIKE and WILLIAM.*

ADMINISTRATOR   Agiluk's cousin?

> *He laughs diabolically. Exit.*

Main Street

SERGEANT GREEN and ESKER MIKE.

SGT. GREEN   Hey! Where are you running to, you toothless mistake for a polar bear?

ESKER MIKE   If I were a bear, I wouldn't have to use my teeth. I'd just knock off your head with my paw, in one swoop.

SGT. GREEN	A policeman's head?
ESKER MIKE	It would come off like moss from a stone, Sergeant. A man tears easy, though you'll have to ask Elijah how he tastes. That's one winter he won't forget.
SGT. GREEN	It was a long time ago.
ESKER MIKE	It wouldn't happen now, would it? Nobody gets lost and stranded now in midwinter. We just radio Inuvik and ask for an airplane or two.
SGT. GREEN	It was his boots or his brother-in-law. So he decided to eat his brother-in-law. And we didn't even arrest him. Why bother the Magistrate with a family affair?
ESKER MIKE	Do you see how calm and warm it is today? It's so warm I can see that spruce tree growing. Sad talk makes me tremble on a warm day like this.
SGT. GREEN	Is that why you were running?
ESKER MIKE	I wasn't running. I was walking fast.
SGT. GREEN	Nobody runs here. Running is suicide. It freezes the lungs. Or it fills them with flies. Only fugitives run in Aklavik. When I see somebody running, I chase him.
ESKER MIKE	You don't have to chase me, Sergeant.
SGT. GREEN	If I don't chase you today, I chase you tomorrow.
ESKER MIKE	What do you mean?
SGT. GREEN	Can't you feel it in your bones? Aklavik is no place for a man who wants to get ahead like you. You didn't trap enough muskrat this season to chink the drafts in your shack.
ESKER MIKE	I must be growing weak. It's the harsh climate.
SGT. GREEN	And you're an old fornicator. You've got all those little mouths to feed.
ESKER MIKE	That's true enough. I find women suitable. I've been fornicating for the best part of my life.
SGT. GREEN	So sooner or later, you're going to try to cheat the government. It follows, doesn't it?

ESKER MIKE	Yes, it follows. Can I stop it from following?
SGT. GREEN	I wouldn't be surprised if you invented a new relative just to collect more welfare on her behalf.
ESKER MIKE	*(waking)* Why would I do a thing like that?
SGT. GREEN	I just told you why. And when I come to arrest you, you'll know the reason. *(he pulls an old pair of handcuffs out of his pocket)* Do you see these cuffs?
ESKER MIKE	The cuffs? You'd better save those for a criminal like Constable Mac who arrests men for nothing at all. Goodbye, Sergeant. I wouldn't do anything wrong. I was just running to meet the boat. The first mate and I are going to make a business deal and become as rich as store clerks. You'll never have to arrest me. I think clean thoughts and do good deeds, every day and in every way. *(he hurries away)* The government! I'd better find a cousin somewhere or I'm in for it.

> *Exit ESKER MIKE. SERGEANT GREEN laughs.*

SGT. GREEN	Look at that dismal specimen of mankind. A true son of the North! Well, one extra cousin isn't so bad. But if he puts another on the list, I'll have to threaten him with a trip to the Outside. *(he smiles)* The Outside! He'd rather be skinned and hung out to dry on a willow frame.

The Mate's Cabin

ALBERT and WILLIAM at a table.
Enter ESKER MIKE.

ESKER MIKE	What do I see? A Hay River rat who's come down North for air!
ALBERT	Air? That's about all. Hay River for me! Lots of tables in the beer parlour. A road to the Peace. And French fries in a box.
ESKER MIKE	I don't see what's so good about that. You live with an Indian woman in Hay River and they call you a squaw man.

ALBERT	Calm down. Relax. I didn't call you a squaw man. God, you people in Aklavik are crazy. Always growling. What's wrong? Can't you keep alive here? *(he grins)* When a white man crosses the Arctic Circle, he changes into another man. You wouldn't know him.
ESKER MIKE	The Arctic Circle's only a line in the air.
ALBERT	I can't say how it happens. Once I told a tourist he was crossing. He looked at me for a while, and then he fainted.
ESKER MIKE	*(laughing)* Stupid! Those tourists are stupid! *(he sits down)*
ALBERT	William and I thought you caught your finger in a trap, so we opened the merchandise.
ESKER MIKE	*(furious)* You opened it?

> ALBERT and WILLIAM laugh. ALBERT produces an unopened bottle.

ALBERT	Made from fine rye grain and Rocky Mountain water. Nine ninety-five. Here's your nickel change. Albert Onchuk's as honest as the day is long.
ESKER MIKE	As the day is long in December, maybe. *(he pulls out an old list)* The price here is five forty-five.
ALBERT	That's in Alberta. This is Aklavik. One thousand miles by water from Fort Providence. You have to pay for your liquor F.O.B. Aklavik!
ESKER MIKE	Four dollars to put this bottle in your bag? Shit! I could get it cheaper from Inuvik.
ALBERT	It's not the weight you're paying for, it's the discomfort. Insects! When we stopped at Wrigley, the flies were half an inch thick on the deck. You couldn't see white. We had to shovel them off.
ESKER MIKE	Those aren't flies. We have flies here that can black out a lantern at dead of night, in five seconds flat! That hunter from New York didn't have a chance.

ALBERT   *(suspiciously)* What hunter?

ESKER MIKE He marked his tent with an oil lamp when he stepped outside to pee. And he *never* found his way back.

ALBERT   *(with deliberation)* Three hundred miles upriver, I killed a mosquito as big as my thumb. A jiggerful of Albert Onchuk's blood! I could have had him stuffed, but he was squashed flat.

ESKER MIKE Ha! I've seen mosquitoes make a man's skin puff like a balloon and kill him with fever. Our Aklavik flies drove Mr. Catack crazy. Now he can walk through a swarm stark naked and come out with no sores at all, but plenty of flies in his mouth. He eats so many flies he doesn't have to eat meat.

ALBERT   Liar!

> *ESKER MIKE grabs ALBERT by the shirt.*

ESKER MIKE You little runt. If worse things don't happen to us every day then the North is the South, and the South is the North.

ALBERT   Okay.

ESKER MIKE And what about that four and a half dollars you robbed me of?

ALBERT   Okay. Okay.

> *ALBERT hands over the money.*

I'm doing this because you're my business partner. What took you so long? I thought you'd be the first one here.

ESKER MIKE I was paying my respects to the law, in the person of Sergeant Green.

ALBERT   The whole town went through this boat in fifteen minutes.

ESKER MIKE If there was a boat every day, they would drop dead from excitement. But I wouldn't give my foreskin for the luxury cruise to Arctic Red River.

ALBERT   On Dominion Day I danced with the Captain. He
                   only knows how to waltz. The men of Fort Norman
                   danced with the men of Fort Norman. We had one
                   woman guest. She was over sixty. Pierre Matoy
                   offered her eighty-five for the night and all he got was
                   a kiss on the cheek.

ESKER MIKE   We know how to dance. William can do the jig and
                   the two-step. I'm best at the Scottish reel. *(to
                   WILLIAM)* Do you mind if Albert takes you around
                   the floor?

WILLIAM   Practice makes perfect.

ALBERT   I'm not fussy. Why should I be?

                   *ESKER MIKE plays his harmonica. ALBERT
                   and WILLIAM dance.*

ESKER MIKE   Now that I've seen you dancing with a man I don't
                   have to see anything else.

ALBERT   Forget it. I can pick up a Loucheux woman and
                   forget about it in ten minutes. I'm trying to forget
                   what a backward dump this place is, so we can get
                   down to business.

ESKER MIKE   Business! *(he pronounces the syllables)* Busi-ness!

ALBERT   We'll fleece those tourists until they have to fly
                   South with the ducks.

                   *They begin to chuckle, and end by laughing
                   uncontrollably.*

                   I'll sign them on at Hay River. The deluxe two-way
                   package tour down and up the Mackenzie! All stops
                   included! Beautiful Norman Wells! Exotic Fort
                   Good Hope! The gay night life of downtown
                   Aklavik!

ESKER MIKE   They can sleep in my lean-to at five dollars a time.
                   One dollar extra for hot water. Eggs, fifty cents each!

ALBERT   Mosquitoes on the family plan!

ESKER MIKE   Muskrat meat à la mode!

ALBERT	Just introduce them to a few live Eskimos and they'll go out of their heads. Americans!
ESKER MIKE	Americans! They'll make me rich! *(grinning)* Esker Mike, trapper and capitalist!
ALBERT	Capitalism! That's a philosophy!
ESKER MIKE	Elijah Kimuit has three washing machines, one mother-in-law and an old schooner. I'm going to buy myself three kickers for my scow and a second-hand carburetor for the stove.
ALBERT	Did I hear you say you were a capitalist? I've been looking at this table, but I don't see any of your capital yet.
ESKER MIKE	*(suspiciously)* Capital? Why don't *you* give me *your* capital? You're supposed to cheat the tourists. You're not supposed to cheat me.
ALBERT	You need a head office to cheat even fat from a grizzly. And all head offices are in the South. Don't you know anything about the tourist business?
ESKER MIKE	No, but I'm learning fast. *(he leans forward menacingly)* I'm learning what a fickle partner you are.
ALBERT	*(coldly)* You can learn lots of things if you want. Even if you can't read. You can look at the pictures in the Eaton's catalogue all your life, and become a professor without leaving your shack. I'll just find somebody else.
ESKER MIKE	You're a Hay River rat all right! *(ESKER MIKE is undecided. He pauses, then empties a pants pocket and throws the contents on the table)* There it is! Genuine Canadian dollars, panned from the gold-laden banks of our local river.
ALBERT	That's some pan that can separate banknotes from silt and rusty junk, which is all you've got for minerals in this place. *(he stares at the table)* I'm not touching crooked money.
ESKER MIKE	It's not crooked. It's just welfare for my wife's cousin, who just happens not to exist.

ALBERT   And the Administrator is just going to lock us up!

ESKER MIKE   Don't worry about him. He's got his mind on other
                    things. He wants me and the ladies in the co-op to
                    take over the Hudson's Bay. I'll be Prime Minister.
                    (seriously) If he pokes his nose around, I'll borrow a
                    sister from William. He can't tell one Eskimo from
                    another in broad daylight.

ALBERT   That sounds like him. I admit it. *(he counts the*
                    money) Not very much. Give me that four dollars in
                    your pocket too.

                         ESKER MIKE does so.

                    You can keep the half-dollar change.

ESKER MIKE   Aren't we supposed to have a contract?

ALBERT   A contract? You don't even have a last name.

ESKER MIKE   I'm only me. That's how I've always been.

ALBERT   You can't make a contract legal without a last name.
                    Take my word for it. Now, are we finished? I want
                    to go visit the town, to see if those cabbages are
                    really two feet wide, and anything else of historical
                    importance and scientific wonder.

ESKER MIKE   I won't stop you from enjoying the pleasures of
                    Aklavik before it's overrun by tourists. William and
                    I will just stay behind in the privacy of your
                    luxurious cabin and celebrate your arrival.

ALBERT   *(rising)* Maybe I'll drop in on your shack and say
                    hello to my old friend Agiluk. With your
                    permission. I know what your rights are now.

ESKER MIKE   Go ahead. Maybe you can put her back into the habit
                    while you're there.

ALBERT   *(gasping with surprise)* Ah! Maybe I can.

                         Exit ALBERT.

WILLIAM   It's crooked money so it's gone to a crooked man,
                    like sun to summer.

ESKER MIKE   William, you don't understand how money works.
               Open a head office and you can step on your
               neighbour the next day. After that, they'll put you
               on the council.

WILLIAM   You shouldn't dream. Once you start, you can't stop.
               It's like falling asleep in the snow.

ESKER MIKE   *You* dream all the time.

WILLIAM   The difference is, I began when I was a boy. One
               sleep of a dog each day. It takes practice, or you lose
               control. But now it's as hard as it was at the
               beginning.

ESKER MIKE   William, I could kill you. I'm just inviting you to
               finish this bottle first. The sound of water underneath
               this boat makes me think of my unlucky youth, and I
               don't feel like drinking alone.

Outside the Boat

TOOMIK   *(singing)*
               Does Idloo kill the bear?
               Idloo is possessed! Idloo is possessed!
               He kills it with a sharp laugh.

               Does Idloo kill the flood?
               Idloo is possessed! Idloo is possessed!
               He kills it with a fast boat.

               Does Idloo kill the dark?
               Idloo is possessed! Idloo is possessed!
               He kills it with a great sleep.

ESKER MIKE   Hey, Toomik! What kind of song is that?

TOOMIK   It's an old song. Are you the Captain?

ESKER MIKE   *(assuming the CAPTAIN's voice)* Why would an old
               woman want to know?

TOOMIK   That's good. You sound like Esker Mike, but it's
               better to be a Captain on an afternoon like this.

ESKER MIKE   What do you know about afternoons like this?

TOOMIK   I know what comes before night.

ESKER MIKE	What else do you know?
TOOMIK	I know that your mate is visiting Agiluk and if Esker Mike catches him, he'll shoot him dead.
ESKER MIKE	I won't do no such thing. I would ordinarily, but a man doesn't shoot his own guest. Maybe I'll shoot you instead.
TOOMIK	Do what you want.
ESKER MIKE	If he puts a finger on Agiluk, she'll jab it like a small trout. Why should I shoot him?
TOOMIK	Don't ask me. I can tell you stories of Agiluk's childhood. I can tell you how she rolled down a hill in a skin when she wasn't much older than her youngest. But I don't know the answers. Don't ask me why.
ESKER MIKE	I won't. I won't even ask you why you're still living, when your teeth are out and you can't see a needle, and when you're going to die anyway.
TOOMIK	Just as well. If you did, I couldn't answer. But there will be others before me. The boat is here and the mate is elsewhere. This morning I smelled rain in the air. Don't you know what that means? You don't, and neither do I.

Exit TOOMIK.

ESKER MIKE	(*calling after*) Old witch! Dried dung of a tern!

In the Shack

AGILUK. ALBERT is drinking tea.

ALBERT	Agiluk, Queen of the North! I knew you wouldn't keep an old friend out.
AGILUK	I wouldn't keep anybody out. This house is as open as no house. Tents have no doors. It's a habit. You could come in at four in the morning. A murderer could come in. I couldn't stop him.
ALBERT	You couldn't stop a twelve year old boy!

AGILUK	*(scornfully)* Yes, if a man came through that door looking for a lay, he would come through the door. If a bow-legged man I once knew came through that door with a bulge in his pants and asked for tea, I would let him.
ALBERT	Nothing's changed!
AGILUK	I would let him wipe out a dirty cup and drink tea from it. That's a man's right. You can't refuse his stomach. But if he tried to touch me, I would do something else.
ALBERT	In the old days, you knew how to do one thing. What else would you do? You still skin your catch on the floor. And the deckhand said you were just as good as I had told him. Good as ever!
AGILUK	They used to say other things. A man alone on a long river can say what he wants.
ALBERT	I'll tell you what he said. He said above the Circle there's nothing like it. Eskimo women are always good, I said.
AGILUK	Here is your man. Here is the snow knife on the table. If that man had a right hand, he was a liar!
ALBERT	You wild bitch! Wild Agiluk!
AGILUK	I am . . . myself. You can run out of here screaming and call for the Sergeant. It will be Agiluk who did it. It was Agiluk who said yes, and Agiluk who is saying no.
ALBERT	Wild! Wild!
AGILUK	I have to defend myself. All of Aklavik knows. Why shouldn't I tell you? I am fighting against my unborn children already, just as if they were in me and alive.
ALBERT	You need a man. If you don't have a man, you'll go right out of your mind.
AGILUK	A man's conceit! I've had three men and you. Esker Mike is a man!

ALBERT	He's a man, and he isn't. He stole money from the government and I've got it in my pocket. *(he removes the money)* It's new enough to break.
	AGILUK stares at the money.
AGILUK	*(dumbfounded)* The government's money? Esker Mike's money?
ALBERT	Albert Onchuk's money! Money that's on its way to Hay River, that booming little city on the shores of Great Slave Lake. Or maybe I'll give you a share. I can see you're going downhill. All the women here are fifty years old, even the ones that are just twenty.
AGILUK	You know where he is?
ALBERT	I know where he was. Underneath a bottle of rye. By now he must be underneath the wharf.
AGILUK	Underneath the wharf?
ALBERT	He's going to slide into the mud like a muskrat, and float away. You can look for him in the Beaufort Sea.
AGILUK	I'll look for him nowhere. *(strongly)* When I am gone, Esker Mike can claim his rights with me for the last time! Not until then!
ALBERT	*(standing up, horrified)* What are you talking about? *(he approaches)* You're hot! Look at the sweat on your arms.
AGILUK	It's a hot day.
ALBERT	It's not that hot. And the stove is off.
AGILUK	It's hot. The tarpaper brings in the heat. It loses it quickly too. The walls of this house are like my own skin. *(distractedly)* I think of what might happen and my breasts ache!
ALBERT	Breasts like old pelts!
AGILUK	They served!
ALBERT	Thighs that could grapple with a bear!

AGILUK   Yes, all muscle and used to bruises. That's how it's
                been ever since I remember. *(melancholic)* Thighs
                like the two banks of our river. Each of my children
                lay like a winter across me. My belly was thick.
                Underneath the blood flowed. And then I pushed
                them out. The river can't stand it anymore, and with
                a great groan, it opens up and new life shows itself.
                Ten children! After comes the summer.

ALBERT   The summer! Those thighs know a tugboat when
                they see it!

On the Wharf

*CONSTABLE MACINTYRE, the
ADMINISTRATOR, ESKER MIKE,
WILLIAM, OOLIK, TOOMIK, the TWO
WOMEN.*

CONSTABLE   How I hate to see that boat go. I hate to see any boat
                go. The only departure I want to see is my own.

ADMINISTRATOR   Why think about it? Nobody leaves Aklavik.

CONSTABLE   *(sullenly)* Are you serious?

ADMINISTRATOR   Well, don't talk about leaving. Talk about how a
                burning man jumped into the river and came out
                frozen like a stick. The river puts all fire out. I'm
                usually quite good-natured. Aklavik will stick to
                your carcass like a dog to a fish.

ESKER MIKE   *(to the crowd)* Next summer there'll be new boats on
                the river. American tourists! Men who can't do it
                anymore and old ladies with veins on their legs and
                cash in their purses!

SECOND
WOMAN   Tourists? Where do they tour?

ESKER MIKE   Aklavik, you ignoramus! Aklavik! Aklavik! The
                sinking city! They'll pay you money just to walk
                into your unpainted shack and see how you live.
                Take some advice. Don't paint your shack whatever
                you do.

TOOMIK — Some shacks are so full of evil, the paint won't stick on them anyway.

ESKER MIKE — The tourists will pay to see Toomik too. They'll pay double!

TOOMIK — Pah! You disgust me. I have some good poems three generations old. Fifty cents each. That's a bargain. I have a fresh story about Agiluk and the mate which costs even less.

ESKER MIKE — I'll wring the seeds out of your neck!

TOOMIK — (*beating her cane in the air*) Don't strike an old woman!

ESKER MIKE — Lies don't hurt.

TOOMIK — These ears hear things no eyes can see. They saw Agiluk standing in her skin outside the shack. She was screaming at the mosquitoes. Or was it to Nagassuk, who knows how to make a stick act like a man, and long for a stone.

> *OOLIK weeps.*

ESKER MIKE — (*crying out*) Agiluk! That skin is going to be covered with bruises tonight!

> *OOLIK moans involuntarily and runs by. ESKER MIKE seizes her by her arm.*

OOLIK — (*struggling*) Let me go! Let me go!

> *He lets go. She runs off.*

TOOMIK — That's the story of Agiluk and the mate. You owe me two bits or a White Owl.

ESKER MIKE — (*angrily*) You can put it on my credit.

TOOMIK — Credit? Pah! Look at these arms. Can you read what they say? I'd pay Toomik right now, and then run home before the knife loses its edge on a bird or a tree.

ESKER MIKE — I'll use the butt of my hand. It's the last boat of the season. I'm going to stay until I can't see it any more.

> *He sits down on a post and sings.*

> Does Idloo kill the dark?
> Idloo is possessed! Idloo is possessed!
> He kills it with a great sleep.

> *To TOOMIK.*

> Do you have any new verses?

TOOMIK (*singing*)
Does Idloo kill death?
Idloo is possessed! Idloo is possessed!
He kills it with a long life.

Does Idloo kill life?
Idloo is possessed! Idloo is possessed!
He kills it with himself.

Does Idloo kill the cold?
The cold is possessed! The cold is possessed!
The cold kills Idloo.

**SECOND
WOMAN** It's gone.

ESKER MIKE (*standing up*) Let's all head for my shack. I need some witnesses.

> *Exit ESKER MIKE, WILLIAM, TOOMIK, the TWO WOMEN.*

ADMINISTRATOR I flew to Edmonton.

CONSTABLE I'm from Dauphin.

ADMINISTRATOR Then I flew to Montreal. I had a mistress. A good, dishonest, lovable wench. No morals! She was all that I could handle, but I handled her nicely.

CONSTABLE Okay.

ADMINISTRATOR I ate *blanquette de veau* every Thursday night. And *coq au vin* the rest of the week. I had a suntan as deep as that! I tried to wash it off but I couldn't. I never felt better in my life. And here I am in Aklavik. I don't want to be anywhere else.

CONSTABLE Aklavik! You can stick it up your ass!

ADMINISTRATOR   Yes, that's where I have it. In my guts. Take it
away and you gut me. Don't you understand? I went
to parties in Montreal. The noise was thick enough
to touch with your hand. Have you ever felt there
were black flies rubbing their legs on the roof of your
skull?

CONSTABLE   I've never felt like that. I'm thinking about
something else.

ADMINISTRATOR   Be careful then, Constable. Beautiful thoughts are
dangerous thoughts when there's so much beauty
already. You and I, we're right in the middle of the
Great Alluvial Flow. The Mackenzie – Mother of
God, and everyone else! Last week I saw J. Christ
float by on a raft, wearing a parka and smoking an
icicle.

CONSTABLE   Look, leave me alone.

At the Shack

OOLIK runs in, distraught.

OOLIK   Agiluk! Agiluk! *(she searches and runs out)*
Agiluk! *(she re-enters)* He'll kill her! He'll beat her
with the shovel! *(she begins to weep and tremble,
then stops)* Where's the baby? Gone! Where's
Natook? Nobody's here! *(she stoops down)* Blood!
It's blood! Everything's clean, but the blood is wet
on the floor. The floor is washed but the blood is
wet. Wet blood! *(she wipes her hands on her dress)*
Here's some more. It goes out the door. *(she
follows it out)*

Outside Aklavik

*AGILUK beside two skin-covered mounds. Enter
SERGEANT GREEN and CONSTABLE
MACINTYRE. AGILUK is absent-mindedly,
fitfully trying to recall a long-forgotten chant.*

CONSTABLE   There she is. Not as crazy as Esker Mike, but crazy
just the same. And two heaps of dead Eskimo. Or is
it whale meat? I'll put the cuffs on her now.

SGT. GREEN	Cuffs? Let's rest awhile, Mac. Things go slow in the North. The ice breaks slow on the River of Disappointment. Fish grow slow. Our justice is slow, though it locks fast, like the grip of frozen brass on a bare hand. This is a funeral. Sit down here on the moss and rest awhile.

    AGILUK tries again to remember the chant, but gives up suddenly and stops.

SGT. GREEN	Hello, Agiluk.
AGILUK	Hello, Sergeant Green. Hello, Constable.
SGT. GREEN	I smell the smell of summer's end. This is a pleasant time.
AGILUK	A time of work. The time to hang up the last of the fish, and bury one's dead.
SGT. GREEN	Bury one's dead?
AGILUK	As deep as we can, the government says. One foot into the soil that's thawed and the rest to be hacked out with a pick. We threw my father into the river, and you could see him on the bank for years after.
SGT. GREEN	Did he look himself, then?
AGILUK	He looked himself. In the winter, he was hard and covered with snow and saw nothing but darkness. In the summer his bones appeared and he saw something else. Blind darkness and blinding light! That was my father. It made no difference that he took himself off, one morning, and wouldn't come back.
SGT. GREEN	He was a brave man.
AGILUK	Brave? He was old. He did what came to him, that day.

    Silence.

SGT. GREEN	What have you got under those skins?
AGILUK	Nothing. Under this one is the body of Natook.
CONSTABLE	Natook!

AGILUK   He was a strong boy, but he was younger than his brothers. And under this one is the body of Rachel. She was a girl. My mother wanted to kill me when I was born.

SGT. GREEN   Two less!

AGILUK   Two less, and two more. One for the baby that will belong to the mate. And one for the baby I have to give to Esker Mike to balance that one. And if I forget again, I'll take away another of my own, maybe this one that's coming now. I will love my children more, and take them away quick. The same ones. That will stop me. The Northern mate won't want to come close to me then.

SERGEANT GREEN looks under the first skin.

SGT. GREEN   Was it fast?

AGILUK   Fast! The snow knife was sharp. I sharpened it myself. It's hanging from a nail by the stove where it always hangs. You can see for yourself how sharp it is. Blood on one side and blood on the other.

SGT. GREEN   Hanging from a nail?

AGILUK   By the stove, so the blade won't rust. Ah, Natook! He was only two and he could run like a man. But when his neck is sliced with a knife, a boy doesn't run. He bleeds. It was like opening a muskrat. These hands knew how to do it.

SERGEANT GREEN and CONSTABLE MACINTYRE look under the second skin.

SGT. GREEN   A neat job, indeed. One cut apiece, and small ones at that, considering the task.

CONSTABLE   *(overcome)* Brutal! Life here is brutal!

SGT. GREEN   Not brutal, Mac. Difficult. Life here is difficult. *(he contemplates the bodies)* Twelve years! I feel a hundred years old. Older. Murder falls on me now like an act of peace, like a wet snow falling on an unsuspecting August.

SERGEANT GREEN picks up one corpse; CONSTABLE MACINTYRE the other.

SGT. GREEN   Come Rachel! Come Natook! We're off to beautiful
                  Aklavik, where the street moves like a swamp and the
                  sidewalks are made out of wood. And where a
                  Hudson's Bay snow knife covered with blood hangs
                  waiting on a nail.

AGILUK   Yes, come to my house. And I'll make you a cup of
                  tea.

                       Exit.

                  Near the R.C.M.P. Post

                       Enter ESKER MIKE and WILLIAM.

WILLIAM   It was a good way to kill them. I couldn't have done
                  better myself, and I was born with a knife in my
                  hand.

ESKER MIKE   And the police acted like police. Murder anything in
                  Aklavik and Sergeant Green will be there. Though it
                  doesn't compare to the time they got Albert Johnson
                  up Eagle River. That was something! Two
                  constables shot through the gut! And a soldier!

WILLIAM   Two constables! Two men of the law!

ESKER MIKE   They didn't take *him* to Edmonton. No hospital and
                  good food for Albert Johnson. Only snow in his
                  mouth.

WILLIAM   *(dolefully)* They might as well shoot Agiluk too.
                  When the hot summer comes, she'll grow sick, and
                  that will be the end.

ESKER MIKE   You're right. It's no use waiting for her. Maybe
                  we'll move in with Oolik. She's Agiluk's step-
                  sister, and she has a stove that could burn the ears off
                  an ice-worm.

                       END

Inuk and the Sun

by

Henry Beissel

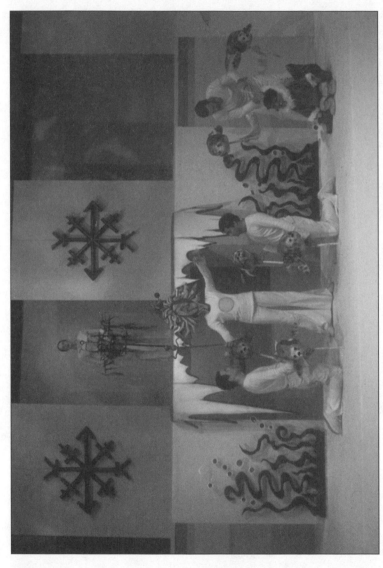

Felix Mirbt's puppeteers, with Silvia Maynard (top), Ian Osgood (left), Jill Courtney (standing centre), Maxim Mazumdar (kneeling), and Mirbt (right).

Henry Beissel is decisive about what North signifies for him in *Inuk and the Sun*: death. Contrary to the rather morbid first impression this connection evokes, however, Beissel's association of North with death is very life-affirming. In conversation with Sherrill Grace, Beissel explained that to him death is just the other side of life, each phenomenon being essential to the other: "You must be able to celebrate death if you want to celebrate life." One of the reasons Beissel wrote *Inuk and the Sun* was to redress what he sees as our denial of the life-force implicit within death, a life-force which he believes Western culture in general, and urban culture in particular, has drifted perilously far from. Inuk's eventual marriage to the Spirit of the Sun is intended to express symbolically our collective dependence on the sun as a life-force. And given our increasing awareness of humanity's relation to the environment, this symbolism has only gained in resonance since *Inuk* first appeared in print in 1974.

Beissel sees *Inuk and the Sun* as neither a regional nor a national play *per se*, but rather as an archetypal play that expresses universal themes: Inuk means "a man" in Inuktituk (Inuit means "the people"). At the same time, however, Beissel feels that *Inuk* is a Canadian play in the sense that North and Canada are so frequently related within a symbolic unity. Beissel supports this equation and believes it to be one that Canadians should appreciate: because we are a northern people, we enjoy a somewhat unique capacity to experience a relatively raw encounter between forces of life and death. Yet in an age when strawberries can be purchased in Calgary in January, when feelings of cold are dissipated by the mere turn of a knob, this is an experience that many Canadians must now seek out and should cherish.

For contemporary readers, the most contentious aspect of *Inuk and the Sun* is undoubtedly the extensive use Beissel makes of Inuit culture — their place, characters, and imagery inform the play profoundly. Beissel sees the writer as part of a world community and defends *Inuk* against criticisms of cultural appropriation along these lines. Yet he is also careful to specify that he understands Inuit defense of their cultural and mythological turf. His vision of the writer as world citizen refers, ideally, to a world in which cultural exchange is mutual and mutually respectful. Given that this has not always been the case with Canada's Inuit people (as Beissel acknowledges forthrightly), claims of cultural appropriation are completely understandable to him, although he stands firm in his conviction that political borders should not be constructed around the artistic imagination.

In fact, when viewed in its entirety *Inuk and the Sun* is the product of considerable cultural hybridization. Elements from the western literary tradition are easily drawn from the play. For one, the linear plot structure and the series of tests Inuk is put to conform to a conventional quest motif. *Inuk and the Sun* can also be read as a classical comedy because it enacts a progression from death (Inuk's father) to marriage. We also witness Inuk's progression from a sense of living in a disordered world, where the lack of abundance leaves him confused and dissatisfied, to a happier, more enlightened view. Although the play's actions do nothing to change the harsh material conditions that structure his world, Inuk's journey alerts him to the presence of an order and justice (however harsh) that was initially indiscernible to him.

From Inuit culture comes not just the setting and human characters, but also the mythical figure of Sedna. Yet the element of Inuit culture that Beissel is most grateful for is what he terms its metaphysics, and particularly the element of that metaphysics that refuses to draw a sharp line between human and non-human life. Thus Inuk's interactions with his family, as well as with animals and mythological figures, are marked by an evenness of tone and an utter absence of incredulity on the protagonist's part. We see the same precocious boy speaking in the same determined tone to his father, to the Musk-ox and to the Spirit of the Moon. It is worth noting that this same metaphysics can be seen in the Tunooniq plays included in this collection.

Beissel drew inspiration for the form of *Inuk* from the Japanese tradition of Bunraku puppetry. Though Beissel does not see puppetry as the only way of staging *Inuk and the Sun*, he does feel that puppets are the best medium for conveying the polarities of light and dark, summer and winter, life and death — polarities which *Inuk and the Sun* highlights with considerable elegance and success.

Within the Bunraku tradition, the puppeteers are clothed entirely in black and, thus, invisible. Beissel modifies this practice to have the puppeteers assume the roles of characters emanating from the spirit world, with the puppets representing the mortal world. Used this way, the puppetry expresses visually two crucial thematic elements of the play. First, because all levels of being are discernible to the audience and can be seen to interact synchronically, this format displays the interdependence of all forms of life. Second, the presence of masked figures manipulating mortal characters expresses, through visual metaphor, the degree to which our collective survival (as symbolized by Inuk) depends on a recognition and acceptance of humanity's helplessness before forces in nature that are beyond our control, forces which challenge and indeed belie the perception that human beings dominate nature. This message is figured neatly by Inuk's personal progression from brashness to compromise, for even the bold Inuk cannot bring his father back from death, nor can he possess his cherished bride, the Spirit of the Sun, for all time. He, like so many Canadians, must endure with forbearance her annual pilgrimage south.

Between 1991 and 1998, *Inuk and the Sun* toured France in the translation by Arlette Francière. It has been translated into Bengali, French, German, Hebrew, Japanese, Mandarin, Polish and Spanish, been made into an opera (with libretto by Beissel and music by Wolfgang Bottenberg). Henry Beissel is a playwright, editor, poet, and translator. He has published over ten volumes of poetry, including the long poem *Cantos North* (1983), which celebrates Canada's northern mythology and identity. He is currently a Professor Emeritus of English at Concordia University.

L.C.

* * *

Inuk and the Sun premiered at Third Stage, Stratford, Ontario on 1 August 1973.

Voice of Inuk	Carole Galloway
Voice of Father and other roles	John Gardiner
Voice of the Spirit of the Sun	Ann Rushbrooke
other roles	Andrew Henderson
other roles	Sylvie Maynard
Puppeteers:	Jill Courtney
	Maxim Mazumdar
	Felix Mirbt
	Ian Osgood
	Ann Rushbrooke

Directed by Jean Herbiet and Felix Mirbt
Designed by Michel Catudal
Puppets created by Felix Mirbt, assisted by Ian Osgood
Special Movements by Jill Courtney
Lighting by Mark Hylbak

To my daughters
Angelica, Myrna and Clara
With Love

INUK AND THE SUN

CHARACTERS

Marionettes:	Inuk
	Father
	Mother
	Raven
	Dog-team
	Polar Bear
	Musk Oxen
	Arctic Fox
	Seals
	Sea Monster
	Sharks
Actors & Masks:	Inuit villagers
	Spirit of the Caribou
	Spirit of the Moon (male)
	Spirit of the Wind (male)
	Spirit of the Dream (female)
	Sedna, Goddess of the Sea
	Spirit of the Ice (male)
	Spirit of the Sun (female)

Author's Note:

Inuk and the Sun aims to conjure something of the spiritual quality of the Inuit people, not to depict their daily life. It is a fantasy which explores on an archetypal level the fundamental human experience of life and death, and of the need to understand and accept our place in nature in order to survive. Canada's First People have much to teach us on that score. It was for this reason, and because the North is a challenge that demands of humans the utmost in courage, endurance and wisdom, that I chose an Inuit setting, Inuit characters and their mythology, to tell a story which is my own fiction.

Though the play was written for all ages, it's more often produced for young audiences. It's meant to be performed by masks, marionettes and actors, so that the audience may viscerally experience different levels of reality. But it's theatrically flexible and has been presented solely by actors, by marionettes alone, and by all possible combinations of the two plus masks. The play can be performed by as few as five actors (plus masks). My preference will always be for the "classical" Stratford production.

For the twenty-fifth anniversary of the play in 1998, I made slight revisions to the text, mainly to heighten the drama and to clarify some of its mythic themes. I also replaced the term "Eskimo" (now primarily used by native northerners in the western Arctic) with "Inuit," and the name of the title character "Inook" with "Inuk," the terms used by the native people of Nunavut.

* * *

Prologue

A stark flat landscape. A few igloos at the edge of an Inuit village. The sun is setting; its warm orange glow fades slowly and is replaced by the silvery ice-blue light of the rising moon. The music evokes the bleak harshness of the land. A flock of wild geese departs noisily as the blustering wind increases in intensity. Wolves howl at close distance.

With a sinister cackle, a jet-black RAVEN appears and circles the stage, chanting in a cracked voice.

RAVEN White is black, and black is white—
Arctic winter, arctic night.
Snow wind, ice wind, wolves at bay:
Man and beast are winter's prey.

Gull and goose have followed the sun,
Moose and caribou have gone,
Whitefish, flatfish, whale and shark—
All have fled the howling dark.

Snow wind, ice wind, wolves at bay:
Man and beast are winter's prey.
White is black, and black is white—
Arctic winter, arctic night.

The RAVEN settles on an igloo.

Episode 1

A light goes on inside the igloo — yellow glow in the sombre polar night. The wind howls. When INUK and his FATHER emerge from the igloo, dogs bark and yelp wildly.

INUK	Quiet! . . . *Nippaitit!* . . . *Nipjarnak!* . . . *(ad. lib.)*
FATHER	The dogs are frantic to be off on the hunt. They're hungry.
INUK	I'm hungry too. *(the dogs yelp again)* Quiet! . . . Down! . . . *(ud. lib.)* We're all hungry! *(wolves howl; the dogs fall silent)*
FATHER	Even the wolves are hungry.
INUK	We must find game.
FATHER	It won't be easy. Most of the animals have followed the sun.
INUK	We'll track down those that stayed behind.
FATHER	A killer wind is blowing. It jumps on the backs of animals and forces them to the ground. Then it covers them with a thick fur of snow. We should wait till the wind is out of breath and grows tired.
INUK	The wind has a long breath, and we need food. For seven days we've waited out the blizzard. I cannot wait any longer. I want to prove myself a man, Father, and a man is a hunter.
FATHER	A hunter knows how to wait.
INUK	Wait? What for? A hunter stalks and kills his prey.
FATHER	*Ayorunu.* Everything happens as the spirits have decreed. That is why we must know how to wait. Wait for the right moment to shoot the arrow. Wait with the harpoon over the ice-hole for the seal. Wait in the igloo for the storm to pass. Wait for the return of the caribou and the sun. Winter is the season of waiting.
INUK	Where does the sun go, Father, when she leaves us?
FATHER	No one knows for sure. She leaps over the edge of the world. Some say, into the sea to warm the fish. Others say she goes to shine for the spirits of the dead. There are even rumours that she is under the curse of an evil spirit. But no one knows.

INUK	Has no one ever followed the sun to see where she goes?
FATHER	We must let the secrets of the world be. It's as the spirits have decreed. *Ayorama.*
INUK	Can the spirits be trusted, Father?
FATHER	There are good spirits and bad ones.
INUK	I think most of them are bad. That's why we go hungry in winter. They make us suffer. Sometimes they even kill us.
FATHER	But the good ones help us, and with their help we can overcome all difficulties.
INUK	Then I want to go and find the sun and ask her to help us.
FATHER	You're too impatient, Inuk, and reckless.
INUK	But the good spirits will help us travel right to the edge of the world and show us the way to the sun.
FATHER	There's no return from beyond the edge of the world.
INUK	The animals follow the sun there every year and they return.
FATHER	And it's animals we must hunt, not the sun. We need food and clothing.
INUK	But if we hunt the sun and capture her and bring her back here, then all the geese and hares and caribou and seals will come back too, and we'll have lots of food.
SPIRIT OF THE MOON	*(shaking with laughter)* He wants to hunt the sun!
	The RAVEN starts up and circles the stage with his sinister cackle.
INUK	*(frightened)* Who's that?
SPIRIT OF THE MOON	You're bold, little one. What's your name?
INUK	I'm Inuk. And I'm not little any more.

SPIRIT OF THE MOON	You bear a proud name, Inuk, but you still have a lot to learn.
INUK	That's true, but that doesn't make me little.
SPIRIT OF THE MOON	So you're human. D'you know who I am?
INUK	You're the Spirit of the Moon.
SPIRIT OF THE MOON	That's right. And don't you forget it. I'm the Moon. I rule this land of the long night. The black sky is my dominion, and the stars are spirits in my service. I make a glittering feast of the night.
INUK	But you're so cold, Moon, so bitter cold.
SPIRIT OF THE MOON	Is that why you want to bring back the sun and drive me out of my land?
FATHER	Inuk is young and foolish.
SPIRIT OF THE MOON	Teach him then that all things have their season. I paint your igloos and your hunting grounds as white as my face so that you should find your way in the long winter night. What more d'you want?
INUK	The sun is brighter and warmer.
SPIRIT OF THE MOON	Yes, of course, my sister, the sun. Everybody loves her. Foolish creatures! Don't you know that her love is deadly? Go ahead, love her and let her burn you up! But me, me you must respect and admire because I shall outlast her. She consumes herself with fiery passion, I am immutable and at peace.
INUK	You're nothing without her. You wax and wane because...
SPIRIT OF THE MOON	Silence! I tell you, I am who I am. I never change.
INUK	Then why do all the animals follow the sun?

SPIRIT OF
THE MOON   They too will be consumed. And so will you!
            (laughs uproariously) A boy hunting the sun to
            banish me! What impudence!

            *The RAVEN circles with cackling laughter and
            flies off.*

FATHER   Inuk is hungry. He doesn't know what he's saying.

SPIRIT OF
THE MOON   You know the ancient customs. If you need food,
            call the spirits for the hunt! *(to Inuk)* And you must
            learn that music and dance triumph where conceit
            comes to a bad end. Remember that, Inuk, remember
            that. *(withdraws)*

FATHER   See what you've done. He's gone.

INUK   Where?

FATHER   Back into the igloo of his clouds.

INUK   Let's go after the sun, Father.

FATHER   We'll do no such thing. Get such foolish and
            dangerous notions out of your head! We shall go on
            a hunt alright, but we shall hunt for food. Let's call
            the Spirit of the Caribou to help us. Start the drums,
            Inuk!

Episode 2

            *Music. The MOTHER emerges from the igloo.
            INUK and his parents perform a ritual dance
            enacting the stalking and killing of the caribou.
            INUK is the caribou and wears an antlered
            headgear. He imitates the movements and the
            sounds of a caribou. His FATHER is the hunter,
            the MOTHER and other Inuit villagers assist.
            Drums, rattles, and clappers. Authentic Inuit
            rhythms. The climax is reached with the mock
            killing of INUK, the caribou, and by the others
            dancing around the "dead body," chanting:*

FATHER   Great Spirit of the Caribou,
            The Inuit are calling you.

MOTHER	When we're by snow and wind pursued You give us fur and oil and food.
FATHER	We Inuit must hunt to live And owe our lives to what you give.
MOTHER	Great Spirit of the Caribou, We sing and dance in praise of you.
ALL	(*chorus*) The Inuit are calling you, Great Spirit of the Caribou, Please come and visit our igloo.

> *A bone rattle accompanies the appearance of the*
> *SPIRIT OF THE CARIBOU. All other music*
> *stops. INUK leaps up and withdraws into the*
> *igloo.*

SPIRIT OF THE CARIBOU	You called me.
FATHER	Great Spirit of the Caribou!
MOTHER	Help us! We're hungry.
FATHER	A blizzard trapped us in our igloos.
MOTHER	We haven't eaten for many days. The wind brings us nothing but snow.
FATHER	And it strangles the bark in the throat of our dogs.
MOTHER	The flame burns low in our blubber lamps.
FATHER	Our days are nights now, and we cannot find game. We need your help, Great Spirit.
MOTHER	Help us, Great Spirit! We are cold and hungry.
FATHER	We're setting out on a hunt. Help us find game!
SPIRIT OF THE CARIBOU	I'm the protector of the caribou. Why should I help you who kill many caribou each year?!
FATHER	We honour the caribou and help you against foxes and wolves. We never kill more than we need to live. That's the law of the north.

MOTHER

We celebrate the grace and courage of the caribou in our songs and dances. Who'll praise you when we die?

SPIRIT OF
THE CARIBOU

That's true. But how can I help? My herds are grazing in the sun. They go south when the Ice Spirit returns. Here, under the moon, the cold wind holds sway. Nothing moves without his consent while he rides the hounds of snow.

FATHER

Speak for us to the wind.

SPIRIT OF
THE CARIBOU

The wind never listens. When he's awake he raises his voice so that nothing else can be heard. And when he's asleep he's deaf.

Unnoticed by the others, INUK has emerged from the igloo with bow and arrow.

INUK

(shouts) You don't want to help us!

SPIRIT OF
THE CARIBOU

I cannot help you. Not until my herds retu-u-r-r-n . . .

He is struck by the arrow INUK has shot in anger and disappears with a scream in a flash of light. The RAVEN returns with his sinister cackle.

FATHER

(choking with laughter) Inuk, you fool! You tried to kill a spirit! Don't you know the spirits are immortal?

MOTHER

Beware! A spirit never forgets insult or injury until he's revenged.

RAVEN

(circling throughout the following song)
White is black, and black is white—
Arctic winter, arctic night.

MOTHER

Gull and goose have followed the sun,
Moose and caribou are gone.

FATHER

Whitefish, flatfish, whale and shark—
All have fled the freezing dark.

RAVEN	Snow wind, ice wind, wolves at bay, Man and beast are winter's prey.

Episode 3

Arctic winter. Arctic night. There is no moon.
The wind is howling. We hear the barking dog-
team offstage.

FATHER	*(offstage)* Ho-o oh! . . . Quiet! . . . *(ad. lib.)*
INUK	*(offstage)* Down! . . . *Nippaitit!* . . . Quiet! . . . *(ad. lib.)*

INUK and his FATHER emerge from the dark.

FATHER	It's too dark to read the map the wind has drawn in the snow.
INUK	Have we lost our way?
FATHER	The moon will tell us — if you harness your tongue to patience!
INUK	I see no sign of the moon.
FATHER	Wait and see. We'll build a shelter here and rest.

They pull the sled into view and set it up as a
shelter against the wind. The dogs start to bark
again.

INUK	Quiet! Or the wind'll give you a whipping!
FATHER	The dogs are hungry.
INUK	So am I.
FATHER	Lie down and sleep. You need no food while you sleep.
INUK	I'm too hungry to sleep.

Addresses the night as though in prayer.

Animals of the long night,
Where are you?
Animals of the long night,
Why do you flee from us?

We're your friends.
We need you.
Animals of the long night,
Come, bring us your flesh.

FATHER   They cannot hear you in this wind. Lie down and
sleep. We must wait for the moon.

There is a spectacular display of Northern Lights.

INUK   Look, Father! Northern Lights! How beautiful they
are! They look like many-coloured waves. The sky
is a big black igloo decorated for a happy dance.
Maybe that's the glittering feast the moon was
talking about.

FATHER   No, Inuk. It's giant spirits playing with the skulls of
our ancestors. The souls of our fathers and mothers
have returned to earth, but their bodies are up in the
sky or down in the sea, and sometimes the spirits
play games with their skulls to while away the time.

INUK   I wish I could join them. It'd be one way to keep
warm.

FATHER   You're too reckless, Inuk. One day the spirits'll
punish you.

INUK   I'm not scared.

FATHER   Sleep now. The moon'll soon be rising. *(lies down
to sleep)*

INUK   *(gets up stealthily and talks to the Northern Lights in
the sky)*

Help me, O Spirits!
I am a shadow
in a land of shadows.
The wind plays with me,
the moon plays with me.
I'm fair game for the dark.
Help me become a man.

Help me conquer my fear
of the moon, of the wind.
Give me the strength
of the polar bear,

the foxes' speed,
and the skill of wolves.
For I want to hunt the sun.

Help me, Good Spirits.
I am a shadow
in a land of shadows.
I'm a boy
at the mercy of the wind,
at the mercy of the moon.
Help me become a man.

> *The wind now howls at full force. Abruptly the*
> *SPIRIT OF THE WIND swoops down from the*
> *sky and suddenly — all is still.*

SPIRIT OF THE WIND So you're afraid of me, are you, Inuk? I'm the Spirit of the Wind.

INUK Yes, I'm afraid of you — but I stand up to you all the same.

SPIRIT OF THE WIND Bravo! Only the brave stand up to me, and I favour the brave.

INUK Will you help me then?

SPIRIT OF THE WIND Perhaps. If you're willing to follow me.

INUK Follow you? Where?

SPIRIT OF THE WIND I'll show you the way to the sun. You're looking for her, aren't you?

INUK This isn't some trick you're playing, is it?

SPIRIT OF THE WIND Why d'you say that? My directions are always true.

INUK You've led us astray too often. I don't trust you.

SPIRIT OF THE WIND Suit yourself. But I don't see how else you're going to get to the sun unless you follow me.

INUK   I can't leave my father alone here.

SPIRIT OF
THE WIND   You'll have to — sooner or later. You want to
                        become a man, don't you?

INUK   Yes, but—

SPIRIT OF
THE WIND   All you have to do is follow me, follow the wind.
                        When the moon rises everything will be arranged.
                        Now, lie down and sleep. It'll be a long journey to
                        the sun.

INUK   *(lies down)* I wish you'd lie down too, Spirit of the
                        Wind, so that we can find some game. My father and
                        I are hungry. Our dogs are hungry too.

SPIRIT OF
THE WIND   Leave it to me, Inuk, leave it to the wind.
                        *(disappears in a swoop that brings back the wind's
                        howl full force)*

                        INUK and his FATHER are sleeping.

                        Episode 4

                        *When the SPIRIT OF THE DREAM appears,
                        the wind falls silent. The story she tells is
                        accompanied by an appropriate play of shadow
                        puppets.*

SPIRIT OF
THE DREAM   Sleep, Inuk, sleep. You'll need all your strength
                        when you wake. I'm the Spirit of the Dream and I
                        can see into the future. You're still a boy, but you'll
                        be a man soon. In between lies a dangerous journey.
                        There! That's the giant Sea Monster. He is blind and
                        ferocious. All the fish, even the whale and the shark,
                        are afraid of him. He's so powerful that once upon a
                        time he climbed out of the sea to break a large piece
                        out of the sky. He wanted to have it for a ceiling in
                        his underwater cave. But the sun blinded him, and he
                        fell back into the sea. Now, in revenge, he snatches
                        the beautiful sun from the sky every year. The wild
                        geese always try to stop him, but he makes an arrow

of them and shoots them way . . .way into the air until they disappear in the clouds. He wants to keep the golden sun imprisoned in his cave until she gives him back his sight, but you'll soon find out what happens.

> *The shadow of INUK himself appears in the shadow play.*

Beware, Inuk! The giant Sea Monster knows no mercy. He cannot see you, but he feels and senses you with his tentacles from the slightest movement in the water. Watch out, Inuk! If he catches you he'll tear you apart, and the sharks will have a feast.

> *In the shadow play INUK confronts the SEA MONSTER. Sharks are closing in. INUK throws his harpoon, but the SEA MONSTER snaps it like a twig, and his silent, sinister laughter metamorphoses into the wild barking of the dogs. The SPIRIT OF THE DREAM vanishes. INUK wakes up.*

Episode 5

> *INUK wakes up to find himself face to face with a POLAR BEAR beset by the dogs who have surrounded and are attacking him.*

INUK   Father! A polar bear!

> *In a flash Inuk's FATHER is up and ready, harpoon in hand, to meet the BEAR who has begun to kill the dogs one by one.*

FATHER   Stay behind me, Inuk! *(to the BEAR)* Come on, pride of beasts — it's your life or mine.

> *The BEAR turns on the FATHER who keeps him at bay with his harpoon. INUK circles and attacks him from behind. He is about to throw his harpoon—*

Don't throw it! You lose it and you're lost. . . . It takes more than one harpoon to kill a bear. . . . Stab him with it!

> *In the ensuing life-and-death struggle, the BEAR kills Inuk's FATHER but is himself killed by INUK.*

(dying) I'm proud of you, Inuk. You've killed your first bear. You're a man now.

INUK O good spirits, don't let my father die.

FATHER Don't grieve, Inuk. . . . *Ayorama.* . . . All is decreed.

INUK Listen, Father! You'll be alright!

FATHER I'm not sorry to leave this world of struggling. . . . I'm tired.

INUK I'll build you an igloo and go back to the village to get help. You'll be alright! You hear me?

FATHER In the Land of the Dead I'll find peace. . . . Perhaps the sun shines there forever.

INUK You'll be alright! You hear me?

FATHER The spirits . . . give warmth . . . and peace. *(dies)*

INUK Father! Father — come back!!! *(shakes him, then breaks down crying)*

> *The SPIRIT OF THE MOON appears and harshly lights the scene.*

SPIRIT OF THE MOON *(laughing)* Your father is dead. *(INUK cries)* Yes, weep, Inuk. A man must know to weep. And you're a man now — albeit a little man. Tears are the price of living. There's much weeping in the mutable world. Every snowflake is a frozen tear.

> *The SPIRIT OF THE WIND swoops down from the sky.*

SPIRIT OF THE WIND *(angrily)* Don't listen to him, Inuk. Look, he's laughing while he tells you to weep! That's how he deceives the living. He hates them because he's dead. But you're alive. Your sorrow will pass. Life is full of joy.

SPIRIT OF THE MOON	Listen to him talk, Inuk! His heart is full of air. You, Wind, envy me because you're condemned to be forever on the move and I'm at peace. You roam the world without rest. Joy, Inuk, passes quickly — like your father, like you!
SPIRIT OF THE WIND	Don't delude yourself, Moon! You're forever on the move too, except that you're locked into the monotony of your prescribed circles. I pity you. You're jealous of my freedom to come and go as I please. Life means change, Inuk, and change brings joy.
SPIRIT OF THE MOON	Some joy — your father's death! Weep for him, Inuk. And weep for yourself because he's at peace now.
SPIRIT OF THE WIND	Bury your father, Inuk, and move on. There's laughter over the horizon.
INUK	*(screams)* Shut up! *(then, frightened by his audacity, softer)* Must you quarrel at my father's grave?!
SPIRIT OF THE WIND	Your father's spirit lives on. It lives on in the Land of the Dead and in your children.
SPIRIT OF THE MOON	That's something we can agree on. The spirit lives on forever.
INUK	Yes, that's right, isn't it. What I bury is only his body. But where has his spirit gone? Where is the Land of the Dead? I want to go there and speak with him. Will you help me go there, Great Spirits? Please.
SPIRIT OF THE WIND	To get there you must travel beyond the edge of the world.

SPIRIT OF THE MOON	Ha! And when you get there you're done for! *(to the SPIRIT OF THE WIND)* Besides, how do you propose that he travel? His dog-team is dead. Will you blow his sled across the ice?
INUK	I can pull my own sled. I'm young and the bear has given me his flesh to eat. I have his strength now.
SPIRIT OF THE MOON	Don't be a fool, Inuk. The Land of the Dead is a long way away for you.
INUK	I don't care. I'll go over the edge of the world. My father said the sun was there too. Will you show me the way?
SPIRIT OF THE MOON	I can't. I won't.
SPIRIT OF THE WIND	I know where you can find the sun. I'll show you the way there.

> *The following song is accompanied by a wind instrument.*

Follow the wind, follow me.
Though heaven is my place of birth
I know every corner of the earth
from the mountains across the tundra to the sea.

I blow from the east
    I blow from the west
I breathe and whisper
    and howl without rest.

I blow from the west
    I blow from the east
I can comfort or kill
    both man and beast.

I blow from the north
    I blow from the south
I blow the very words
    right out of your mouth.

> I blow from the south
>> I blow from the north
> and if I don't have my way
>> I have my will by force.

> Follow the wind, follow me.
> Though heaven is my place on earth,
> I know every corner of the earth
> from the mountains across the tundra to the sea.

SPIRIT OF THE MOON Empty boasts! Empty promises! You listen to the wind and you're lost.

INUK *(to the SPIRIT OF THE WIND)* Will I find the spirit of my father where you take me? And the sun?

SPIRIT OF THE WIND You ask too many questions. Just follow me. Follow the wind!

SPIRIT OF THE MOON You're a fool to trust the wind, Inuk. He's gentle as a summer breeze now to hide that he's a killer at heart.

INUK I'm a man now. I trust my own strength.

SPIRIT OF THE MOON I'll light up the whole length of my long night to watch the wind lead you astray. *(laughs uproariously)*

> *The MOON's laughter is taken up by the RAVEN who returns with his sinister cackle and circles INUK, who begins to pile stones over his FATHER's body as the SPIRIT OF THE MOON and then the SPIRIT OF THE WIND withdraw.*

SPIRIT OF THE WIND Follow me! I'm the breath of the spirits. Follow the wind! *(exits)*

RAVEN White is black, and black is white
Arctic winter, arctic night.
Man kills beast and beast kills man—
thus it was since time began.
Snow wind, ice wind, wolves at bay—
man and beast are winter's prey.

Episode 6

Three days later. INUK is stumbling across the icy wasteland. His feet are sore and he is approaching exhaustion.

INUK   How much further is it to the Land of the Sun? *(silence)* Can you hear me, Great Spirit of the Wind? *(silence)* I've walked three days now. The knife-edged ice has cut my boots, and my feet are cold and sore. I've eaten the last of the bear meat. And the end of the world is as far away as ever. *(silence)* What shall I do, Great Spirit of the Wind? *(silence)* Why don't you answer me? I followed you — now what?

Silence.

I'm a shadow
in a land of shadows.
The wind plays with me,
the moon plays with me.
I'm fair game for the dark.
Help me, spirits in the sea and in the sky!
I didn't come this far to die.

The MOON breaks into prolonged, uproarious laughter.

SPIRIT OF
THE MOON   You see, Inuk, the Wind has abandoned you. I warned you. You wouldn't listen. You should've gone home to your igloo.

INUK   I couldn't return to the village, to my mother, empty-handed. And my father dead.

SPIRIT OF
THE MOON   You're lost now, aren't you. You don't know where to go. *(laughs)*

INUK   I know the direction. There — where the light is the colour of blood! *(points to the horizon where a faint glow of sunlight stains the darkness)*

SPIRIT OF
THE MOON   Well, you don't need my help then. Why don't you go on?

INUK

My feet are sore. I have little strength left. And it seems still so far to go.

SPIRIT OF
THE MOON

You foolish boy — to run after my dazzling sister! Don't you know it's I who rule the Land of the Long Night?!

With a menacing air.

Ice-light brittle
shadows crunch
moonbeam skittle
back and hunch.

Skull faced silence
crack-crazed loon
snow-crust islands
knife the moon.

Black blood river
sickle-starred
glaciers shiver
bonebite-scarred.

Ice-clot spittle
frost harpoon
snow-night brittle:
Hail the moon!

INUK

I'm not afraid of you. You're just jealous of the sun because she's more beautiful than you.

SPIRIT OF
THE MOON

Oh, you find her beautiful, do you? *(laughs)* Don't you know that her fire is fatal. Her light blinds you. Her scarlet rays are nothing but a net of fire in which to trap you and burn you up.

INUK

All I know is that without her we have no food. Her fire is the fire of life. When she comes the ice runs away, the animals return, and the rocks burst into flowers.

SPIRIT OF
THE MOON

Time will tell, my boy. I have no more to say. Speak to the musk-oxen. Perhaps they'll help you. But remember to hail me, hail the moon!

> *While the MOON withdraws laughing, a group of MUSK-OXEN appears.*

MUSK-OXEN   *(picking up the MOON's last line)*

Hail the moon!
Bone-face spirit
ice-crack horn
silver hoof-print
shadow born.

Flaming snow torch
night beast eye
shag-fur frost-scorch—
praise the sky!

> *During this speech a group of MUSK-OXEN enter to the rhythm of a dark, slow drum. INUK waits till their dance is finished before he approaches them. The bull comes forward menacingly.*

INUK   Peace, mighty Musk-ox! I'm hungry but I don't want to kill you.

MUSK-OX   Kill me? You . . . little man . . . kill me? *(laughs; the other MUSK-OXEN join in)*

INUK   Don't laugh! I've killed my first polar bear. I'm a big hunter now.

MUSK-OX   *(amused)* My respects, my respects. . . . But you're still little to me. We can run you into the ground quicker than a blizzard.

INUK   I don't want to fight you. I need help.

MUSK-OX   Lay down your harpoon then. *(INUK does so)* Now we can talk in peace.

INUK   I'm hungry. I need food.

MUSK-OX   What d'you want us to do about it? Food is scarce for us too. We have to scratch through ice and snow for scraps of grass. Not much of a meal.

INUK	I'm hunting the sun. The wind promised to show me the way, but he has abandoned me. I've travelled for three days and I'm lost. Help me find the sun, please. It'll make your life brighter too.
MUSK-OX	Why should I ? What d'you want of the sun anyway?
INUK	I need to bring her back to the Land of the Inuit, my people.
MUSK-OX	She's going to return in her own good time.
INUK	Winter is long and cruel to us. Often we Inuit suffer from the cold, the bitter cold. Our bodies don't grow the shaggy furs that keep you warm.
MUSK-OX	I know. You hunt and kill us for our skin.
INUK	The moon says that's the law of the north.
MUSK-OX	He can talk.
INUK	He says we all have to live by the law of the north — my people, your herds, all living creatures. But I prefer to live under the rule of the sun. Under the sun the land is bright and happy, and there's plenty of food for us all. And everybody is nice and warm.
MUSK-OX	Well, for us Musk-oxen, it does get a little too warm under our thick fur in the summer. But you're right, it is a happier time all round.
INUK	That's why I want to find the sun and bring her back here.
MUSK-OX	She'll come back. You'll just have to wait.
INUK	If we must wait any longer we'll all be dead.
MUSK-OX	She always comes back. Every year.
INUK	There's no game, and my people are starving.
MUSK-OX	Everything has its season.
INUK	Winter is long and cruel.
MUSK-OX	The seasons measure our patience as well as our courage.

INUK   Besides, I'm looking for the spirit of my father. A polar bear killed him, and I want to find his spirit to know when and where he returns to the world.

MUSK-OX   I understand, but I cannot help. We don't know exactly where the Land of the Sun lies. We see her roll along the horizon till she falls over the rim of darkness and disappears. Our ancestors tell us that's where the Land of the Dead is, but how to get there. . . . *(shakes his head slowly)* Sorry. Why don't you ask the Arctic Fox over there? He has relatives in the Land of the Sun. He should know. But beware! He's sly. He doesn't like to give away his secrets.

> *An ARCTIC FOX is discovered sleeping curled up in the snow. INUK bows to the MUSK-OXEN who depart gravely. INUK picks up his harpoon and jumps the ARCTIC FOX, holding the harpoon to his throat.*

INUK   Don't move and I won't hurt you!! Listen! I'm in search of the sun. You must show me the quickest way there — or else!

ARCTIC FOX   *(sly)* Or else what?

INUK   Else I'll kill you!!!

ARCTIC FOX   What good would that do you?

INUK   That's true, but I can't afford to argue. You tell me where I can find the sun. I count to three!

ARCTIC FOX   But I don't know the way there.

INUK   You're lying. You have relatives in the Land of the Sun.

ARCTIC FOX   Well . . . sort of. . . .

INUK   Alright. Then you must know how to get there — ONE!

ARCTIC FOX   But I don't know — honest!

INUK   There's no such thing as an honest fox — TWO!!

ARCTIC FOX   I've never been there. I've only heard talk about it.

INUK	This is your last chance, liar — THREE!!!
ARCTIC FOX	Wait! I know who can show you the way — the whistling swan! He flies there every year. He knows. Look! There's one up there. *(he points over INUK's head into the sky behind him. As INUK turns to look, the ARCTIC FOX slips away)* Happy hunting, Inuk — in the Land of the Dead! *(exits)*

> *The SPIRIT OF THE MOON reappears, convulsed with laughter.*

SPIRIT OF THE MOON	Ha-ha-ha! He tricked you! A little Arctic Fox tricked big man Inuk! A whistling swan indeed! *(laughs)* Don't you know there's not a whistling swan left in all the arctic lands. They've all gone south with the sun before the long night came and took over.
INUK	It's easy for you to mock me, Moon. You're not hungry and tired as I am. . . . But I deserve your mockery. It's shameful for a hunter to be cheated by a fox
SPIRIT OF THE MOON	You're not a hunter yet, my boy. You still have a lot to learn about the world. So what are you going to do now? You're not only tired and hungry, you're also lost. Maybe you'll reach the Land of the Dead sooner than you think.

> *The SPIRIT OF THE WIND swoops down from the sky.*

SPIRIT OF THE WIND	Don't listen to him! His light is the colour of the cruel polar bear, and his heart is a chip of ice. Follow me, follow the wind!
INUK	Follow you where? Where've you been, Spirit of the Wind?
SPIRIT OF THE WIND	I'm busy raising huskies of snow and driving them southward across the tundra toward the sun.
INUK	And you leave me here helpless — without food or shelter. I called you and you didn't come.

SPIRIT OF THE MOON	That's the Wind for you — nothing but noise!
SPIRIT OF THE WIND	Listen who's talking! You've nothing to do but lie around in the black sky sunning yourself and scoffing at those of us who've got work to do.
INUK	Would you please stop quarrelling, both of you. Spirit of the Wind, you promised to show me the way to the sun.
SPIRIT OF THE WIND	Right. And I've taken a short break to do just that. Now look over there! See the seal-hole in the ice?
INUK	Yes.
SPIRIT OF THE WIND	That's a breathing-hole for the seals.
INUK	I know that.
SPIRIT OF THE WIND	Of course you do. Now, tie your harpoon-line around your waist and stand there with your harpoon at the ready. The moment a seal comes up, throw your harpoon. If you hit it, the seal will show you the way to the sun.
INUK	And if I miss?
SPIRIT OF THE WIND	Then you'll have to wait for it to come back. Or for another seal to come up.
SPIRIT OF THE MOON	If you're still alive by then.
SPIRIT OF THE WIND	There's no other way. Good luck! I must be off again. Don't lose heart, Inuk! The world belongs to the brave. And I'll protect you. I have a long and strong arm. *(departs)*

> *INUK ties the harpoon-line around his waist and stands over the seal-hole, poised with his harpoon, waiting for a seal to appear.*

**SPIRIT OF
THE MOON**

I have to admire your courage, Inuk. You, a little
boy, defying me, the illustrious ruler of the night. I
like that. Perhaps you'll grow up to be a man after
all. But so long as you put your trust in the wind,
you're asking for trouble.

*Just before the end of the SPIRIT OF THE
MOON's speech, a SEAL comes up for air.
INUK hurls his harpoon and strikes it. The
SEAL dives quickly and pulls the struggling
INUK into the sea and under the ice.*

**SPIRIT OF
THE MOON**

For you, Inuk, the way to the fire leads through the
water. But I remain behind — immutable and at
peace.

Episode 7

*The action continues from the previous episode,
but it now takes place under water as INUK is
dragged by the SEAL to an underwater cave,
where he is quickly surrounded by other SEALS
who tie him up in his harpoon line and perform a
ritual dance around him.*

SEALS

(*chorus*)
We are the seals,
the cheerful seals.
We sleep on ice
and eat codfish and eels.

All winter we live
under the sea
under the ice—
flipper-de-lee.

We are the seals
with flippers and tail.
We're hunted by man
by shark and by whale.

We're nowhere safe,
so we live with fear,
but all the same
we're full of cheer.

We caught a little man
from the Land of the Moon
and pulled him down
by his own harpoon.

We are the seals,
the cheerful seals—
shall we try and see
if the little man squeals?

    SEDNA, Goddess of the Sea, appears and the
    SEALS scatter. She is ugly and imperious.

SEDNA	What's going on here? *(to INUK)* Who're you? What are you doing here?
INUK	I'm Inuk. I think I've drowned.
SEDNA	Have you ever heard a drowned man talk?
INUK	Well, no . . . but . . .
SEDNA	Don't talk nonsense then! . . . Well then, have you lost your tongue? What are you doing here?
INUK	I don't really know . . . I mean I don't know where I am.
SEDNA	You're out to capture the sun. That's a serious matter.
INUK	*(startled)* How d'you know about that?
SEDNA	*I* ask the questions here, *you* answer them.
INUK	But who are you?
SEDNA	That's the first riddle you must solve.
INUK	I don't understand.
SEDNA	You don't seem to know or understand very much, do you.
INUK	What riddles are you talking about?

SEDNA	Listen. As a special favour to the Spirit of the Wind, and because he specifically asked me to, I'm prepared to help you find the sun. On three conditions! First, you must discover who I am.
INUK	You must be one of the sea witches.
SEDNA	Are you trying to insult me?!

The SEALS are giggling in the background.

INUK	No, but you're so ugly.
SEDNA	Think before you speak, Inuk! Or I shall feed you to the sharks.
INUK	No, please, don't do that. I'll try my best. I promise.
SEDNA	Alright then. Listen to the second riddle: Wind or Moon— who is the groom, who is the bride crying in the tide?
INUK	*(repeats, dumbfounded)* Wind or Moon— who is the groom, who is the bride crying in the tide? That's too difficult. It doesn't make any sense. How d'you expect me to know the answer to something that doesn't make any sense.
SEDNA	The Sea Monster knows the answer.
INUK	The Sea Monster? I can't ask him. I don't even know where to find him.
SEDNA	*He* will find *you*. The Seals will take you to his cave.
INUK	But the Sea Monster is a terrible giant. I dreamt of him. He'll kill me.
SEDNA	A man is known by his trials, and I heard you boasted that you were a man, Inuk.

INUK	Anyway, he isn't going to tell me anything.
SEDNA	It's up to you to make him tell you the secret.
INUK	How am I to do that? He'll tear me to pieces before I can open my mouth. *(outburst)* Oh why didn't I listen to my father! It was foolish to go hunting for the sun.
SEDNA	Aahhh — you're learning.
INUK	Yes, the hard way.
SEDNA	Don't you want to know your third and final task?
INUK	Not if it's as difficult as the first two. I'd sooner go back to my village.
SEDNA	And never see your father again?
INUK	Well, no . . . I mean, yes, I want to find him. But make it something easy.
SEDNA	All it takes is a little courage. Two ferocious sharks guard the entrance to the Great Hall of the Iceberg. Your task is to get past them and enter the Great Hall.
INUK	*(desperately)* O Good Spirits! You have forsaken me. I am a shadow amongst shadows at the bottom of the sea at the mercy of a monster at the mercy of the shark— Oh why is the world so cold and so dark?
SEDNA	Take heart, Inuk. There's no darkness in the Iceberg. Once you're inside the Great Hall, everything will be bright and clear. Because you'll find the sun there.
INUK	Will the spirit of my father be there too?
SEDNA	I told you, *I* ask the questions here, *you* answer them. Now tell me: who am I?
INUK	Please, can I be untied first? I cannot think bundled up in my harpoon-line.

SEDNA	*(motioning the SEALS)* Untie him!
	While the SEALS untie INUK, they furtively exchange signs and gestures with him until he realizes what they're telling him.
SEALS	*(chorus)* We are the seals, the cheerful seals, we sleep on ice and eat codfish and eels. We're happy in winter, we're happy in summer. Are we sad? No! Because we serve the Goddess Sedna. . . . The Goddess Sedna. . . . Sedna, Goddess of the Sea. Happy — yes! Sad — no! Because we serve Sedna, Goddess of the Sea. . . .
	The SEALS carry on till INUK comprehends.
INUK	I'm ready.
SEDNA	Answer me then — who am I?
INUK	*(play-acting)* You are . . . you are . . .
SEDNA	Yes, I am . . .
INUK	You're not a sea witch.
SEDNA	I'm not.
INUK	You are . . . you are . . .
SEDNA	Yes, yes — who?
INUK	You are . . . you are . . . not a sea fairy.
SEDNA	*(increasingly impatient)* I don't want to know who I'm not but who I am!
INUK	Then you are . . . you must be . . .
SEDNA	Yes, I must be . . .

INUK	Sedna, the Goddess of the Sea!
SEDNA	*(furious)* Earthquake and tidal wave!!! How did you guess? Someone must've betrayed me.

> The SEALS are half giggly, half fearful, in the background.

INUK	Betrayed you? There's no one here to betray you. No. I'm Inuk, and Inuk knows how to use his head.
SEDNA	Alright then. I am Sedna, Goddess of the Sea. You have solved the first riddle. Now let's see if your head is a match for the Sea Monster! Remember: Wind or Moon— who is the groom, who is the bride crying in the tide?
INUK	Wind or Moon— who is the groom, who is the bride crying in the tide? How can I find the answer to such a strange and difficult puzzle?
SEDNA	*(to the SEALS)* Take him to the Monster's cave! . . . *(to INUK)* If you pass all your tests, we'll meet again. If not *(gestures ominously)* the more the pity.
INUK	Can't you give me a clue?
SEDNA	Farewell, Inuk. And good luck! *(exits)*
INUK	*(calls after her)* If the Monster doesn't kill me and the sharks don't eat me, we'll meet again. Farewell. *(the SEALS beckon him)* I'm coming, I'm coming. How I wish I were back on firm land. It's better to be hungry than to be eaten.

> The SEALS move off with him.

Episode 8

*INUK arrives in the cave of the SEA
MONSTER. He is terrified by the huge octopus-
like creature.*

SEA MONSTER   *(full of menace)* I sense a presence . . . *(probes the
air with his tentacles, but INUK eludes him)* an alien
presence. . . . I do not tolerate uninvited visitors in
my cave.
(incantation)
I'm the Monster of the Sea.
With my many tentacles
I choke my enemy.
I choke the whale
and I choke the shark—
I'm as mean as can be
because I live in the dark
and I cannot see.

But I can sense and I can feel
every movement in the water
whether it's creature or ship's keel.
Someone's entered my cave,
someone too bold and too brave.
It isn't seal or whale or shark
because I know them in the dark,
I know their song, their whistle and their bark

*The SEA MONSTER has been trying to capture
INUK with his tentacles, but so far INUK has
eluded him. He is now exasperated.*

Who or what thing are you? Are you a giant
crab? . . . A sea urchin? . . . Are you a sting
ray? . . . *(each time he waits for an answer, but
INUK is busy evading the SEA MONSTER's
attempts to catch him)* No, I can sense it. . . .
You're an alien creature plucked from the air. . . .
I warn you! No one enters my cave uninvited and
lives. . . . My tentacles will catch you. Beware! . . .
There! I've got you!! . . . No, you got away again!

INUK   *(trying to put a brave face on a losing situation)* I'm
Inuk, the mighty hunter!

SEA MONSTER   When I catch you, I'll suck the life out of you.
(charges with increasing fury; in self-defence INUK strikes off one of the SEA MONSTER's tentacles)
Ouch. You've cut off one of my tentacles. You must die!

INUK   You watch that you don't die! I've killed a polar bear with my harpoon.

SEA MONSTER   *(laughs)* Are you trying to frighten me? I have polar bear for breakfast.
(incantation)
I'm the Monster of the Sea.
With my many tentacles
I choke my enemy.
I choke the whale,
and I choke the shark.
I'm as mean as can be
because I live in the dark
and I cannot see.

INUK   You've told me that before. But I'll cut off your tentacles one by one till you've none left.

SEA MONSTER   You insolent creature! For every tentacle you cut off I grow two new ones.

> *The struggle between them intensifies. INUK cuts off another tentacle, and the SEA MONSTER immediately sprouts two new ones to replace it. Eventually INUK is caught.*

Ha! I've caught you!! . . . Now you must die.

INUK   *(in desperation, a shot in the dark)*
Wind or Moon—
who's the groom,
who's the bride
crying in the tide?

SEA MONSTER   *(startled)* Who told you that?

INUK   Sedna.

SEA MONSTER   You know her name?!

INUK   The Goddess of the Sea.

SEA MONSTER   Did she send you?

INUK   Yes, she did.

SEA MONSTER   What does she want?

INUK   The answer, the answer to the riddle.

SEA MONSTER   *(very agitated)* Never . . . never! I hate the Goddess of the Sea. It's she who banished me to this black cave. Every year I snatch the sun from the sky, but Sedna takes her away from me and gives her to the Spirit of the Ice, her own son, who keeps her in the Great Hall of the Iceberg. . . . I hate Sedna . . . and since you're one of her band all the more reason for you to die.

INUK   Hold it! I'm not one of her band. I'm Inuk, an Inuit boy. I'm looking for the sun.

SEA MONSTER   You're looking for the sun?

INUK   Yes. To be quite honest, the Goddess of the Sea is ugly and mean. I don't like her any more than you do.

SEA MONSTER   You're just saying that to curry favour with me.

INUK   No, honest! She's set me three difficult and dangerous tasks before I get inside the Iceberg. That's where I hope to find the sun. And my father. A polar bear killed my father.

SEA MONSTER   I'm sorry to hear that. But what do you want of the sun?

INUK   I want to take her back to the Land of the Inuit.

SEA MONSTER   Where is this Land of the Inuit?

INUK   It's the land of my people — up above the ice and by the edge of the sea. Our land is cold and barren without the sun.

SEA MONSTER   And you want to take the sun there?

INUK   Yes. Because when the sun comes to us, our land is full of colour and life and beauty. . . . But I can't get to the sun without knowing the answer to the riddle:
Wind or Moon—
who is the groom,
who is the bride
crying in the tide?

SEA MONSTER   That's my secret.

INUK   I tell you what I'll do. . . . You give me the answer
                       to the riddle and I promise you a special gift from the
                       sun.

SEA MONSTER   What kind of gift?

INUK   Well, for instance, a chunk of sunlight to stick in
                       your ceiling.

SEA MONSTER   *(considering this)* Ye-es.

INUK   Then you'll be able to see again. Because you're not
                       really blind. It's because of the darkness in your cave
                       that you can't see.

SEA MONSTER   And what guarantee do I have that you'll keep your
                       promise once I let you go?

INUK   Cross my heart!

SEA MONSTER   I shall come and tear out your heart if you deceive
                       me!

INUK   I won't deceive you, believe me.

SEA MONSTER   I warn you. I'll know where to find you!
                       I'm the Monster of the Sea.
                       With my many tentacles
                       I choke my enemy.
                       I choke the whale
                       and I choke the shark.
                       I'm as mean as can be
                       because I live in the dark
                       and I cannot see.

INUK   Don't worry, you won't be in the dark any more. All
                       you need is a chunk of sunlight. I'll keep my
                       promise.

SEA MONSTER   Alright then. Here's the story. *(whispers at length
                       in INUK's ear and then lets him go)*

INUK   What a sad story!

SEA MONSTER   Not really. But that's all I can tell you. That's all
                       you need to know.

INUK   Thank you, you kind Monster. You'll have your
sunlight yet . . . provided I survive the sharks that
guard the entrance to the Iceberg! *(departs)*

SEA MONSTER I shall tear him limb from limb if he has tricked me!

Episode 9

*Accompanied by the SEALS, INUK arrives
outside the entrance to the Great Hall of the
Iceberg which is guarded by two fierce sharks.*

INUK   There is the entrance to the Iceberg. But how will I
ever get in? How will I get past those fierce sharks?
They'll tear me to pieces.
Oh Good Spirits!
I'm a shadow
in a sea of shadows
at the mercy of the sea
at the mercy of the dark.
Help me, please,
conquer these sharks.

SEALS   *(chorus)*
Listen to the seals,
the cheerful seals.
No need to conquer the shark.
Just accept the light with the dark.

INUK   I don't know what you mean. I'm only a boy. I
can't fight these ferocious sharks.

SEAL   Oho! You're only a boy, are you? I thought you
were a man — *(sarcastic in a good-natured way)*
Inuk, the mighty Inuit hunter!

INUK   Well, yes . . . but they're so much bigger than I.
And I don't even have my harpoon.

SEAL   We'll see what we can do.

SEALS   *(chorus)*
Listen to the seals,
the cheerful seals,
with flippers and tail.
We'll get you past the sharks
disguised as a whale, a humpback whale.

INUK

Disguised as a whale, a humpback whale? . . . Yes, that's a good idea. They're big enough to scare even the sharks. But how I can disguise myself as a humpback whale? They're a hundred times bigger than me.

SEAL

Exactly. A silly idea! It can't be done. I have a much better idea. We'll trick them.

INUK

Trick them? But how? Sharks are no fools.

SEAL

Maybe not, but we'll outsmart them. You watch. *(whispers to INUK)*

INUK

This I've got to see. I just hope I won't end up a meal for them.

> *The SEALS now move close to the SHARKS, displaying themselves in order to lure them into pursuit and away from the entrance to the Iceberg. This gives INUK an opportunity to sneak around their backs.*

SEALS

(chorus)
We are the seals,
the cheerful seals,
we sleep on ice
and eat codfish and eels.

We are the seals
with flippers and tail,
we're hunted by man.
By shark and by whale.

We're nowhere safe,
so we live with fear
but all the same
we're full of cheer.

INUK

(just before he enters the Iceberg) Thank you, good Seals, thank you. I'll always be your friend. *(exits)*

> *Too late the SHARKS realize they've been tricked. As they swim furiously back and forth in front of the entrance to the Iceberg, the SEALS depart, laughing at them.*

SEALS

(chorus)
You were tricked by a boy,
you silly shark,
your teeth are bright
but your brains are dark.

You were tricked by a boy
and by the cheerful seals
who sleep on ice
and eat codfish and eels. *(exit)*

Episode 10

*A startling, dazzling change of light! We're in
the Great Hall of the Iceberg. Everything
glistens and sparkles in white, silver and soft
turquoise. The SPIRIT OF THE ICE sits in a
frozen position on a block of ice which glitters
golden because the SUN is evidently locked in it;
what movements he makes must be slow and
stiff. Inuk's FATHER lies frozen inside another
block of ice. INUK enters and stares in awe and
amazement at the radiant magnificence of the
Great Hall.*

INUK

Where am I? . . . The light is so bright I can't see!
Like summer snow. . . . And yet it's so cold! . . .
As if I'd fallen into the Moon. . . . How did I get
here? . . . I've never seen anything so sparkling, so
glittering, so beautiful. . . . Now I remember — the
Seals! This must be the Great Hall of the
Iceberg. . . . Oh, Good Spirits, don't let me freeze
to death here!

Spirits of the Sea and of the Sky!
You've pulled me down
over the edge of the world
without telling me why.
I'm a shadow now
in this crystal hall of light:
don't let me die!

He discovers his FATHER in a block of ice.

There's my father! . . . *(runs over to him)* Father,
Father! I've found you. . . . *(the FATHER is rigid in
the ice)* It's me, Inuk! Wake up! . . . *(hammers
with his fist on the ice block)* Can you hear me?
Wake up, Father! . . . Come on!! Shake off the
ice!!! It's me, Inuk, your son!

*The FATHER doesn't move. INUK looks about
distraught and discovers the Sun in another ice-
block. He rushes over to it and shakes it wildly.*

This must be the sun. Get up, Sun! Rise! I've been
looking for you all over the Land of the North. . . .
(the Sun doesn't stir) . . . *(to himself)* If I chipped
off a piece, just a little piece — off the sun I mean, I
could use it to melt the ice that holds my father and
free him.

O Spirits Good and Bad!
I know now that in your hands
I'm nothing but a toy,
you play your games with me
and give me time to enjoy
the warmth and radiance of the sun
until you've had your fun and tire,
then you throw me like a harpoon
back into the winter world of the moon.

*He raises his harpoon and prepares to throw it at
the frozen Sun.*

But when you play with me
you play with fire.
I defy you, Spirits!
While I have life
I must have the sun!

**SPIRIT OF
THE ICE**   *(sharp, loud — like ice cracking)* You're undone!!!

*Startled, INUK looks about and only now
discovers the SPIRIT OF THE ICE.*

You dare raise your harpoon against me, the Spirit of
the Ice, in my own Great Hall?! *(INUK is frightened
and lowers his harpoon)* What impudent creature are
you?!!

INUK	I am—
SPIRIT OF THE ICE	*(thundering)* Silence!!! Do you think I don't know who you are??
INUK	*(timidly)* You asked.
SPIRIT OF THE ICE	You're human. You belong to a race of creatures that thinks the world was made for them alone! That's why you must die. I shall turn you into a block of ice!
INUK	No, no, Great Spirit of the Ice. You've got it all wrong. I'm Inuk. I belong to the people of the North. We think of all creatures as our brothers and sisters. Nanuk the bear, the wolf, the fox, the whale, the wild geese — they all are our brothers and sisters.
SPIRIT OF THE ICE	Then why do you raise your harpoon against me? I too have my place in the order of things.
INUK	I didn't raise my harpoon against you, Great Spirit of the Ice — I was aiming at the sun.
SPIRIT OF THE ICE	You were aiming at the sun? You were going to throw a harpoon at the sun?? That, little human, is even worse than aiming your weapon against me!

> *Unnoticed by either INUK or the SPIRIT OF THE ICE, the SPIRIT OF THE SUN enters and listens to their exchange.*

INUK	I've travelled the whole length of the winter earth to find the sun. My people are starving. The caribou herds have long gone and the sea is frozen. Our land is dark and cold, and we have nothing to eat. We need the sun to survive.
SPIRIT OF THE ICE	You need the sun to survive and yet you raise your harpoon against her. You're mad.
INUK	I meant no harm. I just wanted to take a chip of the sun to melt the ice and free my father.

SPIRIT OF
THE ICE   *(i*ℎ *disbelief)* You wanted to take a chip out of the sun??

INUK   Or maybe capture her and take her back to the Land of the Inuit.

SPIRIT OF
THE ICE   Capture the sun?? The supreme ruler of everything — capture her and take her away??? These are grave offences punishable by death.

INUK   But I wanted to capture her because I love and admire her warmth, her radiance, her—

SPIRIT OF
THE ICE   *(interrupts him)* Flattery will get you nowhere! You've forfeited your life. Prepare to die!

SPIRIT OF
THE SUN   *(steps forward and tells the SPIRIT OF THE ICE)* I pardon him. . . . *(turns to INUK)* I am the Spirit of the Sun. . . . And I like your spirit, Inuk. I like the fire in your eyes.

INUK   It's your fire
that burns in my eyes,
as it's your light
that flushes our skies.

O Great Spirit of the Sun,
I didn't know
you were so beautiful
—and still so young.
Now I understand
why the animals follow you
and joy colours the land
wherever you go.

Come back with me,
drive the long night away,
break the ice-crust off the sea
and wake the lavish day!
Scatter your flowers,
bring back the beasts—
so that in your honour
we may tell our stories
and sing and dance and feast.

SPIRIT OF THE ICE	Enough wheedling and fawning!! How dare you, you impudent little boy — how dare you try to flatter the Sun with empty words!
INUK	They're not empty words.
SPIRIT OF THE SUN	And he's not a little boy, not any longer. Only a man would have the courage and the knowledge to enter here.
SPIRIT OF THE ICE	*(put in his place)* That's true, that's quite true. I have two ferocious sharks guarding the entrance. . . . *(to INUK)* How did you manage to get past them?
INUK	Sedna, the Goddess of the Sea, sent me here.
SPIRIT OF THE SUN & SPIRIT OF THE ICE	*(in chorus)* Sedna?!
SEDNA	*(bursting in)* On three conditions! Two you've fulfilled. You discovered my identity, and you've got past the sharks. The third condition shall determine whether you'll be turned to ice or returned to earth.
SPIRIT OF THE ICE	*(aside)* Good! There's a chance yet that I may keep him.
SEDNA	Wind or Moon— who is the groom, who is the bride crying in the tide?
SPIRIT OF THE ICE	Ha, Inuk. Now unriddle us that riddle!
INUK	That's very difficult.
SPIRIT OF THE ICE	You bet it is.
SPIRIT OF THE SUN	Sedna, you're asking too much of him.
SEDNA	He must solve the riddle or he is lost.

INUK   Well then, I say the Moon is the groom.

SEDNA   And who is the bride?

INUK   I wonder if it is . . . *(hesitates playfully)*

SEDNA   Yes, you wonder if it is . . .

INUK   *(quickly)* You, Goddess of the Sea! You're the
                Moon's bride.

SEDNA   *(taken aback)* And why am I crying in the tide?

INUK   Because you're betrothed to the Moon. But month
                after month the Moon puts off the wedding. You cry
                in the tide because you fear you'll never be married to
                him. You cradle the Moon on your waves but he can
                never be yours.

> *To the accompaniment of bone rattles, SEDNA*
> *quickly changes from an ugly hag to a beautiful*
> *young woman. The SPIRIT OF THE ICE puts*
> *his hands over his eyes as though he were*
> *blinded. INUK watches SEDNA's*
> *transformation in amazement.*

                I don't believe my eyes. . . . How you've changed!

SEDNA   It's you who has changed, Inuk.

INUK   Just a moment ago you looked like an old hag, now
                you're a beautiful woman. How can you change like
                that?

SEDNA   It's you who has changed, not I. Understanding has
                changed you, and courage. The better you understand
                and the braver you are, the more beautiful I and all
                things shall be.

INUK   I'm afraid I don't understand that.

SEDNA   Some day you will — if you think enough about
                it. . . . Now go. You may return to your people.
                And leave the Moon's courtship to me.

SPIRIT OF
THE SUN   And I'll go with you as your bride — if you want
                me.

INUK	Want you? Want you?? I love you, I admire you, Sun. . . . Just imagine — Inuk, the mighty Inuit hunter, married to the Sun!
SPIRIT OF THE SUN	No, not Inuk, the mighty hunter — I go with Inuk, the understanding and loving man.
SEDNA	And let me warn you. The Sun is betrothed to the Spirit of the Ice in the same way that I, Goddess of the Sea, am betrothed to her brother, the Moon. She'll never be wholly yours.
INUK	But why not?
SEDNA	Every year she must return for a time here to the Great Hall of the Iceberg.
INUK	But why?
SEDNA	That's the law. And all things must live by the law, even the Sun.
INUK	It's a cruel law that separates what belongs together.
SEDNA	Some day you'll understand.
SPIRIT OF THE SUN	All things have their season — remember, Inuk?
INUK	All things have their season. . . . Yes, I remember now. . . . A long time ago. When we started out on our hunt. My father said that. *(remembers his FATHER)* My father! What about my father? Can he come with me?
SPIRIT OF THE ICE	*(categorical)* No, he stays! He's locked forever into the eternal ice.
FATHER	*(from within the ice-block)* I'm proud of you, Inuk. You've become a mighty hunter and a man.
INUK	You must come back with me to our people, Father.
FATHER	No, Inuk. My season is done. Leave me to the peace I've found.

INUK	But we need you, Father. I need you, Mother needs you.
FATHER	The living need each other in their struggles. You look after your mother now as she has looked after you before.
INUK	I can't return to the village without you, Father.
FATHER	It's decreed that my struggles are over.
SPIRIT OF THE SUN	He cannot return, but his spirit will be reborn in our first son so that in time he can become the father of your grandchildren when you've gone to rest.
SEDNA	No earthly shape or creature can last forever.
SPIRIT OF THE SUN	But everything returns forever and ever in a different shape.
SEDNA	Everything must forever change and go on changing, Inuk. That's the law.
SPIRIT OF THE ICE	Even I must melt and return in new forms. That's the law.
INUK	Yes, but can't he live just a little longer, please.
FATHER	My time is up, Inuk. *Ayorama.*
INUK	No, no, no!!! You can't leave me alone!!!
FATHER	Don't grieve, Inuk. You're a man now. My spirit will return to your children. That is the law. Farewell, Inuk, and take my greetings to our people. *(dies)*
INUK	Farewell, Father.
SEDNA	You may go now, Inuk. And take the Sun with you.
INUK	I almost forgot. I made a promise—

SPIRIT OF THE SUN	—to the Sea Monster. I know. You shall keep your promise. When we rise above the sea I'll throw a handful of sun-rays into his cave to light it up as bright as a summer morning, but whether it'll cure his blindness. . . . *(shrugs her shoulders)*
INUK	He'll feel the light if he can't see it.
SPIRIT OF THE SUN	Yes. He'll know the season has come round again.
INUK	O beautiful Spirit of the Sun, your fire makes me stronger than whale, musk-ox and polar bear, your light makes me happier than seal or arctic hare. I'm a shadow in a land of shadows no more. I'm Inuk, a man now in his stride, I bring to my people the Sun as my bride.
SPIRIT OF THE ICE	For one short season only!
SEDNA	For a long season!
SPIRIT OF THE SUN	And every year!

> *Music. Drums. The SPIRIT OF THE SUN and SEDNA slowly dance in a circle with INUK. The SPIRIT OF THE ICE stealthily gets hold of INUK's harpoon and suddenly hurls it at him. The harpoon misses INUK and instead strikes the Sun still imprisoned in a block of ice. There is a flash and a thunder clap, and slowly the Sun rises in a blaze of light. Quick scene change without break.*

Epilogue

> *Same set as in Prologue; but now the moon is setting and the sun is rising. The wind is softer, and the howling of the wolves more distant. The RAVEN flies in and circles the scene.*

RAVEN   Summer comes, winter must fly,
the sun is climbing into the sky.
Snow wind, ice wind, pass away,
night must now make way for day.

Gull and goose come back with the sun,
char and salmon start their run.
Herds of caribou return
along with arctic shrew and tern.

Summer comes and winter goes,
winter comes and summer goes,
man kills beast and beast kills man—
thus it was since time began.

> *The RAVEN completes his song when the sun
> has flushed the scene with her burning light and
> flies off with a sinister cackle. Cut lights
> quickly.*

END

Changes

by

Tunooniq Theatre

Tunooniq Theatre is a group that came into being in Pond Inlet because, in David Qamaniq's words, "Young people didn't have enough to do" and "[they] were not aware of how people lived before the traders and the missionaries" (interview, 16 December 1998). What they did was to organize dramatic performances for which they needed the memory and active help of the Elders. *Changes* presents what its title promises, enacting what the Inuit did "before" and what happened when the traders and missionaries came. Tunooniq's plays are, as Sherrill Grace says in the Introduction, "overtly didactic." What the group set out to do and what it does appears in the performances themselves.

At the same time, both *Changes* and *In Search of a Friend* (see pages 279-92) display a dramatic structure so unusual that it is difficult to categorize or classify the plays according to any non-native convention. What both plays emphasize are the depths and complexities of a single situation or moment of existence. The actors' words are not predominant: movement, sound, and visual effects together produce meaning. For example, the first part of *Changes* centres around a seal-hunt and the second around the coming of the strangers, although plot is relatively unimportant. The stage directions do not merely indicate action on stage, or lighting, sound or scenery changes: they flesh out the play. In the "Unsuccessful Hunt" scene, the stage directions read *"After a long time of listening to the wind, there is the sound of Naujak's thoughts as he perches over the seal hole. He is shivering and looks very weary,"* and, a few lines later: *"There is a pause and then the sound of a seal coming to the surface; there is a moment of tension as the boy aims for the hole and misses."* The reader is led to wonder about the sound of a seal coming to the surface and perhaps to link it involuntarily with the sound of a thought.

The principle resource for *Changes* was the Elders who, themselves, directed the drum dance celebrating a successful hunt (Qamaniq, interview, 16 December 1998). What the Elders said is transmitted more or less directly in the dialogue, when, for example, Aqigiq says, "My young daughter, Panikpak, must care for the young children. She, too, will have to be a mother. Older women like Uniluq are most admired by us, for her skills are most important to our survival." However, the play communicates more than the concrete minutiae of everyday life; it deals also, movingly, with the communal experience of historical change, encapsulated in the contest between the Shaman and the Priest in scene 9. The outcome appears at one point to be in doubt, for the Priest *"weakens"* while the Shaman grows strong. In the end, however, the Shaman *"drops to his knees,"* and the Priest directs the people to a burial site. The contest is signified by words and actions, the participants portraying the diminution or increase of power by advancing and retreating, or rising and sitting, or kneeling. Significantly, there is no representation of actual physical combat. Sound adds a dimension to the contest. At the opening of the scene, like an auditory foreshadowing, *"There is the sound of chants and of* ajajaq [songs or singing], *then gradually the sound of prayers is heard."*

With extraordinary economy and strength, sound, words and movement blend to show an entire passage of social history in a few moments. The ebb and flow of the contest, the rise and fall of the chanting, the drum beat and the prayers, the Shaman's defeat and, in conclusion, Uvilik's lament have a formal rhythmic quality that gives to what is celebrated or commemorated a sense of elegy.

Tunooniq is so much a community endeavour that giving credit to individuals presents difficulties. David Qamaniq, who was most helpful in providing production and other background information, says that all the actors took part in scripting and planning the performances. The Elders taught the actors the traditional dance and some, at any rate, of the *ajajaq*, which are described as traditional folk songs (*Canadian Theatre Review*, 73 [1993]: 22). These songs are called for twice in *Changes* (105 and 112) and at the close of *In Search of a Friend* (see 292), and they appear to have a ritual component or to be expressions, even instruments, of power. Examples of these songs, translated into English, are included in Penny Petrone's *Northern Voices: Inuit Writing in English* (1988). Pakak Innuksuk, who had previously started a dance group in Igloolik, provided the initiative for the formation of Tunooniq.

E.D.

* * *

Changes was first performed at Expo '86 in Vancouver, British Columbia, and then toured Banff, Edmonton, Ottawa, and Greenland. In 1986 Tunooniq performed it at the Inuit Circumpolar Conference in Alaska, and, throughout 1988, *Changes* toured with *In Search of a Friend*, in Inuktitut, to Eskimo Point, Cape Dorset, Iqaluit, Fort Franklin, and Yellowknife. In 1989, Tunooniq performed excerpts from *Changes* and *In Search of a Friend* during the Arctic Song Festival in Cambridge, England (*Canadian Theatre Review* [Winter 1992], 54).

The Tunooniq cast was Iga Attagootak, Josia Kilikushak, Kitty Komangapik, David Qamaniq, Oopah Attagootak, Lamechi Kadloo, Malchi Arreak, and Pakak Innuksuk.

CHANGES

CHARACTERS
Aqigiq
Naujak
Uviluk
Panikpak
Nukilik
Taqiapik
Bob
Another White Man
Priest

Scene One — Starting Scene

*The performers file onto the stage. They are
dressed in traditional caribou skin clothing.
Pakak enters last, carrying the drum. They sing
the first ajajaq. As the song ends the hunters
prepare for hunting. Two hunters go in the other
direction and spot tracks. They leave hurriedly.
Two women are in a tent, working on skins.
Another woman is outside the tent stretching a
skin. Several men are poised over seal holes.
There is the sound of the wind howling. It fades
as the woman gets up and looks out at the
audience as if searching.*

AQIGIQ   All we can do is watch and wait. Sometimes the men
are gone a long, long time. This Arctic . . . it's so
unpredictable . . . so unforgiving. Many of us have
died. We have all known the pain of waiting for
animals that don't come. Sometimes it seems, the
spirits of the land forsake us. *(she looks despairingly
around and then goes to the tent)*

Scene Two — Unsuccessful Hunt

*After a long time of listening to the wind, there
is the sound of NAUJAK's thoughts as he
perches over the seal hole. He is shivering and
looks very weary.*

NAUJAK
I have hunted many times now. Why don't the seals ever come to me? I wonder if I will ever be like my father. If only the little seal could come to me! I could be the one to feed our family for the first time! Oh, please, little seal, please . . . come! *(there is a pause and then the sound of a seal coming to the surface; there is a moment of tension as the boy aims for the hole and misses)* Aagh, there it goes! . . . Aaaagghh!

Scene Three — Women at Camp

UVILIK and PANIKPAK are at the tent sewing seal skins. Then AQIGIQ goes out and then walks to the microphone.

AQIGIQ
My young daughter, Panikpak, must care for the young children. She, too, will have to be a mother. Older women like Uvilik are most admired by us, for her skills are most important to our survival. She will teach the young women to prepare the skins for sewing. We must learn to sew the sealskin kamiks and caribou parkas properly. Only these animal skins can protect us from the long harsh winters. *(she returns to the tent)*

The focus shifts to the hunters. The hunters are dejected and leave for home. They walk home empty-handed and the tent is a sad and quiet place as the wind howls.

AQIGIQ
You didn't catch a seal?

NUKILIK
Yes, we waited long time . . . we got close to getting one . . . but we caught no seal.

UVILIK
But where are the others?

Scene Four — Evil Spirit

TAQIAPIK
(goes to the microphone and searches the horizon) Somewhere out there, two of our hunters are missing and I have seen in my vision that they were killed by a polar bear. They will never return to us.

The people cry and comfort each other.

AQIGIQ   They are dead . . . they will never return?

TAQIAPIK   There is an evil spirit in our camp. We must kill it or it will destroy us . . . let's begin.

The SHAMAN gets on his knees and NAUJAK covers him with a skin. The SHAMAN starts to convulse and move around until he lies prone on the floor. There is the sound of ajajaq in the background. After a brief silence, he tries to get up but convulses again, over and over until he throws off the skin. TAQIAPIK / SHAMAN rises and shows the bloody knife to the people and the audience.

TAQIAPIK   I have killed the evil spirit! Now we'll be able to catch seals again!! *(TAQIAPIK gets the hunters ready for hunting and they start going off as UVILIK speaks)*

UVILIK   We wait for so long! Left behind from their hunting trips. We are never sure if there will be food this time. We never fully trust this land . . . but we hope . . . only hope and try our very best. *(she returns to the tent)*

Scene Five — Success!

There is throat music and the men wait. The seal is heard and the young hunter, NAUJAK stands poised with his harpoon ready. He hits it and yells exuberantly: the others rush to help him. Together they dig into the seal, cutting off some of the liver. They are laughing and chatting happily.

TAQIAPIK   My son got his first seal.

NUKILIK   *(with pride)* It looks good . . . let's eat the liver!

NAUJAK goes to the microphone with some liver in his hands. Obviously very happy and full of self-gratification, he finishes his meat and then looks at the audience inviting them to share his pride.

NAUJAK	There is nothing so great as to catch an animal, and sharing it with my people. I've spent my whole life training for this moment. Now I am a hunter! *(happily he returns to the others and they trudge home with the seal)*

Scene Six — Games

Upon seeing the hunters the women are very happy.

PANIKPAK *(excited)* He's coming back . . . he's coming back. Soon we will have some seal.

All join in a feast of fresh seal.

NAUJAK Mother, I caught my first seal!

UVILIK *(turning to the others in excitement)* My son caught his first seal.

AQIGIQ Hai . . . that is a great joy.

NUKILIK *(laughing)* My nephew, when he heard the sound of the seal his legs were shaking. *(he laughs harder)* When he used the grappling hook he almost fell in with the seal. It was very funny.

The others join in the laughter. TAQIAPIK goes to the microphone with a drum in his hands.

TAQIAPIK Today my son caught his first seal. This is the happiest time of my life, for hunting is more than just survival . . . it is the joy of life!

He begins to drum and all join in a happy ajajaq. *After the drum dance TAQIAPIK picks up the sealskin and goes to the microphone.*

It is in our tradition to play games after a boy's first catch. We will have a game and the winner will have this skin.

They play a game of nugluktaq *and while they are competing, a young girl, animated and full of life, speaks.*

PANIKPAK   This is a happy time for us. A time for games and songs . . . for enjoying our love for each other. We have food and we will live another day.

> *When she finishes the strongest hunter — NUKILIK — wins the game. His wife is jubilant.*

NUKILIK   Hai, now my wife can make kamiks from the sealskin. They're going to take me back when we leave this camp.

> *He does a dance with the others singing in the background. Afterwards they play a hitting game of strength. Again, he beats everybody.*

Scene Seven — The Transformation

TAQIAPIK   *(challenging NUKILIK)* Let's wrestle.

> *When TAQIAPIK starts to lose, the SHAMAN transforms into a walrus and chases after NUKILIK. He kills him and the people are shocked and afraid.*

AQIGIQ   What has happened to him?

> *TAQIAPIK then brings NUKILIK back to life. The strong hunter rises, and as he goes to the microphone, he glances nervously back.*

NUKILIK   Among our people there are certain powerful men. In our camp we have a shaman capable of doing strange and awesome things. He can be fierce or he can be helpful. We must follow his advice for it is our law.

> *Right after this speech, the SHAMAN / TAQIAPIK directs the hunters to get ready for hunting.*

TAQIAPIK   Before we run out of seal meat let's go hunting.

Scene Eight — Strangers

*The hunters are about to go off but then
NAUJAK sees some strangers. He shouts
shakily.*

NAUJAK   Look . . . Indians are coming.

                    *His legs shake and he runs behind his father.
                    NUKILIK gets a harpoon and aims it at the white
                    people who come up on the stage.*

TAQIAPIK   Wait . . . I don't think we should be scared of them.
                    Who are you people?

NUKILIK   Who are you people? Where did you come from?
                    Can you not understand?

                    *One of the white people approaches suspiciously,
                    clutching his possessions. But then he takes the
                    initiative and speaks. At first he is hesitant, but
                    he goes ahead and introduces himself.*

BOB   My name is Bob, Bob. *(he pauses)* I'm Bob. Bob!

TAQIAPIK   Baa . . . baaa.

NUKILIK   *(walks around them, touching their clothes)* What
                    kind of clothing are they wearing? They don't look
                    like animal skins.

                    *The Inuit come closer, but are still very hesitant
                    and confused. BOB then looks in his pockets and
                    takes out a mirror. He holds it towards the
                    audience so that it shines. The Inuit pull back
                    and gasp.*

BOB   Look! it's a mirror.

                    TAQIAPIK is very curious and takes the mirror.

TAQIAPIK   *(showing it to NUKILIK)* Look at this.

NUKILIK   Eeh, hai, look there's a person inside it.

BOB takes back the mirror and pretends to pluck his whiskers using the mirror. The Inuit giggle. He shows the women and then motions for TAQIAPIK to get a skin. He takes the skin and gives it to BOB. In return BOB pulls out a knife which he hands to NUKILIK. He looks at the knife amazed and shows the others.

NUKILIK They gave me a good knife.

TAQIAPIK *(ignoring him, he explores BOB's possessions)* I wonder what this is . . . maybe it's a good broth from seal.

BOB gets a seal skin from NUKILIK.

BOB *(inviting them to have a drink of the broth)* This is good medicine! Good medicine!

Everybody has a drink. Then BOB goes to the microphone.

BOB I don't really care if it takes a year of living in this God-forsaken land. But I aim to get my fortune and then buy a big house with plenty of land down South. The trading is easy and so, I gather, are the women. These savages don't know the true value of a skin and to them a knife or even a mirror is ample reward for their labour. While I'm here I'll take a look around for gold and other valuable minerals. By next summer, when the ship returns I'll be laden with enough furs to fulfill all the dreams of the women in Europe and the New World. Yep! I'm going to be rich! RICH! *(he then does a jig and dances with the women)*

TAQIAPIK The white man gives and takes. They stay and change our lives. My blood gets cold because I fear for the changes. I'm old and I cannot change. But the young, they embrace the changes. I wonder, will these changes all be good . . . . *(pauses as the Inuit all start to fall down)* Look at the hunters. Sleeping like babies in the day. How will we survive these changes?

Gradually the Inuit start passing out and wandering all over the stage. The trader collects as many furs as he can and loads them on the sled. He exits to another area, still visible to the audience.

Scene Nine — The Priest

There is the sound of chants and of ajajaq, *then gradually the sounds of prayers are heard.*

TAQIAPIK   Listen . . . . I had a strange vision of the white man. I saw in my vision spirits, not from the land but from the heavens. I have a strong feeling they are coming.

The people look as TAQIAPIK begins to drum, they start singing where they are. Some rise up but others stay seated. They are about one quarter the way through the song when suddenly a PRIEST appears, shouting.

PRIEST   STOP! STOP!! THIS SHAMANISM. For there is only one God who can save your souls.

The SHAMAN, TAQIAPIK, drums towards the PRIEST and the PRIEST seems to weaken for a while.

Jesus Christ lives in you! *(points to the SHAMAN)* You, and you.

The SHAMAN weakens as the PRIEST walks towards the people, but he regains his strength and advances again to the PRIEST. The PRIEST falls down and the people go towards him slowly. The PRIEST rises stronger than before.

In the name of God I demand you to stop. *(the SHAMAN drops to his knees and the people begin to cluster around him)* You must now leave the old ways and live a new way of life. God is now your new leader.

The people sob, and the PRIEST directs them to a burial site at the side of the stage. He recites a prayer. The old woman, UVILIK, looks at her husband and goes to the microphone.

Scene Ten — The Ending Scene

UVILIK   Our leader, the great shaman is dead! What are we to do now? We have always struggled for survival. We used our knowledge and our strength to overcome the cold and the uncertainty. *(pause)* My children will know an easier life and I'm glad. But, will they know a better one? Will they be strong? Will they be wise? Will they be proud of the struggle . . . ?

She begins a very sad song by herself. When she starts another song she motions for her niece to join her and from there the rest join in. The PRIEST and the SHAMAN are the last to join . . . . Gradual fade to black.

END

Terror and Erebus

by

Gwendolyn MacEwen

H. M. S.hips *Erebus and Terror*
Wintered in the Ice in
28 of May 1847 } Lat. 70° 5' N Long. 98° 23' W

Having wintered in 1846-7 at Beechey Island
in Lat 74° 43' 28'' N Long 91° 39' 15'' W After having
ascended Wellington Channel to Lat 77° and returned
by the West side of Cornwallis Island

Sir John Franklin commanding the Expedition

All well

Commander.

WHOEVER finds this paper is requested to forward it to the Secretary of the Admiralty, London, *with a note of the time and place at which it was found* or, if more convenient, to deliver it for that purpose to the British Consul at the nearest Port.

QUINCONQUE trouvera ce papier est prié d'y marquer le tems et lieu où il l'aura trouvé, et de le faire parvenir au plutot au Secretaire de l'Amirauté Britannique à Londres.

CUALQUIERA que hallare este Papel, se le suplica de enviarlo al Secretario del Almirantazgo, en Londres con una nota del tiempo y del lugar en donde se halló.

EEN ieder die dit Papier mogt vinden, wordt hiermede verzogt, om hetzelve, ten spoedigste, te willen zenden aan den Heer Minister van de Marine der Nederlanden in 's Gravenhage, of wel aan den Secretaris der Britsche Admiraliteit, te London, en daar by te voegen eene Nota inhoudende de tyd en de plaats alwaar dit Papier is gevonden geworden.

FINDEREN af dette Papiir ombedes, naar Leilighed gives, at sende samme til Admiralitets Secretairen i London, eller nærmeste Embedsmand i Danmark, Norge, eller Sverrig. Tiden og Stædit hvor dette er fundet önskes venskabeligt paategnet.

WER diesen Zettel findet, wird hier-durch ersucht denselben an den Secretair des Admiralitets in London einzusenden, mit gefälliger angabe an welchen ort und zu welcher zeit er gefundet worden ist.

Party consisting of 2 Officers and 6 men left the Ships on Monday 24th May 1847

Gm Gore Lieut
Chas F Des Voeux Mate

The Victory Point Record is the only official written record of the disastrous Franklin Expedition of 1845. It was found by Captain Francis Leopold McClintock in 1859 at Victory Point on King William Island, and it is frequently reprinted in books about Franklin. Geoff Kavanagh used it (with name changes to include the characters) on the program for the premier of Ditch, *and both MacEwen and Kavanagh quote from this moving document. The original is in the National Maritime Museum in England.*

Terror and Erebus is an iridescent play. When the fabric shifts, moved by music, articulation in a different voice, or change in emphasis, what appears simultaneously, or in rapid succession, is a view of North as bitter challenge and North as the interior of the mind that responds to that challenge.

Gwendolyn MacEwen (1941-87), playwright, poet, and novelist, first published *Terror and Erebus*, subtitled "a verse play for radio," in *The Tamarack Review* (1974); it was broadcast by CBC on 21 January 1975. A later version, included in *Afterworlds* (1987), is subtitled, "Being an account of the search by Rasmussen for the remains of the Franklin expedition." The most recent production of the play was on 17 June 1997, when it was performed as a cantata, subtitled "A Lament for Franklin," with music composed by Henry Kucharzyk. The version of the play reprinted here is from *Afterworlds*.

Terror and Erebus deals with the Franklin expedition of 1845, its fatal conclusion and the reasons for the outcome. Rasmussen's voice frames the story, his search frames Franklin's search, his view frames the Arctic. When Franklin and his second-in-command, Crozier, speak, what they say appears through Rasmussen's consciousness, so that the listener experiences a depth of focus: the immediacy of one man's actual experience, and, simultaneously, the reflective overlay of someone else's mediation.

One of the obvious differences between the 1974 and 1987 *Terror and Erebus* is the presence in the radio version of production directions: "*Music bridge to Franklin, wind sound effects,*" "*On the word* third *a chilling sound effect.*" Their absence leaves directors free to work with the text to the best of their creative ability. The other differences between the 1974 and 1987 versions, with one notable exception, are small adjustments, which significantly alter the focus of the play. Some tighten the lines, by, for example, the removal of repetition. Speaking of the driftwood eyeshades that the Inuit made to cut the glare of sun on snow, Crozier says: "Only those, only those ridiculous / instruments / You need to keep the cosmos out" (1974), which is changed to: "Only those ridiculous / instruments/ That keep the cosmos out" (1987). The metaphysical intention is still there — the human mind cannot endure the unbroken light of unrelenting reality — but emphasized by the plainness of the statement rather than by repetition.

Another change is the redirection of lines, so that where speeches in the radio version are directed at the audience, characters in the later version speak with one another or address the situation at hand. For example, when Crozier says: "Now we come to the end of science . . ." (1974), he is clearly inviting the audience to consider general implications. In contrast, when he says, "We came to the end of science" (1987), the directness of the past tense and the blunt cadence convey a bleak dramatic urgency. At the same time the metaphorical implications remain, reinforced by the next two lines: "Now we leave ciphers in the snow, / we leave our instruments in the snow." These counterbalance Rasmussen's words in the opening lines of the play:

> And sometimes I find their bodies
> Like shattered compasses, like sciences
> Gone mad, pointing in a hundred directions at once—
> The last whirling graph of their agony. (121)

Again, where Rasmussen asks Crozier about the southward drift of the ice, in the earlier version he says: "But the ice, wasn't it drifting south / Itself, like a ship, a ship within a / ship?" where the later version has " . . .like a ship — your ship within a / ship." The change engages the interlocutor, Rasmussen, more profoundly with the dead Crozier, without diminishing the metaphoric strength of the words.

The major difference, however, is the addition of lines to Crozier's comments on snow (and other kinds of) blindness.   In the radio play, he says:

> To select what we will and will not see,
> To keep the cosmos out with layers of cloth
> and strips of leather—
> That's man, I suppose,
> an arrogant beast. Whether
> He is right or wrong is—
> O Hell! Look, Lord, look how
> They fall back behind me!

In the later version Crozier says:

> We select what we will and will not see,
> We keep the cosmos out with layers of cloth
> and strips of leather—
> O Hell! Look, Lord, look how
> They fall back behind me!
> The snow turns red, there are sounds
> of men puking, and sounds
> of knives scraping bone.
> They are eating
> one of their dead,
> They are whimpering; the snow
> Turns red.

Further, in case we miss the point of the prayer, with its "Give us this day our daily bread, and forgive us. .," or its link with "Though all our senses fall apart / we still must eat," it is driven home, savagely, unlike the deliberate and careful ambiguity in the earlier version: "Give us this day our daily bread and forgive us / The kind of bread and blood and meat we've tasted."

Is the refusal to recognize the possibility of cannibalism an example of the mechanism we use to keep the cosmos out? Are we doing the unspeakable and refusing to acknowledge it? Do we begin with false premises about survival? Whatever the possibilities, MacEwen thrusts them firmly into the foreground in these lines.

Rasmussen is the intermediary between the explorers and the audience. His counterpart, the one who interprets the purely physical dimensions of place and circumstance, is the Inuk, Qaqortingnek. For Qaqortingnek, the western metaphoric and literal exploration does not exist: he is at home, dealing only with actuality. "And they did not understand" is a refrain in Qaqortingnek's lines. He does not understand the science and ghosts that inhabit the explorers' minds. "My fathers had never seen white men / And my fathers did not know about ships," he explains, "and they did not understand the dark" (in the hull of the ship). Ships and dark may not be the most appropriate symbols for what Inuit did not understand, more aptly, the "papers," the ship's records, are torn up and scattered by Inuit children. Kucharzyk's music emphasizes the contrast between the complexity and conflict of the explorers' thinking and Qaqortingnek's childlike simplicity of utterance.

In *Terror and Erebus* Gwendolyn MacEwen explores the interior boundaries of the possible and permissible in the human mind, and their echo in action. What she achieves is, in her own words, "a bridge between the inner world of the psyche and the 'outer' world of things" ("A Poet's Journey into the Interior," *Cross-Canada Writers' Quarterly* 8. 3-4: 55).

E.D.

* * *

Terror and Erebus was first broadcast on the program series CBC Tuesday Night on 21 January 1975.

Rasmussen   Henry Ramer
Franklin   Charles Palmer
Crozier   Chris Wiggins
Eskimo   George Ross Robertson
The music was composed and conducted by Morris Surdin.

The cantata, *Terror and Erebus (A Lament for Franklin)* by Henry Kucharzyk, text by Gwendolyn MacEwen, was commissioned by the Canadian Broadcasting Corporation and the Ontario Arts Council and premiered on 17 June 1997. All the characters were presented by baritone Theodore Baerg, with music played by the Northern Portraits Ensemble.

TERROR AND EREBUS

CHARACTERS

Rasmussen
Franklin
Crozier
Qaqortingneq

Being an account of the search by Rasmussen for the remains
of the Franklin expedition.

RASMUSSEN
King William Island . . . latitude unmentionable.
But I'm not the first here.
They preceded me, they marked the way
      with bones
White as the ice is, whiter maybe,
The white of death,
      of purity.

But it was almost a century ago
And sometimes I find their bodies
Like shattered compasses, like sciences
Gone mad, pointing in a hundred directions
      at once—
The last whirling graph of their agony.

How could they know what I now know,
A century later, my pockets stuffed with
      comfortable maps—
That this was, after all, an island,
That the ice can camouflage the straits
And drive men into false channels,
Drive men
      into white, sliding traps . . . ?

How could they know, even stand back and see
The nature of the place they stood on,
When no man can, no man knows where he stands
Until he leaves his place, looks back
      and knows.

Ah Franklin! I would like to find you
Now, your body spreadeagled like a star,
A human constellation in the snow.
                    The earth insists
There is but one geography, but then
There is another still—
The complex, crushed geography of men.

You carried all maps within you;
Land masses moved in relation to
                    you—
As though you created the Passage
By *willing* it to be.
                    Ah Franklin!
To follow you one does not need geography.

At least not totally, but more of that
Instrumental knowledge the bones have,
Their limits their measurings.
The eye *creates* the horizon,
The ear *invents* the wind,
The hand reaching out from a parka sleeve
By touch demands that the touched thing
                    be.

So I've followed you here
Like a dozen others, looking for relics
                    of your ships, your men.
Here to this awful monastery
                    where you, where Crozier died,
                    and all the men with you died,
Seeking a passage from imagination to
                    reality,
Seeking a passage from land to land
                    by sea.

Now in the arctic night
I can almost suppose you did not die,
But are somewhere walking between
The icons of ice, pensively
                    like a priest,
Wrapped in the cold holiness of snow,
                    of your own memory.

FRANKLIN
I brought them here, a hundred and twenty-nine men,
Led them into this bottleneck,
This white asylum.
I chose the wrong channel and
The ice folded in around us,
Gnashing its jaws, folded in
              around us.

The ice clamps and will not open.
For a year it has not opened
Though we bash against it
Like lunatics at padded walls.

My ships, the *Terror*, the *Erebus*
Are learning the meanings of their
              names.
What madman christened them
The ships of terror and of Hell?
In open sea they did four knots;
Here, they rot and cannot move at all.

Another winter in the ice,
The second one for us, folds in.
Latitude 70 ^{N}. November 25, 1846.
The sun has vanished.

RASMUSSEN
Nothing then but to sit out the darkness,
The second sterile year,
              and wait for spring
And pray the straits would crack
Open, and the dash begin again;
Pray you could drive the ships
Through the yielding, melting floes,
              drive and press on down
Into the giant virginal strait of
              Victoria.
But perhaps she might not yield,
She might not let you enter,
              but might grip
And hold you crushed forever in her stubborn
              loins,
              her horrible house,
Her white asylum in an ugly marriage.

FRANKLIN

I told him, I *told* Crozier
The spring is coming, but it's *wrong*
        somehow.
Even in summer the ice may not open,
It may not open.
Some of the men have scurvy, Crozier . . .
        their faces, the sick ones,
        their faces reflect their minds.
I can read the disease in their souls;
It's a mildewed chart
On their flesh.
        But this is no place
To talk of souls; here
The soul *becomes* the flesh.
I may have to send men on foot
To where the passage is,
To prove it, to prove it is there,
That Simpson joins Victoria,
That there is a meaning, a pattern
        imposed on this chaos,
A conjunction of waters,
        a kind of meaning
Even here, even in this place.

RASMUSSEN

A kind of meaning, even here,
Even in this place.
        Yes, yes,
We are men, we demand
That the world be logical, don't we?

But eight of your men went overland
        and saw it, proved it,
Proved the waters found each other
        as you said,
Saw the one flowing into the other,
Saw the conjunction, the synthesis
        of faith, there
In the white metallic cold.

And returned to tell you, Franklin,
And found you dying in *Erebus*,
In the hell
        of your body,
The last ship of your senses.

June 11, 1847.

Crozier took command,
A scientist, understanding magnetism,
          the pull of elements, but
The laws which attract and as easily repel
Could not pull him from the hell
          of his science.

Crozier, what laws govern
This final tug of war
          between life and death,
These human polarities?
          The ice
Is its own argument.

CROZIER

It is September, the end of summer.

Summer, there was no summer . . .
Funny how you go on using
          the same old terms
Even when they've lost all meaning.

Two summers, and the ice has not melted.
Has the globe tipped? The axis slipped?
          Is there no sense of season
Anywhere?

September 1847.
We await our third winter in the ice.

RASMUSSEN

But the ice, wasn't it drifting south
Itself, like a ship — your ship within a
Ship?

CROZIER

The ice is drifting south, but
          not fast enough.
It has time, it has more time than we
          have time;
It has eternity to drift south.
It doesn't eat, doesn't get scurvy,
Doesn't die as my men are dying.

April 1848. The winter is over.
Supplies are to last three months only.
We are leaving the ships for good.

RASMUSSEN
You went overland, then.
Overland, an ironic word.
How can you call this *land*?
　　　　It's the white teeth
Of a giant saw,
　　　　and men crawl through it
Like ants through an upright comb.
Overland. You set out from the ships
In a kind of horrible birth,
　　　　a forced expulsion
From the two wombs, solid at least,
Three-dimensional, smelling of wood
And metal and familiar things.

Overland . . .

CROZIER
April 21, 1848. Good Friday.
Our last day in the ships.
We pray, we sing hymns, there
　　　　is nothing else to do.
We are all of us crucified
　　　　before an ugly Easter.
Civilization . . . six hundred and seventy miles away.

A hundred and five men left. Three months' supplies.
Our Father who art in heaven,
Hallowed be thy name . . .
　　　　six hundred and seventy miles to civilization,
Three months' supplies, a hundred and five men . . .

Give us this day our daily bread
And forgive us . . .
　　　　scurvy among the men,
　　　　we leave ship tomorrow,
Thy kingdom come, thy will be done . . .
　　　　six hundred and seventy miles to
　　　　civilization . . .
For thine is the kingdom, and the power,
And the glory . . .

Our Father
Our Father
Our Father

RASMUSSEN
April 25, 1848. HMS Terror and Erebus
Were deserted, having been beset
Since the 12th of September, 1846.
The officers and crew consisting of a hundred and five
Souls under the command of Captain F. R. Crozier
Landed here. The total loss by deaths in this Expedition
Has been to this date nine officers and
Fifteen men.

So you pushed on, and sun and snow,
        that marriage of agonizing light
Assailed you.

CROZIER
In the beginning God made the light
And saw that it was good . . .
        the light . . .
        and saw that it was good.
My men fall back, blinded,
        clutching their scorched eyes.
Whoever said that Hell was darkness?
What fool said that light was good
        and darkness evil?
In extremes all things reverse themselves.

RASMUSSEN
The naked eye dilates, shrinks,
Goes mad, cannot save itself.
You didn't even have those wooden slits
The Eskimos wore
        to censor the sun,
        to select as much light
As the eye could bear.
Some science might have tamed the light
For you,
        not hope, not prayer—
But pairs of simple wooden slits,
Only those ridiculous
        instruments
That keep the cosmos out.

CROZIER

We select what we will and will not see,
We keep the cosmos out with layers of cloth
        and strips of leather—
Oh Hell! Look, Lord, look how
They fall back behind me!
The snow turns red, there are sounds
        of men puking, and sounds
Of knives scraping bone.
They are eating
        one of their dead,
They are whimpering; the snow
Turns red.

I sent thirty men back to the ships,
Thirty good men back to the *Terror*, the *Erebus*
        for food.
We can go blind but we must eat
        in this white waste.
Though all our senses fall apart
        we still must eat.
Give us this day our daily bread and forgive us
The kind of bread and blood and meat we've tasted.

RASMUSSEN

Thirty good men.
On the way back all of them but five
        died,
Knelt before the sun for the last time
        and died,
Knelt like priests in the whiteness
        and died,
        on their knees, died,
Or stretched straight out,
Or sitting in a brief stop
        which never ended,
        died.
It does not matter now.

Five made it back to the ships
And there, in the wombs, in the
        wooden hulls,
        died.

Five who could not go back,
Who could not a second time
Bear the birth, the going forth,
      the expulsion
        into pure worlds of ice.

CROZIER

The men do not return with food.
We push on, we cannot wait here.
The winds wait, the sun waits,
      the ice waits, but
We cannot wait here;
      to stop is to die
In our tracks,
      to stand like catatonics
In this static house of bone.

Already we look like statues,
      marbled, white.
The flesh and hair bleaches out;
      we are cast in plaster.
This ice cannot bear the flesh of men,
This sun will not tolerate colour;
      we begin
To move *into* the ice, to mimic it.
Our Father who are in heaven,
Our Father
Our Father

One night we saw Eskimos
And they were afraid,
They gave us a seal,
They ran away at night.

We have come two hundred miles from the ships,
We have come two hundred miles.
There are thirty men left.
It is the end, it is
The end.

RASMUSSEN

Now there was nothing more to do,
      no notes to write and leave in cairns,
      no measurements to take, no
Readings of any temperatures
      save the inner

Agony of the blood.
Now Crozier, now you've come
To the end of science.

CROZIER

We scattered our instruments behind us
   and left them where they fell
Like pieces of our bodies, like limbs
We no longer had need for;
    we walked on and dropped them,
    compasses, tins, tools, all of them.
We came to the end of science.

Now we leave ciphers in the snow,
We leave our instruments in the snow.
It is the end of science.

What magnet do I know of
That will pull us south?
   None,
   none but the last inevitable
   one—
Death who draws,
Death who reaches out his pulling arms
And draws men along like filings
   on paper.

It is the end of science.
We left behind us
A graph in the snow, a horrible cipher,
   a desperate code
The sun cannot read, and the snow
   cannot either.

RASMUSSEN

But men can, men like me who come
To find your traces, the pieces
Of your pain scattered in the white
   vaults of the snow.
Men like me who come and stand
   and learn
The agony your blood learned—
   how the body is bleached
And the brain itself turns
   a kind of pure purged
   white.

And what happened to the ships?
It hurts to talk of it.
        The Eskimo Qaqortingneq
Knows.

QAQORTINGNEQ

I remember the day
When our fathers found a ship.
They were hunting seals
And it was spring
And the snow melted around
The holes where the seals breathed.

Far away on the ice
My fathers saw a strange shape
A black shape, too great to be seals.
They ran home and told all the men
In the village
And the next day all came to see
This strange thing.

It was a ship, and they moved closer
And saw that it was empty
That it had slept there for a long time.
My fathers had never seen white men
And my fathers did not know about ships.
They went aboard the great ship
As though into another world
Understanding nothing.
They cut the lines of the little boat
Which hung from the ship
And it fell broken to the ice.
They found guns in the ship
And did not understand
And they broke the guns
And used them for harpoons.

And they did not understand.

They went into the little houses
On the deck of the ship
And found dead people in beds
Who had lain there a long time.

Then they went down, down
Into the hull of the great ship
And it was dark
And they did not understand the dark.

And to make it light, they bored a hole
In the side of the ship
But instead of the light
The water came in the hole
And flooded, and sank the ship
And my fathers ran away
And they did not understand.

RASMUSSEN
And the papers? Franklin's papers?
The ship's logs, the reports?

QAQORTINGNEQ
Papers, oh yes!
The little children found papers
In the great ship
But they did not understand papers.
They played with them
They ripped them up
They threw them into the wind
Like birds . . .

RASMUSSEN
They were right—
What would papers mean to them?
      Cryptic marks, latitudes,
      signatures, journals,
      diaries of despair,
      official reports
Nobody needs to read.
I've seen the real journals
You left us — you Franklin, you Crozier.
I've seen the skulls of your men
      in the snow, their sterile bones
Arranged around cairns like
      compasses,
Marking out all the latitudes
      and longitudes
Of men.

Now the great passage is open,
The one you dreamed of, Franklin,
And great white ships plough through it
Over and over again,
Packed with cargo and carefree men.
It is as though no one had to prove it
Because the passage was always there.
Or . . . is it that the way was *invented*,
Franklin?

        That you cracked the passage open
With the force of your sheer certainty?

        Or is it that you cannot know,
Can never know,
Where the passage lies
Between conjecture and reality . . . ?

END

Ditch

by

Geoff Kavanagh

Greg Kramer as Whitbread (left) and Jonathan Tanner as Hennesey (right).

Like Gwendolyn MacEwen's *Terror and Erebus*, Geoff Kavanagh's *Ditch* joins the long line of Canadian endeavours to put literary flesh on the bare historical bones that remain of Franklin's arctic expedition of 1845. In *Terror and Erebus* MacEwen deploys a wide dramatic lens to critique the technological and philosophical assumptions that informed, and mis-informed, voyages of northern exploration. Kavanagh brings a much narrower focus to bear on this same historical event: he explores it from the perspective of two sailors left in a ditch to make their peace with their culture, their sexuality, and each other. The result is a work of tremendous contemporary resonance, emotional power, and humour.

A good deal of *Ditch*'s dramatic power derives from Kavanagh's skillful use of ironic reversal, and particularly from his consistent shifting of the traditionally marginal to front and centre. His choice of title is a case in point. While Kavanagh relies on our common understanding of the ditch as a place that is entirely lacking in connotations of honour or prestige (it is perhaps the spatial antonym of the pedestal or precipice), by the end of the play, we come to associate this humble space with the positive qualities of authenticity and compassion.

For those unfamiliar with traditional narratives of northern adventure and of the myth of the North that nourishes them, a brief sketch of this sub-genre's features will help to demonstrate the degree to which Kavanagh undercuts this tradition. Within this narrative schema, protagonists are represented typically as rational agents of the highest order and of the highest rank; they are shining examples of the European male at his peak of physical endurance and emotional invulnerability. Though such men invariably encounter dangers, these challenges are overcome with equal invulnerability. Needless to say, such heroes are unfailingly represented as heterosexual. Indeed, the only desire acknowledged typically by such heroes is that which draws them upward and onward towards terra incognita. And given that such lands are frequently gendered as feminine, even this desire is rendered heterosexual (see *Terror and Erebus*, 123).

Kavanagh overturns these conventions with parodic abandon. In *Ditch* we hear not of success but of utter failure; here our dramatic focus is not on captain or officer but on Whitbread and Hennesey, two common sailors. These men are neither brave nor strong. Whitbread is gravely ill and Hennesey is lame; despite the rifle at their side, they live in continual fear of wolves, bears, and of the crewmen who abandoned them. Further-more, it was neither Empiric idealism nor a thirst for the heroic that guided these two towards the historically infamous site where we encounter them. The only principles that have drawn Whitbread and Hennesey to the Arctic are economic necessity and Murphy's Law: being down on their luck, they had the misfortune to find employment as seamen aboard the *Terror* and *Erebus*. And last but not least, Whitbread and Hennesey are gay, and, despite Hennesey's reluctance to admit it, they are in love. In *Ditch*, desire is felt not for terra incognita, nor even for the Empire's homeland, but rather for the loving human touch, for authentic communication, for sexual intimacy, and for a world in which these desires could be acknowledged, expressed and respected. A terra incognita of a wholly different sort.

Despite this virtually endless string of ironic reversals, I do not wish to suggest that while the traditional narrative of northern exploration got it all wrong, Kavanagh has set the record straight. That was neither his intention nor the result he has achieved with *Ditch*. In a 24 June 1998 letter to Sherrill Grace, Kavanagh classified *Ditch* a "semi-absurdist comic drama." It is absurd in that Whitbread and Hennesey's physical and emotional energy levels are not consistent with the context of death-by-starvation and illness Kavanagh situates them within. Such victims are without the emotional energy to quest for meaning and resolution, let alone the physical energy to consider swimming in Arctic waters or engaging in sexual activity.

There are unquestionably strong parallels between *Ditch* and that classic of absurdist theatre, Beckett's *Waiting for Godot*. Both works feature two bickering male protagonists engaged in a series of futile attempts to exercise agency, and both are set in a near-barren landscape. Yet we must note Kavanagh's classification of *Ditch* as "*semi*-absurdist." He points to Whitbread and Hennesey's sense of historicity as the feature which distinguishes *Ditch* from Beckett's play: "their historicality is a large factor in the play," Kavanagh told Sherrill Grace, "whereas in Godot history is nullified." And despite Kavanagh's decision to end the play on an absurdist note ("There's nothing . . ."), in *Ditch* meaning is not only sought after. It is found in the love for Whitbread that Hennesey is finally (if tragically) able to acknowledge to himself, and to the ghost of social authority his mind conjures to sanctify this love.

In the end, I think it is Kavanagh's decision to represent the final, torturous days of the Franklin expedition with such spareness of character and setting that gives *Ditch* its allegorical power. An array of thematic landscapes awaits the wandering interpretive eye. When this eye rests on the two abandoned sailors in a fearful land with a boat full of European junk, *Ditch* becomes an allegory for cultural displacement in which North functions as a metonym for Canada. When this eye focuses on Whitbread and Hennesey's sexuality, the fearful world surrounding them, and their abandonment in a ditch, the play becomes a poignant expression of the degradation and isolation gay men must endure in a homophobic society. Add to this the themes of illness and death that pervade the play, and *Ditch* can easily be interpreted (as it has been by reviewers) as an allegory for the isolation and despair caused by AIDS.

Geoff Kavanagh was awarded a Chalmers Award for *Ditch* in 1995. His other works include *Canoe Lake*, a play about the death of Tom Thomson set in Algonquin Park, and most recently, *The Water Crawlers*, a play set in Toronto. By moving his plays progressively closer to his own time and place, Kavanagh is exploring the contemporary resonance of North within a nation whose citizens are overwhelmingly situated along its southern border.

L.C.

* * *

Ditch was first produced by Inkenstink Productions at the Tarragon Mainspace as part of the SummerWorks Festival in Toronto, Ontario 26 August 1993.

| Whitbread | Greg Kramer |
| Hennesey | Jonathan Tanner |

Directed by Colleen Williams

DITCH

CHARACTERS

Hennesey	late twenties
Whitbread	late twenties
The Captain	to be played by Whitbread

SETTING

The setting is the far north. Hennesey and Whitbread are two of the last members of a doomed Northwest Passage expedition. With their ships trapped in the ice for nineteen months, the surviving men begin a desperate trek hauling a lifeboat south to find one of the Northern rivers. Action starts after Hennesey and Whitbread have just been abandoned; starving, the healthier men have tried to return to the ship to find whatever food they can. They have left Hennesey and Whitbread with the boat which contains an assortment of useless articles. Whitbread is near death yet lucid, and Hennesey has a broken foot. His foot was broken when the sledge fell on it; he can no longer walk well enough to keep up with the other men. They have left, promising to return.

SET

The set should convey the early summer of the Arctic. Its two principal elements are the lifeboat and the ditch. Only the bow of the lifeboat need be seen, however there has to be room enough for Whitbread to be propped up realistically within it, and to be dragged in and out by Hennesey. It may be placed horizontal to the audience with only the right side showing.

The ditch itself can be conveyed in several ways; if several different levels of playing area are used, then it might only need to be suggested by the higher levels. If only one level is used, then the lifeboat may be seen to be coming out of the end of it. It should be combined of materials which suggest the ice, snow and muddy conditions of the Arctic at this time of year.

At different points in the play, the men suggest that they are in a valley, on a beach or upon a plain. This is meant to suggest the lack of any cognition upon their part of where they actually are. The set, therefore, need not necessarily appear realistic, and any abstract elements which the designer sees fit to use to convey the sense of cold and vastness which is the Arctic are perfectly acceptable.

Scene One

WHITBREAD is sitting up in the boat.

WHITBREAD (*reading a piece of Royal Navy bottle paper*)
Whoever finds this paper is requested to forward it to
the Secretary of the Admiralty, London, with a note
of the time and place at which it was found . . .

Stops reading.

Fucking hell . . .

Reads.

Or, if more convenient, to deliver it for that purpose
to the British Consul at the nearest Port.

Pause.

Fucking China . . .

Springtime, 1848; a place that'll have to wait till
someone gets famous finding corpses here to be
named. I, Able-Bodied Seaman Whitbread, will not
have this place named after me; for despite the fact
that the ground is now swollen with them; humped,
their arses sticking skyward the highest things to be
found on this desolate plain; I haven't got the
strength to catalogue the event; won't be given a
roast beef luncheon at the Royal Geographical
Society . . .

> *Lights up on HENNESEY at Stage Left, using a*
> *rifle as an ill-suited crutch. He waves it in the*
> *air, mock cheerfulness, but can't support his*
> *weight without it.*

There is no roast beef — geography for dead men . . .
Historians will have to play this game — how two
men out of a hundred and five became separate from
the rest and died in a ditch together. A gruesome
discovery for the searchers sent out; a puzzle to be
marvelled at behind any more fashionable news of
war . . .

HENNESEY (*yelling at the departed men*) Of course it's no go!
Look at what dragging that bloody boat did to my
foot. Broken; and now I can't keep up. Somebody's

got to look after Whitbread — the state he's in.
Don't worry boys — we'll be fine. Just don't . . .
Don't forget us! Find the bloody ship and then come
back, no point in dragging the boat back there, a
straight line — that's what we need. Find the
straight line boys! Find the straight line you sodding
bastards — as if there's any straight lines out here.

>   *Pause.*

WHITBREAD "I could count four corpses without moving my
head." Somebody could be knighted for saying that
— a whisper in Victoria's ear and he'd earn the
gratitude of the realm simply for stating the remains
of this . . . "Most confounding, your Majesty, were
the two sorry fuckers we found in a ditch." " 'Sorry
fuckers, in deed' . . ."

HENNESEY Nineteen months stuck in the ice trying to find the
quick way to China! It wasn't much though, was it?
We had fun, didn't we — watching everybody go
mad, get sick, start dying? Wasn't that worth the
quick route?

My broken foot. It's only a sprain, sure to be mended
by the time you get back! You fucking pricks; I
could keep up, I couldn't pull, sure; but I could keep
up. You shits! "Stay with the boat, Hennesey, give
yourself time to mend and look after Whitbread,"
Was that some kind of joke? Whitbread's half-dead
you sodding bastards!

>   *Pause. He hobbles over to the boat and takes in*
>   *their surroundings.*

They didn't even haul the boat out of the ditch. They
left us in the ditch to drown in our sleep in the first
high tide.

>   *He grabs a rope attached to a ring at the bow of*
>   *the boat and attempts to pull the boat up,*
>   *obviously to no avail. He collapses on the*
>   *ground holding his foot in pain.*

Bastards! You left us in a ditch to die!

WHITBREAD Don't you think the boat will float?

HENNESEY What?

WHITBREAD	If this ditch fills up with water then the boat will float.
HENNESEY	That's right, we could wake up miles from here — how would they find us then? Did you hear that you shits? You didn't even secure the boat for us!
WHITBREAD	We probably won't float much farther than where you're standing.
HENNESEY	It's a bloody ignoble thing, getting left in a ditch. How the hell are we supposed to keep a look out from down there? How are we supposed to defend ourselves — against the savages and bears?
WHITBREAD	We haven't seen any bears in months.
HENNESEY	They wouldn't hang about with a hundred men all ready to shoot them. But there's only two of us, they might figure it's worth the risk now — fuck all that we can do about it.
WHITBREAD	Can't we shoot them as well?
HENNESEY	How the hell are we going to do that, two little men with a couple of rifles? A decent bear will keep coming with more than two shots in him, unless we get him in the heart or brain. Could you shoot the heart out of a bear, Whitbread, especially if it was running at you?
WHITBREAD	I suppose not.
HENNESEY	Likely bloody not!
WHITBREAD	Maybe the noise would scare it away.
HENNESEY	Listen . . . All you hear out here is noise, the wind and that ice breaking up. I'll tell you what'll happen. We'll be lying in that ditch, thinking how nice it was that those sodding bloody bastards left us here to rot together. And the bears will be over there, rolling bones for our belongings; when one or two of the lucky ones will get up, come over here and fucking eat us. Promise you'll do me a favour, Whitbread.
WHITBREAD	What's that?

HENNESEY   If you see a bear running at us please don't try and
                  shoot it, shoot me. I'll be standing right next to
                  you, you won't be able to miss.

WHITBREAD   What'll I do then?

HENNESEY   The other gun will be here, you can shoot yourself.
                  I'd do the same for you except I haven't got the
                  courage. A real bleeder, that's why they stuck me
                  here with you. They knew I'd look after you, not
                  bash in your head the second they topped the rise and
                  go hobblin' after them screamin' Whitbread's done
                  bought it . . .

                  It'd be easy, you know . . . ? I could do that, you
                  know . . . ?

                       He picks up a conch shell at his feet.

                  I could do it with this!

                       Pause. Realizing what's in his hand.

                  What the fuck is this doing here?

WHITBREAD   Someone dropped it.

HENNESEY   One of the men—

WHITBREAD   He got it out of the boat just before they left. It's his
                  lucky conch . . .

HENNESEY   You mean we've been dragging some bastard's lucky
                  conch all over this shithole?

WHITBREAD   *(throwing items out of the boat)* We've been
                  dragging something lucky for everyone. Where were
                  you when the officers decided how many lucky
                  possessions were needed to ensure our success? Their
                  books — very lucky books . . . Plates; you
                  wouldn't want to starve to death without empty plates
                  around to remind you of the fact; and there's a change
                  of clothes for every man in case the savages throw us
                  a party — we could all share this toothbrush and
                  comb for a bit of sprucing up . . .

HENNESEY   But a fucking conch . . .

WHITBREAD   (*holding up a sponge*) Look, a sponge to go with it. Could you imagine having a lucky sponge?

HENNESEY   At least a sponge doesn't weigh that much — this thing must be five pounds!

WHITBREAD   (*finding another conch, different shape*) He had a set; though they don't seem to match. Do you think he fancied himself a bit of a collector? Then why would he only take the one out of the boat?

                 He pokes his fingers into the pink opening.

                 Maybe it reminded him of home . . .

HENNESEY   We've been dragging this codswallop for a hundred miles. Men have died and haven't even been buried because everyone's knackered from pulling this boat full of rubbish.

WHITBREAD   Not all of it's rubbish. Here's a pair of slippers that've hardly been worn.

HENNESEY   Who was it? Who was it that had this fucking conch? I'm going to kill him with it when they get back.

WHITBREAD   I thought you were going to kill me . . .

HENNESEY   I could kill you first and then go after them . . . Whitbread's bloody dead and did anyone drop this? Smash in his teeth with the cold bit of comfort that looks like a cunt from home.

                 Pause. Looks it over carefully.

                 Do you think that's what it was? That's bloody perverse, isn't it? (*beat*) A perversity of nature — out of one of the Captain's Sunday sermons. "It's important, gentlemen, to stay all such perversities . . ." That's you and this bastard, only he's at least natural, isn't he?

WHITBREAD   This one looks like it has teeth.

HENNESEY   You were having a laugh through those sermons,
                  weren't you? If the Captain only knew what
                  perversities were sitting in front of him — looking
                  like the holiest pricks in the place. How many times
                  did he ask you to lead us in a hymn?

WHITBREAD   I was the only one with any choir training . . .

HENNESEY   Choir training my arse. He'd finish giving his
                  sermon and look about to see if anyone had paid
                  attention. You'd be sitting, eyes closed, hands
                  clasped and rocking back and forth like you'd been
                  praying. Prayin' — you . . . I'd want to grab you
                  and throw you out of there myself but what right did I
                  have — a heathen, I didn't believe in any of that shit
                  anyway. I don't know how you managed . . . You
                  don't fancy yourself some kind of saint, do you
                  Whitbread?

WHITBREAD   No.

HENNESEY   The patron saint of perversities. Saint Tim
                  Whitbread; martyred in a ditch by the heathen
                  Hennesey because he was half-fucking dead anyway
                  and a pervert to boot . . .

WHITBREAD   If you're going to martyr me then you'd better hurry
                  — you won't catch the men otherwise.

HENNESEY   Who's the one who's bloody martyred us — brought
                  us down into this ditch?

WHITBREAD   You won't be able to move very fast — and they
                  won't be dragging anything.

HENNESEY   Except themselves — whereas I'll be dragging you.
                  It'd be a bit of a race — wouldn't it? How soon I'd
                  be able to forget killing you — how much lighter my
                  steps would get the farther away you became.

WHITBREAD   I could start crawling in the other direction — I don't
                  expect I'd last long.

HENNESEY   That wouldn't be like me killing you though, would
                  it?

WHITBREAD   You could shoo me away — be the cause of my death
                  that way.

HENNESEY	Start screamin' "Get away, ya bastard!" "You'll soon feel ma boot in yer arse!" Something like that?
WHITBREAD	"I'll chowder yer noggin' with me cunty conch!"
HENNESEY	Would that scare you?
WHITBREAD	Your leaving would scare me . . .

       Pause.

HENNESEY	Then let them go — it's more important that I be a witness to this, don't you think? I wonder if there's ever been the like . . . Two such sinners with nothing to do but pray? Just the two on the little crosses next to Christ. What were their names? You should know, you studied for the clergy.
WHITBREAD	Schoolmaster.
HENNESEY	There must have been religious education for that . . .
WHITBREAD	I wasn't at it very long.
HENNESEY	Well let's pretend we're them, then. I'll be from Germana and you can be from Sodom — and they've stuck us up next to Jesus because we were out of town when God got pissed off and burnt up all our kin. How do you think we should go about asking to be saved?
WHITBREAD	We could repent . . .
HENNESEY	Say we're sorry . . .
WHITBREAD	Ask to be forgivin . . .
HENNESEY	It wasn't us, really. It was two other blokes. Henbread and Whitessey . . .
WHITBREAD	I don't think that would work.
HENNESEY	Not even worth a try?
WHITBREAD	Our fate's in this ditch.
HENNESEY	You're spoiling it now — just cause Christ's not here doesn't mean he's not listening.
WHITBREAD	I don't think you're sincere.

HENNESEY	That's because I'm not dying, am I? I'm waiting for the men to come back.
WHITBREAD	They won't be coming back.
HENNESEY	Of course they'll be coming back — we've got all their lucky stuff, don't we? How the hell do they expect to get out of here without their lucky stuff? Somebody's wife will kill him if he gets home without those slippers . . .
WHITBREAD	They've probably forgotten all about us . . .
HENNESEY	How do you forget two of your mates and a boat that you nearly died dragging? Tell me! You're just being a bastard, right — trying to destroy my hope?
WHITBREAD	It's your hope that I love most about you. My love feeding it. I'll be dead soon, then there won't be any.
HENNESEY	Don't start . . . Don't you dare start talking like that . . .
WHITBREAD	About dying?
HENNESEY	The other thing.
WHITBREAD	Love?
HENNESEY	That's it! Keep your love to yourself — I'm supposed to be repenting.
WHITBREAD	I can't do that even sitting here it's what I think about.
HENNESEY	You're going to keep bringing that up, aren't you?
WHITBREAD	I only said I love you.
HENNESEY	Well I don't love you! No matter what's happened . . .
WHITBREAD	Nothing's happened.
HENNESEY	That's right — not a damned thing. Two years stuck in that ice and a lot can be forgiven — forgotten . . . Do you hear that, Saint Tim; it can all be forgotten . . . Think about something else for Christ's sake.

Pause.

Everybody else was doing it, weren't they?

WHITBREAD No.

HENNESEY Don't make it sound like that — like I was the only one . . .

WHITBREAD You weren't?

HENNESEY They were lined up to have a go at you. We used to draw lots for it in the mess — who's going to fuck Whitbread? We were going to string a blanket up, give you your own little corner where you wouldn't have to freeze your arse but it became such a game, hunting you down, the whore up on deck; half-frozen but still ready . . .

WHITBREAD You always stank of rum — it disgusted me at first.

HENNESEY You stank of soap — it was worse.

Pause.

I've changed my mind. I think I'll shoot you if I see a bear coming; it'd be nice to do something pleasant before death . . . "There — that's the end of that bastard Whitbread — that's the end of my hope." It'd be pretty stupid to greet a bear with a look of hope on my face, wouldn't it? I'd hate to think I did anything stupid out here, wouldn't you?

WHITBREAD I doubt there's anything stupid left to do out here. Not after the first winter when they made us keep watch . . . Those bloody winter months stuck in the ice, in the dark. Keeping that watch just so they could call the day something.

HENNESEY *(authoritative tone)* "Discipline, Whitbread. You can't survive out here without discipline."

WHITBREAD There wasn't anything to see, not even to look at — men went mad up there staring at nothing; the officers told them not to look anymore, to keep their eyes to the ship. They had to double the watch just to keep us from walking off.

HENNESEY Going off for a romp, more like.

WHITBREAD   You're what saved me from deserting, walking
              off . . . That's all you have to do to kill yourself out
              here; walk off for a few hundred yards and you'll be
              dead in hours; frozen, eaten — pitching headfirst into
              a ditch like this. "Death by misadventure —
              madness . . ."

                  Pause.

              Promise you'll shoot me if I go mad.

HENNESEY   I'm the one who's mad; going barmy listening to you
              — "Love's all I can think of!" I could shoot you for
              that. I could shoot myself for listening.

WHITBREAD   If I don't know who I am; who you are — this
              place . . .

HENNESEY   You'd be a lucky bugger.

WHITBREAD   I don't want to forget. I'm happy, really — that it's
              ending like this, the two of us together.

HENNESEY   You're happy . . . We're rotting in a ditch and you're
              happy . . .

WHITBREAD   How many of the others ended up with no one;
              falling down and the only notice taken was of
              something to step over.

HENNESEY   And what notice will be taken of us?

WHITBREAD   We'll be a puzzle for historians when our bones are
              found.

HENNESEY   We're a puzzle now. It's enough to make you believe
              in Jesus — some sort of holy sick sense of humour.
              "I think I'll be especially nasty to Hennesey and
              Whitbread" — fuck them up the arse just to show
              that there's nothing Christian about that sort of
              business . . .

WHITBREAD   Christ had nothing to do with it — it was the men
              that left us here.

HENNESEY   Christ had everything to do with it — you picked us
                  out this lovely grave just because you're a holy little
                  prick at heart, needing a proper burial . . . I suppose
                  you'll want me to say a few good words and kick a
                  bit of dirt in on top of you when you're done. Maybe
                  I shouldn't wait then if you're so eager.

                  I could start filling that ditch in now, if you'd like.

                  HENNESEY finds a small pebble and throws it
                  at WHITBREAD.

WHITBREAD   Here! Are you still trying to smash my skull?

HENNESEY   I'm entertaining myself with the thought. There's
                  not a hell of a lot that's entertaining out here.

WHITBREAD   Do you think the boys would have you?

HENNESEY   I'll tell them what you said — who would blame me
                  for killing you then? "Hey boys — you wouldn't
                  believe what the little bitch was talking about!"

WHITBREAD   They'd send you back. It took days to find this ditch,
                  it's the perfect size for us, the two of us together . . .

HENNESEY   I gave him one with the lucky conch!

WHITBREAD   Bashed in his head with a bit of that plate!

HENNESEY   Smothered him in some party clothes!

WHITBREAD   Forced that sponge down his throat . . .

HENNESEY   Oh . . . You shouldn't talk about eating. We're
                  going to starve here if they don't come back.

WHITBREAD   They left us some food . . . *(holding up two parcels)*
                  Look — a bit of chocolate and some stinky
                  pemmican.

HENNESEY   It was all they had you ungrateful bastard; they won't
                  eat till they find the ships.

WHITBREAD   Then they'll starve. The ships are empty.

HENNESEY   There's a hold still full of tins! Everybody knew
                  that.

WHITBREAD   All of it spoiled. All of it torn apart by the ice by
              now — nothing'll be there . . .

HENNESEY   They've left us the damned boat; how the hell do you
              think they're going to get out of here without the
              damned boat?

              *The sound of a wolf calling is heard. They are
              both frozen as they wait for the sound to repeat
              itself; after a few seconds it does.*

HENNESEY   What the fuck is that! It's a wolf, isn't it? A
              fucking wolf! What the hell is a wolf doing up here?

WHITBREAD   I didn't think they lived this far North.

HENNESEY   Bloody right — there's nothing to eat!

WHITBREAD   I've heard there's hares, and mice — do you think a
              wolf would eat mice?

HENNESEY   I know what he'd rather eat. Us, right? Us!

WHITBREAD   Funny none of us ever saw any hares — even on
              watch.

HENNESEY   Who gives a bloody shit about hares — there's a
              fucking wolf over there — do you think he's thinking
              about hares right now?

              The cry is heard again. They whisper.

WHITBREAD   Sounds like he's moving off.

HENNESEY   What! He's practically on top of us.

WHITBREAD   It was definitely fainter that time.

HENNESEY   You're sitting in a ditch — how the hell can you tell?

WHITBREAD   I can still hear things.

HENNESEY   Do you think you'd be able to shoot a wolf?

WHITBREAD   It's not as big as a bear . . . But if it got close
              enough . . . The noise would definitely scare it —
              don't you think?

HENNESEY   Not the bloody noise again — do you think you
              could shoot anything?

WHITBREAD	I could shoot myself.
HENNESEY	Really? I don't think I could do that.
WHITBREAD	I'm not going to live anyway — why kill a perfectly good wolf?
HENNESEY	Because that perfectly good wolf might kill me! What do you think he's doing over there — singing? He's calling to his friends, "Hello, I've got supper on!"
WHITBREAD	I could kill myself now if you'd like. You could drag me a little ways and then hide while the wolves eat me.
HENNESEY	Think of something else.
WHITBREAD	We could turn this boat over — hide underneath it. It weighs about half a ton — that's a quarter of a ton each to lift. I'm game.
HENNESEY	You're game! You can barely stand up!
WHITBREAD	I could lie on my back and use my legs.
HENNESEY	Your legs don't work!

The wolf cry is heard again — much fainter.

WHITBREAD	(*loudly*) I barely heard it that time. They must be moving off.
HENNESEY	Shhh . . . ! Maybe they're being tricky — I've heard wolves are very cunning.
WHITBREAD	What? Like send one of them off to have a shout while the rest sneak up on us?
HENNESEY	Something like that.
WHITBREAD	That's stupid.
HENNESEY	Stupid? I wasn't the one who wanted to turn the two ton boat over.
WHITBREAD	Do you think they knew we were here?

HENNESEY   Shooting yourself — that's stupid! "Just drag me a
                ways" — and see if the bloody clever wolves don't
                find me when they're done with you!

WHITBREAD   They could come back.

HENNESEY   That's brave, isn't it? Shoot yourself and leave me
                here to deal with whatever comes along. I like that!
                Sounds like the bloody coward's way out!

WHITBREAD   If they come back we'll try to shoot them.

HENNESEY   You're just saying that now. I'll think you're behind
                me and really you'll be taking your head off with that
                thing!

                > *A large rumbling sound of ice breaking up
                > begins to grow. The men become quite agitated
                > as they shout over it.*

HENNESEY   I can't stand this!

WHITBREAD   Come back in the boat.

HENNESEY   The boat! As if the boat's any comfort . . .

WHITBREAD   It's better than being out there.

HENNESEY   It's a bloody grave — you won't catch me in it.

WHITBREAD   It's where we belong. Down in the muck.

HENNESEY   Don't start that again.

WHITBREAD   The muck of men like us — it's where they'd want
                us.

HENNESEY   Where who'd want us — the men? They're fucking
                starving, dying. No, it's what you bloody
                wanted . . .

WHITBREAD   I wanted you alone.

HENNESEY   And this was your only chance . . . ?

                > *Fade to black as the noise of the wind picks up
                > and they are dwarfed by the elements.*

Scene Two

*As the lights come up WHITBREAD is singing
a hymn. His singing is timed with
HENNESEY's slow wakening. As he finishes
the hymn he pulls a Captain's hat up from the
contents of the boat and puts it on.*

WHITBREAD   *(loud, brash tones)*
Eternal Father, strong to save.
Whose arm doth bind the restless wave.
Who bidst' the mighty ocean deep
It's own appointed limits keep.

    *He sings in a very authoritative manner,
imitating the Captain.*

Oh hear us when we call to thee
For those in peril on the sea.

    HENNESEY wakens with a start.

HENNESEY   What the Christ . . . ?

WHITBREAD   *(authoritative tone)* Do you realize what day this is?

HENNESEY   *(laughing)* The Captain! I'm bloody dead, aren't I?

WHITBREAD   It's Sunday morning, and you're sleeping.

HENNESEY   I starved to death, or was it the wolves? It was that Whitbread — he killed me, I became overly attached to some bastard's conch in the night and he got jealous.

WHITBREAD   Your language is reprehensible, Hennesey. Especially for the Lord's day.

HENNESEY   What difference does it make? I'm dead, aren't I? You must be a busy bastard, if they've sent you to get all your dead seamen.

WHITBREAD   We're going to have a Sunday service.

HENNESEY   Sunday service — is that what you want to call it? How about ushering old Hennesey down to the gates of hell. `Ere, did you see the way I died? Can you tell me what happened? It must have been a lousy death any way you looked at it.

WHITBREAD	We could begin with a prayer together.
HENNESEY	I was never much for the prayers.
WHITBREAD	I was going to talk of monogamy . . .
HENNESEY	Fine. I'll start. I knew a whore once who didn't half mind me as much of the rest of the seamen . . .
WHITBREAD	Your problem, Hennesey, is that you never partook of the sweet goodness in having a family.
HENNESEY	I partook of whores —
WHITBREAD	It's obvious you're in your present state because of your failure to abide by the divine example. Of Jesus, Mary and Joseph.
HENNESEY	I thought they were Irish swear words.
WHITBREAD	Your mental health is a disgrace.
HENNESEY	True, I was driven mad listening to a lunatic who insisted he loved me in a ditch.
WHITBREAD	A filthy business . . .
HENNESEY	He was a whore as well; though of all of them, I'm sure he loved me the best.
WHITBREAD	There's time to repent! When you get out of here I'd like you to have a family.
HENNESEY	You'd like that would you?
WHITBREAD	*(holding up a plate)* You can keep their picture in a frame. *(kisses it)* And be faithful to that whenever temptation calls.
HENNESEY	What if we both get out of here?
WHITBREAD	You could call your first son . . . *(beat, takes off the hat)* Little Tim, after me. *(beat)* But you wouldn't want a son that took after me, would you?
HENNESEY	The men will be back soon — we could be ready to go with them.

WHITBREAD	I'd rather have a son that took after you — full of hope always, that would be a charming thing in a boy, wouldn't it?
HENNESEY	We only need a bit of rest — that's what they said, wasn't it?
WHITBREAD	He could show up at the door with half-dead things — turtles and birds that the family cat had mauled, and tell you he'd like to keep them as pets till they healed. You'd put them in a little box together and you'd watch with him as they died, saying the whole time that they were going to be all right. You'd be good at that, wouldn't you? You could be a lying bastard to him, couldn't you?
HENNESEY	My foot's just sprained — and you're only tired . . .
WHITBREAD	I can barely walk!
HENNESEY	We could throw out all this shit from the boat — take you along that way.
WHITBREAD	Better you bashed my head in now than keep telling me that.
HENNESEY	*(begins scattering the items out of the boat)* What's more important — some fancy clobber, bloody plates and books, slippers and fucking sponges, or taking you with us.
WHITBREAD	You'd only die dragging me along.
HENNESEY	There's shit in there weighs three times what you do . . . We won't be taking any of this with us.
WHITBREAD	I'd like to make a confession.
HENNESEY	A confession — you were the one doing the service.
WHITBREAD	You can make a confession to anyone — all that counts is that the words be spoken and someone listens.
HENNESEY	Then could we go back to talking of whores?
WHITBREAD	I'm glad we're here — it makes me happy, no delirious, that you're with me.

HENNESEY	That's not much of a confession. I thought you'd tell me a sin.
WHITBREAD	You don't think it's a sin — to be happy in hell?
HENNESEY	If this was hell then it'd be impossible to be happy.
WHITBREAD	It could be your hell. To die in misery next to a fool — an idiot. What could be worse?
HENNESEY	You could be morose about the whole business.
WHITBREAD	I've cursed us, haven't I? Corrupted you . . . Please come down into the boat.
HENNESEY	I said I wouldn't.
WHITBREAD	I don't think I'll live much longer.
HENNESEY	Then you'll be dead — and I can start filling that bloody hole in.
WHITBREAD	It's a filthy business, this dying; makes me terribly light headed. *(beat)* I'd like to hold you again.
HENNESEY	You shouldn't talk of that.
WHITBREAD	What else do you want to talk about — our salvation? You said you didn't believe in that; "Drag me down to the gates of hell." This is hell, my happiness at your expense, come down and complete it.
HENNESEY	I can't . . .
WHITBREAD	I'll guide you, like the first time. Unbuttoning your trousers and reaching in for your cock — pulling you closer, uncontested in the dark. Your appeals mute, caught in your throat until your gasps of pleasure.
	"It's just like a fucking cunt, isn't it?"
	Funny how those gasps can be repeated by dying men; the not quite dead corpses that we staggered over on the way here — their final breath escaping them with a violent shake; their faces in the muck, their arses springing heavenward as if on offer.

	Don't think the other men didn't notice that — if they come back here they'll want to see that you buried me properly, turned over, so the filthiest part of me doesn't go up amongst them.
HENNESEY	They'd be hard pressed guessing the filthiest part of you.
WHITBREAD	That's right — you liked it just as well in my mouth, didn't you? I wonder if they'll realize that. They might have to snap my neck making sure that I don't offend, that every degraded part of me points towards hell.
HENNESEY	I saw a woman at a carnival once — could stick her own head next to her arse. Her legs tied up in a bow over her head while she walked around on her hands.
WHITBREAD	I wonder what the Queen will think when the searchers tell her that. "One of them had obviously fallen from a great height, your Majesty. He was all twisted with his head tucked into his arse."
HENNESEY	If you stuck about later she did the whole show naked, but it'd cost you plenty to see it.
WHITBREAD	Do you think her Majesty will appreciate how far we've fallen?
HENNESEY	From the pick of the Royal Navy to this bloody ditch . . . If she wants to see it she can come and pay plenty.
WHITBREAD	They could have a little tour for her amusement — "This is where six of them died on a single afternoon; this is where the two queer ones ended up in a ditch together . . ."
HENNESEY	"Notice how one of them's been shot and the other torn apart by wolves."
WHITBREAD	"And over where the ships used to be — we'll see how the rest of the men had to eat themselves."
HENNESEY	Don't start about that.
WHITBREAD	"There was nothing else for them to eat."
HENNESEY	The bloody ships will still be there!

WHITBREAD	"Notice the knife marks on the bone, Ma'am. They obviously started carving the fleshier parts first. We'll be having a nice bit of flank steak on the yacht tonight to commemorate the event."
HENNESEY	It's being in that fucking ditch that's making you talk like that, being in that fucking grave!
WHITBREAD	"The two in the ditch died exhausted, trying to turn the boat over on themselves. Everything out here wanted to eat them, it seems — everything but the mice and the hares."
HENNESEY	Get out of there! Get out of that bloody boat!
WHITBREAD	It comforts me to be in it.
HENNESEY	It's turning you into a lunatic!
WHITBREAD	You promised to shoot me if that happens.

> *HENNESEY walks over and grabs WHITBREAD roughly by the shoulders.*

HENNESEY	I'll bloody drag you out!
WHITBREAD	Don't!
HENNESEY	I won't listen to this shit any longer!

> *HENNESEY drags a protesting WHITBREAD to Centre Stage and props him up.*

HENNESEY	Now sit there and keep your bleedin' trap shut!
WHITBREAD	Hand me your gun.
HENNESEY	Just shut-up.
WHITBREAD	I'll try putting a clean hole between my ears. You could drain my brains into a boot and save them for them when they come back.
HENNESEY	(*holding up the conch*) Don't you keep this up! Don't you bloody well dare keep this up!

> *Blackout. The sound of the ice breaking up is heard.*

Scene Three

HENNESEY is building a pile of rocks about four feet in front of the boat. WHITBREAD is standing, propped up with a long oar which he holds like a standard bearer.

WHITBREAD   We wouldn't be in for long . . .

HENNESEY   *(preoccupied, testing the strength of his rock pile)* We wouldn't last a minute.

WHITBREAD   It's important, Hennesey.

HENNESEY   What's so bloody important about it?

WHITBREAD   Not acting like we're dying . . .

HENNESEY   And killing ourselves is going to keep us from that?

WHITBREAD   Not killing ourselves, acting like the living . . . It's pathetic really . . . "When are the men and the wolves coming back? Who's going to eat us . . . ?" I can't stand it any longer; it's degrading.

HENNESEY   You feel degraded by a bit of fear, do you Whitbread? Well, I'm sorry I'm not braver, I've never really prepared myself to be eaten by a wolf, it's not exactly a common way for a seaman to die. Anyway, we're not going to be degraded any longer; we'll prove ourselves useful by getting this boat out of the ditch. I'll need that oar in a minute.

WHITBREAD   Prove ourselves to who?

HENNESEY   The men! They'll come back and see what we've done. "Hello, those two are useful still." That's what they'll say. "Those two are of use."

WHITBREAD   Sounds just like them.

HENNESEY   *(piling another stone up)* And what'll they say if they see us out there bathing?

WHITBREAD   That those two have some dignity left. They might appreciate a bit of that.

HENNESEY   That's the last thing they'd want to see though, isn't it? After sticking us in this degrading ditch . . .

After hogging all the dignity for themselves by
walking those miles of glory back to the ships . . .
To come back and find us acting like the Governors
of Jamaica splashing about in our private pool.

WHITBREAD   We'll just dip in and be out again; it'll be too cold for
anything else.

HENNESEY   Maybe they'll think we're drowning ourselves like
the couple of bony runts that we are. This ditch
they've abandoned us in not good enough . . . "We
were waiting for a rich girl to stop her carriage after
hearing our cries, but none happened along. So we
thought we'd do the proper thing, tied ourselves up in
a sack and in we went." Like a fairy story.

WHITBREAD   More like a leper parable.

HENNESEY   Did you ever hear of rich girls in carriages stopping
for a couple of lepers?

WHITBREAD   Taking them home and giving them a saucer of milk
in front of the fire.

HENNESEY   Then they were cured and became the Lord Mayors of
London.

WHITBREAD   Or the governors of Jamaica.

HENNESEY   Always wanted to be called Guv'nor; crop in one hand
and a pint in the other. Big fat arse stuck to my
saddle as I rode with the hounds. A fine figure of a
man . . . Can you imagine me with a big fat arse?
(*lifts up his coat, drops it quickly*) Course you
bloody can. It's all you've been doing since we got
here.

 WHITBREAD takes off his coat, shivers
 uncontrollably.

HENNESEY   (*rushing over and putting his coat back on him*) Put
your bloody coat back on! I told you I was having
none of it. (*WHITBREAD tries to shrug the coat off*
but HENNESEY holds it on him; half hugging him
as he does so) What will the men think?

WHITBREAD   Who gives a damn what they'd think? Righteous
                 bastards. I'd watch them, pretending to be looking
                 for the ships; they'd be standing on a rock, not
                 looking at the horizon, trying to make out the masts,
                 they'd be staring at the ground looking for a grave for
                 us, anything that we could both fit in to.

HENNESEY   They must have gone miles out of their way.

WHITBREAD   Then they let go to catch your leg beneath the boat.
                 Your screams taking the last of me — they knew
                 that'd happen; that we'd stay here together . . .

HENNESEY   And them with a smile on their lips along with an
                 apology to the Queen. "We really scuppered it, your
                 Majesty; but at least we fixed those bastards . . ."

WHITBREAD   You don't believe me . . .

HENNESEY   (letting him go) It was you that brought us to
                 this . . . You were the only one that let go . . . The
                 boat slipping into the ditch and they were all
                 screaming just as much as me.

WHITBREAD   They were shouting — happy . . .

HENNESEY   You're the one who's happy . . . Acting like we're
                 here on holiday . . . "Just a dip, Hennesey. That's
                 all it'll take and your dignity will be in place again."
                 My dignity's going to be getting this bloody boat
                 out. Just give me that oar, we'll show them.

                        *HENNESEY takes the oar and props the thinner
                        edge underneath the front of the boat; it lies
                        across the rock pile extending out with the paddle
                        being an obvious seat for WHITBREAD.*

WHITBREAD   It'll show them that we're still men, won't it? Still
                 two of the boys. That they can't just bury us.

HENNESEY   (checking the strength of his rock pile) Not when
                 we're the two most useful buggers up here. " 'Ere,
                 did you get that out all by yourselves?" Put your
                 weight on it.

                        *WHITBREAD sits on the paddle with his back to
                        HENNESEY*

HENNESEY	That's bloody useless.
WHITBREAD	*(trying to stand up on it)* I could stand on it if you'd hold it still.

> *He struggles for balance, HENNESEY holds him steady. WHITBREAD gives a triumphant cheer as he gets his balance. The boat doesn't move. They both stare at it for a moment.*

WHITBREAD	It's not working.
HENNESEY	We'll both have to get up there.
WHITBREAD	There isn't room for that.
HENNESEY	I'll get the other oar then.
WHITBREAD	They took the other oar.
HENNESEY	What?
WHITBREAD	They were using it for a tent pole.
HENNESEY	They weren't—
WHITBREAD	Or maybe they knew it'd be the only way to get the boat out. They couldn't have that, could they? They must have taken it with them and pitched it half a mile away. *(beat)* There's a clear patch of water out there, not too far.

> *(HENNESEY lets go of WHITBREAD and he loses his balance again, falling off the oar. Beat. HENNESEY pulls the coat off WHITBREAD and begins to remove his own.*

HENNESEY	All right, we'll go have a bathe, Whitbread . . . We'll jump into that frozen pisspot out there and have a bit of a scrub up.
WHITBREAD	*(eagerly joining in)* Like two Greeks swimming the Hellespont.
HENNESEY	Like two old chums, hand in hand, slipping out over the ice till we reach open water and can do a couple of headers in . . . or were you planning a swallow dive?
WHITBREAD	Just a dip; I've waited all winter.

HENNESEY pulls his coat back on angrily.

HENNESEY   No! Bloody fuck. I'll get up there, I weigh more than you do. *(HENNESEY begins to get up on the oar; kneeling at first)* C'mon, give me a hand.

WHITBREAD holds him steady while he stands on the end of the oar.

WHITBREAD   It's only a little swim.

HENNESEY   A little swim, he says! Try sitting on it in front of me here.

WHITBREAD   What are you afraid of?

HENNESEY   Fucking drowning! A wholly natural thing for a seaman to be afraid of, in my opinion. That and the cold, I'm freezing already.

WHITBREAD sits on the oar in front of HENNESEY. HENNESEY maintains his balance by holding him the whole time.

That's it. Let's try bouncing a bit. *(they begin to bounce up and down)*

WHITBREAD   It's not working.

HENNESEY   Try harder . . . I can feel it giving, can you feel it?

WHITBREAD   No.

HENNESEY   It's bloody frozen in that ditch.

WHITBREAD   Of course it is; they all had a good piss on the sides before leaving.

HENNESEY begins bouncing harder.

WHITBREAD   You'll break the oar.

HENNESEY   *(stops bouncing)* Why didn't they just piss on us then, eh? "You two get down into there; down amongst the scented soaps and the curtain rods. We'll show you what your kind's worth." Better yet, why didn't they just slaughter us? Nobody would've known. It would've been kinder wouldn't it?

HENNESEY is dejected, sits on the oar behind
WHITBREAD.

WHITBREAD   We shouldn't just sit here . . .

HENNESEY   Sit here and get better. That's what the men said
when they left, wasn't it? Part of some bloody joke
they were playing. But why do that when we can
have a frolic? God knows everyone else is frolicking
out here. The men . . .

WHITBREAD   It's our last chance . . .

HENNESEY   For what?

WHITBREAD   To wash some of this muck off.

HENNESEY   That'd make you feel better, wouldn't it? Nothing
like getting the muck off when you're starving to
death. Try feeling a bit of fear. It's done wonders for
me.

> *WHITBREAD begins to cough violently and*
> *shiver, HENNESEY quickly wraps his clothing*
> *around him.*

WHITBREAD   It would be good to be clean again. Just for a
moment . . .

HENNESEY   Good! When were things ever good? Not since we
left the Thames . . .

WHITBREAD   It couldn't be that cold . . . no colder than in
Scotland. Monks and scholars bathe there in the
middle of the winter.

HENNESEY   Monks and scholars must be fucking bonkers.

WHITBREAD   It clears their heads.

HENNESEY   And what happens when our heads clear? We'll
realize we're as potty as a bunch of Scottish monks.
Besides, I hate bathing. I'm always afraid I'll be
swallowed by a whale, like Jonah.

WHITBREAD   It was the only thing I loved about school — bathing
in the river before breakfast.

HENNESEY	Three days Jonah spent in the belly of that whale — eating nice fish suppers I suppose . . . Till he got spat up on a beach no harm done to him at all.
WHITBREAD	All of us stripped and screaming; pretending to be the Greeks.
HENNESEY	You'd have to think God was doing Jonah a bit of a favour, wouldn't you? Where was it that he got spat up — it was probably not more than a few yards from home . . . everybody gathering around: "Hello, you're home early."
WHITBREAD	"God stuck me in a whale."
HENNESEY	"Oh, of course he did, Jonah, you drunken bastard."
WHITBREAD	The river was frozen at the banks and we broke the ice in order to swim. Me and another . . .
HENNESEY	Another what — scholar? I bet he was no fucking monk.
WHITBREAD	He drowned.
HENNESEY	Then you should have learned your lesson. Like Jonah, I bet he didn't go mucking about after God taught him a thing or two.
WHITBREAD	Do you think we're being taught something, Hennesey?
HENNESEY	Morals — that's what this place is teaching us.
WHITBREAD	*(laughing)* What about all the other men?
HENNESEY	They weren't that moral either.
WHITBREAD	Then we're nothing special . . .
HENNESEY	Special — we're the two Greeks swimming for Jesus in Hell's pond, aren't we?
WHITBREAD	Hellespont . . . *(beat)* "Swimming for Jesus . . ." *(taking off his shirt again)* Then we should give him a run for his money, shouldn't we!
HENNESEY	Right — his walking on the water against our surviving a swim in it! It's worth a wager.

WHITBREAD   All those holes in the bastard; he won't be walking
far this time!

HENNESEY   Jesus, Whitbread . . . You'll get us eaten by
something out here yet . . .

WHITBREAD   I'm going to try for a whale, Hennesey! A bloody
great whale big enough for both of us . . .

> *WHITBREAD runs a few steps towards Stage
> Right while pulling off one of his boots. He
> falls. He tries to rise but can't. Long pause,
> HENNESEY hobbles over.*

WHITBREAD   Hennesey . . .

HENNESEY   What . . .

WHITBREAD   I don't think I can walk anymore . . .

HENNESEY   You've gone and done it now . . .

WHITBREAD   It's just like Jonah, being punished for his
blasphemy.

HENNESEY   You tripped on your lace.

WHITBREAD   I'm frightened, Hennesey. I don't want to be
punished anymore.

HENNESEY   *(helping him back into his clothes)* That's it —
degrade yourself.

WHITBREAD   My one swim with Jesus . . .

HENNESEY   Bloody buggered it, Whitbread . . .

> *The sound of the wind and the ice breaking up are
> heightened as the lights dim to quarter level.
> WHITBREAD begins to slowly crawl towards
> Centre Stage; HENNESEY takes a longer route,
> again moving very slowly, peering out into the
> audience. He takes his harmonica out of his
> pocket and tries to warm it beneath his arm; he
> clutches himself, obviously very cold. When
> WHITBREAD reaches Centre Stage HENNESEY
> is there and helps him to a sitting position, he
> then sits down with his back against
> WHITBREAD's. The sound fades and the lights
> go to black.*

Scene Four

HENNESEY and WHITBREAD sitting back to back at Centre Stage. As the lights come up WHITBREAD is holding up the bottle paper and HENNESEY is rolling pemmican into small pill shapes — laying them out on a plate in front of him.

WHITBREAD Somewhere in this margin I should write about Hennesey — they could name this ditch after him. Would his soul be happy with that; laid to rest — or would it be happier among the others: the 105 that departed the ships and quickly met their deaths . . . There's not much room in this margin — "Hennesey, one of the strongest, chose to stay with his friend Tim Whitbread when he knew that death was certain, unavoidable . . ."

HENNESEY There's enough for a few days here.

WHITBREAD You might as well take it.

HENNESEY There's equal shares — we'll both have the same.

WHITBREAD It could save you but it won't help me.

HENNESEY We've got the chocolate too. When I was a lad I always wanted to live off chocolate.

WHITBREAD You should save that for the men coming back — it wouldn't do, you looking all stuffed and happy.

HENNESEY There's plenty of food where they are.

WHITBREAD Of course . . .

HENNESEY Imagine if we shot a bear — how long we could live off that?

WHITBREAD Why don't you go hunting?

HENNESEY Because we're the bloody hunted — aren't we? We're bait.

WHITBREAD The about to be eaten . . .

HENNESEY What the whole fucking world's trying to eat—

WHITBREAD   Do you think we'll be able to hold them off with our
              guns till we starve to death? That would be eating
              away at ourselves, wouldn't it? Beating everyone to
              the punch.

HENNESEY   *(handing him the plate with the food)* Here — eat
              this.

WHITBREAD   *(refusing it)* I'd rather gnaw on me own thumb —
              speed things up a bit.

HENNESEY   Don't be so bloody thick!

WHITBREAD   It won't help me.

HENNESEY   *(keeps offering)* I'm not going to eat a damned thing
              until you do.

WHITBREAD   That's stupid.

HENNESEY   Stupid again! Well I'm not the one who's trying to
              starve himself when six dozen dead men managed
              without any effort at all.

WHITBREAD   I'm not going to live much longer.

HENNESEY   How long do you think I'll last with you bloody dead
              in that ditch; getting ripe — every bear and wolf
              that's around howling for your bones . . . That's a
              pretty picture, isn't it? But why would you give a
              shit, you'll not be here to see it? You'll be all safely
              gnawed through by yourself by then — won't have
              your throat ripped out while you're running away.
              No, dragging my bloody self away — I've got a
              broken foot, haven't I . . . Christ, the wolves will be
              up on a hill having a laugh, saying let the pups go
              and get him . . . *(he attempts to grab the paper)* Give
              me that bottle paper — I'll write the ending to all
              this.

              *WHITBREAD keeps the paper. HENNESEY
              continues anyway.*

              Hennesey, after his friend Tim Whitbread had gnawed
              himself to death, was torn apart by sixteen bears —
              eleven wolves, four rabid hares and a family of mice.

WHITBREAD   *(begins to crawl towards stage right)* I'll be off then.

HENNESEY	"I'll be off," he says! Like he was going to toddle off down to the pub for a pint or two . . . Or maybe you're heading off for another wash . . .
	Pause. Watching.
	Where the hell are you going to go — there's everywhere to go and nowhere out there?
WHITBREAD	I don't think it should make much difference. Do you think a mile would do it — I don't think I could get much farther than that.
HENNESEY	A mile would be fine — make sure it's a full mile though, no cheating.
WHITBREAD	How long do you reckon' it would take — going at this pace?
HENNESEY	*(walking over and standing beside him)* At that pace . . . probably a week.
WHITBREAD	Oh — I think I'll be dead before that.
HENNESEY	I imagine we both will — look how your legs are dragging; you'll be going round in a big circle; drawing us a target for the crows to come and peck our eyes out.
WHITBREAD	*(collapsing)* I don't think I can do it . . .
HENNESEY	No — really? I thought you were setting quite a pace there for a while, tiring a bit at the end, mind; but you soon would have had your second wind.
WHITBREAD	Don't be such a bastard.
HENNESEY	Will you go back there and eat something?
WHITBREAD	*(his face near a small pile of rocks)* There's stuff on these rocks we can eat.
HENNESEY	What — bugs? I'm not eating any bugs.
WHITBREAD	No, some sort of plant. I remember the Captain telling us about it in one of his sermons.
HENNESEY	Oh — right. "Intestinal fortitude, gentlemen. I lived for two months eating nothing but my own soil."

WHITBREAD	No, it was some kind of lichen; it was all they had to eat when they were starving on his last expedition. Tripe de roche — that's what the Voyageurs called it.
HENNESEY	I don't want to eat any bloody French moss. *(prodding the rocks with his rifle)* I'd just as soon eat bugs as that shit.
WHITBREAD	You'd eat it if you were hungry enough.
HENNESEY	*(dragging WHITBREAD back)* That's right. I'd eat anything, wouldn't I — according to you . . .
WHITBREAD	I didn't say that about you.
HENNESEY	No — it was just the other lads that were going to come back here for a bit of a nosh, wasn't it? Well, don't worry; I'll treat them to a bloody great Frenchy dinner of that shit on the rocks over there. I'm sure we've got the proper forks for it in the boat.
WHITBREAD	I was only saying . . . if you think about it . . . what else is there?
HENNESEY	There's not thinking about it, that's what there is. Piss on thinking about anything out here — there's no point.
WHITBREAD	Maybe if it came down to all that — they wouldn't want us with them. We're different, after all.
HENNESEY	Sensitive you mean — like I might start weeping when they had a go at you.
WHITBREAD	Like they might not find us all that palatable.
HENNESEY	You're wrong there — it's always the ones that are different get mixed up in the first bit of nasty business. Like that bloke they made carry Christ's cross — just cause he was from out of town. What was his name?
WHITBREAD	I don't know.
HENNESEY	Blimey — you'd think in all that time you spent praying you could have looked up a few names . . .

> *HENNESEY again offers WHITBREAD some food. This time he takes it.*

HENNESEY	That's better.
WHITBREAD	I'll stay alive as long as I can. It'd be killing myself if I stopped eating, wouldn't it?
HENNESEY	Certainly would — there'd be no salvation for you. Not that your type gets much of a chance in the first place.
WHITBREAD	If I just dragged myself off though, so that you could have the food and maybe survive — do you think that's the same thing?
HENNESEY	What if the men were just over the rise — heading back with sacks of food: and they would've said — "Pile our mate Whitbread into that boat; we'll take him with us." It would've all been for nought, wouldn't it?
WHITBREAD	What if I drag myself up to the rise and see if they're there?
HENNESEY	You don't know which bloody rise they took, do you?
WHITBREAD	They could be over any of them — sharpening their knives.
HENNESEY	Making wolf sounds — trying to scare us to death.
WHITBREAD	I could plead with them to take me, but to leave you alone.
HENNESEY	But they wouldn't want us; we're spoiled meat, remember? All the tricks we've got up to — I wouldn't fancy a bit of your flank steak.

        The wind picks up and the sound of a male choir can faintly be heard singing the same hymn that was sung in Scene Two.

WHITBREAD	I think I can hear them?
HENNESEY	Who?
WHITBREAD	The men — they're coming back, they're singing.
HENNESEY	Singing? You're going bloody bonkers, there's nothing . . .

The music picks up.

WHITBREAD *(sings along)* Da ta da da . . . Da ta da da . . .

> *HENNESEY begins to move about trying to hear what WHITBREAD does. He becomes extremely agitated, as if affected by the music.*

HENNESEY There's no fucking singing!

> *The music gets louder. WHITBREAD adopts a beatific look, humming along.*

HENNESEY There's nothing except for the damned wind!

WHITBREAD It's the men coming to get us.

HENNESEY The men!

WHITBREAD We'll be butchered now!

HENNESEY *(grabbing his gun and looking wildly around)* You shut-up!

WHITBREAD Or maybe they've found the food and are singing harvest songs!

HENNESEY *(levelling his gun at WHITBREAD)* There's no fucking singing — say it! *(the music gets very loud)* There's no fucking singing out here!

> *Blackout. The music stops with the black and the sound of the ice breaking up is heard, it is louder than the music.*

Scene Five

> *Lights up on HENNESEY holding WHITBREAD in his arms again. WHITBREAD is very close to dying and HENNESEY is trying to keep him occupied (maybe stave off death) with his story telling.*

WHITBREAD There wasn't a sign of them?

HENNESEY There was nothing.

WHITBREAD I heard them . . . I heard them singing.

HENNESEY	I'm sure you did. I could hear wisps of it myself sometimes.
WHITBREAD	Then they must have been near here — they must have passed close by.
HENNESEY	They were singing an opera, weren't they — the men? I used to love the opera.
WHITBREAD	When did you ever go to the opera?
HENNESEY	I never went — I used to have a soup cart, onion soup — to hide the liquor on the lords' breath before they went home to the ladies. I'd tour around the fashion spots with it; always starting out at the opera. Not that I ever sold any there, mind; but I'd drag my cart right up in front till they'd send me off — said the whole lobby stank of onions . . .
WHITBREAD	Some of that soup would be good now.
HENNESEY	I was famous for that soup — practically a whole onion in each cup. There used to be a queue for it when the clubs closed — all the bloody toffs rolling about in the streets, half of them with their tongues stuck in each others' throats — old school chums . . . I had a couple offer me half a crown to go home with them one night. No bloody way — they wouldn't let me take my cart with us; it would've been nicked and then what the hell would I have done?
WHITBREAD	I used to love onions.
HENNESEY	I could never see an onion again and it'd be too soon. I used to stink of them. Me mum said I was getting old from it — the two bloody great lines down my face from the afternoons spent bawling as I peeled, my hands stained brown and never getting home till dawn. "Why don't you join the sodding Navy," she'd say. Then my cart got stolen by a gang of toffs who wanted to take turns sitting on it while the others rolled them through the streets.
WHITBREAD	(*extremely agitated*) I got expelled from school!
HENNESEY	Got kicked out? I never gave them the chance; one day I said I wasn't going and that was it — never missed it.

WHITBREAD	I never went home again!
HENNESEY	Don't worry — you'll get your chance. You'll be a bloody hero. "Once again a fine example of the sort of hardships that our British sailors can endure. The two in the ditch were in particular quite brave — holding off hordes of hungry animals while chatting of the opera and onion soup . . ."
WHITBREAD	The men . . .
HENNESEY	"Seem to have forgotten their two companions. Perhaps they were jealous of their elegance."
WHITBREAD	The men . . .
HENNESEY	Are not walking by singing!
WHITBREAD	The men!
HENNESEY	Will not be coming back, will they!

       Pause. HENNESEY tries to feed WHITBREAD.

       'Ere . . . eat this

WHITBREAD	I can't.
HENNESEY	You said you'd try. Pretend it's some of that soup you said you'd like.
WHITBREAD	I don't want to pretend.
HENNESEY	There's not a hell of a lot else to do out here.
WHITBREAD	I dragged us here, didn't I?
HENNESEY	Pulled against everyone.
WHITBREAD	I was the one standing on the rocks, looking for a ditch.
HENNESEY	You were hard at it — had no one fooled.
WHITBREAD	I'm the one that let go of the boat; so that you'd have to stay here with me. I broke your foot.
HENNESEY	It's only a sprain.
WHITBREAD	And then I was happy about the whole thing. You must think I'm a real bastard.

HENNESEY	A daft bastard, Whitbread . . . But then why shouldn't you be? You've not been anymore fuck-arsed than anyone else out here — the person who thought this whole thing up in the first place. What was the friggin' purpose, did you ever wonder? They knew there wasn't any trade route through here years ago — it was all just to get to the other side. For what? So that we could say we did it; so we could sit around the pub for the rest of our lives talking about the years we spent in the fucking ice. *(beat)* I should have joined the army; I would've had some real stories to tell then . . .
WHITBREAD	You don't think this is real . . .
HENNESEY	Nah . . . this is all just pretend, remember? Pretending there's some purpose to it. That you bloody love me — that's good enough for now. We'll pretend we're here cause you love me — that of all the places we could've ended up here was the best cause we've had the most privacy. And that the friggin' boat rode over my foot and down into that ditch at the moment that you stopped walking cause it was all meant to happen this way. That's what love's all about — ending up in a sodding ditch together.
WHITBREAD	I can't take anymore . . .
HENNESEY	Anymore what?
WHITBREAD	Pretending.
HENNESEY	Then you've really poxed it, haven't you? I'll tell you another one . . . We're here to find the Northwest passage for the glory of ol' England! I was wrong — it's out here somewhere; and once they've plotted the great line across with our dead bodies they'll save a month's time getting tea into the Queen's teapot and silk onto the backs of society's maidens. We'll be a part of that, you and I; maybe they'll name something after us.
WHITBREAD	This ditch.

HENNESEY   Nah . . . Something more grand . . . "The Two
             Wolf-Eaten Bastards in a Ditch Tea Company . . ."
             "Broken Foot Stockings or Buggers
             Handkerchiefs . . ." *(pause)* That'll be the real puzzle
             for the historians, won't it; guessing which one of us
             was buggering who . . . It could become a parlour
             game for the school chum set; they'll put out the
             lights for four months and see who doesn't end up in
             someone's arse. You'd need an odd man, wouldn't
             you — to be the loser? He could play the starving
             one after the first game's finished; doesn't get any
             food for six weeks — they'll see what he ends up
             with.

             Pause.

WHITBREAD   Hennesey . . .

HENNESEY   What?

WHITBREAD   I don't think . . .

HENNESEY   I told you not to.

WHITBREAD   Soon it will be dawn.

HENNESEY   And . . .

WHITBREAD   I don't think I'll see it.

HENNESEY   You don't have a choice, do you? You'll have to sit
             there and wait for it, the dawn or nothing.

             *Pause as the lights go down, HENNESEY and
             WHITBREAD both staring straight ahead.*

Scene Six

*WHITBREAD has died. HENNESEY is
attempting to smash through the hard ground
with the butt of his rifle; he moves some rocks
around where WHITBREAD had said the lichens
were; then tries to scoop the earth with one of
them. At Centre Stage is a bundle of clothing
shaped into the figure of a body. WHITBREAD
is standing Stage Left in the shadows,
HENNESEY has his back to him. He is wearing
the CAPTAIN's hat with a more elegant coat. It
should be evident that he is an hallucination on
HENNESEY's part.*

CAPTAIN   Be careful with those lichens!

HENNESEY   Sod the fucking lichens!

CAPTAIN   They may be all you have to eat in the end.

HENNESEY   Then I won't eat anything, will I?

CAPTAIN   Then I'll tell you that they're not the right kind
anyway. I thought it might give you some hope if
there was anything else here to eat. That's part of a
Captain's job, you know — giving his seamen some
hope.

HENNESEY   I don't need any bloody hope.

CAPTAIN   You think the other men will return for you, don't
you?

HENNESEY   They said they would. Why wouldn't I believe them?

CAPTAIN   They're all dead as well.

                      Pause.

HENNESEY   *(stops digging)* Hope is one thing — what kind of an
idiot would I have to be to have any hope left now?
But a bit of doubt, an expectation, that I might have
been left with . . . that — I wouldn't have
minded . . .

CAPTAIN   I'm sorry; I thought you wanted the truth.

HENNESEY   The truth of this place would drive you mad . . .

CAPTAIN	You've seen it though, haven't you?
HENNESEY	*(banging his rifle butt into the dirt)* That's right — I've heard the music. The harvesting songs of the dead men come to butcher us — the stink of an onion opera. I heard it all with him . . .
CAPTAIN	Are you sure you don't want to save him?
HENNESEY	Save him?
CAPTAIN	For — you know . . . ? *(beat)* It's not the right kind of lichen — you won't have that.
HENNESEY	To eat, you mean?
CAPTAIN	Soon there won't be anything else.

Pause. Hennesey resumes digging.

HENNESEY	Do you want it back?
CAPTAIN	What?
HENNESEY	The truth.
CAPTAIN	Not really.
HENNESEY	I loved him.
CAPTAIN	I was afraid of that.
HENNESEY	I loved him more than I ever loved anything . . . more than Jesus, Mary and Joseph; bloody Ol' England or even me mum . . .
CAPTAIN	It's not proper!
HENNESEY	Not cricket, is it? Not Christian? I don't give a toss. I'm going to bury him then build a bloody great cross out of that shit your officers threw into the boat. Those murderers — we might have made it out of here if it weren't for them.

Hennesey bangs furiously at the ground.

CAPTAIN	You'll kill yourself.

HENNESEY   *(stops banging)* It's what he wanted, a Christian
                burial. Though what Christ would be doing out here
                would be a mystery . . . He might as well have a
                heathen's send off — I could put him in the boat with
                all his possessions and light the whole thing on fire.
                He'd have a better chance at some sort of salvation
                then, wouldn't he?

CAPTAIN   It'd be easier than digging that grave.

HENNESEY   You'd have me just leave him, wouldn't you? Just
                like we left all the others. "They're in God's hands,"
                some git of an officer kept saying. They were bloody
                dead in the rubble, nobody even turned them over . . .

CAPTAIN   *(coming out of the shadows and standing over the
                bundle)* I wonder if they all smelled so badly . . .

HENNESEY   *(looking at him for the first time)* It's that bloody
                soap.

CAPTAIN   No — I think he died of something quite foul. Are
                you sure he didn't soil himself?

HENNESEY   I remember about you and all that.

                    *The captain throws his coat into the boat, places
                    his hat on the prow.*

CAPTAIN   *(lying down on top of the bundle, immediately
                assuming the presence of the dead WHITBREAD)*
                You'll have to wash the body . . .

HENNESEY   *(balking)* Do you think he'd be the first called up
                with a bit of shit in his drawers? I mean, Jesus . . .
                Does it really matter? I don't think he would've
                cared . . . He wasn't all that clean to begin with —
                up to all sorts of filthy business all the time,
                remember? *(HENNESEY kneels down, turns the
                body over)* What did you bloody die of? I can't smell
                anything . . . . *(he picks up the sponge near the
                body, begins wiping it down)* I can still smell that
                soap! *(sniffs the sponge)* This was your bloody
                sponge, wasn't it! You're no better than any of
                them! We were supposed to find the river — we were
                going to float down it and be saved! You all had the
                bloody party planned though . . .

HENNESEY   Can't possibly be saved without looking like
            gentlemen, without looking learned and having a
            book or two to lend those Frenchy Voyageur
            chaps . . .

            Pause.

            Your back — I've never seen your back. I always had
            your shirt thrown over it . . . We could fuck now if
            you weren't . . . Is that what you wanted — "Come
            down into the boat." I should've done it — what
            would it have mattered? It would have been the first
            time in the daylight for us, where we could see each
            other — damn the cold — we did it in worse, didn't
            we? Your back is beautiful; I would have run my
            tongue up and down it when I was inside you, bitten
            at it and bruised your shoulders with my hands. We'd
            definitely be fucking now if you weren't . . .

            Pause. Throws the sponge away.

            I'm a worse fuck-arse than you, aren't I? Really
            ballocked it, keeping you alive . . .

            *HENNESEY drags WHITBREAD back to the
            boat with great difficulty, propping him up
            inside to assume the same position he had at the
            start of the play. In the rest of the scene it
            should be evident that HENNESEY's mind is
            failing. He is now imitating the CAPTAIN
            during certain parts of his monologue as if the
            CAPTAIN were still there.*

HENNESEY   You could give us a hand . . .
            The wolves and hares will have him for sure . . .

            "It's no go — helping him . . ."
            I'm putting him in the fucking boat.
            "There's nothing Christian about that — about the
            ditch either."
            So sod being a bloody Christian. I just don't want
            him out here . . .

As soon as he's in I'm leaving.
"Which direction?"
South — to the river.
I'd be better off in the ditch — nicer death, not falling
on my face like all the rest.
I've got to go . . .
"Got to leave, can't stand starving with all that food
in the larder?"
I've got to try . . .

"Being stronger than all the rest. And lead me not
into temptation. You've already done that — you're
the last one left alive. What's dying on the way to
that river going to do for you?"

I can't just sit here.
There's sitting there or there's nothing — that's what
I told him.
To him — I can still walk, I can get out of here.

I can't . . .

    He holds up the CAPTAIN's hat.

You could help me.
You! You were sent to get me, remember?

At least tell me the way!

    He fits the hat onto WHITBREAD's head.

"The Father sent his only son to atone for our sins."
Jesus . . . !

"His mother Mary and his father Joseph — the divine
example."
That's the way . . .

    He knocks the hat off.

That's bloody useless . . .

"They're the good words you'll be saying over
me . . ."

That's bloody evil — spreading that around out here.
It's vile. Temptation; trying to make me say that I
didn't love him and that it was all a mistake, an error
in judgement and that I'd like to repent . . .

I might be saved . . .

I can't be saved . . .
There's nothing . . .

> *Fade to black as the choir singing the hymn can again be faintly heard.*

END

Who Look In Stove

by

Lawrence Jeffery

*Gary Reineke as Jack (on roof), Dan Lett as Harold (in cabin),
and Glyn Thomas as Edgar (left).*

In the summer of 1928, prospectors discovered the bodies of John Hornby, Harold Adlard, and Edgar Christian at a cabin by the Thelon River in the Northwest Territories. They had starved to death after misjudging the migratory patterns of caribou. We know this because Christian, the youngest member of the group and a distant relation of Hornby's, kept a diary, and shortly before his death he placed the note, "Who look in stove," on top of the stove and the diary inside it. Lawrence Jeffery discovered Edgar Christian's diary in the early 80s. This moving document left a lasting impression on him and, in March 1993, he visited Dover College in England, where Edgar had attended school and where the diary is now kept. The first edition of the play, published by Exile Editions (1993), included Jeffery's Preface and Edgar's diary, with his two last letters to his parents.

In *Who Look In Stove* Jeffery combines imaginative speculation with details from Christian's diary to dramatize the final months of these mens' lives. The result is a gripping play because of its haunting subject-matter and the intellectual depth and dramatic skill with which Jeffery tells the story. It is strikingly elegant in its steel-cold precision, and Jeffery's refusal to sentimentalize either the events or the historical personages he dramatizes, only increases the play's poignance.

Perhaps it is inevitable that a play about three men starving on the Barrens should have a substantial psychological component. Before reading Jeffery's play I would have thought that the only plot-generating device offered by such a scenario would be the exploration of psychological inscapes. Starvation is a pretty boring phenomenon, or so I thought. However, I found the practical detail that Jeffery uses about how to resist starvation riveting.

These details are made even more compelling by the deftness with which Jeffery uses dialogue to add a metaphoric dimension to the theme of starvation. Through recollection of family histories, a psychoanalytic semiotic begins to structure our understanding of the relationships among the three men: mothers come to be associated with love and food, and fathers with the denial of these forms of nourishment. As the cold, silent leader of the group, Jack embodies male authority, and Harold's and Edgar's regard for Jack is shaped by their unresolved feelings for their own fathers.

Jeffery develops a philosophical dimension in the play by expanding the theme of starvation to include speech and writing. Just as the withholding of paternal love is often expressed through a lack of communication, so Jack's authority extends at times to his denial of Harold and Edgar's right to speak and write. It seems that the extreme idealism fuelling Jack's determination to survive leads him to equate language with reality. As winter approaches and supplies dwindle, Harold suggests that they make a run for safety while weather permits. Jack insists on silence because "naming something makes it real." Harold answers Jack's idealism with his own bellicose brand of materialism: "Like what? Hunger? Fear?" Because only Jack can lead the group to safety, Harold and Edgar are forced to try to survive on Jack's terms. Though Harold displays his resistance through petulance and non-cooperation, Edgar offers none.

Because Jack's philosophical beliefs prove a tragically insufficient means of coping with the long winter, *Who Look In Stove* constitutes a brutal critique of the stoical, life-denying idealism that nourishes the myth of the North. Yet I think Jeffery's probing goes beyond philosophical debate to a critique of any abstract system that attempts to explain human interaction without accounting for the psychological complexities of subjectivity, and thus for acts of apparent irrationality.

The character of Edgar is crucial here. Just as it is the written words of Christian's diary that mediate between real-life experience and Jeffery's dramatic representation, so it is Edgar who mediates between Jack and Harold to determine whose view will hold sway. It is not philosophy but psychology that explains Edgar's inclinations, and his inequality lends him a power he never utilizes. Jack feels a responsibility for his young and inexperienced relative that he does not feel for the older, tougher Harold. Were Edgar to have grasped the gravity of their situation in time and taken a decisive stand with Harold, Jack might have relented and the three might have lived to record their "failure." However, Edgar's remembered interactions with his father reveal that he does not question authority or strategize independently. Jeffery also suggests that Edgar is in love with Jack. It is, therefore, less rational calculation than psychological conditioning and incipient erotic desire that predispose Edgar to resist Harold's view of events and move towards Jack's — towards stoicism, silence, and death.

Jeffery could not have found a better spatial context within which to explore the philosophical and psychological dimensions of human interaction. In the far North the dictates of material circumstance cannot be ignored; yet the North's very extremity exercises an inexorable pull over idealists seeking a worthy "opponent." And the hungers that accompany this challenge are so ritualized and universalized that they inevitably open a well-spring of deep-seated psychological associations. Yet in the end it is Jeffery's use of time that impresses me most because this factor balances the play's intellectual precocity with a compassionate humanity. Because the fates of the characters are sealed before we gain familiarity with them, and because there is no scene or act break to relieve the relentless inevitability of events, the audience is trapped in the same situation as Jack, Harold, and Edgar: we must watch, powerlessly, as the consequences of a decision, which slipped by before being fully grasped, takes its inexorable toll.

Jeffery was born in Vancouver, but now divides his time between Toronto and Shanghai. He is senior partner with Stonecutter Publishing in Toronto, which produces *China Business Monthly*. His publications include *China, the Consumer Revolution* (1997), *Hong Kong: Portraits of Power*, with photographs by Lord Snowdon (1995), and *Four Plays* (1992). He has written a biography, *Simon Murray: Three Decades in the Heart of a Dragon* (1999) and is working on a new play called *Gweilo* (meaning "foreign devil" and referring to a white person), which is set in China.

L.C.

* * *

Who Look In Stove premiered at PlayRites 94, Alberta Theatre Projects' Annual Festival of New Canadian Plays, in Calgary, Alberta 6 February 1994.

Jack	Gary Reineke
Harold	Dan Lett
Edgar	Glyn Thomas

Director	Bob White
Lighting	Harry Frehner
Set Design	John Dinning
Costumes	Carolyn Smith
Composer	Paul Bagley

WHO LOOK IN STOVE

CHARACTERS

EDGAR	eighteen
HAROLD	twenty-eight
JACK	forty-six

SETTING

The cabin is represented by a 14' square recessed 10" below the surface of the stage. There is an exit facing stage right. Minimal representation of exit and walls, perhaps only the four corner beams that hold up a flat platform roof. The roof is made up of only a few beams, enough to bear someone's weight, but not enough to completely block out light from above. There is a small square stove in the middle of the cabin, a stove pipe leading up from it to the roof. All this minimal, spare, abstract.

> *JACK is working on the roof. EDGAR and HAROLD are inside the cabin filling pots with earth to hollow out the cabin floor. They are digging out the floor to give more headroom. They are using cooking pots, when full they carry the pots out the cabin door stage right. They pour the earth at the base of the exterior walls. They begin at the wall to their left of the door as they exit and proceed across the wall facing the audience. This hollowing out process ends when a line of earth has been laid against the exterior walls from one edge of the door opening around the perimeter of the cabin to the other edge of the door opening. The earth serves to define the exterior walls and the door opening.*
>
> *JACK stops working. He listens. He rises from his knees to a low crouch. He waits. He jumps up and down on the roof twice. EDGAR and HAROLD stop, they look up and then at each other.*

EDGAR   What?

HAROLD   Shh.

EDGAR	*(whispers)* What did we do?
HAROLD	He thinks we're talking about him.
EDGAR	But we weren't.
JACK	*(shouts)* No talking!

> *Silence. Short Pause. JACK resumes working. He works nervously, frantically.*

EDGAR	*(whispers)* We weren't.
HAROLD	Never mind.
EDGAR	What's wrong with him?
HAROLD	Just do your work.

> *HAROLD exits with pail of earth, begins pouring earth against wall to his left as he exits door. JACK peers down at HAROLD.*

HAROLD	*(without looking up at JACK)* We weren't talking.
JACK	I heard you.
HAROLD	*(still not looking up at him)* Only after your fuss.
JACK	I don't want you talking.

> *HAROLD escapes into the cabin.*

JACK	*(shouting after him)* Listen to what I'm saying . . . . Listen to me!

> *HAROLD throws his pail down and kicks EDGAR'S over. EDGAR stands.*

EDGAR	What?
HAROLD	Shut up.
EDGAR	But what did I do?
HAROLD	Stop asking so many questions! That's all you ever do. Why this, why that? Think. Just think for once.
EDGAR	But . . .

HAROLD	What?
EDGAR	What's wrong with him?
HAROLD	Think!

> *Short pause.*

EDGAR	I don't know . . . . What did I do?
HAROLD	Never mind.
EDGAR	But Harold I—
HAROLD	Go back to work. Never mind, forget it, just, here *(he picks up EDGAR'S pail and hands it to him),* just go back to work.

> *HAROLD turns and picks up his own pail and goes back to scraping out the floor. EDGAR stands silently holding his pail looking down at HAROLD. EDGAR cries.*

JACK	*(to himself)* Surely you two have said all you can say to each other by now? After all these months? What more is there to say? . . . If it's about me I don't want to hear it . . . . You'll do it or else . . . . You'll just do it.
HAROLD	*(without looking up)* You're not crying are you?
EDGAR	*(sniffling)* No.
HAROLD	Look, it's just getting a bit tense, that's all. It'll get better once the cabin's done and the food's in for winter . . . . Just please stop crying, please.
EDGAR	Sorry.
HAROLD	You don't have to be sorry.

> *Short pause.*

EDGAR	Why doesn't he want us to talk?
HAROLD	It doesn't matter why, he just doesn't. *(he hands EDGAR his pail)* Here.

> *EDGAR takes the pail, HAROLD takes his, EDGAR exits, empties pail against exterior wall.*

JACK   There's no room for doubt. Not now . . . . All talk
                    does is breed doubt. Makes things where there's
                    nothing.

                    EDGAR looks up at JACK, watches him.

EDGAR   How's it coming? Pretty good? . . . I guess it'll
                    hold a lot of snow if it can hold you as steady as it
                    does. We've done a good job on it after all. Haven't
                    we? It'll bear up for sure. Won't it? . . . Jack? . . .
                    We're almost done inside. Won't be long now. It's
                    not such a hard job. It's tedious. A bit of a bore
                    really. Same thing over and over. But not a hard
                    job. Nothing to complain about is what I
                    mean . . . . I'm not complaining . . . . Jack?

JACK   Do as I say and it'll be fine . . . . I've been through
                    worse than you could imagine . . . . Worse and it
                    was never as good as this.

EDGAR   Jack? . . .

JACK   This is luxury if you want to know.

                    *Pause. HAROLD comes out of cabin with pail,
                    he looks at EDGAR, EDGAR quickly enters
                    cabin. HAROLD empties pail against wall.*

JACK   What are you doing?

HAROLD   Banking up the earth. Just like you said Jack,
                    banking it up.

JACK   You were listening to me.

HAROLD   Were you talking? Were you?

JACK   Yes.

HAROLD   To who?

JACK   You were listening.

HAROLD   There's no one out here, Jack, no one right now but
                    me. If you were talking then I guess I was the one
                    listening . . . . But I never heard you Jack. So what
                    are you saying?

JACK   I'm saying . . . . Get back to work . . . .

HAROLD	You've been talking to yourself, haven't you Jack, silent in your mind or out loud but still just to yourself. Right? Am I right?
JACK	No.
HAROLD	You've been talking to yourself . . . . You won't say two words with us, won't answer the poor kid anything but with grunts. And should we talk, if we dare speak, you stare at our lips like it's something you're aiming at down the barrel of a gun . . . . And the second they stop moving you shoot . . . . That's right, isn't it Jack? Hold your aim on the beast as it moves, shallow breaths as it runs, as it slows a deep breath, hold it, and when it stops, shoot. Right? . . . That's how the professionals do it, isn't it? At least that's what you said . . . .
JACK	Words are dangerous things.
HAROLD	It's all we've got lots of, Jack. Words. Lots of words.
JACK	Naming something makes it real. Doesn't matter if it exists or not, naming it makes it as good as real.
HAROLD	Like what? Hunger? Fear?
JACK	Shutup!
HAROLD	I'll talk if I want to talk, Jack. Course if some day you find me mumbling to myself on the roof shoot me. Okay? Just shoot me . . . . Asshole.

> *HAROLD goes into the cabin, EDGAR comes out. They work silently for 60 seconds filling pails and pouring earth around the perimeter. The light slowly changes to dusk. JACK sits on his heels on the roof staring out at the sunset. HAROLD empties a pail of earth, enters cabin, EDGAR exits cabin with a pail of earth.*

JACK	Edgar.
EDGAR	Yes.
JACK	Are you listening to me?
EDGAR	Yes. I'm listening.

JACK	You see the light now? Right now?
EDGAR	Sunset.
JACK	Dusk. Let's call it dusk. Or twilight. I don't like it called sunset. The sun never sets really, it's just shining somewhere else . . . . This light is an important light, Edgar. It's important because it's slipping away . . . . Are you listening to me?
EDGAR	Yes, Jack . . . . It's slipping away.

> *Short pause. HAROLD appears at the cabin door, he hands EDGAR his pail, takes EDGAR'S empty pail back into cabin to be filled.*

EDGAR	You mean the light is fading? . . . Making shadows?
JACK	Things lose their edge, blend one into the other . . . . You have to work at seeing, at recognition, it reminds you, as it slips away, of what you'd come to take for granted.

> *Short pause.*

EDGAR	It's my favourite time.
JACK	Why?
EDGAR	I like the colours.
JACK	There's more beautiful.
EDGAR	No, I like this best, I think.
JACK	You said you'd never seen anything as beautiful as the Northern lights.
EDGAR	Yes. Yes, they're splendid . . . .
JACK	*(mocking)* Splendid.

> *Short pause. HAROLD hands EDGAR another pail.*

JACK	Why do you like the dusk?

> *Short pause. EDGAR stiffens, thinks.*

JACK	*(hard)* Tell me . . . . Be precise.

EDGAR   It means supper. It means we stop working. It means food and sleep, I suppose.

JACK   Suppose?

EDGAR   No. That's why. That's why I like it.

> *Short pause.*

JACK   We're not in a bad way. We're not. You have to trust me.

EDGAR   I do. I do trust you.

JACK   You can't imagine hardship, real hardship. Someday I'll tell you. I'll share it with you, share my memories of it, tell you what others knew . . . this is nothing.

EDGAR   I'm not worried, Jack. After all, I didn't come to Canada for cricket on a pleasant green, did I?

JACK   No.

EDGAR   I came to be with you, learn from you, go where you've gone, see something of the country you know so well . . . . I'm not worried, Jack.

> *Short pause. HAROLD hands EDGAR another pail.*

JACK   Three's not a good number, that's the problem. Two can surrender just enough of themselves to the other to make it work. Like a three-legged race, simple as a schoolboy's game . . . . But three . . . three is odd man out . . . .

EDGAR   Harold isn't so bad, he's a good chap at heart . . . I like him. I think maybe he's just a bit spoilt is all. He's used to the good life is all . . . . Don't you think?

JACK   Who said anything about Harold?

> *EDGAR is still, waiting, looking up at JACK. HAROLD exits cabin.*

JACK   (*to EDGAR*) You're finished now. Light the stove . . . . Go on.

EDGAR enters the cabin and prepares to light the stove. HAROLD empties his pail then begins splitting wood for the stove. He splits wood while he talks to JACK.

JACK   What's he writing in that book of his, have you read it?

HAROLD   Why should I want to read it?

JACK   You haven't looked?

HAROLD   Have you?

JACK   No.

HAROLD   But you think I would.

JACK   I want to know.

HAROLD   So ask him.

JACK   He says it's a diary.

HAROLD   Yeah?

JACK   So why now? All summer it stayed shut at the bottom of his pack. Now it's out. Now I come in find him curled round it scribbling. What's it mean?

HAROLD   His father told him to keep a journal, that's all.

JACK   Why now? Why didn't he start from the beginning?

HAROLD   I don't know Jack.

JACK   It means something that he's doing it now.

HAROLD   That's what you think, it means something?

JACK   Yes. Something's happened in his mind. It's turned him to writing.

HAROLD   It's obvious what he's doing.

JACK   What? What's obvious?

HAROLD   He can't speak so he writes.

JACK   He can speak.

HAROLD	Not freely, you won't let him.
JACK	That's your opinion is it?
HAROLD	It's true. You set traps for his tongue . . . . Ask questions, twist meanings, put him on the spot then turn and walk away. He never knows where he is with you. What do you expect him to do?
JACK	What do you expect me to do?
HAROLD	He's your responsibility. I didn't make promises, assure his parents or bring him thousands of miles, you did. And now, when he needs your reassurance, you turn away.
JACK	I'm here.
HAROLD	No Jack, the more he needs you the more you push away. You turn away, like from a bitter cold wind.
JACK	I am responsible.
HAROLD	Yes you are . . . .
JACK	You're turning him against me, aren't you?
HAROLD	You're not listening, Jack. It has nothing to do with me.
JACK	If I catch you there'll be hell to pay . . . .

> *Short pause HAROLD stops at door to cabin with an armful of wood, he looks up at JACK.*

HAROLD	Jack . . . Jack?
JACK	What?
HAROLD	Tell me honestly . . . tell me . . . have we got a chance?

> *Short pause. JACK looks off into the fading sun.*

HAROLD	I mean where's the caribou? We missed the caribou, didn't we? Or there never were any . . . . Whatever it is there's 7 long months of winter ahead. Little I know I know that.

Brief pause.

So what's your plan? 350 miles to Fort Reliance and snow any day . . . . Not that? No mad dash out? No, I didn't think so. So what's the plan? What's the secret? What's the magic that'll get us through? . . . Jack? . . . Seriously Jack, I'd like an answer . . . .

JACK   You're welcome to leave.

HAROLD   You know that's not an option. I don't know any more about this country than you've taught me which isn't a hell of a lot. I wouldn't stand a chance . . . .

JACK   You answered your own question.

HAROLD   Yeah, which one?

JACK   You know nothing about this country . . . . Do what you're told, that's all. Do what you're told and you'll be fine . . . .

HAROLD   I've heard that before.

JACK   Not from me.

HAROLD   From men just like you. Men expert at holding themselves at a safe distance from danger.

JACK   I'm not afraid of anything.

HAROLD   You're afraid of us. Every day more and more you're afraid of us.

JACK   Do what you're told!

HAROLD   *(in a military way)* Yes Sir!

> *HAROLD enters the cabin with the wood. Fade to black except for an orange light on JACK's face as he continues sitting on his heels staring at the fading sun. A few moments of JACK's face only then all black. Short pause then lights up on HAROLD and EDGAR in cabin. JACK absent.*

HAROLD   What's he like?

EDGAR   He's big.

HAROLD   Fat?

EDGAR   No . . . . Heavy. Solid.

HAROLD   Strong then.

EDGAR   Yes.

HAROLD   Do you like him?

EDGAR   I love him.

HAROLD   But do you like him?

EDGAR   He's my father. I don't know . . . . What do you
              mean?

HAROLD   Do you like being with him? What's it like being
              with him?

EDGAR   Okay . . . . One thing I never liked . . . always
              waiting for him. He could never be on time.

HAROLD   Like Jack.

EDGAR   Yes. We always had to wait dinner for him. He was
              always late. We were always hungry. But Mother
              insisted. We had to wait. And when he did finally
              get home we were starving. So hungry no one said a
              word, they were too busy eating . . . . That made
              him mad. He wanted us to wait, then he wanted us to
              pretend we hadn't.

HAROLD   Like Jack.

EDGAR   I used to grind my teeth. Especially if it was beef. I
              could smell it. I could imagine the meat and I'd grind
              my teeth . . . . I was so hungry.

HAROLD   Then you couldn't like him. How could you like a
              man like that?

EDGAR   He's my father.

HAROLD   Right.

EDGAR   What about yours? You talk like he's dead.

HAROLD   No. Not dead . . . . When I was young I was always
              frightened of him. That's all I ever felt. I'd hear his
              feet moving up the gravel path, his key in the door
              and my heart would start to race. I'd think: What
              will he be like? Will he be silent, angry or sad? I
              could never just be with him. When I was with him
              I was always only concerned to try and please him.
              That's what my childhood was about. Trying to
              make him happy.

EDGAR   He had great responsibilities.

HAROLD   I'm the age now he was then. Responsibility had
              nothing to do with it. He was a prick is all.

EDGAR   But he's your father!

              Short pause.

HAROLD   I don't feel that way any more. The fear's gone . . . .
              Now it's hate. I hate him.

EDGAR   Harold you can't think that.

HAROLD   Hate and anger. It started when I was about your age.
              I'd try and talk to him you see. I'd come up to him,
              reading his paper, and speak to him. From behind his
              paper he'd answer: Yes? . . . And I'd try and try but
              all I could do is after a while start to cry. Couldn't
              get anything out but tears . . . . But I got over that.
              I went from snivelling to screaming. I realized he
              really couldn't hurt me after all so I started yelling at
              him. Oh it was ugly . . . . God I hated him. Now
              it's heading somewhere else. New territory. I'm
              somewhere between hate and the next thing.

EDGAR   And what's that? What's the next thing?

HAROLD   A shape on the horizon right now. Something
              moving in the distance . . . . Jack knows . . . . It's
              where he is. It's what he feels . . . . I expect.

EDGAR   It must be the War makes you feel this way.

HAROLD	It's not the War .... Maybe it is. But only because medals make no difference to men like that. The fathers we had .... You give them everything they want. You do everything they ask you to do, the perfect son, and still they don't love you .... Don't or can't doesn't matter it's just not there is the point .... You do it all but you're all alone anyway. What's the point? ... Think Edgar, think about him ....
EDGAR	What about him?
HAROLD	What you feel when you call up his face in your mind. The first thing, what is it?
EDGAR	Well .... I am always a bit nervous around him. But I feel that way round Jack too. They're my superiors, aren't they? ... I must respect them.
HAROLD	Why?
EDGAR	They're older .... I'm not saying he's perfect. I'm not saying that. It is mean to make children wait for their food. Children .... The table's set, the food's been ready for hours .... But Mother refused to start without him. She wanted us to eat as a family is all.
HAROLD	Some family!
EDGAR	We were starving. We were children. This one time, I was 5 or 6, and it was hours we waited. Hours! And when we complained, and when we squabbled amongst ourselves — because we were hungry of course — she got angry. We were children! ... She was livid when he finally walked in the door. Livid. They fought. Screamed. He turned to us standing there waiting to eat and sent us off to bed. He yelled at us — sent us running off to bed .... After the fighting stopped he came up to say goodnight. I remember his silhouette in my door. He was so big he filled it. He said go to sleep now, your mother's upset. It's nerves she's got and she needs you to give her some peace .... He leaned over to kiss me goodnight. I could smell the whisky on his breath. He was drunk. He'd been drinking.

Short pause.

HAROLD	What did you say to him?
EDGAR	Nothing. I went to sleep.

Pause.

HAROLD	Let's make a promise Edgar. Between us. Just between us. Can we?
EDGAR	Sure . . . . What promise?
HAROLD	Let's not talk about food anymore. Let's not mention it. I don't mean the food we eat here, I'm not saying let's not say we're hungry. I'm just saying let's not talk about meals with family . . . . Christmas or beef . . . . Can we leave that out of the conversation? Can we make that promise you and I?
EDGAR	*(laughs)* Yes. I promise.
HAROLD	It brings too many memories.
EDGAR	It does doesn't it.

Short pause.

EDGAR	Harold, you were in the War, weren't you?
HAROLD	Yes.
EDGAR	You saw men die.
HAROLD	I've seen men die . . . . Why?
EDGAR	I wonder. I keep thinking . . . when a man dies . . . . When we die do our thoughts seep out in a single line the way we think them, and do our memories leave one at a time the way we form them . . . or does it all rush out in a great chorus? . . . I mean what happens?

Short pause.

HAROLD	You die. That's what happens. You just die.

> *Short pause. JACK appears from stage right.
> He is wearing heavier clothes than in the scene
> before. He carries a rifle and a pack and wears
> gloves. He carries the skinned haunch of a
> Caribou over his shoulder. His face, clothes and
> hands are smeared in blood. He enters the cabin.
> He leans his rifle against the wall by the door, he
> drops his pack on the floor, he throws off his
> gloves. He lifts the bloody haunch of meat off
> his shoulder and holds it up above his head. He
> glares at HAROLD then at EDGAR.*

JACK Meat . . . Meat . . . Meat!

HAROLD No, really?

> *JACK throws the meat at HAROLD'S feet.
> JACK takes a step toward HAROLD.*

JACK I don't like your attitude. It's getting on my nerves.
What is it with you anyway. What is it?

HAROLD I'm vegetarian.

> *EDGAR laughs. JACK swings around violently
> and slaps EDGAR hard across the face. Silence.
> Pause.*

EDGAR *(stunned)* I'm sorry . . . . I'm sorry, Jack.

> *Short pause.*

JACK No.

> *JACK moves to touch EDGAR; EDGAR steps
> back, away from him.*

JACK I'm sorry. I . . .

> *Silence. Long pause. JACK removes his coat,
> washes his face and hands. EDGAR picks the
> meat up off the floor and puts it on the table; he
> finds a carving knife and begins to butcher it.
> HAROLD puts on his coat, goes outside, lights
> a cigarette.*

JACK Were you writing in your diary today?

EDGAR No.

JACK	It's alright if you do. It's what your father wants you to do, isn't it?
EDGAR	He said it would be a good idea . . . . To keep a record.
JACK	Yes. It is. I have one.
EDGAR	A diary?
JACK	A diary, a journal.
EDGAR	You never said.
JACK	From another trip, not from now. A friend's diary . . . . From a trip we were on together . . . . I don't know why I carry it with me I just do.
EDGAR	Can I see it?
JACK	No . . . . No you couldn't make it out. The handwriting. It would make no sense.

Short pause.

JACK	I'm sorry about . . .
EDGAR	It's okay. It was my fault.

Short pause.

JACK	It's important to write things down as they happen. It's no good later. They change in the telling, are transformed through retelling . . . . I know a man at Reliance tells a story from a trip we were on together when I hear him tell it now I don't recognize it. It's nothing I was part of, not the way he tells it now.

HAROLD enters.

HAROLD	It's getting colder . . . . Looks like snow again . . . .

JACK puts on his coat.

EDGAR	Where are you going?
JACK	To get the rest of the meat.
EDGAR	I'll come with you.
JACK	No. Stay. I can do it.

EDGAR   Are you sure?

JACK   Stay . . . . If I'm not back in 2 hours don't wait.
               It'll be the snow. I'll spend the night at the cache.
               I'll be back by noon tomorrow at the very latest.

                    JACK exits.

EDGAR   He's angry with me. That's why he's leaving . . . .
               What did I do?

HAROLD   If he doesn't need help it means he only shot one
               Caribou. Only one Caribou! That won't last a week.
               One! . . . If there had been more he'd want us out
               after them. Shit!

                    *Pause. HAROLD moves beside EDGAR at the
                    table, he looks down at the meat and pulls out
                    his knife.*

HAROLD   Are you hungry?

EDGAR   Yes.

HAROLD   So let's eat . . . .

                    *They stand with their knives out staring down at
                    the meat. Blackout.*

                    *The next day. Jack is outside splitting wood.
                    EDGAR is inside the cabin sitting at the small
                    table working on his diary. JACK picks up an
                    armful of wood, carries it into the cabin and piles
                    it by the stove. JACK looks at EDGAR writing
                    then goes back outside. JACK brings in another
                    armful of wood.*

JACK   What are you writing?

EDGAR   Things that happen. Sometimes specific things. The
               temperature, the direction of the wind, how much
               snow fell. Sometimes, more and more, thoughts.
               Things that come up in my mind.

JACK   What things?

EDGAR   You know when you're on the telephone, especially
               long distance, you can barely hear, it's all static, and
               you're straining to hear? You know that?

JACK   Yeah. I guess.

EDGAR   You have a conversation. You try and get across the distance, you shout what you mean to say. And then when you're finished . . . when you hang up . . . there's this silence . . . . There's suddenly this odd silence. And the words from the conversation you just had float past you like leaves . . . catching your eye . . . . It's those things I write down. The stuff that stays in the air after you've finished talking.

JACK   Me?

EDGAR   Or Harold . . . . He says things that make me think. They stay in my mind and make me think. You do too. That's what I write about. That's what I try to write down. What floats by after you pass, the dust in the air swirling behind you . . . . And the wind, the temperature, the time the sun comes up and the time it goes down.

JACK   You're writing about me in your diary? About what I said?

EDGAR   Sort of.

JACK   Don't.

EDGAR   Why?

JACK   I don't want you to.

EDGAR   But you said it was a good idea.

JACK   *(points at the page EDGAR has been working on)* What's that? What have you written today?

EDGAR   About the fish.

JACK   What about them?

EDGAR   *(reading from the diary)* Jack dug up all the fish left 60 in all which will last just 2 weeks and then if we have no meat we will be in a bad way . . . .

JACK   What else?

EDGAR   That's all.

JACK   I don't want to see you writing any more. You want
                to keep a diary, fine, but don't do it around me,
                understand?

EDGAR   Yes, Jack . . . . I'll stop if you want?

JACK   No. No, it's what your father wants. You keep it.
                Just not around me.

> *JACK exits quickly. Short pause. EDGAR*
> *looks down at his diary, he reads a few earlier*
> *entries to himself then closes the diary. He*
> *stands, picks up the diary, walks to the door and*
> *looks out. He turns back into the cabin and puts*
> *his diary away in a small trunk at the end of his*
> *bed. He closes the trunk, he stands, looks around*
> *the cabin, moves to the stove, kneels, opens door*
> *to stove, pokes at fire, puts more wood in the*
> *stove, watches the flames, closes the door to the*
> *stove. He stands and moves around the cabin*
> *restlessly. He lies down on his bed, he stares at*
> *the roof, he rolls onto his stomach, he tries to*
> *make himself comfortable. He grinds his hips*
> *into the bed. He moans. He sits up on the edge*
> *of the bed. He stands. He moves around the*
> *cabin restlessly. He stops and looks out the*
> *door. He steps outside without putting on his*
> *jacket and looks around quickly for JACK or*
> *HAROLD. He goes back into the cabin. He*
> *checks that the door is closed securely. He goes*
> *back to his bed. He lies down on his back and*
> *pulls a blanket up over him. He prepares to*
> *masturbate. He suddenly jumps up and moves to*
> *the door. He looks out nervously, he closes the*
> *door and takes one of the rifles leaning up against*
> *the wall beside the door and jams it up against*
> *the door. The door is blocked shut. He tests it.*
> *He moves quickly back to his bed, covers*
> *himself with the blanket and again prepares to*
> *masturbate. After a few moments HAROLD*
> *enters from stage right. HAROLD tries the door.*
> *He is surprised to find it locked. He shakes it.*
> *EDGAR jumps up off the bed frantically trying*
> *to fold the blanket. HAROLD bangs on the*
> *door. EDGAR races to the door, pulls the rifle*
> *away from the door and opens it for HAROLD.*

> HAROLD *looks at* EDGAR *then at the rifle then walks into the cabin.*

HAROLD   What were you doing?

EDGAR   What?

HAROLD   What were you doing?

EDGAR   Sleeping.

HAROLD   With a gun?

EDGAR   No.

HAROLD   What were you up to?

> HAROLD *moves over to* EDGAR's *bed, he looks down at it.*

HAROLD   Sleeping? I don't think so.

EDGAR   Jack doesn't want me to write while he's around so I blocked the door . . . . So he wouldn't catch me at it.

HAROLD   At what? *(short pause)* Writing? . . . Or something else?

EDGAR   No. Ask him. He just doesn't want to see me doing it.

HAROLD   I'm sure.

EDGAR   Ask him.

HAROLD   Where is it then?

EDGAR   What?

HAROLD   The diary . . . . First you say you're sleeping, then you say you were writing. If you were writing, Edgar, and not doing something else where is it? Where's the diary? *(short pause)* You're blushing . . . . My my, finally the truth. You're beet red Edgar, you're a bloody sunset.

EDGAR   Stop it.

HAROLD   Was it good?

EDGAR   Harold!

HAROLD	Was it a good one or did I interrupt? . . . Were you finished? All done?
EDGAR	*(screams)* Harold stop it!

> *JACK enters from stage right. He enters the cabin, takes off his pack, props up his rifle and begins to remove his outer clothes.*

JACK	I saw them.
HAROLD	What? What did you see?
JACK	So close I could see the steam from their breath.
HAROLD	Caribou? How many?
EDGAR	You saw Caribou?
HAROLD	Let's go.
JACK	No . . . . It's too late . . . . In the morning.
HAROLD	How many did you see? . . . How many were there?
JACK	It took me a while before I recognized them. It's been so long since I last saw them . . . . Years it seems. And there were others with them I didn't recognize. Strangers.
HAROLD	Jack?
EDGAR	What's he talking about?
HAROLD	He's mad.
JACK	I'm telling the truth!
HAROLD	What did you see, Jack? What exactly?
JACK	I was waiting. I knew they'd come. I was very still. The wind blew snow to cover me. They couldn't have seen me . . . . I was downwind. I waited . . . . And they came. I knew they would. Hundreds.
HAROLD	Caribou?
JACK	Yes.
EDGAR	Hundreds?

JACK	Seemed like it. But perhaps not quite. Perhaps 80 or 90.
HAROLD	Caribou? You saw 90 Caribou?
JACK	Yes.
HAROLD	Did you shoot? Did you get a shot off? How close were they?
JACK	I could reach out and touch them.
HAROLD	How many did you get?
JACK	I didn't shoot. I couldn't.
EDGAR	Why?
JACK	For what? To get one or two, three if I were lucky? . . . They'd have spotted me, it wouldn't have taken 30 seconds and they'd have had me in their sights. No . . . . No, that's not the point, is it?
HAROLD	*(sotto voce)* He's in the War, he's in the fucking War. *(to EDGAR)* Go see what you can see.
EDGAR	*(to JACK)* Where, Jack?
HAROLD	Go down to the river, go up 100 yards and down a hundred yards. If you see anything come get us.
EDGAR	We've got time, we could catch them.
HAROLD	No. It's dusk. Go . . . . Go!
JACK	I know exactly where they are.
HAROLD	*(sotto voce)* Shut up you damned fool.
EDGAR	Where?
HAROLD	Go!
JACK	*(to EDGAR)* Hey you! . . . Don't give yourself away. They'll be bedding down for the night. With luck we can hit them before dawn with sleep still in their eyes. A few dozen could do it. A dozen.
HAROLD	Go, Edgar.

> *EDGAR exits, moves off stage right. Long pause. HAROLD finds a cup and puts heaping spoonfuls of sugar in it.*

JACK   Easy with that.

HAROLD   It's for you.

JACK   I'm not hungry.

HAROLD   Come sit down.

> *JACK finishes removing his outer clothes and sits down at the table. HAROLD pours some hot tea into the cup and stirs it.*

JACK   I saw them.

HAROLD   Yes, I know . . . . Drink this.

JACK   Tea?

HAROLD   Yes. Drink it down.

> *Short pause. JACK takes the cup.*

JACK   My hands are stiff. I sat so still I didn't dare move or even breathe.

HAROLD   Drink.

> *JACK drinks. HAROLD sits in a chair opposite JACK.*

HAROLD   We have less than 100 pounds of flour. And fish for only two weeks.

JACK   I know.

> *Short pause.*

HAROLD   We're in a bad way here.

JACK   Yes.

> *Short pause.*

HAROLD   What did you see?

JACK   What?

HAROLD	On the barrens? Caribou? . . . Did you really see any Caribou?
JACK	No. None. But I don't want to frighten the boy.
HAROLD	Don't do it again.
JACK	What did I do? . . . I only said . . . . What did I say?
HAROLD	Never mind.
JACK	Oh God.
HAROLD	Drink.

> *JACK empties the cup, puts it down on the table, he looks at it a moment then buries his face in his hands.*

JACK	Oh God.

> *Short pause. HAROLD prepares another cup of tea with lots of sugar for JACK. Blackout. Brief pause in black then lights up.*
>
> *JACK and EDGAR and HAROLD are lying in their bunks. The light is low; the cabin lit by an oil lamp.*

EDGAR	Food . . . was always dead when I ate it or thought about it. It had taste and smell but it was dead. Now it is a living thing that I must kill. I think of it now as always a living thing.

> *Pause.*

HAROLD	Tell us about your girls, Edgar.
JACK	Girls?
EDGAR	I haven't got any girls.
HAROLD	Oh, surely one?
JACK	Do you?
EDGAR	No.
HAROLD	Have you ever done it with a woman, Edgar?

> *Pause.*

JACK	You asked that before.
HAROLD	He never answered.
JACK	Leave him alone.

Short pause.

HAROLD	Have you?
JACK	Ignore him.
HAROLD	Don't be shy. Tell us.
EDGAR	Well.
HAROLD	You do know how to do it?
EDGAR	Yes.
JACK	Course he does.

Short pause.

EDGAR	But . . . I think . . .
JACK	Never mind him.
EDGAR	I think it means nothing without love.

Pause.

HAROLD	Christ! . . . Love!
EDGAR	It's important!
HAROLD	Have you ever loved a woman, or a girl, have you?
EDGAR	No.

Short pause.

JACK	I have.

Pause.

JACK	At least I thought I loved her . . . . I still dream about her, sometimes . . . .
HAROLD	I dream of waking up beside a warm body. I dream of her skin, her hair, her smell. That's my only dream . . . . And food.

Short pause.

JACK   The minute our eyes met we knew. We wanted each
                        other. We wanted to taste each other . . . . She still
                        excites me. *(short pause)* I thought I loved her. I
                        thought she loved me. We couldn't keep our hands
                        off each other . . . . But she watched me enjoy her
                        body from a distance. She watched it and was
                        amazed. What she wanted wanted her . . . . But there
                        was always this distance . . . . *(short pause)* We
                        never stopped being excited. But that's all there
                        was . . . . We never entered the other's mind . . . .
                        We never needed the other's eyes to complete a
                        picture.

EDGAR   And if you had, it would have been love?

JACK   It would have been love if the thought of her, of her
                        face or the sound of her name, had been enough to fill
                        me with joy . . . .

                        Short pause.

EDGAR   Doesn't your family do this for you? When you
                        think about them?

JACK   When I go home to England we sit and talk. We ask
                        each other about our lives and always seem pleased
                        with the answers we get. But it's the fact that you
                        answered that pleases, not what you say. They don't
                        listen to what you say. I tell them things, important
                        things, and I know to them it's just my lips moving.
                        It's just a sound they hear. It doesn't touch
                        them . . . . They nod and move off . . . . It's not
                        love . . . . Whatever it is it's not love.

                        Short pause.

EDGAR   I love you Jack. *(short pause)* Jack? *(short pause)*
                        I've never felt this for anyone, not my father, my
                        mother, my brothers or sisters. No one . . . . *(short
                        pause)* I love you.

                        Pause.

JACK   Love's only between a man and a woman. The real
                        love.

> *Short pause.*

HAROLD   Real love has sex.

> *JACK leaps out of his bed, pulls out his knife and jumps onto HAROLD. HAROLD grabs onto JACK's arms, keeping the knife only inches from his face.*

HAROLD   Jack! . . . Jack!

EDGAR   *(standing up)* Jack don't . . . . Jack, what are you doing? *(he starts to cry)* Jack!

> *EDGAR sobs, he falls to his knees, he cries uncontrollably. JACK and HAROLD stop struggling and stare at EDGAR. JACK gets off HAROLD and puts the knife away.*

HAROLD   Edgar . . . it's all right now . . . . Edgar?

> *EDGAR continues to cry. JACK bends down to him, puts his arms around him, rocks him.*

JACK   I'm sorry. I'm so sorry.

HAROLD   Get him back to bed.

JACK   Come on, get up . . . . Come on, I'll fix you a hot whisky. That'll set you straight.

> *JACK helps EDGAR back to bed, HAROLD prepares hot whisky.*

HAROLD   *(he holds up whisky bottle for JACK to see)* This is it.

JACK   So?

> *HAROLD pours some into cup then takes a shot from bottle then offers bottle to JACK. JACK takes bottle, looks at it, pours more into EDGAR'S cup then drains bottle himself. HAROLD carries cup to EDGAR.*

HAROLD   Drink this now. Sit up. *(EDGAR sits up)* Be careful. It's the last of it. Enjoy it.

EDGAR   *(he drinks some then speaks)* Please don't fight.

HAROLD   We won't . . . . Drink . . . .

JACK   You mustn't get down Edgar. We'll pull through
                this. The days are getting longer, a few months and
                it'll be spring . . . .

                Short pause.

HAROLD   Drink . . . . Finish it.

JACK   This is nothing!

HAROLD   Quiet!

JACK   It's nothing.

                *JACK moves quickly to his trunk, he opens it
                and searches for something. He pulls out a diary.*

JACK   Remember the diary I told you about? Remember?

EDGAR   Yes.

JACK   Well listen. I'll read you something.

HAROLD   Jack. No. No, it's all right.

HAROLD   It's late.

EDGAR   No, let him read. I want to hear.

JACK   *(he reads, but slowly, awkwardly, as if the words are
                barely legible)* Here we are . . . . "9 am. Situation
                is now very serious. Walter last night told us that he
                felt he was sinking fast and might pass away at any
                moment so he talked to us as to what should be done.
                I promised him I can carry on for 5 days on
                Wolverine hides doing heavy work and hunting.
                David took a walk after Ptarmigan last evening which
                proved he can walk so Walter has told him he must
                go on to the barrens and dig up the Caribou paunch.
                I am myself capable but do not know even where they
                are" . . . . And then later he writes: *(JACK turns the
                pages)* "This morning I used the syringe with
                comparative success for the result was that I got rid of
                a quantity of matted hair off Wolverine hide" . . . .
                They were eating hide and fur!

EDGAR   What does he mean syringe?

HAROLD	You shoot soapy water up inside yourself.
EDGAR	Why?
HAROLD	Clear the system.
JACK	They're eating bones, hide and fur!
EDGAR	Then what?
HAROLD	I think that's enough.
JACK	Wait, wait.
HAROLD	Jack, that's enough.
JACK	Right. All right . . . . You see, you see what we have here is nothing. We have inconvenience is all.
HAROLD	It's time to sleep.
EDGAR	I see what you mean Jack.
JACK	Do you?
EDGAR	Sometimes I forget how bad others have it.
HAROLD	*(to EDGAR about drink)* Finished?
EDGAR	Yes. Thanks.
JACK	Never you mind. A good night's sleep and the world will be a different place entirely.

> *HAROLD puts cup on the table and is about to turn off the oil lamp.*

EDGAR	Could you leave it on?
HAROLD	*(he turns it down low)* How's that?
EDGAR	Fine.

> *Pause. JACK is sitting on the edge of his bed. EDGAR stares at the ceiling, HAROLD climbs into his bed and makes himself comfortable.*

I know now what it is to be poor.

HAROLD	Go to sleep.

> *Short pause.*

EDGAR   I'm hungry all the time. I never have enough to eat.
              And I'm cold. And I'm tired.

HAROLD   We're all tired.

EDGAR   Poverty is a terrible thing.

JACK   That's not poverty.

EDGAR   What would you call it?

JACK   Poverty is being without hope. *(pause)* It has
              nothing to do with hunger or cold or hard work.
              (short pause) Poverty is a man no matter how hard
              he works can't make enough to clothe and feed his
              family. Poverty is no one to turn to for help. No
              family, no friends to cushion the hard times. No one
              to turn to. That's what poverty is . . . . Poverty is
              disconnected, alone . . . .

                  Short pause.

JACK   This. This is inconvenient. A big inconvenience. A
              dangerous one. But we had a choice coming
              here . . . . And we have people on the outside who
              will always be there for us.

                  *Pause. JACK gets into bed and pulls the covers
                  up around him. They are still and silent, staring
                  at the ceiling.*

HAROLD   It's my birthday today.

JACK   Is it?

HAROLD   Yes.

EDGAR   How old are you?

HAROLD   28.

                  Short pause.

EDGAR   Happy Birthday . . . .

HAROLD   Thank you.

                  Short pause. Blackout.

Lights up. HAROLD lies in his bed. There are bones on the plates on the table. EDGAR is pounding bones on the floor, breaking them up with the back of an axe then putting them in a pot.

EDGAR   None of us feel well . . . . You think Jack does? *(short pause)* I hate it when he leaves. I think he's not coming back. I hate it when I have to leave. It's hard to want to go far. I get dizzy if I can't see the cabin. *(short pause)* Aren't you going to speak today? . . . You haven't said two words . . . . It's rude . . . . I don't know what you think you're doing. It's just rude.

HAROLD sits up on the edge of his bed.

EDGAR   Are you going out? *(short pause)* Cut some wood then. At least cut some wood.

Short pause. HAROLD stands, puts on his coat.

Where's the syringe? You had it last . . . . Harold?

HAROLD points to it. Short pause.

EDGAR   I feel all cramped and stuck . . . .

HAROLD exits, walks off stage right.

EDGAR   You could at least say goodbye! *(he stands, goes to the door, looks out)* You're not the only one having a hard time of it! . . .

EDGAR picks up a few sticks of wood from outside and quickly brings them in and shuts the door behind. He puts the wood in the stove. He stands.

What was I thinking? Something. Something came into my mind . . . What?

Short pause. EDGAR gets to his trunk, takes out his diary, sits at the table, turns the pages then prepares to make an entry. He waits. He holds his head in his hands. Pause. He sits back in his chair. He stands. He moves about the cabin. He stops. He moves to the door, he looks out.

He shuts the door and goes to JACK's trunk. He opens the trunk and looks through it for the diary JACK read from. He finds it. He stands. He leafs through it. It is blank. He kneels and looks through the trunk for another but finds nothing. He stands. He turns the pages frantically. He stops. He takes a few steps. He looks up. His eyes roll up into his head. He falls back onto his back the diary still in his hand. Blackout. 5 seconds then lights up. JACK stands over EDGAR, looking down at him.

JACK   Edgar?

Short pause. JACK bends down and picks up the diary. He looks at it.

EDGAR   *(hoarse)* Jack.

JACK   Get up now.

EDGAR   You lied to me.

JACK   Get up.

EDGAR   You made the whole thing up. It was a story. You lied.

Short pause. JACK puts the diary back in his trunk.

JACK   I saw a raven flying north. It means Caribou . . . . Soon. *(short pause)* Get up . . . . Please.

EDGAR   No . . . . I can't.

JACK   I didn't lie . . . . What I told you did happen. Just because it wasn't written down doesn't mean it didn't happen. *(short pause)* The truth is a feeling Edgar, not a fact . . . . It's understood by the heart, not the head . . . . I could tell you the details of my life, the when where and how of it, but that wouldn't be the truth about it . . . . Truth is about belief . . . . And belief comes from trust . . . . And trust from love . . . .

EDGAR   How could you lie to me?

JACK	Because you needed to hear it. Didn't you? . . . And it gave you strength, didn't it? Better than if I'd said straighten up, be strong, right? Am I right?
EDGAR	Yes.
JACK	Well that's the point isn't it? I did it for you. Because I care about you.
EDGAR	Do you love me Jack?

Short pause.

JACK	Yes.

Short pause.

EDGAR	And you did it because you love me?
JACK	Yes. *(short pause)* I'm awfully tired.
EDGAR	I'll get up. *(he does not move)*
JACK	I'm sitting down . . . . I'm going to bed . . . . I'm all done in . . . .

They are still. Blackout.

Lights up. JACK and HAROLD are sitting by the stove. They are very still throughout the scene. They speak with difficulty, taking breath is laboured. EDGAR lies asleep in his bed.

HAROLD	He can sleep.
JACK	Yes.
HAROLD	I wish I could . . . . Why can't we sleep? . . . I'm exhausted.
JACK	I don't know. It happens. No food . . . the system makes no sense any more.

Short pause.

HAROLD	Always I've heard, because of the cold, you mustn't sleep, you mustn't give in to sleep. You'll freeze. You'll not wake up . . . . Now I pray for sleep. I want to sleep Jack, I'm so tired.
JACK	It'll come.

HAROLD	*(he does not move)* I'm going out.
	Short pause.
JACK	No.
HAROLD	I can't just sit and wait.
JACK	You won't come back.
HAROLD	I will.
JACK	You won't.
HAROLD	Come with me then . . . . We'll both go . . . . Come with me.
JACK	The boy . . . . I won't leave him alone.
HAROLD	I have to go out.
JACK	If he wakes up and we're not here he will be frightened . . . . He asked me not to leave him alone.
	Short pause.
HAROLD	How long . . . . How much longer?
JACK	For what?
	Short pause.
HAROLD	For something to happen.
	Short pause. Blackout.
	Lights up. HAROLD in bed asleep. EDGAR kneels by JACK's bed, JACK in bed, EDGAR rubbing his legs.
JACK	They feel broken . . . . Splintered.
EDGAR	But this helps?
JACK	You should rest now.
EDGAR	Does it?
JACK	Yes . . . . We should have stayed here . . . .
EDGAR	It was worth a try.

JACK	I should have made you stay here.
EDGAR	No . . . . I won't be left behind.
JACK	But they were here. Tracks all around the cabin. You could have shot one from the window . . . . Put them by the door.
EDGAR	What?
JACK	The rifles. Load them. Put them by the door. They'll be back you see. They will.
EDGAR	I heard a raven this morning.
JACK	You see?
EDGAR	Yes.

Pause.

JACK	I keep thinking of my father.
EDGAR	Do you?
JACK	I thought he was a God . . . . I thought he was so good, so strong. A great man.
EDGAR	He was.
JACK	I don't know.
EDGAR	He was a great man. Everyone loved him.

Short pause.

JACK	When I saw him laid out in his coffin . . . . When I looked at his face . . . . I was so angry.
EDGAR	Why Jack? Because he died? Because he left you alone?
JACK	No . . . . I don't know why . . . . But not because he died . . . . I wanted to spit in his face. I wanted to hit him. *(angry)* Do you understand?!
EDGAR	No . . . . I don't . . . .
JACK	No?
EDGAR	No.

JACK

I want to get up now.

> *Pause. JACK does not move. EDGAR
> continues rubbing his legs.*

I want to get up.

> *Pause. Blackout.*

> *Lights up. HAROLD lies in bed staring at the
> roof. EDGAR lies in bed also staring up at the
> roof. JACK is gone.*

HAROLD

I don't . . . want to talk any more. *(short pause)* I
can't. *(short pause)* I just can't do it. *(pause)* Don't
ask me why. *(pause)* I'll tell you . . . . *(short
pause)* My thoughts . . . and what I say . . . and my
dreams . . . . These things are all the same
now . . . . I don't know if I'm dreaming, or thinking
or talking out loud.

> *Short pause.*

EDGAR

You're talking out loud.

HAROLD

I'm not sure . . . . I'm just not sure any more.

EDGAR

But it's me . . . . It's Edgar . . . . I'm here, Harold,
beside you . . . .

> *Short pause.*

HAROLD

Oh . . . . Good.

> *Short pause. Blackout.*

> *Lights up. All three lying in bed.*

JACK

Edgar . . . . I'm going now . . . . I'm going.

EDGAR

But we're April.

JACK

Too late for me.

EDGAR

I heard Harold firing. He saw Caribou . . . . More
than ever.

JACK

No . . . . Well, maybe a few more days then.

> *Short pause.*

HAROLD	I couldn't focus my eyes . . . . I could steady the gun, I could see them, I could focus, but couldn't line them up in the sights . . . . I look at my hand it's a blur. It takes a few moments to come clear. I look up, in the distance, and it's a blizzard of images . . . . It takes time to clear . . . .
JACK	Never mind.
HAROLD	And the sun is so bright.
JACK	It won't last . . . .
EDGAR	I'll go out tomorrow.
JACK	It's too late . . . . Even with food it's too late for me now . . . . The system has shut down. I can feel it.
EDGAR	Do you want me to rub your legs? . . . Should I rub them?
JACK	When I'm gone . . . . Close my eyes . . . . That's all I ask.
	Pause.
EDGAR	It's raining . . . . It's spring, Jack.
JACK	The roof is leaking.
EDGAR	It's rain.
	Blackout.
	Lights up slowly. Sound of water dripping through the roof. The light is warm. The sound of birds. EDGAR and JACK in bed. HAROLD standing.
HAROLD	Wait . . . . Wait . . . . Wait. (*short pause*) No, wait.
EDGAR	Harold.
HAROLD	Wait.
EDGAR	What are you doing?
HAROLD	There's . . . I remember now . . . . What I want to know is . . . Jack . . . Jack!

JACK   *(hoarse)* Yes.

EDGAR   Leave him alone.

HAROLD   No . . . . No I want to know this. *(short pause)*
                What I want to know is . . . . You're so smart, Jack.
                You're such a clever man. You can tell me things
                about myself I didn't know were there . . . . What I
                want to know, Jack, is how a man so wise, so full of
                experience, how can he make such a mistake as
                this . . . . Tell me that . . . . Tell me.

                Short pause. HAROLD collapses onto the floor.

EDGAR   Harold?

HAROLD   I'm okay. I'm okay.

JACK   Harold.

HAROLD   Yes, yes. You tell me . . . .

JACK   You know the answer.

HAROLD   What?

JACK   You know it. *(short pause)* Something told you to
                come here with me, something just as strong said
                stay away . . . . So . . . . You tell me . . . . Why?

                HAROLD curls up into fetal position crying,
                wailing in pain. This crying continues for 90
                seconds, fading to a whimper near the end.
                Silence for 15 seconds.

JACK   Get him off the floor. *(short pause)* Get him back to
                bed.

EDGAR   Harold . . .

JACK   Edgar . . .

EDGAR   Jack . . . Jack . . .

JACK   Harold . . .

EDGAR   Harold.

                Short pause.

JACK   Edgar. *(short pause)* Edgar?

EDGAR	I'm too tired to get him.
JACK	Edgar?
EDGAR	Yes?
JACK	I'm sorry . . . . I'm sorry about this . . . .
	Pause.
EDGAR	It's alright, Jack . . . . Never mind.
	Short pause.
JACK	Forgive me . . . . Please.
	Pause. Blackout.
	Lights up. EDGAR in bed. Harold at JACK's bed sewing JACK up in a canvas shroud. Only JACK's face is still exposed.
EDGAR	He wants his eyes closed . . . .
HAROLD	When you're stronger . . . take him outside . . . . And bury him . . . .
	Pause.
EDGAR	He called out . . . . I went to him. He looked up at me and his lips moved. He wanted to say something . . . . I kept him company. I spoke to him . . . . I would say a name and I could see a wave of feeling spread out across his face . . . . I kept looking into his eyes . . . . Only his eyes . . . . And then, near the end, I leaned over and reached under and held him to me. He was no heavier than a loaf of bread. I could feel his heart beating under my hand . . . . I kissed his cheek . . . . I couldn't move. I couldn't break away. I was frozen there, holding him . . . . He tried to speak . . . . He breathed into my ear . . . . And then he was gone . . . .
	Short pause.
HAROLD	Are you watching what I'm doing? . . . Are you paying attention?
EDGAR	Why?

HAROLD	You'll be doing this for me.
EDGAR	Are you going to die, Harold?
HAROLD	Yes.
EDGAR	Please don't.
HAROLD	You don't need to move us out right away . . . . We'll be fine for a while . . . . But bury us . . . . Bury us.
EDGAR	(*alarmed*) Harold?!

> *HAROLD moves back to his bed slowly. He gets into his bed and makes himself comfortable.*

EDGAR	Harold?
HAROLD	I'm too tired Edgar.

> *Short pause. Blackout.*

> *Lights up. They have not moved.*

HAROLD	It's raining.
EDGAR	It's just bone and hair.
HAROLD	You got some out?
EDGAR	Yes . . . . Will you try?
HAROLD	Yes.
EDGAR	It's hair blocking us up and making us so weak.
HAROLD	Yes. Cramps.
EDGAR	If we could only have a good meal. Some fresh meat. If we only had some good grub. A warm soup.
HAROLD	Please . . . . Shut up.
EDGAR	I just meant. (*short pause*) Do you want to use the syringe?
HAROLD	Later.
EDGAR	I'll help you.
HAROLD	Later.

EDGAR   Do you?

                   Short pause. Blackout.

                   Lights up. EDGAR sitting up in bed facing
                   audience blood streaming down from his nose
                   across his mouth and chin and down his front.

EDGAR   Harold! Harold! Harold! . . . Oh . . . . Oh . . . .
                   Harold!

                   Blackout.

                   Lights up. EDGAR walking stiff limbed around
                   the cabin. He walks as if blind, bumping into
                   things and feeling his way. He walks around the
                   cabin clockwise twice.

HAROLD   Stop it.

                   EDGAR walks around cabin and passes by
                   HAROLD's bed for a second time.

                   Stop it . . . .

                   Blackout.

                   Lights up. EDGAR is sewing HAROLD's
                   shroud. 60 seconds of EDGAR sewing. He
                   stops. He looks down at HAROLD.

EDGAR   There now. *(short pause)* All done. *(short pause)*
                   Goodbye then . . . .

                   Blackout.

                   Lights up. EDGAR is sitting on the edge of his
                   bed. He is holding his diary and some letters.
                   He has had another nose bleed. There is fresh
                   blood down his mouth and chin and front.

EDGAR   All set. *(short pause)* All done. *(short pause)* Make
                   preparations . . . . *(short pause)*

> *EDGAR tries to stand but can't. He falls to the ground. He lies very still for a moment as if unconscious. He begins to move. He crawls toward the stove. He pulls himself up by the stove. He opens the stove door. He sticks his hand in and feels inside the stove. He pulls his hand out. He holds his hand up and looks at it. It is chalk white from the ash. He places the diary and letters in the stove and closes the door. He puts a piece of paper on the top of the stove. He holds up his pen. He tries to focus on the paper. He leans over it and brings his pen to it. As he writes he pronounces the word:*

EDGAR Who . . .

> *He stops, leans back and examines the paper. He repeats:*

Who.

> *Pause. He stares at the paper. He writes another word and as he writes it pronounces it:*

Look.

> *He continues writing slowly, pronouncing the words as he writes them.*

In. *(short pause)* Stove.

> *EDGAR places the piece of paper on the top of the stove. He puts his pen down on top of the piece of paper.*

Good . . . . Good.

> *EDGAR crawls back to his bed. He climbs in. He pulls the blankets up around him. He stares at the roof.*

All done. *(short pause)* Preparations . . . . *(short pause)* Finished . . . .

Music begins. EDGAR slowly pulls the
blanket up over his face. The sound of water
dripping. Birds singing. The light goes bright
and warm then brilliant white then fades slowly
to black as the music ends.*

END

* The last verse of the 5th song of Mahler's
Kindertotenlieder. When the verse is finished,
blackout.

In this weather,
in this storm,
in this horror,
they are resting, they are resting,
as if in their mother's house,
where no storm frightens them,
where God's Hand shelters them,
they are resting, they are resting,
as if in their mother's house.

Free's Point

by

Philip Adams

Philip Adams as Mick.

The North would not be *North* without stories of lost explorers, crazed miners, and mad trappers. Robert Service encouraged this popular conception of the Yukon in his *Songs of a Sourdough* (1907), but the association of the North with madness stretches back into the last century to poems such as C.D. Shanly's "The Walker of the Snow" (1859), to Ojibway myths of the Windigo, and to real people and events. Earle Birney's "Bushed" is based on fact. Albert Johnson, the mad trapper of Rat River, has been re-created and interrograted in books by Rudy Wiebe, among others, and he is commemorated in the name of an Inuvik bar.

In *Free's Point*, Philip Adams gives us another of these madmen drawn from life. The play recreates the final moments in the life of Michael Oros, who tried to live alone in remote bush south of the British Columbia/Yukon border. Oros, from all accounts an intelligent but deeply disturbed man, grew violent in his isolation and so paranoid that he murdered another trapper in 1981. The disappearance of Gunter Lishy led to an RCMP investigation and manhunt in which Oros, like Johnson, killed a Mountie before being shot by police. Oros is interesting because he kept diaries detailing his thoughts and experiences between 1972, when he arrived in the North, and his death in 1985; these diaries form the basis of lawyer Vernon Frolick's account called *Descent into Madness: The Diary of a Killer* (1993). In *Free's Point*, however, Adams draws upon his personal knowledge of Oros's life, complemented by the diaries and police records, to create Tahltana Free Mick from the man who called himself Sheslay Free Mike.

The beauty of this play lies in Adams' expressionist dramatization of madness. With a minimal set (the Nakai production used a long ramp with a pile of sticks), Adams relies on speech, lighting, and sound effects to create a reality distorted by Mick's deranged perceptions and haunted memory. Heinz (the Lishy figure) is a figment of this mind, and yet his physical presence on stage is essential to the action and themes of the play. When the play begins, Mick is already mad, has already set fire to a cabin and his girlfriend, has already murdered and buried Heinz, his dogs are dead, and he is alone with the sound of his own voice, waiting for the end. What we witness is a replay of the events leading up to this moment, a replay contained within the freeze frame of Mick's monologue, which opens and closes the play. Heinz materializes to goad Mick into remembering, reiterating, and finally re-enacting significant scenes from his life.

The key to this play lies in the figure of Heinz who, in true expressionist style, is the concrete externalization of an inner state, fear, or problem. Heinz can carry this weight because, as Adams recreates the Oros story, this older man is Mick's double, at once a father figure to be feared and hated, a mirror image of Mick's own desire to succeed (with Julie, with the bush), and the companion who relieves his loneliness but threatens to encroach on his fragile sense of physical and psychological space. There is even a suggestion of homoerotic tension in Mick's ambivalent view of Heinz, but a privileging of this aspect of Mick's replay of events would depend upon emphases and gestures in performance. Through Heinz, the audience or reader sees, not so much an etiology for Mick's state, as the depths of his self-deception, the consequences of his paranoia and violence, and, ironically, his fundamental lack of freedom. Mick has come North to find peace, purity, and freedom. What he finds is violence, corruption, and entrapment in the berm of his own mind.

If there is a hero in this play, it is not Mick. Adams is not asking us to sympathise with, let alone condone, this man's behaviour. At best, Mick is an anti-hero, a figure of southern, civilized humanity run amok. It is not the bush that has driven him mad but his own illusions, selfishness, and egocentricity; he is like Margaret Atwood's pioneer in "Progressive Insanities of a Pioneer," hating everything that resists him and screaming to get out. The unacknowledged hero, the mute protagonist opposing Mick, is the northern bush itself, the "little bit of sandy beach" on a northern lake that will survive Mick but will not free or cleanse or save him.

Philip Adams, artistic director with Nakai Theatre in Whitehorse from 1994 to 1998, was also artistic director for the first New Theatre North playwrights' festival, held in 1996, which presented 35 new plays written in and about the North. He is proud of the vitality of theatre in the Yukon, which he has done so much to support. In the North, he tells us, "each person is a 'real character' and plot means staying warm in January" (Adams, "Why Theatre, Lawrd?" *Theatre Memoirs*. Playwrights Union of Canada, 1998: 45), but when asked what northern theatre *is*, he demurs: "Hunting moose on stage just ain't as exciting as the real thing" (44). What he is certain of is that northern theatre is about local stories, community, and a frontier desire to do something new.

Adams has published *Tears, Mama* (1992), a tough one-act play about a transsexual musician in a homophobic world, and *Shakedown Shakespeare* (1997), which he co-wrote with Yvette Nolan. "Shout Love," his 15-minute one-hander about Canadian poet Milton Acorn, was produced by Longest Night in 1996. He is currently writing a libretto for "Flukes," an opera about whaling in the western Arctic that will unite his interests in music, theatre, and the North.

S.G.

* * *

Free's Point was first performed at the Nakai Theatre in Whitehorse, Yukon on 21 February 1996.

Tahltana Free Mick	Philip Adams
Heinz Selmer	Roy Ness
Directed by	Yvette Nolan
Lighting design by	Joanne Lantz
Set design by	Alyx Jones
Sound design by	Daniel Janke
Costume design by	Georgina Brown
Stage managed by	Sharon Shorty

FREE'S POINT

CHARACTERS

Tahltana Free Mick   Age 35 to 45
Heinz Selmer   Age 45 to 55

Scene 1

In black, from far in the distance, a small plane is heard. The sound slowly, ever so slowly gets louder and louder until it feels that it is right in the auditorium, in our laps, in our faces. Lights up very slowly. It is morning. The stage is covered with dirt, sticks, rocks, and a small stretch of beach. Small pads of loose papers are stuffed under some rocks. These are Mick's journals. It is a sandy point of land on the side of a lake. There are a few trees, mostly poplar and willow. There is a bermed cave with a few sticks and branches leaning against it. A full moose carcass hangs from a tree. On one side of the point there is a pile of sticks and on the other a mound of dirt. Even though MICK acts as if "Rowdy" is present, there is no dog; "Rowdy" is long dead and exists only in MICK's mind. As the sound of the plane recedes MICK explodes from underneath the pile of sticks. The plane passes and is finally gone.

MICK   Fuck. They're at it again. Fucking assholes. Don't worry, now. Come here, Boy. They missed us this time. They didn't even see us, did they. But they keep trying. It's like they are on some kind of mission, or something. They don't want to know what's down here, really. You'd think with nothing much to do up in those planes that they'd get bored. At least have enough time to look down once in awhile. I mean they don't have to stay between any lines or anything. No guard-rails. Ain't much on-coming traffic. Fuck 'em. Good dog. That's a good Rowdy boy. There now, it's OK, boy.

MICK   Well, it's not *OK*. It's just the way it is. It's the
way this all went down. We don't have to stand for
this shit, Rowdy. Look at it, eh. Just look at it.
You got to be blind to not know what's going on
down here. Either that or just plain stupid. That
plane is gone but any time now it'll be back, just
you wait. Then it'll be coming down all over us
again. Eh, Rowdy. They can't leave us alone, can
they. You see what this shit does to them? It gets
them fucking paranoid. You know? They get it into
their heads that they are in some kind of danger. That
I am some kind of threat. Then they come in here
looking for me. They leave no stone unturned. But
they're just looking to look. Visitors is all they are.
They've got this burning desire, this uncontrollable
urge to come in here and put things right. It takes
over. Becomes an obsession. It'll be something to
make them all feel like they've done good for the day.
Something to tell their children. Go back home.
Dinner on the table. Wife in the kitchen there
whipping up the grub. Kids all pissed off that
nothing's happening in this two bit town. Daddy
comes in through the door, tired, full of pride. Full
of his world. Full of himself for what he has done.
Spreads his hands on the table. Mom's walking in
with corn on the cob. Oh, I love that corn. And he
says, "I saw him today." Long silence. Well, it's
chow time; who's listening to him? "I said, I saw
him today. Spotted him from the plane." Little
Jamie on his way to snaggin' a cob spills his juice.
Mom's on her heels headin' back to the kitchen for a
rag. Dad grips the edge of the table. "Down at the
bottom end of Teslin. There on that little sandy
point." Jamie's chompin' and the girls, just sittin',
hands in their laps, heads slunk down over their
plates, sayin' "Corn is boring," and Mom is pissed
because no one but her is moppin' the juice. And
then it's over. That's it. That's all he gets for a
day's work. "No one but me understands," he thinks.

*A plane suddenly flies low overhead. MICK
takes out the sheet of plastic which he has been
hiding under the sticks and pulls it over him.*

MICK   You can never be too sure about what's gonna happen
next around here. They come sweeping down over us
here, you know, real low like, spraying us with that
testicide they use. It's all fucking poison. I mean,
why else would they do it, eh? Why else would they
fly around like that, back and forth like they are on
some kind of weaving machine. *(he crawls out and
writes in one of his journals)* Hey, that's good.
"Plane again today. Sneaking up at dawn. Real low
this time. Straight into the wind. May have spotted
us. Some of it got on us. They are flying the
pattern, now. Back and forth on a sky loom." I like
that one. "Sky loom." Hey, an air loom. You see
it, Rowdy? There it is there. You see it with your
eyes. That brown stuff spewing out the back. Then
it settles down all over everything. Just when you
think you're out here alone, they're back at you
again. Just can't fucking leave you alone. Hey,
we'll show 'em, won't we Rowdy. Free Mick.
Sidekick. Old fella. Yeah. That's a good boy.
That's what freedom is all about, ain't it. Yes it is.
It's all about paying attention to what's closing in on
you. It's knowing when to leave. Ain't it Heinz.
It's all about timing. See how close they were this
morning? Sneaking up like that. Ah me, I'm afraid.
I see them all the time out there and I am afraid. See
all this testicide shit they laid down on us? You
know what this shit does? It shrivels your nuts.
Shrinks the skin up tight until it squishes all the
blood out. Then there's nothing left. No more juice.
Just a sack of stinky gunk. That's what happens to
you. That's what that fucking testicide does to you.
I know. I seen it happen. Well look, look what
happened with Julie. Remember her, Rowdy? Sure
you do. You know Julie and the Belly Rub. Well,
you know how she wanted my babies. Oh, she was
right on the money she was. Big Time in the Big
Top. She knew that babies were real freedom. We
would be free for a whole generation. This is what
those genes do and that DNA stuff, Rowdy. Two
people come together in harmony and make little
speakers inside our offspring. That way we can
whisper to them. Say little things into our
microphones and they'll hear us. "I love you.

MICK   I love you Julie. They are half me and half you."
With the babies, that's where it all comes together.
Inside of them. They got the speaker system; you
got the volume control. They hear and react. Feel
and react. Smell, react. They don't have to think
about it. We give it all to them. Made in our own
image. They are us. That's what Julie knew. But
what good did it do her? I had to save her. Oh yes, it
was all up to me. That's what I did, all right.
Walked right up to her place that night and plucked
her from the fire. When he first looked in he didn't
notice anything out of place. All he saw was a lump.
An old sleeping bag piled up in the corner. Then he
realised, "Yes, it's her!" The rise of her hips.
Unmistakable. It was her foot, all right, sticking out
of the end of the sleeping bag. Delicate. The smoke
was still high in the ceiling and she was going to
sleep right through it. Hey, she was lucky he
happened to be there, passing through. And
remember that big door? Heinz, you built it for her,
didn't you. Yeah. Christ, it's like you didn't want
anyone else to get in or something. All to yourself.
The fire was into the rafters. So he does. He walks
right in as if it doesn't matter to him. She is too
close to the flames. And she is so light. So fragile.
She'll go up like dry toast. Little crumbs gone
invisible and then ground down into the earth.
Breathe her in like that. Turned to powder by the
wind, my sweet. Flakes of white ash floating in the
air. Like summer snow. She doesn't weigh much.
About as heavy as a dog only longer. A little harder
to carry too. People bend in different places than
dogs do. It's easier to carry a dog. Pick her up. The
beam lets go. Sparks fly up into his eyes, stinging
skin. He can't see. She lay in his arms. Still.
Sweet morning smells coming from her sleeping bag.
Musty. Jet black hair. God. He can feel her
breathing. Actually feel her breath. Her body tight
to his. Her lungs pushing her ribs out. Filling her
body. Her heart flushes the blood down through her
lungs. Then sucked back out. Pushing the air up and
out her nose. Her sharp, little, tilted nose. A tiny
pimple on this side. Here, let me squeeze it for you.
Exhale. Her body going small again. Tiny and frail.

MICK

She stirs. Awake, like that, as if it is morning. Blinking and licking her lips. A crust of mucus at the corner of her mouth. She looks up. Sees him. Tahltana Free Mick. Smile. Scrunches her face and curls up into his arms. Where to turn now? He knows it's now or never. In the corner with no windows. He can't see the door. It has to be somewhere behind that beam. The fire in between. He cups her into his body and plunges through the smoke, the fire, and brimstone. Over the beam. Hair burning off around his face. Smelling like . . . like . . . . Then he sees it. Arh, it's not the door. The stove. If he hits it, that will be it. The only thing between him and the sharp edges is Julie. Handles. Corners. Knobs. He spins to his left. Pulls Julie close to his body. Pulls her up high to his shoulders, presses her into his chest. Hard iron hit thighs. Slowly rip pants. Gouge thin strips. Flesh peeling off. Peeling away. Rolling off the edge. Bits of muscle stuck to hot steel. Down through the smoke. Falling. A bundle of Julie tight in his arms. *(silence)* The next thing I remember is the cool air passing over my face. It feels like my head is in a stream. I had bounced off the stove and fallen through the doorway. My head rests on the door mat. The bristles stiff. Hurt my face. I tuck up my legs and push us along the ground. Then the whole roof crashes in. The air disappears. I can't breathe. Then, in one full, bright, beautiful moment, it explodes. Sparks jet stream into the night air Stars and sparks. A thousand suns of fire. Oh yes. After that she wanted babies. At least I think that's what happened. It was either that or play tiddly winks. I'm not trying to be funny, Rowdy. She really did like tiddly winks. You remember. Sure. Hey, what do you do? Do you tiddle when you play? Or is it winking? Or is it full out tiddling and winking? "Hey tiddle diddle the cat's in the middle. The cow's left holding the spoon." No, that's how Heinz used to sing it. No, that's not it. Tiddle. Diddle. Diddle diddle. "Mick! Stop that diddling." "Can't help it, Mom. My leg just does it all by itself." Ah, come on Rowdy. Help me out on this one. God, she was perfect. We were perfect. I miss that about her.

MICK	She wanted all the babies we could have. And there were plenty out there. But she couldn't keep them. I can see them all running along the shoreline. The sun heating up the holes in the sand where we step. There are all kinds. Wee blondies. Copper-topped. Dark and moody ones. The lakes are warm and our skin full of sweat. Swimming in the warm. See what I mean? She was all softness, you know. She was all kindness and pleasure. Julie. She was my sweet liberty there for awhile. She was. . . .

> *Offstage a branch snaps. He freezes stalk still. He reaches for his .22 rifle which was with him under the pile of sticks and takes dead aim at the point where the snapping sound came from. He freezes again. Soundlessly, from behind him, Heinz approaches. He is carrying a large pail. He stops and watches MICK aiming in the opposite direction. Then like a cat realising its prey is just beyond reach, MICK lowers his rifle.*

HEINZ	Look both ways.
MICK	Jeesuz! How the fuck?
HEINZ	Caught you again, now didn't I?
MICK	Get out. Get the fuck out of here. I didn't want you here.
HEINZ	Jah. Jah. It's OK. Slow down. I'm only playing, only fooling around, and besides, I just got here. Why would I leave so soon? Don't be crazy.
MICK	Jeesuz fuck. Get out of here, I said.
HEINZ	Take a moment, OK Mick? All right, I'll leave. I got this extra sugar I thought you . . . . I'll leave it right here on the ground, OK? I'll just leave it here so that you can take it or leave it, Jah? It's just over there if you need it. I'll leave. Jah? Jah.
MICK	Yeah. Get.
HEINZ	Come on now, Mick. It's me. Don't be so mean. You always said just to drop by. Besides, we're used to this. This is not the first time for this. We've done this already. But I will go.

MICK	*(calmed)* Don't go. Jeesuz, Heinz. Why did you sneak up like that? You, of all people. And at a time like this. Just don't do it again. I'll fucking kill you, if you do.
HEINZ	Well, then I should leave shouldn't I.
MICK	If you know what I know, you will.
HEINZ	"Do you see what I know, what I know, what I know." Jah, OK, OK. I see this. We used to play this game, you and me. I find you — you find me. "Don't sneak up on me." Ha! That's a funny one you got there, Mick.
MICK	What?
HEINZ	You sneak up on me all the time. What did you do down at Paddy Lake? Well, Mick? What did you do? You even had a cup of coffee poured in your mug, in your own mug, before I knew it. Now that was a good one. *(HEINZ starts to set up an area for himself by the lake, humming "Lili Marlene")*
MICK	Where're you headed?
HEINZ	Here.
MICK	What?
HEINZ	Here. I've come here.
MICK	What for?
HEINZ	Because this is where I was coming.
MICK	Don't jerk me, Heinz!
HEINZ	I'm not. I was coming here to this point. I wasn't coming here to you. I don't want you. I don't even want to see you really. The fact that I do see you is kind of funny, you know. Ironic, wouldn't you say, considering the last time. This time round I only want to be here. On this spot. It's not that I don't want to see you — see you; that's not what I mean. No. I do have these eyes and I am seeing you. But this time it is different. What I mean is, I want to be here on this point. This little bit of sandy beach here where I was a couple of months ago.

HEINZ	On my way to Dease Lake. Passing through I found this spot here and I liked it. You liked it too because you came back. I wanted to come back. Here. So now I am. Here. *(hums and continues to make camp)* Nice, isn't it?
MICK	I don't recognise it.
HEINZ	Of course you recognise it. It's very familiar to you because you are here already.
MICK	No, the song, asshole. I know this place. I don't know the song.
HEINZ	Oh, that little ditty. It was something my mother used to sing to me. It goes... *(sings)*
MICK	Don't! I don't want no mother's song! How long are you staying?
HEINZ	Don't know. Do you?
MICK	Yeah. You're staying just as long as it takes you to pick up your bucket of things there and move on.
HEINZ	No, this is not what I mean. I mean how long are *you* staying here?
MICK	Just long enough to watch you go. Make sure you are really gone. Then I'll leave.
HEINZ	You want me to go, I'll go.
MICK	I want you to go.
HEINZ	You want me to stay, I'll stay.
MICK	No, I'll stay.
HEINZ	Go? Stay! Stay? Go! Ah, these questions.
MICK	Go!
HEINZ	Go? Go where? Where would I go?
MICK	Away!
HEINZ	I've been away. Now I'm back.
MICK	I want you to go.

HEINZ	Why? Why do you want me to go?
MICK	Because I am tired of repeating myself. I have to tell you all the time, go somewhere else. And when you get there, you won't find me there. There is lots of room out there.
HEINZ	But you need me, Mick. Without me you wouldn't be able to go through with this. I know what this is. You don't like me. Awww. *(pulls a second bag of sugar from his bucket)* Right now, you don't want me. "I vant to be alooone!" She was beautiful, wasn't she. And alone, I might add. You need the sunglasses though, a silk scarf, we have this make-up, and do something with that hair, dahling.
MICK	Don't stop now. Please. More. More.
HEINZ	*(as Dietrich)* I remember the first moment you came into my life. It was, how do you say, a miracle, dahling. *(cross fade dialogue with MICK)*
MICK	... That day in the harbour, just as we were about to set sail for the islands off Cape Verde. A little trip round the Horn and you came striding down the pier....
MICK	Yes. Yes. And don't forget all the girls who were there too. Waving and crying. They were all with me.
HEINZ	Yes, yes there were — girls. Plenty of girls. But you — you were the only woman, *(together with MICK)* Dahling.
MICK	No. That isn't how it went. We didn't talk through that part. *(put scarf on HEINZ)* You just put on that scarf and stood over there. And as I remember it, you were the one that was made up. Yes, that's it. *(puts lipstick on HEINZ)*

> *They dance together, but from far apart. HEINZ, still as Dietrich, starts to laugh and then mocks MICK.*

MICK	Come on, Rowdy. Let's go.
HEINZ	As for me, now that I'm here like this, I will stay.

MICK stops still. HEINZ, takes off scarf, wipes lipstick, fusses and makes himself at home.

MICK *I really didn't mind him. He was fun to have around from time to time.* That was Gordie who flew over awhile ago, wasn't it?

HEINZ What? In a plane, you mean?

MICK No, on a swan's back. Just a few minutes ago. Scared the shit out of me. Even Rowdy got scared.

HEINZ Rowdy?

MICK Rowdy!

HEINZ Row-dy!?

MICK My fucking Rowdy dog. Scared you, didn't it boy. They flew right over top of us. In low. Spraying. Spraying testicide. That's how it will end. Some tourist will stumble in on our camp and find us all with sucked out balls. Skin all tight up. From this *(hands on cheeks, pushing his mouth together in a pucker)* to this. *(stretches skin taut the other way)* It's OK now, fella. Yeah. There you go fella.

HEINZ I thought you knew, Mick.

MICK What?

HEINZ About Rowdy.

MICK You got something to say to me, Selmer? He's a good dog, aren't you Boy. Had him since he was a pup. Just a little wiener, you were. Been right here with me all this time.

HEINZ I thought you knew. About Rowdy. Don't you remember?

MICK I don't remember nothing. That's what it's doing to me. They put all this shit in the air to get me. You see it, don't you Rowdy. You got eyes. You got good eyes. You see that brown stuff coming out of the back of those planes? That's the spray. That's the stuff they're laying down all over this area to shrivel your nuts. Keep you limp. *(to HEINZ)* Don't look at me like that. It's working on you too.

MICK   Remember what happened to Rowdy. He couldn't
              even do it to McCullough's bitch there in town. Her
              tail was all cranked over to one side and everything
              and he couldn't do it. He had to sit down. Right
              there at the end of the road. She just walked away,
              looking over her shoulder at him with those glassy
              eyes. It's the same old shit. Looking kind of limp
              yourself, Heinzie.

HEINZ   You're going crazy, you know that, Mick. You've
              been out here too long on your own. All by
              yourself. We are old friends but I've never seen you
              like this. Those are just planes. Period. Nothing
              more. They get you from here to there. There's
              nothing dangerous about them. Oh, they fall out of
              the sky sometimes, but that's about it. Don't waste
              your time thinking about this funny stuff. You used
              to know better than this. All this didn't used to be a
              problem for you. And it shouldn't be a problem for
              you now. What's done is done.

MICK   I know. That's what I mean. This wasn't a problem
              before. Neither was the taste of the water. Or these
              hot summers we've been having. Was the winter
              cold enough for you? Open your eyes!

HEINZ   I'm looking. What am I looking for? Is this the
              looking part? Looking for what I can't see? We did
              agree to look, didn't we? Let's go back.

MICK   We can't. OK, let's go back.

HEINZ   Jah. Sure we can. I was looking, right? You were
              telling me to look at these problems that you saw.
              This bad water. The trouble with the air. Too much
              the chopping down of trees. I look where you tell me
              to look *(looks skyward)* I don't see anything. I ask
              you to explain to me; you talk nonsense. Here, this
              water is good.

MICK   Square hole. It's all up in them planes. Everything
              that's wrong is in them. Remember when they
              finally caught up with me? Gordie landed right in
              front of my camp there on Hutsigola Lake. Spilled
              all that oil on the beach. And when they took me
              away in the plane, I saw barrels of the shit stowed in
              the back. They knew what they were doing, all right.

HEINZ
No, Mick. I know planes. I know engines too. This is simply exhaust from the engines. The colour you see is waste.

MICK
I know it's waste. It's wasting me. And it's wasting you. I don't care what you call it. It's still the same ol' shit. Yeah, "it's just waste" he says. Don't you see what we are up against?

HEINZ
Jah.

MICK
Jahvol, all right. Rowdy, heel. Good boy. *(MICK exits with his rifle and knapsack)*

HEINZ
Mick! Mick! Jah, Tahltana Free Mick. What a stupid thing to call yourself. Jah, Herr Mickey Spilane. Sounds Irish to me. What will it be tomorrow, uh? Meziaden Mickey? Teslin Tiny Tim? Liard Lost Larry. Brook's Brook Bob? What does that make me? What? Heinz 57? Heinz pickles? No, I am Heinz. I will always be Heinz.

> *He stands waiting for an answer. He starts to sing "Girl From Ipanema" but as "Tahl and Tana, and young and lovely ...." Hearing no response from MICK, he picks up his pail and gets some water. He goes up to a tree and, with his handkerchief, he starts to wash down the trunks of the trees. He is methodical and meticulous. Lights dim as he goes about his task. He sings "Me and My Shadow."*

Scene II

> *There are now more trees in the playing area. HEINZ is busy making a lean-to close to MICK's berm. He has a neat pile of peeled pine poles which he stands up in a tee-pee. He goes to the mound of dirt and clears some debris away. As he is lashing more poles together, MICK enters in behind HEINZ and knocks the tee-pee over. He is pointing his rifle right at HEINZ's head.*

MICK
You're an asshole, Heinz. You not smart either. For a Kraut, you're a pretty dumb fuck.

HEINZ	Just hold on a minute, Mick. Just hold it. Where have you been? I knew you'd be back, but I thought I'd hear you coming.
MICK	(*imitating the sound of a rifle hammer*) Click.
HEINZ	This is silly. Pointless. Now put down the .... Look, the site is all cleaned up now. See I started to build a little place. And no more brown spray stuff. Poof. Gone.
MICK	That's my line.
HEINZ	Jah. You are right. I was just quoting you. Can I get you a cup of coffee or something?
MICK	Coffee eats your guts.
HEINZ	I know, but so do other things you do.
MICK	Your guts are supposed to eat things, not get eaten. (*MICK goes for a pee*)
HEINZ	Eat. Get eaten. Law of the jungle. "You say, Yes. I say, No. You say, Why? I say, No one's nose. Oh, oh. Oh-oh-oh."
MICK	Oh, fuck off.
HEINZ	What's wrong with you?
MICK	You.
HEINZ	What do you mean?
MICK	You don't even know the words. Sing something you know. Don't go singing some goddamn Limey song.
HEINZ	Remember, without Hamburg, they'd be nothing.
MICK	You mean, like einz fries and swie Cokes at the A & W Hobnob? Don't talk to me about being nothing without Hamburger.
HEINZ	Huh?
MICK	Square fuck. You are a stupid fuck with square hole. Stupid square-holed fuck.

HEINZ	What's your point?
MICK	You're the fucking point. You're here. *(to himself)* Why didn't he see it coming? Why didn't he leave?
HEINZ	Jah, and I will remain.
MICK	What does that mean?
HEINZ	It means I am here.
MICK	I thought you left.
HEINZ	Just like that? Poof? Gone? You are really deep, you know. *(mocking)* Why, there must be something in the water this morning. You always say the water's going bad. The snow water doesn't taste the same. The willows are getting all waxy. You point these things out and yet nobody else sees it. Nobody cares. You say the earth is going for a shit but nobody cares, Mick. Face it.
MICK	You wanna know the real problem? It's her, Julie Dante. The problem is she used to reach up under my shirt, right there on Main Street, and pinch my nipples hard between her fingernails as if no one else could see what she was up to. She knew to stick her finger up his ass when she wanted him to come in her mouth. And she cried every night the big lights came out. She loved being out here. Out here in this. Some days she would just sit way up there on the ridge and just watch him. Just doing the little things. Everyday stuff. Puttering around. Wood. He'd be way down by the creek there, and then for no reason he would look up from what he was doing, and wave at her. A sparkling jewel. But then something happened. Oh, he wanted her to like it. To want him that way. Big Time under the Big Top want. But she couldn't. It was all too much for her under those big lights. They all run away. She'll be back. I know she will. *(pause)* OK, so this is the game we are playing now eh, Heinz Swie Drie Frier Fumph Baby. Here's the rules: two people. One here. One there. Let the dance begin.
HEINZ	Mick yells at her, "Why? I don't get it?"

MICK	"It's too close," Julie says. "It's all too much. I don't want that much."
HEINZ	"How can it be?" he cries. "I was only starting to fall in love with you."
MICK	Julie pleads, "Why did you wave at me then?"
HEINZ	Mick says, a bit too coldly, I think, "Why did you wave back?"
MICK	You see? Now, if two people like to dance, why stop the music?
HEINZ	Is this a game? This is not a game.
MICK	Well, then, what's in the bucket?
HEINZ	The same things. My gun, my few things, the camera, my books....
MICK	I don't want no fucking camera here, OK. Put it away. Yes! Down. Down in the bucket.
HEINZ	Mick, it's in the bucket.
MICK	So, what's in the bucket then?
HEINZ	The same things. My gun. My few things. The .... My books. Some sugar. Hey. Let's do this together, Mick. I know it's not much, but if we want, we can share this place. I mean, we don't have to have it all on one side or the other, do we? We don't have to have it one way or the other. If we separate, pull apart just a little, like this then, we won't crowd each other out. Won't be in each other's way. See? Like this. I am here. You are there. There is plenty of room over there to move around. I know this. We both know this. Besides, I didn't come out here empty handed. I have things for you.
MICK	I don't need "things."
HEINZ	But I have things which I would like you to have. Things from before. Things that will help us get through this. That will guide us. Look.

> *He takes a photograph out of his bucket. It is a picture of MICK and HEINZ.*

HEINZ Look at this! This, I carry with me. See? This is us together. Remember this time? This was a good time. This is how friends are. Friendly. I like you Mick. Not many people do. But you know that already. That is why I am here. I like to spend time with you. Be out here with you. Jah. Good photo, what.

MICK Who are you kidding? That's not me.

HEINZ Sure it is, Mick. Look. Your hair was longer then and I was a little heavier, but without question, that is you and that is me.

MICK It's not fucking me and it's not even fucking you.

HEINZ OK. Then it isn't. "You say potato and I say potato. You say tomato and I say tomato." This isn't us right here either. Not together. Not like this. Not like that. Fred and Ginger no more. "Let's call the big thing off." Not with our arms around each other. No. I can see it now. That is not us. And neither is this. What? Do you think someone just came in here? Took this picture and it is not true? That it is only half true. Ha. What a funny thing. Half true. How can this be? This is a photograph. It is real. Just as real as the person who took it. This paper here — you can count on it. It is a memory of our past. When we were together. Living proof that the past was there.

MICK Well let me tell you something — the past ain't what it used to be.

HEINZ That's what I mean, Mick. See? We do have a past. We've done things together. You can't deny this.

MICK I do deny it.

HEINZ How can you? This is proof.

MICK I don't see it as proof. I see it as lies. "Memory is a thing of the past. All we remember is our state of mind at the time, not the actual event. Your mind just makes up the little details as it goes along."

HEINZ "Nothing is ever forgotten completely. It is just stored differently." I remember many things we did.

MICK	Like what?
HEINZ	We travelled up to Quiet Lake and helped Rick build his cabin. Remember that summer? All the flies?
MICK	Nope.
HEINZ	Ah, sure you do. Then the time we .... Oh, jah remember that young girl who came out here? You must remember her?
MICK	Nope.
HEINZ	Sure. The same girl who died in that fire a couple years later. The smoke got to her first, they said. At least she didn't burn to death.
MICK	Nope. *(collapsing)*
HEINZ	Oh yes, she burned, but not to death. She was dead already. Out here in the bush with no one else around. It's to be expected that something would go wrong.
MICK	That was me. That was all me. I was the only one there. I saved her.
HEINZ	No, as I remember it, she died.
MICK	She left. She .... No ...
HEINZ	Oh, Mick. What's going on with you? What's the trouble?
MICK	... she went to Halifax .... I wrote it down ... somewhere....
HEINZ	Here, now. That's OK. Sit down here for awhile. You OK? What did you eat today, Mick? Mick? *(MICK slumps)* Mick? Mick!

> *Throughout, HEINZ gets the unconcious MICK comfortable. Retrieves camera and props it up on a log to take a picture. He uses the delayed shutter release so that he is included in the shot. He lifts MICK's head up the way a big game hunter does with his fresh kill.*

HEINZ   Oh, Jesus. What is this? Are you OK, Mick? Here lie down. That's it. Put your head here. Do you want a blanket? God, you are cold. You're so cold. Just like it used to be. Only you used to be awake. Now look at you. Half dead. There's not so much left to this story. Probably just a bit more. I am happy to be here. For you. For you. You need to go through this. If it weren't for me, the ants would already be in the ears. The flies would suck the veins dry. Making dirt from all this wet stuff. Then what would you be? Just a pile of stinky fly poo. It could be worse. But then again, maybe not. This is why I need to be here.

           He picks up one of MICK's stashed journals. He is amazed at what is written. MICK wakes up.

MICK   Hey ... hey ... wha ...?

HEINZ   There now. It's going to be OK. *(tucks journal inside shirt)*

MICK   What's going ...? What are you doing?

HEINZ   It's OK, Mick. You had a little ... nap. Now, just lie back down, there. Put your head—

MICK   Don't fucking touch me like that.

HEINZ   I'm only trying to help.

MICK   I don't need no help.

HEINZ   It's OK. Sometimes we all need a little assistance. A gentle, guiding hand on occasion. A little mothering, way out here in the—

MICK   I don't need no mothering! Especially from you.

HEINZ   OK, then what am I supposed to do? Sit here and watch you go into another one of your fits? Is this it?

MICK   I didn't go anywhere.

HEINZ   Well, what just happened then? What came over you just now and made you pass out? Huh?

MICK	It was a nap. I was taking a nap. I only had to shut my eyes for a bit, is all.
HEINZ	I. Don't. Think. So. OK then, who am I? Huh? Someone who happened to come past here and spotted you, and with a "oh darnit, I interfered. I leave?" Jah. I could have easily kept on going, you know. Just walked and been somewhere else by now.
MICK	Why didn't you?
HEINZ	Jah. "Just walk on by. Wait by the corn field."
MICK	Hey, Heinz. Let's go back a bit here. In hindsight, you said you were the one who found her in the fire. You said that, didn't you.
HEINZ	Jahvol.
MICK	That was me. And Julie didn't burn up in the fire. How could she have died like that? I was there to save her. I was the one. I should know. And that's how I remember it. *She'll find her way back.* OK. Start.
HEINZ	As you wish. It was the same girl who almost died in that fire a couple years later. The smoke was getting to her and it was lucky for her that someone came ...
MICK	That was me. That was me! Big Time under the Big Top.
HEINZ	... that *you* came along and got to her first. I made that door for her. A big thick one. I helped her lots during our time together. So at least she didn't burn to death. Out there in the bush. With no one around.... No one but you, that is.
MICK	Big Time. Big Time. *My jewel.* Perhaps you tell me why you are here. Perhaps you just sit right down there. No, over there! Now, explain this thing to me because I don't get it. You came right up here fucking next to me like that. Now, Heinzie. Do you like this place?
HEINZ	Jah. It is a good place here. It is like a ...
MICK	A garden.

HEINZ   ... a garden. Jah.

MICK   Jahvol baby. It is a garden. It's a sweet, delicious horn of plenty. It's not really a neighbourhood. So why isn't everybody out here?

HEINZ   Because if everyone was here, then it wouldn't be here?

MICK   It's easier than that.

HEINZ   It's because they're afraid, that's why.

MICK   Now you're getting it.

HEINZ   They're afraid of who they might run into out here. It might even be someone they know.

MICK   Yes, people you know, they're different. These people get inside you. I lose bits of myself every time I talk with someone I know. Strips of my skin disappear. Bones. Then guts. Gone. I used to get all nervous when I hung around people I knew, but now I just get skinny. See, it's the ones who keep coming around that you got to worry about. They start finding out things about you. And then they have you.

HEINZ   Hook, line, and sucker.

      MICK goes into his berm. Throughout, HEINZ cuts a chunk of meat off the carcass and, like a bear, buries the piece under branches and dirt. He also hides MICK's journal, which he has had in his shirt. He removes a few more sticks from the mound of dirt. He sings "I Fall To Pieces."

HEINZ   Now, what game will we play today? I think we might play Guess That Tune. Or maybe musical chairs.

MICK   *(from inside)* I'm busy.

HEINZ   Oh that's OK then. I will play with myself.

MICK   Ain't nobody else gonna play with that thing.

HEINZ	That's naughty. OK, then. We will play Guess That Tune. I know this tune, see. I hum a bit of it. You guess what it is, Jah? OK? OK. *(hums "I Fall To Pieces")* Mick? Are you there? Mick!?
MICK	Take a siesta, Heinz. A Heinziesta.
HEINZ	*(starts to do a Spanish dance)* ¡Olé!
MICK	Sounds like you are dancing again.
HEINZ	Nein. Nein. Just stomping . . . ah . . . the burying beetles. Burying beetles. They were covering me up. Jah.
MICK	*(emerges from berm)* Hey, Heinzo. Who's Nelson Rockerfeller?
HEINZ	A asshole.
MICK	Who's Sherwin Williams?
HEINZ	A bad asshole.
MICK	Ghandi?
HEINZ	A kind asshole.
MICK	A kind of an asshole?
HEINZ	Nein. Nein. A kind, gentle asshole.
MICK	He wasn't a Gentile at all. He was from India. Who's Gordie?
HEINZ	A flying asshole. But he takes you for free. He's · one of the best pilots around.
MICK	It's because I am free. Tahltana Free. Free. Nothing to do with him. That makes him even more of an asshole. He doesn't even know when he's losing money and when he's making it.
HEINZ	Oh Mick, you sure are stubborn sometimes.
MICK	*(sees the meat HEINZ has stashed)* Why is Gordie coming here anyway?
HEINZ	Oh, he's dropping things off.
MICK	Why?

HEINZ	Because he has things he needs to drop off.
MICK	But why here?
HEINZ	Because this is where he needs to drop them off. This is where he was told to make the drop. Is this a problem? He's always done this for me. And for you too for that matter.
MICK	You know Gordie's been looking for me.
HEINZ	Since what time?
MICK	Since the boat. He's still mad because he thinks I did it. He still claims I cut his boat loose and let it go down river. Well, I didn't.
HEINZ	Well, so you say. But no one can prove it any which way, now can they? And besides it happened in the past, and you said that you don't trust the past. Or your memory of it. So there is no proof, really. No one even remembers it any more, let alone go looking for the proof.
MICK	Proof? Who needs to prove it? That's the way they remember it. At least I can remember what I did and didn't do. I know that much. That's the thing about telling the truth — you never have to remember what you said. It just is.
HEINZ	I was talking with Betty the other day, you know, Gordie's wife. She said they'll be leaving soon. She's pregnant and doesn't want to have the baby in the North. She says it would be too cold. Must be warm-blooded or something. She's going to have the baby somewhere hot. Give it a fighting chance, you know, right from the start. I can't see why they would have them in the first place. It's not like it is easy. At least, that's what I hear. And then it is years of grief, what with them growing up and all and then just walking away. I don't ever want to have kids, you know. I am not motivated to do this. Now don't get me wrong. It is not that I can't ... you know ... do it. It's just that the end result doesn't feel as good as the actual sticking it in part. That's the good part, Jah.

MICK

How would you know about that? Don't talk about not wanting kids and sticking it in and all. That's just rude talk. You don't have it in you. You'd like to think you could but I know you can't. And I didn't even touch the fucking boat. Why can't they leave me alone?

HEINZ

They gave up on that boat thing long ago. Didn't you know that? "I vant to be alooone." Well, there you are now. Alone. *(exits)*

MICK

Heinz! Yeah, alone, he says. Well, let me tell you something, I've been on my own since I was 14. Four-fucking-teen, Heinzie. My mother, see, was always worried if we got too close to the water. Any water at all and she'd get nervous. But it was only after Jimmy Swales got drowned. When she was off shopping I'd sneak down and sit on the spot where he slipped. Right off the rock and got sucked in. The only way they knew was by his foot. Caught up on a willow branch. One of them low sweepers. Then he just dragged in the water. Sticking up in the air like a prayer flag. A little blue runner bobbing in the water. Jim The Dad chopped it out just after the funeral. He wasn't about to have no stick remind him of his only begotten son. Everyone was all choked up when he walked right through the centre of town with that axe in his hands. Me, I just laughed. He looked so stupid, hanging out over the water like that, chopping away at the poor tree. The willow bouncing around. Not staying still for his axe. It's a willow; what do you expect? I had reasons to hate that tree too, but I wasn't about to go hacking at it like some crazy idiot. I mean, if his boot hadn't got caught no one would have known. He would be washed up on some beach somewhere off and no one would have looked at me like they did. Yeah. Jimmy Senior. All lord high muckety-muck. Man o' God and all. Out saving their souls, pumping the manly hand in the night-time, and humping the handy wives in the daytime. Well, Jim The Dad had it all figured out all right. Get 'em all juiced up in the evening service, just loving the sound of his Sweet Jesus voice. Sweet Jimmy in Jesus Heaven. The power of the Lord was in him. They'd be down on their knees, believing when he prayed.

MICK	And then later on they'd still be on their hands and knees believing it. Taking it up backwards. Even moaning like a dog. Whimpering for it. Well, I saw it! I fucking saw it with my own eyes. Mom's fat ass waggling all over the kitchen floor and Big Jim just bucking away in it. And to think that Little Jimmy could do no wrong. A little fucking angel. Well, he's an angel now, all right. Little fuck. Slipped on a rock. And went for a swim that day. The water was fast. Filled up his ass. . . . Ha! And washed all my troubles away! Yeah! Do they think I'm fucking stupid? Assholes. Fucking . . . . I mean I couldn't let him get away with it, right? I had to do something. *All I did was watch. I didn't know what else to do. The water would have taken me too. I was a good boy.* It was wrong. And my fucking eyes had to see it, didn't they. Right there on the kitchen floor. Chop that kitchen down, Jimmy. Rip up that old lino. Go after it, Big Time under the Big Top. She just left. Took off down the road with that Preacher Jim. Why didn't somebody else see it? And now all this shit going down out here. The water. The testicide. No one else sees it. I tell them and then they don't leave me alone. Why don't you leave me alone? I said, why don't you leave me alone!
HEINZ	*(enters on the other side of the stage from where he exited)* Oh, you mean me. Ah, jah. Jah. Alone. Um. I have my reasons. Jah. I have something for you too.
MICK	What?
HEINZ	It's . . . a surprise.
MICK	I don't want it.
HEINZ	Well, part of it is a surprise, but the other part is . . . a message. That's the gift part. But the first part of this gift experience is the surprise. Not knowing becomes part of the gift itself. And if I were to tell you what it is, then you wouldn't enjoy it half as much. I mean the actual gift is one thing, but the surprise, that's something else. I like you, Mick. I consider you a friend. Jah. This is true.

HEINZ   I couldn't give this to just anyone. Just you. *(sings "Only You")* Don't you feel the need to talk out here? Just sit down and quietly talk with someone?

MICK   Yeah. I got Rowdy. I got my Rowdy dog.

HEINZ   But Rowdy is gone. They shot him, remember.

MICK   Yeah, right. Man, you are sick. You are a fucking sicko.

HEINZ   Me? Here, let me call him. And if he comes over to me — he knows me, right — then he's here, OK?

MICK   He wouldn't do it. Not my Rowdy. Sit, Rowdy. Stay, Rowdy.

HEINZ   Here Rowdy. Come on Boy. Come on. *(pause)* See? Nothing. No dog. No sounds of his feet on the gravel. No dog tracks.

MICK   I told you he wouldn't come to you.

HEINZ   Remember how he would always chase stick? Well, let's try that. Here. Here's a stick. Stick, Boy. *(goes to throw it)*

MICK   Don't! *(tackles HEINZ)*

HEINZ   Oh. *(everything stops)* You touched me.

MICK   Hush. Quiet. Something's there. *(points)*

HEINZ   You touched me.

MICK   Shhhh. Someone's coming. *(nothing)*

HEINZ   There was a moment . . . a touch . . . . Maybe it's Rowdy. Off chasing a squirrel. There's nothing there. See?

MICK   Shut up.

HEINZ   I know you can hear the sound of my voice. It is filling this space between us.

MICK   You want space? You got all the space you need. But over there. Not here. Over there. And there. And there too. That's what you've got. Not here. Now, do you like this place?

HEINZ	Jah. It is a good place here. It is like a garden. I've got all that part down.
MICK	And I have you.
HEINZ	Ah now. You see. You really do need me.
MICK	I don't want you, Heinz.
HEINZ	You said it. You just said it. It was just there in your mouth.
MICK	I did not. I never said it. I would never say something like that because I don't even feel it.
HEINZ	I heard you. You said, "I have you." My ears heard it. They were open and they heard it.
MICK	Nope.
HEINZ	I want to hear it. Say that thing you always used to say: "Nobody has Tahltana Free Mick." Here, I'll sing it for you. *(sings it to "Nobody Knows the Trouble I've Seen")*
MICK	Oh cut it out. *(pause)* What do you want from me?
HEINZ	I only want to be here on this point. I told you this.
MICK	I'm tired of this. You don't dance with me any more.
HEINZ	No, that's not true. I sing to you all the time. You love it when I sing.
MICK	But I said dance.
HEINZ	Jah. And I said, I dance with you all the time.
MICK	Look, look. I know what you said. You said, sing.
HEINZ	So let's dance *(they dance as HEINZ sings, "On the Street Where You Live")*
MICK	*(intimately)* OK, now you just tell me. Straight out. Don't make it up. Don't say something just to make me happy. Use your own words, ma cherie. *(angrily)* Why are we here?
HEINZ	Out here? In this bush? Or here-here? On this point? *(they stop dancing)*

MICK	Jeez, OK. Out here. Start there.
HEINZ	To answer your first question: This is important to me. *(reads from MICK's journals)* "These rocks that I see are totally beyond recognition. When I first arrived back here, I didn't recognise a single one of them. Someone had come along and moved them. They changed them. So, I straighten things up a bit. I put them back. This is why this place needs me. People go through this country and they think nobody knows. Nobody notices these things. Heinz Selmer left a real mess down on the Nakina three weeks ago." Not me.
MICK	Yes, you.
HEINZ	"He moved up river to the Silver Salmon, and then down past Dickie's camp on Paddy Lake." Dickie Feldman? He doesn't have a camp on Paddy Lake? "Up Gladys Creek and then around the backside of Snowdon and on into Hall Lake. He spent two days in there with his moose, there in the marshy part at the end." I never got a moose in there. What are you talking about? *(MICK starts to panic)* "I saw him trying to haul it up but I couldn't help. Then he would have known that I was there. So I just sat and watched. He dried his clothes off on that rock until the clouds came in. There is a big poplar right down by the water where he always liked to sit, and so he did. He had that stupid green shirt . . . ." Green? My shirt is always red. *(they look at MICK's green shirt)* "that stupid *red* shirt hanging in the tree all afternoon. Something to keep the sneak arounds away." Sneak arounds? "I was there because of the rocks. The rocks needed . . . replacing . . . ?" Is that word really replacing? Yes. OK. "Heinz was so reckless. A person like him does serious damage. Erosion. Tons of rock and earth end up at the bottom of the lakes every year because of people like him. Rocks get turned over, expose their soft bellies to the new heat of the spring sun." This is poetry. "And the branches and trees . . . ." Illegible. ". . . past. They are lonely when . . . ." That's illegible too. "The winter has been too . . . ." Illegible. ". . . and the summer . . . reaching out to touch the sunlight slowly arching up.

HEINZ	You come along . . . ." Illegible. ". . . snap and they are gone. Broken . . . ." Scratched out. "Dead . . . . They must be killed." Killed? Who must be killed, Mick? This is serious. You really got yourself worked up writing this stuff, didn't you. I can't even read it. "It is my job to make things right. The sun . . . ." Can't read that part. "To put things back in their place until . . . ." You didn't even finish that sentence. "I am clean and I am . . . ." Now that one's all crossed out. ". . . caught in the way things are from the beginning." Hey, Mick? What does this symbol mean?
MICK	Don't do this.
HEINZ	OK. Then I will go on. Now to answer your second question: Why am I here-here? Because I have something for you. Something which is important to you. I have a note here. For you. From someone. Special. *(he doesn't produce anything)*
MICK	What?
HEINZ	I told you. It is a note. A letter for you.
MICK	Well? Where is it?
HEINZ	Here. *(taps chest)*
MICK	Are you going to give it to me?
HEINZ	Of course. *(doesn't move)* Yes. It is yours after all. And you deserve to have it.
MICK	Let me have it then.
HEINZ	Well, I can't really.
MICK	What do you mean?
HEINZ	I can't actually give it to you. It's not really here to give. It's not a piece of paper in here anymore. I know what was on it. The words that were written down. And who wrote them down for you.
MICK	Give me the fucking letter!
HEINZ	I can't.

MICK	Why not? What the fuck is going on here?
HEINZ	I wish I knew. I wish I could answer that question for you, Mick. Especially now that Julie is coming back. I mean there are going to be lots of questions going around now. People in town are really happy to see her back. She looks good. Healthy. *(MICK collapses)* She was in Halifax or so she said. Living with her Mom and doing some art thing there. Even sold some of her pottery.
MICK	She really was a tiny person. You forget how small she was.
HEINZ	I forgot how tiny she was. Time will erase some things. Make the details fuzzy. Make things different. Anyway, that's why I am here.
MICK	*It said, "Hello Michael. I'm back for a couple of weeks. Meet me at Haalstad's for a Friday night. Missed you. J."*
HEINZ	And now this is what this is. It's a place for Julie. And me. And you. All together. Just like it used to be. Only things are a little different now.
MICK	*I found it on him afterwards. After all this. (pause)* Julie? Julie is gone. That ain't Julie you were talking to. No.
HEINZ	Jah. Her. Julie.
MICK	I tell you, she is gone. She went back to Halifax. He followed her back East. She told him her mother was sick and her Free Mick believed her. He was worried about her. But in Halifax she didn't know him. *(HEINZ starts to walk around reading one of MICK's journals, ripping pages out and saying "illegible . . . scratched out . . . too messy")* She pretended she didn't recognise him. She even ignored him. They met down in the Historic Properties one night. By accident. Someone's party he didn't know. There was this skinny little guy from PEI all over her. Couldn't stop drinking either. She was in a bad way and he tried to help. The guy was really desperate and wanted her bad. Started clawing at her.

MICK	So Mick stepped in between them. Thinking he'd help out. He thought she needed him. Thought she wanted him to.

> *HEINZ removes the last remaining dirt and sticks from the mound. It is the badly decayed corpse of himself.*

HEINZ	*(to corpse)* Hello. *(turns back)* I don't think you are seeing things too clearly, Mick. Are you sick again? Going to have another nap?
MICK	He thought . . . that she . . . that he . . . .
HEINZ	Who is this guy who went to Halifax? I don't know about him.
MICK	I got to write it down. Tell, tell, tell. Write. *(goes into berm)*
HEINZ	Now just a second here. She is not gone. She's back. Well, jah, she is gone from here. She is not here right now, no. But is she gone from there? From across the lake? No. She is there. I saw her. I spoke with her. I took that note from her. We talked about these things. And she said she was happy to be coming back. Looking forward to being with me again. It was a long time ago, you know Mick. You and her. A lot has happened since then. Oh. Oh. You haven't heard. You've been out here so long on your own. Funny, jah. There is no way you could have known. Julie is going to have my baby, jah.

> *MICK emerges with a primitive symbol painted in mud on his bare chest. His hair is wild.*

MICK	*(simultaneous with HEINZ)* You were too busy with all those rocks. Building little walls. Damming the creek. And then you started putting that shed up. Right in front of my place. Right from the start you said you weren't staying long. But then you did. We took care of this place. Everything was nicely spaced out. *(picks up rifle)* Then you had to come up with this homesteading idea.

HEINZ	*(simultaneous with MICK)* Jah. She is getting big now. She wants to have it out here. It is a good thing she is going to produce this child soon. I am glad you are so excited about this. I was wondering how you were going to react. I can see it now. This will be a wonderful place to bring them up in. It is so quiet and serene. The air is good. And the meat is clean. And you have so much to teach them, Mick. You would have been a good father.
MICK	You are lying to me. It wasn't your baby. It was that skinny guy from PEI.
HEINZ	*(falsely)* Please. It will mean so much to Julie and me. You know, this will make you an uncle, in a kind of way. Once she has the baby, that is.
MICK	No. I don't think it went that way. You were mad at that skinny guy yourself? You said so. Say it again.
HEINZ	That little pip squawk. If I ever see him, I will block his knock off.
MICK	Ha! "Block his knock off." Jeez, Heinz.
HEINZ	Jah. Then Julie said she was coming back.
MICK	Oh but didn't you start moving over there towards your sticks?
HEINZ	"She'll be coming over the mountain when she does."
MICK	Yeah. Only you were moving a little faster cause you were more afraid. And then you said something about me being an uncle.
HEINZ	No. Me? Call you an uncle? It would not be like me to say that?
MICK	Yes. I distinctly heard you say it.
HEINZ	You know, "this will make you an uncle in a kind of way. Once she has the baby that is."
MICK	And then you stopped and turned.
HEINZ	Did I? I thought I just kept going down to the lake.
MICK	No! You stopped!

HEINZ	Look, relax a bit Mick. You are getting upset for no reason.
MICK	Funny, I don't remember it that way. I recall having a really good reason. I think I caught you lying. Lying right to my face. Making up all those little details as you went along.
HEINZ	Look, this is simply ridiculous. I am not making this up.
MICK	No, I know you aren't making any of this up. This is just how it happened, isn't it?
HEINZ	Yes, but I think you were a little more angry, weren't you?
MICK	Um. No. I think ... no, I wasn't angry. It was more a feeling of being sprayed. *(cocks rifle)* By you.
HEINZ	I would never do anything like that. Spray you with what? It's OK, now. Look, Mick, whatever you might think, I never meant you any harm.
MICK	No, I know you didn't intentionally do anything.
HEINZ	You can do anything you want with the rocks. You can stay on this point here. It is yours. It's yours.
MICK	No, I think it's ours. And so it shall remain.
HEINZ	I don't want anything from you anymore. Look.
MICK	*(looks in bucket where HEINZ has stashed journals)* Didn't you take my writings too?
HEINZ	Look, I'll leave now, OK? OK. I will leave. But this will not make Julie happy?
MICK	Get out!
HEINZ	She was really looking forward to being here.
MICK	Then why isn't she here now? Why didn't she stay?
HEINZ	You were too much for her. You said so yourself.
MICK	That wasn't me. That wasn't me!
HEINZ	Yes it was. It was you. All of it was you.

MICK	Weren't you over there?
HEINZ	Yes. OK.
MICK	But then you forgot your bucket. You came back and got your bucket.
HEINZ	I'm leaving now. Just going. *(starts to leave humming "My Way")*
MICK	A little further to your right.
HEINZ	Jah. Jah. Look. Somebody had to point it out to you! Somebody had to show you!

MICK shoots. HEINZ falls dead on the corpse.

MICK	He was so far gone. I could put them on the shelf of a Chinese drug store right then and there. As an aphro-fucking-disiac. Hey. That kind of works, doesn't it. I mean, that's what they are for. But he was lying to me about those kids. He sat right over there and told me he didn't want to have any kids. Can you see it now, Heinz? Without children we're lost. Our souls out there forever. Aimless. That's what Julie wanted. This is what we both knew would save us. This is how we go on. That's how poisoned you were. It's not in you. It ain't in me and I'm out here just like you. Just like Rowdy was. Look what happened to him. You think you avoided getting sprayed, didn't you. Well, you didn't. You thought maybe you could just wash it away. Just stand in the river and let it all go somewhere downstream. Just like Little Jimmy Swales had a good cleaning. Well, he just happened to slip, didn't he, and his Daddy wasn't there to help him, was he. He was dirty, just like his Daddy. Dirty. Dirty Little Jimmy Swales. Died for the sins of his Holy Father. God the Father; God the Son. Shall we rise and sing: "Are you washed? In the blood? In the soul cleansing blood of the Lamb?" Sing it for me Heinz. He stole my meat. Look, look where he stole it from. You just don't do that up here. You don't steal the only thing that is clean up here. Heinz was OK in a way. But he stole my writings. My words. My books. I was saving all these thoughts.

MICK   Seven years of work and he stole it. There was
                  something about Heinz that I liked. He was the only
                  one who could move like I move. A mutual respect.
                  Special understanding that comes with being out here.
                  But I didn't really pay much attention to him. Or
                  Julie for that matter. I didn't care about that story.
                  He could tell it all he wanted and I still didn't care.
                  They've all left me. All gone. And now they are
                  flying in low. They're sending me over the edge with
                  their stupid talk. They won't let up. Remember
                  when they came in here to get me the first time?
                  They thought I was crazy, didn't they. Evil and off
                  my rocker. They brought in all those pigs just to get
                  me to Vancouver. Just to see if I was nuts or
                  something. And me? I just walked out with them,
                  clean as day. Without even so much as a breath. But
                  then I came back. And it was only then that I got
                  mad. They'd shot all my dogs. Every last one of
                  them. Except ol' Rowdy, my ol' buddy pal.
                  McCullough said it was because they didn't know
                  what to do with them since they figured I was going
                  to be away so long. I was only gone a month. One
                  month and no one would feed them? McCullough
                  said he would have taken them had someone asked.
                  But they didn't even ask. They just came in here and
                  shot them up! Now they're coming around here
                  again. Always checking me out. They know that
                  I've got something and they want it. *(suddenly a
                  plane flies directly overhead, buzzing the camp)*
                  Tahltana Mick just tasted liberty.

                              Scene III

                  *The actor playing HEINZ is gone and all that
                  remains is the half-buried corpse.*

MICK   Come on. Come on! What's taking them so long?
                  (dogs bark in the distance) Dogs. Those poor dogs.
                  They should not do that to their dogs. It's not good,
                  how they train them. Over and over they beat them.
                  They force them to hate. Hate the smell of their
                  prey. Cheap meat for hate. Trained to live for it.
                  Die for it. Trapped in dark cages, feeding them
                  chemical meat and rotting guts. Dragging them out

MICK

to the light just for their noses. They should be set
free. We need to be set free. Dogs are the only
things we can always trust. *(dogs are getting closer)*
Ah, my sweet jewel. There is nothing that we
weren't. We were all. We were it. I had to let her
go. Flakes of white ash floating in the wind. Like a
summer snow storm. She said she was sorry but that
it was too late by then. "She hath washed my feet
with tears and wiped them with the hairs of her head.
Thy faith hath saved thee; go in peace." He had to
keep her with him forever. Breathe her in. Her
breath. She was with him then. She was inside him.
The water was inside Jesus Sweet Jimmy Swales.
Washed him clean. Clear. Willow and rock. Pillow
rock. Sweet sleep of reason. Sleep of treason.
Sweepers. Got caught. Rock. Body in the gravel.
Body in the gravel bar. Gotta find the body. Gotta
find the Free Mick. Gotta find 'im. Gotta find 'im.
You can't see me. See you. See you. See you.
You. You. You. You. Coming in. Feel 'em
moving. Moving on in. Spraying the shit.
Spreading the word. Spreading the legs. Sneaking
around. Scare 'em off. Scaring 'em to death. "In
death shall ye know him." Free Mick still is. Still
on the sidehills. Still moving. Always moving.
Always moving up. Floating. Bird's wings. Sweet
songs. Pure air. *(as a bird chirp)* Pure. Pure.
What's that? Motor bird. Chatter box. Looking.
Looking. Spraying shit. Burn me up. Inside out.
All fired up and no place to go. Burn it off. Fire
break. Smoke in the ceiling. Save the girl. Save
the world! Lift her up. Light as a feather. Bones of
a bird. Bones of the father, the son, and the holy
smoke. Gone for good. Wiped off the face of the
earth. Live on forever. Living in the Free world.
The children of the Free Mick. "Free at last."
Jahvol, baby. It is a garden. Free Mick knows there
are no limits to his freedom. Yes! Dropping like
flies to bad meat. *(he fires and tries to reload but his
rifle jams)* It all comes around now. Free Mick is
the land. He is the sun. He is the water that rushes
clean and pure. We are clean in our souls, pure in our
minds. We are made ready for the day when the sun
heals the wounds of our transgressions, when the day

MICK   and the night become one, healing the sad souls, the broken bodies, when the land takes its sweet victory and we are made one with the wind, there are no other blessings we can receive that take us to where we are perfect, cleansed, yes. Yes! YES! Now!! NOW!!

A loud string of shots from a semi-automatic rifle. Blackout.

END

In Search of a Friend

by

Tunooniq Theatre

It seems fitting that Tunooniq should follow up *Changes* (see pages 101-13) with a work portraying one of the consequences of the historic and social events shown in that play. *In Search of a Friend* is a play about addiction, represented not as an individual disease but as an evil enchantment, something like the famine of the old days: to get the better of it, the individual needs powerful help from a stronger enchantment, the support of the community, and his or her own fortitude. In the play's seamless transitions from what is actual to what is metaphoric or magical, these three — beneficent magic, companionship, and spiritual strength — are strongly associated. The play is about a troubled young man, Puju, whose problems include being a teenager confused by clashing cultural values, parents who don't understand him, and a "friend" who remains aloof, refusing to help him or to try to find out what is wrong. He takes refuge in drink and other drugs, and is rescued by a friend, Qiatsuk, and by "*a frightening old man*" (never exactly identified). Qiatsuk, the true friend, withstands mockery (which may be interpreted as actual taunts of peers or the metaphoric taunts of temptation), and exposes herself to the dangers of the drug-and-alcohol environment to reach and help Puju.

Even more than *Changes*, this play relies on movement, and on the active, almost balletic, representation of forces whose interaction makes up an inner reality. Scene 3, for example, consists entirely of action: "*Puju comes running in again, he's caught by Layli [the unconcerned friend] and pushed towards the other creatures. They hurl him across the stage. He spins around centre stage*," and so on. By running (literally and metaphorically), Puju tries to escape problems — such as low self-esteem and conflict with his parents — problems depicted as "*creatures*" who "*hurl him across the stage*." The Singer succeeds in calming Puju, but at the same time prevents him from truly experiencing the outside world ("*the light goes off . . . the sound is cut*") and substitutes seductive song for that world.

The characters who perform the actions represent more than individuals. The Singer who quiets Puju and later has him fast bound in ropes is clearly his addiction. Layli, who thrusts him into the arms of his tormentors, is an unsympathetic young woman, a teenager like himself, who speaks in clichés such as "He's old enough to take care of himself" and "I've got my own problems." Besides being an individual, she might personify a community whose members are too self-involved to support one another, or even the spirit of an unsupportive community. Similarly, Qiatsuk might represent a good friend, a supportive community, or good communal spirit. And the frightening old man wearing caribou clothes, who promises Qiatsuk to be with her "until the end," and who helps Puju see his own soul: who is he? His dress implies tradition; his toughness and constancy, survival; and his frightening appearance, *real* life (as opposed to the dream life of addiction). Although the character is never explained, he brings to mind a suggestion of the shaman.

David Qamaniq says that the production of these plays "has helped [Inuit youth] to know our past and present, but [they are] also meant for all of Canada, to see how our lives have changed dramatically" (interview with Qamaniq, 16 December 1998). In production, they also provide a unique portrayal of contemporary social realities in Arctic communities.

E.D.

* * *

Throughout 1988, *In Search of a Friend* toured the Northwest Territories along with *Changes*. In 1989 Tunooniq performed excerpts from both plays in Cambridge, England. For a fuller account of Tunooniq, see the introduction to *Changes* (103-04).

IN SEARCH OF A FRIEND

CHARACTERS

Puju
Qiatsuk
Layli
Singer
Old Man
Spirit
Creatures

Scene One

The set is pulled out. Back curtain 1 is painted blue and white, like the sea. The side curtains on both sides are painted to look like high mountains. A fast rock beat is heard, fading in.

A young teenager PUJU enters from stage left. He is running, and looks back over his shoulder to see if anyone is following. He stops at centre stage and rests for a while, catching his breath. All of a sudden at stage right a creature, clothed all in black with a bright mouth, grinning, enters. He sees PUJU and runs to him, poking him, laughing and then running off again. PUJU flinches and turns to run towards stage right but another creature comes out. He pushes PUJU. The other creature pushes him too, soon they are pushing and laughing at PUJU.

PUJU   Please stop. Please. Why are you always bothering me? Leave me alone!

PUJU starts to cry and runs away, exit stage right. The music gets louder. One creature leaves laughing, the other, LAYLI, stays on stage.

Scene Two

The music slowly fades. Still in her mask and black outfit LAYLI stands facing the audience, close to stage right.

QIATSUK   *(enters from the audience, calling PUJU's name)* Puju, Puju, Puju. Has anyone seen Puju? *(she spots LAYLI on the stage and runs over to her)* Layli, Layli, have you seen Puju?

LAYLI   No. *(she turns away from QIATSUK)*

QIATSUK   I'm really worried about him. *(she hurries over to LAYLI, moving to stage right, trying to get her attention)* He's acting so strange.

LAYLI   He's old enough to take care of himself. *(she turns away again and crosses to stage left)*

QIATSUK   *(hurrying over to her again)* But we have to try and talk to him. He's so changed, he doesn't want to do anything!

LAYLI   What's his problem?

QIATSUK   I think he's feeling like he's no good. He dropped out of school this year and he isn't even looking for a job. His parents are always down on him. I think he feels that everything is against him.

LAYLI   *(turning away and moving across to stage right)* His parents should try to talk to him.

QIATSUK   *(moving to LAYLI)* But that's part of the problem. He can't seem to talk to his parents. And they don't understand him at all.

LAYLI   I'm not a professional counsellor. There are people paid to take care of those problems.

QIATSUK   But he needs people who know him and care about him. He needs his friends. Isn't that what friends are for?

LAYLI   I've got my own problems. I don't have time for his.

The music fades up again. LAYLI turns her back and walks away, exiting stage left.

Scene Three

*PUJU comes running in again, he's caught by
LAYLI and pushed towards the other creatures.
They hurl him across the stage. He spins around
centre stage. The rock music gets louder and
louder and PUJU tries to cover his ears. The
light comes up behind the back Curtain 1, where
the shadow of a frightful creature looms larger
and larger. PUJU is very frightened. All of a
sudden the light goes off, the SINGER pulls
back the curtains and the sound is cut. The
SINGER begins her song. It calms PUJU. He
follows the SINGER and then exits stage right.*

Scene Four

*QIATSUK enters from stage left. She is
searching for PUJU. The white material is
floated above in waves like clouds. It shows that
she is walking and searching. The SINGER
enters, singing her song and tries to catch her.*

QIATSUK	*(pulled by the lovely song, but resisting)* What are you doing?
SINGER	I'm making you feel better. Just relax. *(she continues singing her song and dancing around QIATSUK)*
QIATSUK	*(she feels pulled by the SINGER for a while, and moves as if in a trance, but then stumbles downstage centre)* No. No. You're making my head spin!
SINGER	I will make all your problems disappear. I will make you laugh and sing. I will make you sure of yourself. You won't be afraid of anyone if you dance with me. *(she moves around QIATSUK pulling her and almost forcing her to dance)*
QIATSUK	*(screaming loud and defiantly)* No! I will not go with you. You'll take me away from my life. You'd like to hurt me. I know you. *(backing away from the SINGER and SPIRIT)* You're not beautiful, oh you look beautiful but you're ugly inside. You destroy us humans. You'd like to own our souls.

SINGER stops dancing and wheels around, looking angrily at QIATSUK. She lets out an evil hissing sound.

SINGER   You make me sick! You don't know how to have fun. You're boring and old-fashioned. You're afraid to dance and you don't know beauty. You're nothing. Nothing, nothing. I don't want to waste my time with you. There are many others who want to hear my song and they would love a chance to dance with me. *(she moves to exit stage right)*

QIATSUK   *(running after the SINGER trying to grab her)* Wait. What about Puju. Did you take him somewhere?

SINGER   Oh, the boy with all the troubles. Poor boy. Nobody understands him in the real world.

QIATSUK   Give him back. You have no right to take him. I demand that you give him to me right now.

SINGER   *(laughing evilly and hissing again)* No. You can't demand me to do anything. Everyone is free to choose between the real world and me. Nobody can make the choice for another.

QIATSUK   Take me to him then. Please. I'm his friend. He'll want to know I'm looking for him.

SINGER   Puju is happy. He doesn't need you any more. I give him everything he wants. Get out of my way. *(she pushes QIATSUK off and exits stage right)*

QIATSUK   *(sadly calling out)* Puju. Come back. You can't go with her. She'll destroy you!

QIATSUK sadly walks away, stage left. But all of a sudden a frightening OLD MAN enters stage left. He wears caribou clothes.

OLD MAN   Where are you going?

QIATSUK   Home.

OLD MAN   You can't leave Puju alone with her. You'll have to go find him.

QIATSUK   But how can I find him? I don't know where he is.

OLD MAN

I can bring you there. But you're the only one who can convince him to come back. You're his friend. You love him.

QIATSUK

Who are you?

OLD MAN

You'll find out. Now let's hurry, we can't waste any time. Every moment he's with her makes her more powerful and him weaker. Come! *(QIATSUK starts to run stage right but he stops her)* This way.

> *OLD MAN pulls the curtains back, revealing Back Curtain 2. It appears to be a passage surrounded by icebergs. The OLD MAN disappears, stage left. There is an eerie sound of spirits. PUJU is lying on the floor. He has two ropes tied around him. He has passed out.*

QIATSUK

(running over to PUJU and holding him up) Puju, are you all right? Get up, let's go. Let's go home.

PUJU

(in a dazed voice) What? What are you doing here? Oh. It's you, Qiatsuk.

QIATSUK

Come on. Hurry. Before she comes back. What have you taken?

PUJU

Who, me? Just a little something to make me feel better. Everything's fine. I've got everything under control.

> *PUJU stumbles and falls against QIATSUK. The SINGER enters stage right. She swoops over and holds PUJU. She looks cruelly at QIATSUK.*

QIATSUK

Let go of him. Look what you've done. You've changed him. *(QIATSUK tries to take PUJU, but the SINGER is stronger and gives the ropes to the creatures and LAYLI and they pull PUJU to the other side of the stage)* Oh, Puju. Don't you see what's happening to you. You've got to take off the ropes.

PUJU

I tried that, but I can't. They're too tight.

QIATSUK is crying now. The creatures are pulling PUJU off the stage, and the SINGER is directing them. All of a sudden the OLD MAN enters, stage left. His face looks older and scarier, his clothes are more tattered, his hair is wilder. He looks angry.

OLD MAN   Puju, before you go with them. I want to show you something. *(he points to a place on the stage where a warm blue glow is shining)* Look, look!

PUJU tries to see, but the creatures are pulling him. He tries to strain against them and comes closer to the hole.

SPIRIT   He isn't interested in what you can show him. He wants the good times that only I can offer.

OLD MAN   Puju. I said look. You must look down the *aglu*.

There is a seal hole in the ice.

PUJU   I don't have to do anything. What's down there anyway?

OLD MAN   I can't tell you. You have to look for yourself. All I can say is that it is very important. If you don't look you will become lost in this place where human beings don't belong. Look!

QIATSUK   Look, Puju, please.

SPIRIT   *(getting worried)* That is enough. Come, away from here. Come Puju, I have something that will take your mind off these worries.

The creatures drag PUJU off, stage right. PUJU looks a little nervous, but is anxious to have what the SPIRIT has. QIATSUK walks downstage towards the audience, the OLD MAN has disappeared at stage left. She sings a song about PUJU. When her song finishes, the OLD MAN appears again; this time he looks wilder than ever.

OLD MAN   Are you ready?

QIATSUK   Ready for what? Puju wants to be with the White Spirit. He doesn't want to come back.

OLD MAN	I don't think so. But you must help him to get to the *aglu*, if he looks down he will have the strength to come back to the real world. If he doesn't I'm afraid of what may happen to him.
QIATSUK	Do you think she might kill him?
OLD MAN	She can do many things to hurt people with her substances. She has destroyed families and made bodies sick. And yes, she can kill him. She has killed before.
QIATSUK	Then take me to him. I'll try to help him.

The OLD MAN takes her upstage and pulls back the curtain, revealing Curtain 3. It looks like the northern lights, green, yellow and red. There is the eerie music again. PUJU is tied up with more ropes, he looks very bad, his head is lolling to one side. Before QIATSUK can run to him, the land (streamers of cloth) begins moving and catches QIATSUK up. The land rolls like waves, the Creatures come out holding the ends of the cloth and laughing, they tangle QIATSUK up in the cloth. Finally the SPIRIT enters and the cloth is dropped and QIATSUK, exhausted, stumbles out.

SPIRIT	*(laughing evilly)* I told you to leave him alone. We don't want you at our party.
PUJU	*(looking at his friend)* Qiatsuk. Hi. I missed you.
QIATSUK	Oh Puju. *(she tries to run to him, but the SPIRIT stops her and they wrestle at centre stage)*
PUJU	Stop it. Don't hurt her. Qiatsuk, get up.

Finally beaten and crawling, QIATSUK moves downstage sobbing. The Creatures take PUJU by the ropes and lead him off stage right.

PUJU	*(sobbing)* Qiatsuk, I'm sorry, Qiatsuk. I'm sorry. I didn't want to hurt you. Please forgive me Qiatsuk. I'm sorry. I'm sorry.

> *The SPIRIT swoops behind PUJU who is led off stage left. The OLD MAN enters, looking more frightening still. He stands above QIATSUK who is still crying. She looks up at him.*

OLD MAN When you are ready we will go again.

QIATSUK No, she's won. I tried my best. But she is too strong. He can't break out of those ropes. It's no use!

OLD MAN Love can give a person incredible strength. You must try one more time. If Puju wants to leave her, he still has a chance.

QIATSUK Will you come with me? I need your strength and guidance.

OLD MAN Yes. Of course. I'll be with you until the end.

> *The OLD MAN moves upstage and pulls back the curtain revealing Curtain 4. It is bright, and flaming northern lights are glowing on PUJU who is thrashing at the ropes which tie him. When he sees QIATSUK, he stumbles forward and falls at centre stage.*

QIATSUK Puju, are you ready to come now?

PUJU *(in a weak voice)* Yes, I want these ropes off. Help me Qiatsuk. They are so tight. *(QIATSUK rushes over to help him. The SPIRIT enters hissing)*

SPIRIT Don't touch those ropes. Puju put those ropes on himself, only he can take them off. If he can.

> *The Creatures rush at QIATSUK and pull her off to the side, holding her.*

OLD MAN *(pointing to the glowing light)* This is your final chance, Puju. The *aglu*. Look.

> *PUJU tries to run toward it but the rope yanks him back and he falls. He struggles and gets some ropes free, but then gives up.*

PUJU I can't. You'll have to carry me. I'm too weak. I can't make it.

SPIRIT

Yes. Why don't you take him if you are so strong.

OLD MAN

(angrily) You know I can't take him. He has to go himself. Puju, untie your ropes, you can make it. You have to try.

QIATSUK

Come on Puju. Try. Try.

OLD MAN

I know it is hard. There are hard times in life but you can't give up. You have to struggle, struggle to get rid of the ropes!

PUJU tries and he moves forward, stumbles, falls, tries again to pull at the rope. Then he falls down again, sobbing.

SPIRIT

(comforting PUJU and offering him something to drink) He can't do it. He's mine now. You've lost again old man. Get out of here now so we can continue with our party.

OLD MAN

I may not be able to take Puju to the *aglu* but I can show him what you really look like.

The OLD MAN rips off the SPIRIT's mask to reveal an ugly face. The SPIRIT screams and hisses. Everyone around is frightened of her, even the Creatures run away. PUJU tries to get away from her. He pulls at the ropes. QIATSUK who is free now runs to him, helping him to untie the ropes.

QIATSUK

Puju, you have to get to the *aglu*.

OLD MAN

Look Puju, look.

SPIRIT

(in a meeker voice, trying to pull at PUJU) Puju, come with me. I have something for you.

PUJU shakes her off. She floats around but moves further and further away towards exit right.

QIATSUK

Look, Puju, look.

PUJU is crawling now, he gets closer to the aglu. He finally reaches it.

PUJU   *(looking down he gasps)* It's the most beautiful
                  thing that I've ever seen. What is it?

QIATSUK   Don't you know? It's your soul. *(they are smiling)*

                  Blackout.

                  *Sound of an Inuit drum is heard getting louder
                  and voices singing* ajajaq *get closer and closer.
                  When the lights go on, the stage is pulled in.
                  The side curtains show mountains in the distance
                  and a green summer meadow. Three people are
                  talking and picking berries. An OLD MAN
                  enters and talks to them, asking to see their
                  berries. NAUJA and QIATSUK enter from stage
                  left, smiling and going up to the people who
                  share their berries. One friend pours tea and they
                  laugh. When the drum fades one of the friends
                  begins to play his guitar. He starts to sing the
                  song about PUJU, they all laugh and join in the
                  song. By the song's end, they are holding hands
                  in front of the audience. They stretch out their
                  arms to the audience.*

                  Blackout.

                  END

The Occupation
of Heather Rose

by

Wendy Lill

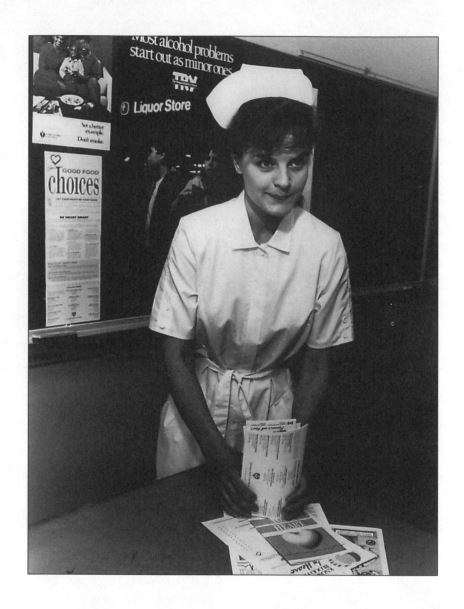

Tamsin Kelsey as Heather Rose.

Wendy Lill's *The Occupation of Heather Rose* is a play for and about southern Canadians, especially those who think they know something about the North. Lill's nurse, Heather Rose, has come back from nine months on an isolated reserve in a provincial north, and from madness, death, and darkness — as does Conrad's Marlowe — to make us see, above all to make us *hear*. This one-act monologue of memory, re-enactment, confession, and angry accusation is a tour de force for the actress playing Heather, and, when the part is performed well, it is an extraordinary experience for listeners. I say listeners advisedly because this monologue is also a dialogue between Heather and the other characters, whose roles and voices she creates to tell the story, and between Heather and us, the members of her southern audience who, unlike the bureaucrat Miss Jackson, have shown up to hear her report.

The plot is loosely based on Lill's 1977 experiences as a consultant for the Canadian Mental Health Association in Kenora. She went there to assess health needs, but quickly decided that another southerner doing another study was unnecessary; after six months, she quit, although she stayed in the area for eighteen months to write for the Sioux Lookout newspaper *Wawatay News*. While there, she listened to the stories and voices of whites, who were trying to work in the isolation of the North and who desperately needed to talk. The play began as stories for four voices, including a nurse, a geologist, and a bush pilot; in *The Occupation of Heather Rose* Heather tells the others' stories as part of her own.

The stories she does not tell are those of the Native inhabitants of Snake Lake. In "Letters Out," an interview with Robin Metcalfe, Lill explains that,

> there's a lot of Natives who can put words into Native peoples' mouths and tell the stories that they want to tell. I'm more familiar with the impact that my culture, the white dominant culture, has had on other people. I like to explore that: to make people as uncomfortable and as sensitive as possible.
>
> (*Books in Canada*, March 1990: 24)

This point is important because some reviewers criticise Lill for *failing* to create Native characters. But like Judy Smith in *Native Blood* (1994), Dara Culhane Speck in *An Error in Judgement* (1987), or Dorothy Knight in Betty Lee's *Lutiapik: The Story of a Young Woman's Year of Isolation and Service in the Arctic* (1975), Heather's rage is not with the Indians but with her own romantic ignorance and Florence Nightingale arrogance, with the indifference of doctors and civil servants, and with the racist, imperialist assumptions that underlie interference in Native culture.

The mirror Heather holds up to her audience reflects the white face of this southern indifference and ignorance. Heather remembers flying into Snake Lake with dreams of adventure and images of Barrie summer-camp life, but before the long winter ends she realizes that this is not the "Land of the silver birch" and that there is "no connection between the Romance of the North and [her] tired lonely existence as a Northern Nurse." During her nine months up North, she learns that white industry has contaminated the water, that medical supplies do not arrive, that liquor is available through the white bush pilot and store-keeper, that her notions of a healthy diet for *her* Indians are absurd and presumptuous, and that she cannot save the lives of those she is there to serve. When she surfaces from a nightmare of reality and winter, she is *dis*illusioned, honest, angry, and occupied by the ghosts of Camilla Loon and Naomi.

The play is tightly organized around four key ideas: Indians, Whites, Culture, and Alcohol. Each of these intersecting and overlapping concepts is explored through its connection with the others. In addition to these organizing ideas, Lill uses strategic intertexts to thicken the message of the play and to unify the action. Thus, the references to *Alice in Wonderland* alert us to Heather's unrealistic expectations and the inadequacy of her cultural preparation for this journey North, while reminding us about the terror of finding oneself in an alien world, where none of the landmarks is familiar. The allusions to Florence Nightingale are even more pointed. This 19th century symbol of female self-sacrifice and service is also the sign of middle-class British assumptions about superiority, assimilation, and imperialism. Florence has taught Heather to shoulder the Whiteman's burden, a lesson she must unlearn. However, it is Conrad's *Heart of Darkness* that is the most important literary/cultural intertext in *The Occupation of Heather Rose* because it provides a model for the style and structure of the play. Heather is like Marlowe in many ways. She enters the darkness of imperialist aggression within her own country and survives to bring us her cautionary tale — a tale about the horror of her past experiences, recreated in our shared present.

But the larger story that Lill recapitulates and dismantles is the southerner's story about the North. Instead of giving us a tale of masculine adventure and heroics, ending in victorious endurance or transfiguring death, Lill gives us a woman's story in which there is no room for heroics; madness is a two-week binge, and what dies with Naomi is a set of destructive southern illusions. In *The Occupation of Heather Rose*, Lill exposes the familiar tale of romantic adventure in the far North for the construction it is, and she demonstrates the danger of such constructions for white southern Canadians who perpetuate them and for northerners who try to survive the stereotypes.

Wendy Lill has written filmscripts, award-winning radio documentaries and dramas, poetry, stories, and several stage plays including *On the Line* (1982), *The Fighting Days* (1983), *Memories of You* (1988), *Sisters* (1989), *All Fall Down* (1993), *The Glace Bay Miners' Museum* (1994) and *Corker* (1998). *Heather Rose* was first published in *NeWest Plays by Women* (1987) and, with revisions, in *Modern Canadian Plays II* (1994). It was nominated for a Governor General's Award in 1987 and has received numerous productions across Canada (including the North) and in Europe.

S.G.

* * *

The Occupation of Heather Rose was first produced by Prairie Theatre Exchange in Winnipeg, Manitoba on 27 February 1986.

Heather Rose   Laurel Paetz

Director   Kim McCaw
Lighting Design   Larry Isacoff
Original Music   John McCulloch

"What sort of people live about here?"

"In that direction," the cat said, "lives a Hatter and

in that direction lives a March Hare. Visit either one you

like. They're both mad."

Alice in Wonderland

"I went a little farther . . . then still a little

farther — till I had gone so far that I don't know how I'll

ever get back."

Heart of Darkness

THE OCCUPATION OF HEATHER ROSE

CHARACTERS

Heather Rose
   who also plays
   Ramsay
   Lorraine McCain
   Mary Kwandibens

Scene

The mid-1980s. A classroom or training area in a government building, in a southern Canadian city.

HEATHER ROSE enters the room wearing a light jacket over a nurse's uniform, carrying a brown paper bag. There is a table and chair in the room, a blackboard, promotional posters for Northern Medical Services, Indian Affairs, Ministry of Natural Resources, Northern Affairs, etc. on the walls. HEATHER looks around at the posters, puts down her paper bag, and looks at her watch.

HEATHER ROSE (*to herself*) I wonder if I still look the same. I asked her to meet me at nine o'clock. But I'm always early.

Oh, I'm not ready for this.

She turns toward the audience.

I have always been an optimistic cheery type of person. I take after . . . both my parents on this score. On Saturday mornings, the three of us competed to see who could be the most bubbly, the most cheerful at the breakfast table.

That's probably why my sister left home so young. She just couldn't stand the pressure.

It began nine months ago. No, of course it didn't. It began long before that.

My mother had been a nurse in the slums of London. And my dad was a high school principal, the kind everyone visits years after with things like plastic ice cubes with bugs inside. Every Christmas, we had refugees from the International Centre sent over for turkey dinner.

So when I told my parents I was going to work on an Indian reserve, they were positively bubbly. I guess they thought I was . . . following in their footsteps.

I remember that first day barrelling through space in that hollow hairspray can of a plane, the sound of a thousand mosquitoes approaching my pillow in the dark, the hard cold metal wing vibrating against my thigh, long pink and purple tubes of land forming then breaking off into water, then land, more water, more wing . . . and in front of me, Ray, the pilot, lighting one Player's after another, blowing lazy circles of smoke back towards my waiting nostrils.

Did he know how sexy I thought he was?

"What's it like being king of the skies, Ray? Carrying the Royal Mail and life-giving medicines, on the lookout for red handkerchiefs and downed planes and forest fires and horny . . . living out one's dreams?"

"You must really love your work, Ray. No speed limits, no parking tickets, no Sunday drivers." What a flirt.

"Who me? What brings me here? Oh, I've always been attracted to the North . . . like a firefly to light. No . . . never this far before. Mainly the Barrie area, but it's a lot like this. One-sided trees, fiery sunsets, loons . . . . You've heard of Camp Cocano?"

The bugger didn't answer me. Just laughed. And turned the nose of the plane down. Suddenly I was on the Salt and Pepper Shaker at the CNE, giggling and holding onto my pockets so my money wouldn't fall out!

I was going down, down, downward into another place, another time, falling through a rabbit hole into a green and silver world below. I was Alice in Wonderland. Shall I fall right through the earth? Splashing into a shower of diamonds and purple morning mist and water . . . bobbing up and down in a plane which had miraculously become a boat.

"No Ray, I didn't mind. Rough? Was that rough? Hey! I love *rough*. Excitement, danger. Makes me feel like I've really arrived! Really alive!"

And I had.

Arrived.

Nurse Rose had arrived. The metal door swung open and the sun blasted in. And there below me, on the dock, was a sea of brown faces all looking up at me, in my slingback pumps and my seersucker dress. What made me suddenly feel that my heart would fall out, that I would die on the spot? And also, that I was . . . the Queen?

HEATHER gives a regal smile, even a wave.

But not for long.

"Holy Jesus Mary . . . what the hell have we got here?"

He stood there inspecting me like a catfish just hauled in off the bottom. Then he laughed . . . no, he snorted at me.

"Name's Ramsay, Miss Rose. The local freetrader, skirtchaser, swindler, philosopher and long-term survivor. Welcome to Snake Lake."

Suddenly back in the present, HEATHER looks at her watch, then towards the door. She seems agitated, uncomfortable, then retreats back into her recollections.

The nursing station. It had such a nice ring to it, I thought. The nursing station. Where the nurse was stationed. Where she was present and waiting for people in distress. In need of help. The first thing I did was unpack Mother and Grandmother. I mean their pictures! I set them up on the arborite desk with their nursing caps and serene smiles to guide me in my work at Snake Lake. Then I began to plow through Nurse Bunny's eight months of medical records. I've brought back a couple of entries to show Miss Jackson.

She takes some rumpled papers from the bag and reads.

"March 10. Jobit Loon died of a shaking fit. Out on his trapline with a beaver in his mitt. And no toque on. The day was dark when they brought him in, his skin grey, his wife watching. Her eyes a long way away."

That's quite poetic I think.

She holds up the paper. Then a sketch of a broken snowshoe.

Bunny did a lot of things like that. Sketches, cartoons. And cigarette burns. Bunny was a chain smoker. And this. *(reads another)*

"March 15. Moonias Turtle died of exposure. Frozen stiff like a chicken you take out of the freezer." Imagine someone even thinking a thing like that? But Bunny did. Then this one.

"May 15. Entire bottom end of reserve has diarrhea. Toilet backed up. Closed early." *(laughs)* That one always killed me! Entire bottom end . . . toilet backed up . . . .

Then a series of "closed earlys." Translation: "Hung over." But I only learned that later. Once Miss Jackson gets a better picture of the place . . . .

HEATHER turns and sticks the pages up on the bulletin board. Then she turns back to the audience, looking nervous.

I don't really drink. *(not completely convincing)* But Nurse Bunny did.

Lorraine McCain, one of the Snake Lake teachers, came by ten minutes after I arrived at my trailer with a bottle of scotch and a bag of chocolate chip cookies . . . "just to welcome the latest lamb to the slaughter." Immediately started telling tales out of school about Bunny — about what a *good head* she was, and about how they'd had to take two cartons of Jack Daniels empties out of our trailer after she left. I'd been told that Snake Lake was a *dry* reserve and I thought that meant *dry*. No alcohol. When I mentioned that to Lorraine, she just gave me sort of a fishy look, said I could be as dry as I wanted, or as wet.

(friendly) "Would you like some herbal tea? I've got Spicy Apple, Morning Thunder, and Sleepy Time somewhere in my suitcases, if I can find it . . . ." I really said that. Yeah, I did.

"Never touch the stuff," she said. Tugged down her bra, hauled herself up off the chesterfield. Said she'd better let me get some sleepy time myself. And then was out the door . . . with the bottle of scotch.

Rough and tough Lorraine. What a character. But I felt sort of rough and tough myself. Gutsy. Ready for anything. I unpacked, got my posters up on the wall, toothbrush in the little holder in the bathroom, shoes lined up in the closet. Uniform pressed and ready for the morning. My Indian Affairs parka was waiting for me in the closet — all downfilled, the hood trimmed with animal fur. When I put it on I felt like I was inside the stomach of a wolf or a bear. I remember I wandered from room to room, touching everything, and when I caught sight of myself in the bedroom mirror, I couldn't help smiling. No . . . grinning! It was like "Hey, look at me. I've really done it! I'm *here*! In the middle of an adventure."

And then it was night. Black night. There were no street lights. No big blue neon "H" from the hospital bathing my room with light 'til I closed it out with sleep. No strains of Tina Turner coming through the flimsy residence walls. A gentle autumn breeze

stirring the pines outside . . . sh-h-h-h-h . . . the drip
drop drip drop of the nylons I'd hung to dry in the
shower stall. Were there animals out there in the
darkness? Bears, wolves, moose? Were there Indians
out there? My patients? Was there a world outside in
the shadows waiting for me? Of course there was.
But what was more important right then was what
was going on *inside* me! I've heard women describe a
feeling that comes over them right after giving birth.
Sort of a humming. That's how I felt that first night
lying in the dark. Kind of a humming.

> *Big sigh. She looks at her watch and paces,
> clearly agitated.*

I think it's really shitty to keep people waiting. I
flew eight hundred miles to be here this morning and
I'm ten minutes early. Miss Jackson just lives a
couple of blocks away. And she's already ten
minutes late. I guess she wants to keep me waiting.
Well, I'm used to it. I probably won't be able to
really talk to her anyway. I tried on the phone one
time but she wasn't "amused." Might as well have
been talking to a brick wall, or a wooden . . . .

> *HEATHER goes over to the blackboard and
> writes the word* INDIANS.

Indians.

One night in the middle of winter I wrote that word
four hundred times on my dining room tablecloth.

My first patient was Camilla Loon. She arrived with
Mary Kwandibens, the nurse's aide. Mary and her
beautiful daughter Naomi. Camilla and Naomi. My
first patient and my last.

Camilla's face was like a worn old leather purse
without the coins. And when she opened her mouth,
soft little noises came out, like coos from a dove.
Her wooden leg was hurting her.

"Well no wonder Mrs. Loon. I've never *seen* such an
old prosthesis! We'll have to get you fitted for a new
one, and while we're at it, how about a new set of
false teeth."

*HEATHER looks pleased with herself,
competent. Then she looks behind her.*

"What is she looking at Mary? Does she understand
what I'm saying?"

At orientation, Miss Jackson told us Indians don't
look you in the eye. And it's true. She was at least
right about that. Camilla Loon looked at the top
button of my uniform as if it had some mysterious
power over her. And Mary K. looked at my feet
when I tried to shake hands with her. But that didn't
bother me 'cause it gave me a chance to study them.

Mary and Naomi Kwandibens for God's sake. Loon.
Moonias. Atlookan. Quill. Makoop. Names that
hold laughter one bubble below the surface. Names
out of the blue, out of the any old where . . . soft,
velvety names like their eyes. Which don't look into
yours.

Indians.

Mary Kwandibens is very fat. Her skin is very brown
and there is so much of it. And when she laughs, her
whole body jiggles and she was laughing a lot that
day. So was Naomi. So was Camilla. She probably
felt great about ordering up a new set of legs and
teeth. They were eating their lunch at the diagnostic
table while I kept on with old Bun's medical records.
But really I was studying them.

All my life I'd wanted to have hair like Naomi's.
Black and silky like a raven's. Not this dirty old
mop. And other things too. I'd wanted to be dark,
not fair. Straight, not curly. Enigmatic, mysterious,
not an open book. It wasn't that I wanted to be an
Indian, but I sure wouldn't have minded being a bit
more complex.

As I watched Mary and Naomi and Camilla sitting
there, I had this overwhelming urge to hug each one
of them. To engulf then. As if some of the good
things might rub off them onto me. And vice versa.
I'd learn their customs and they'd learn mine. About
my Scottish grandmother, my highland dancing
lessons and Robbie Burns' poetry. And we'd all get

on like a house afire. And when I caught Naomi's
eye and she smiled, I remember thinking she was
going to be just like my little sister.

"Move over, Naomi. How 'bout letting me try some
of that bannock!"

I went to see the chief.

"This is a real honour, sir. Chief Red Sky. I've
never met an Indian chief before. I guess I was
expecting you to be . . . older. Kind of like Dan
George.

"Where did you get those topaz rings? God, they're
so beautiful! I love it here. It's . . . beautiful!
The air smells so fresh, and the birds, and the
wildflowers . . . ."

(to the audience) He'd already heard about my order
for artificial limbs and false teeth.

"Oh heavens, they'll show up. I ordered them
through Northern Medical Services. They promised
them within four to six weeks!"

Unlike most Indians, the chief had eyes that looked
into yours, sort of drew you in then pushed you away
again. Maybe that's why he got to be chief. Told
me it was getting harder and harder to eat well and
stay healthy at Snake Lake. That the fish were full of
chemicals from the paper plant up the river, that the
wild rice didn't grow since the government put in the
hydro dam. And that it was hard to keep your kids
clean when there wasn't enough money for proper
sewage. And that . . . .

HEATHER holds up her hand to interrupt.

"Hey! Excuse me, Chief! But I *know* all about the
problems. (I learned it all at my orientation week.) I
want to talk about *solutions*. I've been thinking
about an exercise club for women to improve their
self-image . . . women always need to improve their
self-image. And a good food club to work on our
eating habits now that fish and wild rice have been
kind of blown out of the water. Ha ha. We'll draw
up a list and get Mr. Ramsay to start stocking more

nutritional foods . . . . I mean I've taken a look at his store and . . . . *(gesture of dismissal)* Cling peaches and red hots are all right, but a little goes a long way . . . .

"And at orientation, I heard your alcohol and drug abuse committee has kind of lost direction. So I want to join that and add some life to it. *(big confident smile)*

"And as for the teenagers, well, they just don't have anything to *do*! When I was that age, I'd have gone *crazy* without camp. If we could get a drop-in centre happening at the high school — do some arts and crafts, show movies . . . . *(listens)*

"I'm twenty-one, sir. I guess you're thinking that I'm kind of young and inexperienced. But I like to think I've got a fresh new outlook.

"Mr. Chief Red Sky, I know there are some really terrible problems here but . . . look at me! I managed to scrape through nursing school and I'm no Einstein! And I've been dieting for ten years so I wouldn't look like an elephant leaping about in my kilt at dancing competitions.

"Things can get better, can't they? Well, can't they?"

> *HEATHER walks around the room, musing over the experience in her mind. She goes to the blackboard and writes the word WHITES.*

WHITES.

That's a funny expression, isn't it?

Whites. 'Cause we're not really white, are we? We're sort of pink and beige. The whites at Snake Lake dress in Saturday-at-the-laundromat clothes seven days a week, and they march purposefully about, from store to community hall, to church, to canteen, to dock, to teacherage . . . .

"Hiya Janie, how's by you!"

"How's she goin' Ray?"

"Takin' her easy are ya?"

Pushing the Indians off the roads as they barrel from place to place. And always visiting . . . no . . . checking on one another.

Lorraine lived in the teacherage, a pink townhouse complex built, she said, to lure teachers to the North. Wall-to-wall carpets, central heating, glass doors on the shower, wrought iron bannisters, cathedral ceilings, but according to Lorraine, the units were cold in the winter and not bright enough. They needed skylights and more cupboard space, more this, more that . . . .

I would have sold my soul to the devil to live in one of those units. I'd hang spider plants and wandering jews from the ceiling, swish up and down the broadloomed staircase in my velour robe . . . who needs skylights?

"You're gonna kill yourself and then what'll they do for a nurse?"

Lorraine was visiting with her cannister of gin gimlets, watching me puff my way through my Jane Fonda workout. Filling me in on the Snake Lake gossip. About the legendary teacher Annadora.

Apparently Annadora "did it" with anything that wore pants. Every Friday night, she'd make a batch of butter tarts, then bellow over to Ramsay to come help her eat them. By ten o'clock, they'd be riproaring drunk, full of tarts and chasing the cat up and down the redwood staircase.

Annadora laughed backwards like a donkey. And as the evening wore on, the sound of her laughter rose higher and higher so that it kept the whole reserve awake. You'd think that would have been enough of a reason to fire old Annadora, but in fact, what finally did her in was something else.

Annadora began inviting Indian boys over after school. That's when Joe Red Sky told Education Services that they didn't want Annadora teaching their children anymore. In fact, the Indians actually carried her down to the dock and shoved her on the plane. Goodbye Annadora.

Lorraine said she got "hooked" on brown meat, that Indian men were different than white men. That they smelled different, and that they had warm skin and that they were better in bed. I could tell she was trying to shock me, so I just kept doing my exercises all the harder, my face to the wall.

"Got a boyfriend, honey?" She actually called me honey!

"No, but I'm keeping myself in shape in the event that someone might come along."

(*as LORRAINE*) "You have to take what you can get here. I have a little thing going with a Mountie stationed at Sioux Falls. 'Bout Thursday I start praying for hunting accidents or drownings, so he'll fly in for the weekend to investigate. Rest of the time, I make do with Ray, the bootlegger. Keeps me in gin."

(*as HEATHER*) "Do you mean Ray, the pilot Ray?" None other. He was probably carrying booze that day I arrived, not antiseptic and the Royal Mail. So much for living out one's dreams.

Lorraine and her Mountie, Annadora and Ray, and then Ramsay. Ramsay! When I went to see Ramsay about stocking brown rice and fresh vegetables . . . .

(*as RAMSAY*) "Nice to see a new tail wagging around my humble emporium. I hear you're stuffing hygiene down their throats like there's no tomorrow."

"There's nothing wrong with good hygiene, Mr. Ramsay." You should try it yourself sometime, I wanted to say, but I didn't.

(*as RAMSAY*) "Guess not, but it's kind of hard to stay clean when there's shit floating up your water intake pipe."

Hold on, Heather. "I don't like talk like that, Mr. Ramsay. It sets a bad example. Surely even you know what to do when you have water with impurities."

Beat. HEATHER smiles.

"You boil it."

(as RAMSAY) "You go fucking boil it!"

And then he came up really close to me. "Why don't
we be . . . friends? Hmmm? It's hard living on an
Indian reserve. Your friends in the South forget you,
your magazines never come. People hear every word
you're saying on the radio telephone so you can't be
intimate with someone a long way away. Everyone
will talk about you, even laugh at you. It'll get to
the point that you even think the ravens are laughing
at you, and when that happens, come and see me.
Old Ramse will give you a shot of stamina."

Thanks but no thanks. What were all those people
doing at Snake Lake? Not exactly the type you'd
invite home for Sunday dinner. Not exactly sparkling
representatives of our culture. They were there
because they didn't fit anywhere else. But they'd be
the last to admit it.

Lorraine told me she didn't much like Indians 'cause
they were a "broken people" but not to worry, 'cause
they didn't like us much either.

Well what's to like, I wanted to say. If all you're
getting is leftovers, how do you know whether you'd
enjoy the meal. I was determined not to be like
them.

> *HEATHER writes the word* CULTURE *on the
> blackboard.*

Culture.

At orientation, we spent a whole afternoon on
culture. Miss Jackson told us that going from white
to Indian culture was like going from your rumpus
room into your fruit cellar.

She said that cultures were all about imagining. For
example, she told us when Indians looked out on a
lake, they imagined shaking tents and spirit visions
and powwows and canoes filled with braves moving
silently across the water, thunderbirds circling
overhead . . . .

Whereas when we look out on a lake, we see
something different. When I looked out on Snake
Lake, I imagined hundreds of bodies lying elbow to
elbow on little sandy towels, sailboats and air
mattresses bobbing, tiny voices emerging from sandy
radios . . . .

Culture.

Norma Redbird lived with her new baby, her parents,
her brother, her wrinkled grandmother, and five
assorted others in a white frame shack no bigger than
my kitchen nook and living room combined.

Part of my culture was to feel uncomfortable about
barging into other peoples' homes uninvited, but that
was my job, so I swallowed hard and . . . .

(cheery) "Hi, Norma! How's the new mom! I'm
here to check you and the baby! What are you doing
inside on a beautiful day like this? This is Indian
summer. *(laughs)* I've heard about your winters that
last from October to May. You and little Dolores
should be outside getting some fresh air, some
exercise while you still can!"

Watching *Let's Make A Deal* reruns is what they were
doing, all of them, including the five-day-old infant.

> *HEATHER looks uncomfortable, smiles, shifts
> about.*

"The baby looks good. Good colour. Alert.
Curious. That's a cute top she's wearing. I think
she could use some eyedrops. Why don't you bring
her in this week and I'll give her a thorough
checkup."

A huge piece of frozen meat thawing out in front of
the TV; Monty Hall making jokes with two women
from South Dakota dressed up as chickens; me in my
nurse's uniform yacking away about cute tops and eye
drops.

How did I feel? Like a spaceship which had landed in the middle of their living room, sending out little beeps.

"Spaceship Rose to earth . . . . I've located the Indians . . . . What am I supposed to do now?"

Focus on food. Highlight hygiene. Win them over. Make connections.

"Oh-h-h-h . . . it's so *dark* in here. I saw some calico at the store for two-fifty a yard . . . . It would make nice curtains for those windows, and if you had some leftovers, you could make a tablecloth to cover up that oilcloth. Really brighten up the place. *(smiles nervously, fidgets)*

> HEATHER *pulls out some filecards from her brown bag.*

"What are you having for dinner tonight? Oh . . . I'm not inviting myself. I just saw that piece of meat thawing on the floor. I've never *seen* such a large roast. It looks so *fresh*! Wild! But I'm trying to cut down on meat. Have you ever heard of cholesterol? It's very bad for us. Very. These are some suggestions to help us all be a little less meat-dependent. I'll just leave them here to help you with your meal planning."

> HEATHER *shudders, rips up her meal plans, tacks up the pieces on the bulletin board.*

That day, at Norma Redbird's, was the first time I really began wondering about . . . a lot of things.

Someone was lying and I wasn't sure who.

Miss Jackson told us that part of Indian culture was close family ties, and that was why they lived in such cramped quarters. Bullshit. They were poor. They had no jobs. And nothing to do all day but watch reruns. And nothing to do tomorrow either. No prospects. I had never seen or tasted or smelled poverty before, and it scared me.

What did she know about Indians or family ties, or poverty or culture? All that shit about rumpus rooms and fruit cellars. And imagining. What were the Redbirds imagining — me standing there with my *Canada Food Guide* and sunburned nose, trying to out-shout two women dressed in chicken suits, telling them their house was dirty and their food disgusting. Who the hell did I think I was?

Saying someone has a different culture is just a polite way of saying they're *weird*. Not special, not privileged. Not exotic. Not mysterious at all. They're inferior. And therefore need to be helped. Translation: Altered. So much for culture! *(rips up Canada Food Guides)*

> *Distraught, pacing.*

An Indian reserve is not a nine to five place. Nor a September-to-June place. It's a hanging-around place. I watched Naomi the Raven and her silent stalking friends in their bright satin jackets that said DEF LEPPARD and METALLICA, sauntering around the reserve in their Nikes and blue jeans, quiet; making long-legged circular treks along the dusty roads that went nowhere. They went in and out of school like casual visitors. They never carried books or pencil cases. Even though Naomi was in Grade 10, she could hardly read. Mary said she was getting into trouble. That she was a bad girl. "Oh Mary, who isn't *bad* at that age? Everyone wants to be bad!"

So bad! I did. But I wasn't. In fact, I was still trying to be bad six years later, but without success! Instead, I settled for gourmet dinners on Friday nights with Nancy Anderson, the gym teacher. My only *real* friend at Snake Lake. The first time I met her, she was jogging along the beach in sweatpants and a t-shirt that said HAVE AN INDIAN AFFAIR!

Nancy and I were kindred spirits. She was helping me with the women's fitness program, which after eight weeks of promotion still just brought out two women — Nancy and me. We were both on the alcohol and drug committee. Trying to get some action on the reserve's bootlegging problem. Apparently Ray flew the booze in and Ramsay sold it at any hour, and at any price. Both of us had written off the "white trash" at Snake Lake; and both of us were saving for trips to Europe. We talked for hours about Eurail-passes and adapters for hairdryers, and the Orient Express and running into Jean Paul Belmondo on the Champs Elysée. It passed the time. Summer was gone and the nights were getting longer and longer . . . .

There was a cold mist on the lake in the mornings when I opened the station.

I felt kind of lonely, adrift . . . .

She mimics picking up a phone.

"Hi Mom! Hi. I sound far away? Well I guess that's because I am! Ha ha. I sound *funny*? It must be the line. No. There is nothing wrong. No, I just called . . . to talk. To talk! *Talk*. You know . . . *talk*. I'm fine. Great. Oh yeah . . . lots of fun. Lots of buddies. Lots of fun. Tons. I said *tons*! No, it's just the line. It's a radio phone. That's why it's so fuzzy. Gloomy? No, I'm *not* gloomy! Great. Put him on. Hi Dad! No . . . it's just the line. Oh yeah. Cold . . . brr . . . . Frost in the air! How's Skippy?"

She hangs up the phone and begins pacing.

There was more than frost in the air.

Naomi the Raven and her friends stopped frequenting school altogether. There was a rash of vandalism on the reserve. Nancy Anderson had her tumbling mats slashed. She cried one whole evening in my trailer. Lorraine was happy. Her Mountie flew in two weekends in a row.

One night, there were gunshots outside my trailer. I lay in the dark waiting for the end. Hoping that it was a nightmare and I was going to wake up. But it wasn't a nightmare. It was the real thing. Someone shot out the windows of the Catholic church. It sat there like a scared, hapless, toothless face against the cold autumn sky. What kind of people shoot the windows out of churches? I was getting discouraged

about our Indians. Things weren't working out.
They still seemed so far away . . . yet their problems
were so *close*! The drinking, the fights. I dreaded the
weekends. The nights. The nightmares. I dreaded
what I was going to see in the morning. I dreaded it
all . . . .

Except when the plane arrived. That little silver
sliver of wing cutting through the clouds and it was
magic every time. It became a day blessed with . . .
possibility.

November 2nd. I remember because it was my
birthday and I was at the dock waiting to get a present
from my parents, waiting for my medical supplies,
my order of teeth and legs . . . my *Chatelaine*
magazine, maybe for the results from the water
samples.

And there was a man framed in the doorway of Ray's
plane. A white man. But he was really brown. I
mean *tanned*. And he had the clearest robin's-egg
blue eyes in the northern hemisphere.

I closed the nursing station an hour early so I could
rush home and have a leisurely bubble bath. Wash
my hair. The works. Put on my tweed slacks, my
most clingy sweater. Then fashionably late, wandered
over to the community hall where Mr. Blue Eyes was
giving a talk about land claims. Why not? I was a
member of the community. Sort of. Wasn't I? I
was trying to make connections.

(flirtatious) "Hi! I'm Heather Rose. The resident
Florence Nightingale! I had no idea that aboriginal
rights and treaties could be so stimulating . . . so
pressing . . . so . . . ." *(sexy)* "Like I really feel the
need now to probe even deeper. Why don't you come
home with me and we can . . . ."

No such luck. He was tied up all night with the
Indians. Velvet-eyed Camilla in her red beret, tapping
her cane on the floor, and dozens more weathered old
souls, one after another talking about the good old
days before the white man.

(growing realization) I'll be as honest as I can about this. All I wanted to do at that moment was to take that particular white man back to my trailer. Take off his clothes . . . and mine . . . and forget about Indians and land claims and hideous social conditions. But the hours ticked away. And my hair went limp. I felt embarrassed about my silly fantasies. That's all they were. Fantasies. There was no connection between the Romance of the North and my tired lonely existence as a Northern Nurse. I'd been tricked somehow. So like old Bun probably did a hundred times before me, I went home alone.

I've tried not to even think about Greek Night. Let alone talk about it.

Nancy and I cooked up *dolmathes* with cabbage instead of grape leaves, and pork *souvlaki*, and Greek salad without the *feta* cheese and black olives; wearing the Greekest things we owned; listening to Nana Mouskouri, planning our four hundredth trip to Europe. The candlelight glowed softly around the table, the music blocked out the endless wind outside. Suddenly, the door flew open and there was Lorraine's big shiny face leering at us through the candlelight. Bulgy, lurid Lorraine and gin-running Ray just come for a visit, just come to see how we were enjoying our *petite soirée*.

(as LORRAINE) "Got anything to drink besides this horse piss?" Meaning the fruit punch. "What kind of a nurse are you if you don't have any medication? You must have something! I mean, what do you do here every night if you're not drinking? The two of you. That's the sixty-four dollar question here at Snake. Play scrabble? Play with each other?"

Now why did they say that? Why did they even think that? Why did they have to destroy the only real comfort we had?

> *HEATHER is silent, reliving this painful memory, almost grieving.*

Nancy left a week after that. Went back to Thunder Bay to work in a junior high school. Said she didn't like being away from her home and family. Said she missed her boyfriend. She left me all of her books including a cookbook called *Two Hundred Ways to Make Hamburger Sing*. Isn't that a funny title?

> *HEATHER looks vulnerable, almost in tears, suddenly trapped.*

Oh, it's sweltering in here!

> *HEATHER starts to exit — stops. Pause.*

I realize that I still haven't been very honest about this. It's all still a bit romanticized, polished up. I haven't got to the heart of this. And if I don't, you'll never understand . . . .

Snow. Snow white.

Sometimes, during the winter, my fantasies weren't much different than my reality. I'd see a raven or I'd dream a raven . . . and each evoked the same aloneness, the same gaping separateness.

I'd see an Indian boy a mile out on the lake, walking towards me, a boy with a red toque and a fur parka, perfectly placed in the light between the sky and the world. Walking across the lake, across a bright white desert. His legs would move but he never seemed to get any closer . . . or further away.

Mary Kwandibens told me — that was before she stopped talking to me — that winter was a time of holding on, that the soul went underground to lie like a woman long and straight upon a bed of ice, to sleep and be restored, to rise up new and refreshed in the spring like a young girl.

But that makes winter seem like a time of peace and it wasn't. It was a horrible onslaught.

One-thirty on a dark afternoon and Ramsay is down on his hands and knees working on his snowmobile.

(as RAMSAY) "Well, if it isn't Miss Nightingale. Relax, I won't eat you."

He got up and lurched towards me. The smell of scotch nearly knocked me out.

"Mr. Ramsay, your dog just bit Louis Loon as he was leaving your store."

He laughed. He seemed . . . almost pleased to hear it.

(as RAMSAY) "Well, he must have been trying to steal something. Come here and let me have a look at you. What are you so nervous about, you're twitching like a little rabbit. Jesus, you've got a lousy bedside manner! How come? You're from the city, aren't ya? You're a sweet city woman . . . like Annadora. She had a real gut on her from eating all those tarts . . . . It's hard to tell what you got under that parka."

"That's none of your business."

(as RAMSAY) "No? How come it isn't? How come you find it so easy to resist my offers? You've been here for three goddamned months . . . . What are you afraid of? That one of my dirty thoughts might seep into your lily-white head? Hmmm? Or that one of them Indians is gonna sneak into your trailer and scalp you . . . or even worse . . . ?"

"Shut up! Shut up!" A strange hysterical voice echoing in my brain and I realize it is me screaming and crying. And then a door slams in the wind and he's gone, then a familiar voice. Mary Kwandibens standing beside me with her big warm arm around me. It smells like soap.

(as MARY) "What's this . . . you're a funny little mouse. You should cry! It's good to cry. You let everything build up inside you till you explode!" Rocking me, soothing me . . . . Naomi watching me. Always watching.

(as Mary) "Here, let's cheer her up, eh. I'll read your cards. That'll cheer you up. *(MARY turns the invisible cards)* Is Heather Rose the mouse ever going to get married?" Turn the card.
"Hmmm . . . maybe.
Who on earth will she marry?
Is she going to marry a soldier? No, not a soldier.
A sailor? No.
A tinker? No. What's a tinker?

A tailor? A lawyer? Definitely not!
An Indian chief? Maybe."

I close my eyes and I'm bouncing my rubber ball
against the brick wall at school.

(as MARY) "Is Mary going to lose 80 pounds before
breakup?" Turn the card. "Yes!"

Laughing like a big tongue licking me.

(as MARY) "Is there a storm gathering on the lake?"

Yes, and the wind never stops, and then the big warm
arm, the smell of soap going away, taking her
laughter away and a handful of chocolate bars.

(as MARY) "I'll take these over to Louis Loon to
cheer him up. We'll charge them to Ramsay, eh? He
won't miss them, he's already got too many, maybe
that's his problem, maybe he's got chocolate bars in
his pants instead of you know what." Naomi
giggles. "Don't worry little mouse. We'll get
someone to take care of the dog."

Then just as they leave, Naomi comes over and places
an O'Henry bar in my hand. That's all she did. And
then they were gone. But not the wind, the wind
never stops.

> *HEATHER writes the word* ALCOHOL *on the
> board.*

I do know something about alcohol. On New Year's
Day, I joined with two of the teachers in a rum toddy,
to welcome in a brand new year. If only I could
describe how *good* it tasted. Hot, fiery, sensual,
merry, hospitable. For the first time in my life I
felt . . . witty!

"A little rum? Why not? To warm our cockles,
wherever the hell they are!" *(laughs)*

Leslie Walters, the new gym teacher, arrived at the
end of February. I beat Lorraine over to her trailer
with my bottle of Bluenose. I desperately needed an
audience.

"Oh, it's not a bad place, if you don't mind scraping
ice from your bedroom window in the morning just
to see out." *(laughs)*

"What d'you want to know? Heather Rose tells all.
The church? The natives got restless and there was a
big shoot-up one night. It really does look like hell,
doesn't it? I guess everyone prays in private
now . . . . I'm not exactly a practising anything.
The last thing I practised was the flute in grade ten."
(laughs)

"Run into Ramsay yet? He's part of the landscape
here like the garbage around his store. He's harmless
unless you've got a heart and soul. What else do you
want to know?"

"The Indians? Hard to know what they're thinking.
Blow hot and cold like the frigging winds. Pardon
my French. They're a broken people. It is really
sad, given how beautiful the land is up here and all
but . . . like it's not an *ideal* reserve, eh, otherwise
none of us would even be here, I guess that's how
you gotta look at it. Hey! Don't look so glum!
Lighten up! Want another drink? Don't mind if I do.
Don't mind if I do. Don't mind if I do."

With difficulty, an admission.

After being witty, with Leslie Walters, or just with
myself — I thought I was the best audience of all —
I put a towel over the bathroom mirror. It made the
mornings easier.

Indians.

I remember when I was small, Mom told us not to
talk to any of the men who changed buses at the
corner of our school. They were Indians. From
Munsey Reserve who worked at the mill. I wonder if
I'm prejudiced towards Indians because of that?

Our next door neighbours had a daughter named
Donna who studied archaeology at UBC and married
an Indian. I remember Donna's father sitting in the
back yard with my dad. I was under the picnic table.
He was drinking a lot and he was crying. I remember
him saying that digging bones with Donna was one

thing, but he sure as hell didn't want one of them
plugging her.

HEATHER smashes the table. Very agitated.

Where is Miss Jackson? This is just like it was up
there. No one to tell things to. To help straighten
things out. I needed help. I did! Heather Rose! I
planned on talking to the fly-in shrink when he came
to see the Snake Lake crazies, tell him about the
drinking, how I was losing my temper in front of the
patients, the missed days at work.

"Doctor Allen," I rehearsed this, "I'm finding the
isolation here sort of . . . getting to me."

But after Mabel Turtle told him about her husband
appearing in a vision and Albert Loon describing the
animals running around inside his head, and all of us
sitting on orange plastic chairs around the great white
doctor, and the wind howling and the windows like
teeth rattling and the room spinning, all I could do
was excuse myself and run out of the room — just in
time to get to the bathroom.

What did he know about those people? About spirits
on Snake Lake, about visions, and animals running
around inside your head and long nights and dark days
and crying jags and ravens that laugh at you and
freezup and no mail and . . . what the hell did he
know?

All those fucking high-paid whites coming through
to help the Indians — not little me! Flying in and
out, in and out, in and out, consulting on this,
consulting on that, flashing their million dollar
smiles, stalking about the reserve from plane to
community hall, to band office, to plane, with their
Indian friends, being helpful and advisory, then back
in the air. Once a month old Blue Eyes came and
went, his tan always the same. Perfect. Probably
used a sun lamp. Hope he gets skin cancer.
Probably played squash, told women in satin shorts
about his latest junket to desolate Indian reserves . . .
about what losers we all were . . . . There was no
help for me, except my rum toddies. Want another
one? Don't mind if I do.

HEATHER sits down heavily.

Sometimes when I'd lie in bed at night, I'd think the wind was trying to crack the backbone of my trailer. I'd think it was trying to pull off the roof and I'd be sucked out across the lake dressed only in my nightgown, sucked into a whirl of wind and ice and laughter . . . . Annadora's laughter and the wind . . . .

I felt like a wild animal was running around inside my head. Or maybe a wild bird flying against . . . . Bang! Bang! . . . bang . . . . *(slamming her hand against her forehead)* Trying to get out into the light . . . .

> *HEATHER seems to be reliving something painful. She is hearing Camilla's singing and rocking back and forth.*

Oh this is hard.

The occupation of Heather Rose.

"Mary? Mary? What is Camilla doing here, Mary? Why is she singing like that? Mary?"

Something registered in Mary's big dark face but I didn't know what. She used to make me bannock in the mornings, but not anymore. Not after I yelled at her for leaving the station unlocked. It was only for half an hour, but I yelled at her, in front of her daughter Naomi, and called her a stupid . . . . Oh God!

"Mary! Answer me! I'm the nurse here. You're supposed to be helping me!"

Camilla Loon was holding a sit-in. An occupation. She was going to occupy the nursing station 'til her new leg and teeth arrived. She'd waited eight months and was tired of waiting. She was going to stay right there on that orange chair as a reminder. That she had been depending on me.

Jesus Christ, I was angry. That's right. Angry. Was it my fault that her new leg had gone to a bush camp by mistake and by the time it was shipped back, it wasn't fit for a moose to strap on? Or that the second leg got waterlogged sitting in a leaky warehouse. Or that the Department's policy was that they were only allowed new dentures every four years, so that they wouldn't be filling orders every time an Indian got drunk and dropped . . . . Hey! I didn't make the rules!

Was it my fault that the goddamned plane took the leg to the wrong place. That half the time, the plane couldn't land because of the wind . . . that things got lost in snowstorms or landing strips or alcoholic blackouts; that pilots forgot shifts or their windshield wipers wouldn't work or they couldn't take off or didn't care enough to.

"So! You think you're going to *occupy* the nursing station. Well it is *my* nursing station. My orange chairs that you stick your Bazooka gum on. My tile floors that you spill your ice cream sandwiches on. I change the toilet paper in the washroom, scrub the waiting room at the end of the day after dozens of you sit with your big snowmobile boots and silent dark eyes waiting . . . for service."

Well if I was going to service them they would have to take what I had to dish out.

"You know what really bothers me about you people? You expect me to stitch you up, give you pills, send you out to the hospitals, wipe your bloody noses and I have never once heard anyone say what you're supposed to say when someone does something *nice* for you."

"What do you say? You say 'Thank you!' To just once hear 'Thank you Miss Rose' would be music to my ears! But instead I get silence. Dark eyes. Secrets. Why is that?"

"I never know what you're thinking. Never know what you really want from me. Should I stand on my hands, tell jokes, disappear? Are you glad, sad, mad when you see me? Do you like me, hate me, laugh at me, pity me, blame me?"

"ANSWER ME!"

"You know what I think you are? I think you're all
snobs. Yes, SNOBS."

"You think you're the only ones with a goddamned
history. Whenever I've tried to talk about my
family . . . about being Scottish . . . things my
grannie told me, little stories, or some beliefs . . .
whenever I've tried to share my life . . . nobody
shows any interest. Nobody gives a good goddamn
about me!"

"And you never bloody LOOK at me! Look at me! I
know you watch me, but you won't look at me. And
you talk about me, don't you? Don't you?"

"You've been talking to your chief. He came to see
me, said he'd heard about problems with the new
nurse. NEW! That's a laugh! I feel about as NEW
as the frozen dog shit all around this place. You
don't come right out and SAY things. You never let
things really pour out like we do! We whites! You
don't do that, do you? It's all indirect with you.
Well, I'm tired of it. Tired of this goldfish bowl . . .
big brother, sister, aunt, uncle watching me . . .
judging me, as if I've done something wrong, as if
I'm responsible for the pitiful states of your
lives . . . . Jesus! When in fact I've had the charity
and decency to try and help you. And I told your
chief that. And I told him that I didn't want to see
the next sad-eyed dark-skinned Indian coming through
the door. That I wanted to see a smiling, bouncing,
blonde-haired, lacy, pregnant white woman . . . who
would yack away about how her baby was kicking
inside, and the little clothes she was buying."

"And you know what else I told him? I told him that
if he didn't like the quality of my nursing care, he
could kiss my ass! And that goes for the rest of
you!"

*HEATHER looks mad, then slowly changes to
look shaken, sickened by what she's said.*

I became attached to a particular label on a bottle of
white rum. A perfect picture of a perfect ship on a
perfect horizon.

What I especially liked was the way the sky kind of
lit up the background. That's one of the redeeming
graces about Snake Lake. In winter. The sky. And
the ravens.

I spent two weeks drawing ravens. To hell with
nursing.

> *HEATHER digs through the paper bag,*
> *brings out sketches of ravens and holds them up*
> *for people to see.*

Black ink on thick white Medical Services paper . . .
white like the whiteness all around me.

Ramsay came by. Like a mongrel dog that's caught
wind of a scent. Just for a visit, he said. Looked at
me, at my bottle, then he laughed . . . no, he snorted.

"That's not a fucking ship," he said, "that's an eye.
The iris of a blue-eyed woman."

Took off his snowmobile suit. Then he asked me to
sit on his lap. And he kissed me. Said he brought
me some stamina. And we . . . partied. For two
weeks.

I didn't go near the nursing station. For two weeks.
Sick leave.

The onslaught.

> *Expansively, drunkenly.*

The North has always fascinated me. Ever since I
was very very young. Its wilderness. Its mystery.

> *She begins singing a camp song.*

Land of the silver birch,
Home of the beaver,
Where still the mighty moose,
Wanders at will . . . .

> *She laughs.*

"Who the hell is Will?" Ramsay'd say, and I'd laugh
every time.

Blue lakes and rocky shores,
I will return once more,
Boom did ee ah ah . . . boom did ee ah ah . . .
Boom did ee ah ah . . . boom!

And so it would go . . . me telling him about our
house on Highland Crescent with the grey shutters
and the Queen Anne's lace on the trellis and the dance
competitions at the Tam-o'-shanter and him telling
me about eating lard sandwiches in Timmins. And
then we'd flip on the *Edge of Night* and watch Mrs.
Turner get leukemia and her husband get caught in a
homosexual roundup of a subway men's room.

> *She gets to her feet.*

"Wanna see me dance, Ramse?"

> *HEATHER attempts to dance the Highland
> Fling, but loses her balance, trips, and perhaps
> falls to the floor.*

(to RAMSAY) "Don't laugh you ignorant pig.
Colleen Stewart and I won the Junior Girls for that
dance when we were fifteen. And my parents took us
out for dinner after, to . . . . I can't remember the
name of the place! How could I forget? That was the
nicest restaurant I ever went to."

> *She phones Mom and Dad.*

"Hi Mom? Hi. Yeah hi. Yeah it's me. Hi. Sure,
get him on the extension. Why not? The more the
merrier. Listen, the reason I called is 'cause I can't
remember the name of the restaurant we went to after
I won the Junior Girls. *(shouts)* Oh God! Of
course! It was the Latin Quarter. *(to RAMSAY)* It
was the Latin Quarter. *(to parents)* Yeah, I've got
someone with me. Yeah . . . for dinner. *(to
RAMSAY)* What time is it? *(laughs)* Is he male or
female? I guess you could call him male! So what
else? I got your postcard from Malaga and the
castanets. Yeah, real cute. I said CUTE. Why the
hell did you go to Malaga anyway? Why don't you
stay where you belong. Right here in Canada. If you
want to see colourful culture, you could come North
for a weekend, see the Indians. They're poor, sick,

unhappy, uneducated, fucked over . . . oops . . . sorry
about that! Good photo opportunities. And I'm sure
the storekeeper would honour all major credit cards.

I sound like I've been drinking? *(laughs)* Yeah well I
have. I've been drunk for two weeks. Because it's
too insane here to stay sober. God you sound far
away. I don't know when it started happening . . .
but I've fallen apart. Completely apart. *(she listens;
her face changes; her voice becomes more vulnerable)*
Well I'll try to. I know you do. I know. I love you
too."

HEATHER *turns to* RAMSAY.

"Get out."

I had to get my ducks in a row. People have
difficulties and then they rally. They get back on
track. People think they'll never recover and then six
months later, they can't even remember what they
were upset about. They pull themselves together.

"Hold on Heather, get your ducks in a row." That's
what Dad always said. I was bushed. That happens
in the North in the winter. And six months later, I'd
laugh about it.

I cleaned the trailer. I cleaned the walls. Cleaned the
shower curtain. The kitchen drawers. Sewed the
hems and all the lost buttons.

People throw themselves into work. Work is
supposed to get people through the rough spots. It
was all still there waiting for me. Camilla was still
there, her eyes a long way away. And Mother and
Grandmother. Still smiling at me. *(to photos)* I had
such a steady diet of nurses. Clean, competent,
responsible, healthy women. How did you manage?
Who cared for you? Bandaged you? Hold on Heather.
And the wind still howling and ripping around outside
the nursing station. And Annadora's laughter still
inside my head. Hold on Heather. And the big
cheese poster still on the wall and the t-bone steak,
the wet lettuce . . . and a dozen messages from Miss
Jackson like little pink petals all over the desk.

HEATHER steels herself, then picks up the phone.

"Hello, Miss Jackson? Hi. Heather Rose. Just fine. 110 percent! Just catching up on my paper work. I see you've been calling, but I've had the flu. A bug. Some kind of a bug. I'm all right now though, really. The chief called you? No, I'm all right really. I've got my ducks in a row. I was derailed temporarily but I'm back on track. *(shouts)* Jesus Christ! I said BACK ON TRACK! Why the hell can't they get decent telephones in the North."

"You what? You want me to come out? No. I'm not coming out. I'm staying right here. I have a job to do here and I'm going to do it. There is no question that these people need medical attention. No question at all. I have five vaccinations to do this week and there's always lots of business on the weekends. I don't care who you talked to. I won't. I can't. Go back to what? There's nothing for me to go back to. It's all distorted now, twisted . . . . *(listens)* Who do you think you are? God? Parachuting little people hither and yon, then scooping them out again whenever you please. It makes them crazy.

"Fuck you, Miss Jackson. There's an old woman here with a wooden leg and I've got to make hot meals for her. There's an ancient Indian with a wooden leg occupying the nursing station and Nurse Rose is going to join her."

Crossfade. The sound of CAMILLA LOON singing.

Break up. The breaking up of winter — that winter that I thought would never end.

Break up.

That's what they call it when winter finally ends. Because the ice on the lake begins to break up like a hundred million ice cubes.

Outside, the sound of drums coming from the community hall. There was a powwow going on. A coming-through-winter festival.

> *HEATHER remembers the pulse of the music, tries to reproduce it. She listens to the music.*

It wraps them up, their music. It puts a spell on them. But it drummed me out. It felt sad to be an outsider. So sad. I remembered lying in bed at home on Highland Crescent and hearing the garbage trucks grinding their garbage as they moved along the streets in the darkness. *(pause)*

Darkness everywhere. Dark except for the flashlights going back and forth, back and forth in the darkness . . . and the glow from the community hall.

When I looked out into that darkness there was a glare from the window and I looked . . . different. Looked like a photograph of me . . . only as an old woman.

> *HEATHER sighs and takes a plastic bag from her paper bag. She holds it up for the audience to see.*

This is how they do it. Like this.

> *She demonstrates gasoline sniffing to the audience.*

They brought Naomi in. Found her in the corner of the washroom at the community hall, stinking of gasoline. Yellow fluid all over her face. Her beautiful face. Wearing her red satin jacket, her mother behind, carrying her navy blue mitts.

> *CAMILLA'S song continues under.*
> *HEATHER's face is transfixed as she remembers NAOMI's body being brought into the nursing station.*

"Oh Naomi, what have you done? What have you gone and done?"

At orientation I'd learned all about this . . . but not the horror.

"Naomi, wake up! Say something if you can hear
me. Talk! Look, your mother and Camilla are here!
Talk!"

And I was shouting her name over and over and
slapping her face.

"Naomi! Hey! *(claps hands)* Hey! It's good to talk.
I always talk when I'm having troubles. That's what
I do. Talk! Talk. Please, Naomi. Tell me what you
did today before you . . . . Hey!"

But she was floating in another world.

"Hey, what do you want to do when you grow up?
When you finish school?"

She was drowning.

"Hey! You're in love, aren't you Naomi? With
Clarence Loon. I know because I've seen you
holding hands with him. Think of him. Live for
him. For Clarence. Live for me. Please Naomi!"

But her eyes were closing.

"No! I demand you open your eyes. Damn it! Open
them! Naomi. Hey! It's spring. Rise up! You're
supposed to RISE UP! It's your legend. You're not
allowed to die, Naomi. To give up. You can't do
that. You've got to survive. We've got to survive.
That's all that matters . . . ."

Naomi's heart stopped.

> *HEATHER puts her head down and cries. She
> looks up at the audience, wearily.*

Miss Jackson's not coming. But what did I think
would happen here? That I would somehow be able
to unload this. I can't. It's inside me now.

Camilla's artificial leg arrived on the same plane that
I left on. But not her false teeth. And that's about it,
I guess. The occupation of Heather Rose.

> *Lights go down on HEATHER.*

END

Trickster Visits the Old Folks Home

by

Sharon Shorty

Jackie Williams as Anna.

Trickster Visits the Old Folks Home is a work in progress, telling the story of works in progress, of what has happened and is happening to people in a clearly identified northern community. Anna, the protagonist, is an aging Tlingit woman who has to make the transition from her traditional way of life in the bush to a senior citizens home, a non-native institution, in Whitehorse.

Anna embodies the Trickster of the title, a spiritual being common to many native legends, creator and mischief-maker, sometimes coyote, sometimes raven, a life force, a force of survival, often subversive: unexpected, tricky, representing and requiring constant adaptation. The other spirits in the play are earthy, part of Anna's reality, like the spirit of her husband in the cabin she leaves, or of the "uggy" cat in the institution. (For a comparable treatment of spirit figures, see the introduction to Beissel's *Inuk and the Sun*, 51-53.) The spirit that persists is Anna's own, the spirit of the Trickster.

In the process of adapting to her new setting, Anna tests and questions it and its values. She has with her her "Jesus Picture" and "the Lord's Word." She already knows and appreciates some of the other attributes of white western culture, such as Kentucky Fried Chicken and comic books. Some, like the relentless (and, in her view, intrusive) cleaning and tidying, she comes reluctantly to accept. Others, such as institutionalized care for the aged, she cannot change, but her questioning of it remains valid for non-native as well as Native society. While she may not be able to change the nature of the institution, she can and does modify it to make it more livable for herself, and incidentally, more human, much as peripheral society influences the dominant. The amiable satire with which her view is presented has an affinity with that of Tom King and Drew Hayden Tayler, the subversive humour of those on the periphery. Shorty's Trickster is a blood relation, although not a descendant, of King's Coyote.

In the process of asserting herself and her values, Anna takes charge of Barbara, a younger Tlingit woman in nominal charge of her, who is professionally and naturally a care-giver, but unaware of her traditional heritage, and even of her "Indian" name. Questioning the loss of Barbara's Tlingit identity, Anna says: "That Barbwire — gee, I feel sorry. Nobody teach her anything, I guess. I can't see how — I know... her grandma. She teach her good. Yuh, I remember that. Gee, what happened?" What happened is partly explained later by a reference to Barbara's enforced attendance at "that church school in Carcross," where she forgot her true name. In helping Anna, in acceding to her sometimes outrageous Trickster-like demands, Barbara rediscovers her heritage, including her lost name, which Anna knows and restores to her. She inherits Anna's drum, and by implication, her songs. Her professional life is enriched, not rejected or lost; it, in turn, enriches her new-found identity. But Anna's question,

"What happened?" can be more expansively answered, in part by the action within the play and in part by the very fact of its writing.

Some of the details of Anna's settling-in are simply funny, like the positioning of her spitcan. Others present Tlingit custom: the first thing she does is to cleanse her room of past spirits. Next, she moves her bed so that her "feet face the water." Significantly, she tells Barbara to do the same, instructing her in the traditions of Tlingit women. Some of her settling-in process provides ironic insights. For instance, the discussion about how the call-bell should be used elicits Anna's view. In an instant of comic revelation we come to see things as Anna does. She didn't come to that place to pull strings; she is not there to become part of a bureaucratic system, an activator of machinery; she is a human being and will not assent, whatever the convenience, to the diminishing of her humanity.

The play itself embodies both native and non-native traditions. Western in form, it includes Tlingit beliefs and practices, and Tlingit song and dance. It follows oral literature in being didactic, telling to native and non-native a story about the elements of a live tradition that must not be laid aside, whose continuation is vital to its practioners and to the larger community. Story-telling and drama, satire and teaching are firmly and intricately related; all find their place in this play as it represents and reflects upon its dynamic environment.

Like Anna, Sharon Shorty is an imparter of traditions. Her representation of Anna honours her grandmother. It is important to her that what she writes and performs be approved by the Elders: the cultural identity conveyed by her work must be consistent with the vision of the guardians of tradition (interview with author, 12 August 1997). She is currently Story Producer at Northern Native Broadcasting. She and Jackie Williams, who acted Anna in the original performance, produce skits for various occasions, in which they, as two old women, Sarah and Suzie, continue Anna's Trickster-like existence, ambling into banquets, board rooms, and schools, commenting on everything, from the size of the buildings and the quality and quantity of work performed in them to the kind and quantity of refreshments offered.

E.D.

* * *

Trickster Visits the Old Folks Home was first produced by Nakai in Whitehorse, Yukon as part of the New Theatre North Playwrights Festival on 11 April 1996.

Anna	Jackie Williams	Directed by Yvette Nolan
Barbara	Katherine Linklater	Set design by Alyx Jones
Spirit Dancers	Brittaney Irea-Rose	Sound by Daniel Janke
	Yolanda Carlick	

TRICKSTER VISITS
THE OLD FOLKS HOME

CHARACTERS

ANNA	Traditional native elder, feisty, bossy, and lovable all at once. Born in the Yukon bush and lived there most of her life.
BARB	Young native nurse, just got her Occupational Therapist degree at a University in the South. Went to a residential school and is not too close to her family or the old way of life.
FELINE SPIRIT	An embodiment of the old folk's home. Bothers ANNA and gets into her food.
SPIRIT DANCERS	A few dancers in button blankets, who represent tradition and ANNA's old way of life.

Scene One: Present day Teslin

SPIRIT DANCERS *surround ANNA, and we see their silhouette. She is the lead singer with the drum, and is singing a Tlingit song. ANNA is upright, to represent her youth. As the DANCERS leave, quietly singing, ANNA takes the blanket off and takes her cane. She enters her home with drum and puts it up on the wall.*

ANNA's home, small and cozy, filled with knitting, hanging dry fish, small fridge, hot plate with pot of moose stew, table with teapot, miscellaneous representations of Jesus, pictures of family on wall, spitcan, lots of bags, wood stove, and so on.

ANNA is sitting in her chair knitting. Persistent horn honks.

ANNA   What the heck is that? Sounds like geese! Honk! Honk!

Honking continues.

ANNA   Geez! Better go check, must be crazy people.

                  *Walks to door to check it out, peers outside and
                  sees BARB standing outside.*

ANNA   Hey! That you make all that noise?

BARB   *(reluctant to get closer to the door)* Hello, I'm
                  Barbara. I'm the nurse from the Yukon Home.

ANNA   I say, who's that anyways?

BARB   Barbara.

ANNA   *(leans closer to BARB's ear)* Barbwire?

BARB   *(to ANNA's ear)* Barbara.

ANNA   Barbwire.

BARB   No. it's Barbara.

ANNA   Hmm. Barbwire. Just like rabbit wire, you got
                  Barbwire. Funny name. Okay then, come in.

BARB   Well, the car's running. We really have to go, Anna.
                  Are you all packed?

                  *ANNA walks out a few steps as if ready to go,
                  but she grabs BARB's arm and swings around
                  into the house.*

ANNA   C'mon, I just made some fresh tea. And I got lots of
                  pilot bread.

                  *BARB is looking at her watch, and looking
                  around for ANNA's stuff to take.*

ANNA   Sit down! You look like a beaver, you rush round
                  my little place. Now, who you people, anyhow?

BARB   My mom was from Carcross.

ANNA   Oh, is that right? Then you my people too. You
                  Tlingit, huh? What's your real name?

BARB   Umm, Barbara.

ANNA   Not that whiteman's name! What kinda Indian name
                  your gramma give you?

BARB	Oh, I don't know.
ANNA	Gee, you don't know. *(gets tea for them)* Here's your pilot bread. You want Cheeze Whiz on it?
BARB	No thanks. We really have to get going soon. Where's your suitcase?
ANNA	Never mind, yet. What kinda place you gonna take me to? What kinda food they got, anyways?
BARB	It's pretty good there. We have a nice room for you. There's lots of activities for you. We take residents to community events every week. There's even a place to get your hair done.
ANNA	Which way that room face? What about the food?
BARB	Your room faces the road.
ANNA	Ah shucks! I mean, does it face the south? I gotta have light in my room. Can't hardly see any more for my knitting. And that food. You got any Indian food?
BARB	I'm not sure which way it faces, but I'm sure it will be just fine, Anna. Sometimes we get donations of moose meat or salmon.
ANNA	Oh, you cook it? You Indian, eh, you know how to cook it!
BARB	No, we have a cook.
ANNA	Who's that? Indian?
BARB	No.
ANNA	What then? Whiteman? Aww no! How's he gonna know how to cook our way? I better take my hot plate. I don't know; I don't think he's gonna know how to cook my fish eggs. Go ahead, pack up my little stove.
BARB	Anna, you won't need it. We'll feed you . . .
ANNA	Ah you, I'm gonna starve. I gotta have that hot plate to cook. It's the only thing that keeps me going. If you not gonna take my stove, I'm not going.

BARB	Anna, look, it'll be okay. You can't bring that hot plate. We got regulations.
ANNA	What's that, "regations"?
BARB	It's our rules for the home.
ANNA	I guess I'll be okay if I stay here then. *(sits down)*
BARB	Okay then. We'll take it. *(she moves to get the hot plate, but doesn't know what to do with the pot of stew)*
ANNA	Good soup that one. Go ahead, try some. My grandchild gotta moose last week. I tell him just where to hunt, shucks, he always get that moose. People ask him how he know where to hunt. It's pretty easy to remember where-all I used to hunt. I still hunt, me! I set snare for rabbits down that trail; sure enough I get one last night. Go ahead, look at that rabbit meat. It's in my fridge.
BARB	*(moving hot plate, rushing)* That's okay.
ANNA	Go ahead, look at it! I tell the truth, what you think?

> *BARB looks in fridge, which contains a skinned rabbit minus a leg, boxes of Kentucky Fried Chicken, jars of fish eggs, and popsicles.*

BARB	You like chicken?
ANNA	Yuh, I like that whiteman's grouse. Nice and fat.
BARB	Sure is.

> *BARB starts to carry the hot plate, and ANNA blocks her way with her cane.*

ANNA	What kind of shoes you got?
BARB	Nurse shoes.
ANNA	Geez, you can't hunt in those shoes!

> *BARB exits. ANNA starts to pack some stuff.*

ANNA	Boy, this teapot, pretty old now. I got it from Percy, he come through our camp with his dog team. I see him and I wonder, who's that? My daddy, he say

that's old Percy. He just come from that Hudson's Bay Fort, got lots of stuff for all his winter traps. We look after him good, feed him good, give his dog some fish. Boy, Percy just happy, tell good story about our family. Everybody gonna know, people come see us, they treated good. So when time to go, Percy, he open up a box and give my daddy a good trap, my momma a good stew pot and then me, he give me this teapot. He say, gold all around it. I feel pretty good. Long time now, I lost its little hat.

BARB

(returns) Okay, Anna. What else should I take?

ANNA

Take that 1942 suitcase. That's the one my daddy give to me when I'm gonna get married. Put that Jesus picture in it, and the Lord's Word, and that Vicks. *(BARB moves fast and drops something)* Hey! Don't bust up my stuff! Gee! Then, next, my teapot, some cups, that sugar, my fish cutknife, that fishnet. Get that gunnysack in the porch, put that dry fish in it. See, I can hardly see, but I still cut my fish good. I make that fish better than Ethel.

BARB

Who's Ethel, your friend?

ANNA

Yuh, she's my friend all right. But she try to beat me for who make better dry meat, who sew better, who got more grandchilds. Ah, she's silly. Everyone know I can make better dried meat. I even win that contest, I cut the best fish fillet! They give me that ribbon and that knife there. Boy, nice knife. That Ethel, just the same she try steal my knife at fish camp. Go ahead, pack it up, okay.

BARB

You mean that lady who's at the Home — Ethel?

ANNA

Yuh, I hear she stay there too. At least I have one friend there, maybe.

BARB

What else should I take?

ANNA

Well, we gotta take that fridge. Otherwise my food's gonna spoil up. Who's gonna eat it if I'm not here?

BARB

We have a fridge there you could store things in.

ANNA

No, I gotta have it close by. What if I get hungry at nighttime? How far away is that fridge?

BARB	It'll be down the hall, in the dining room.
ANNA	No, I better take it. It's pretty small. You got 'nuff room in your car? What kind of car you got?
BARB	It's a sedan, four door, from work.
ANNA	Oh, I hope it's got 'nuff room for my stuff. C'mon, pack up that fridge.

BARB picks it up and begins to carry it out. It's heavy.

Gee, what's the matter? You young yet, must be strong enough.

BARB exits to load car.

ANNA is packing her bags and as she bends over an unseen spirit, her husband, grabs her bum.

ANNA   Oh, it's you. Yuh, gotta pack up everything now. They gonna look after me. Nobody here to look after me, Mary Rose gotta go to school. I need help now, my husband. No, Anna can't do everything now. Not the same anymore. Besides, pretty lonely, be stuck by myself all the time. I don't know, some kinda place she gonna take me there. Lotsa people stay there, even that Ethel stay there. I don't know, I try to get along with her, this time. I be okay, oh yah. I got my little fridge and my hot plate. Oh yah, I be okay, I guess.

BARB enters, looks at watch.

BARB   C'mon, are you ready to leave? I'm warming up the car.

ANNA   Gee, don't have to rush. Pretty hard leave my home. Take my little dresser, it's got my clothes. And my slippers, my knitting bag and that radio.

BARB follows instructions and tries to take ANNA's purse.

Not that one — don't just grab anything! Take that chair, only one I like to sit in when I sew, and that little table. Oh-oh, you better not forget to get me some ashes. Go get it, in the stove, okay?

BARB   *(walks to cooking stove)* Where's the ashes? What do you need them for?

ANNA   *(dismisses BARB, walks to wood stove)* Ahh you! Don't you know? Ashes! Ashes! Our people use them for protection! Gee — you don't know!

       Opens wood stove, scoops ashes into a can.

       Here, put it away. I'm gonna use in that place you take me.

BARB   Sorry, I'll be right back. The car's running. *(exits)*

ANNA   Ah, let that damn car run away! *(looks around house)* It's empty now. I raised up eight kids in this house. Now nobody. *(BARB enters)* Pretty soon we go. C'mere, I wanna show you something.

       Look over there, by the lake. I used to go there with my gramma when I was little girl. We hunt gopher, we singe them on the camp fire; we roast them, we fry them and we dry them till I can't eat them anymore. We stay maybe six or seven days. Then my gramma say time to go to next camp. So we go. Long time ago now. I always look out there when I sit here and sew. Must be thirty years I never see nobody camp there anymore. Must be that gopher nice and fat now!

BARB   Are you ready now?

ANNA   *(picks up her bag, and looks at the empty house)* Barbwire, pass me that drum. Time to go, I guess. *(walks to door)* I'm gonna sing a song — gonna be last time I'm gonna sing in this house, I guess. Yuh, I'm gonna say good-bye. *(sings good-bye song)* No more I see you, so I say good-bye.

       One strong beat on drum, and she exits with BARB.

Scene Two: Old Folks Home

       BARB and ANNA enter doorway, BARB is laden with bags, etc.

ANNA	Boy, this place sure stinks. Eww! Gosh — I feel lots of spirits everywhere. Oh-oh, where's my ash can?
BARB	See, this is your room. There's a coffee room, just across there. You can have coffee and visit other residents, cards, books, and . . .
ANNA	Can't you know?! I don't read. How am I gonna see that books? Got any comics books? That's the one I like, Jughead. He's got a funny hat and he likes to eat lots. Now, never mind; I gotta work now.

> *Sprinkles ashes in doorway.*

Now we can go in.

> *Walks around, feeling spirits.*

Whew! Boy, need lotsa work here. How many people die here, and you never clean it out!

BARB	It's clean, Anna.
ANNA	How come it stink then! *(laughs)* No, Barbwire, I mean our way! Boy, I gotta teach you. You don't know nothing! Okay, go get everything now! Gotta get my fridge, I'm hungry.

> *BARB exits. ANNA sprinkles ashes.*

ANNA	I don't know — lotsa old people here. What kinda place? Gee, funny way they got my bed too hard too. How am I gonna live here? Whiteman cook, I see them nurse. They men! I get shame. I can't let them help me. Gee, it's only my husband who see me naked. Crazy people! And I see cat. Oww. He sure is uggy. Fat. Them cats are no damn good for anything. They pee on everything. Damn thing, better stay outa here. That Barbwire, gee, I feel sorry. Nobody teach her anything, I guess. I can't see how — I know her grandma. She teach her good. Yuh, I remember that. Gee, what happened?

> *BARB enters with fridge, bag.*

ANNA	Finally, you come, Barbwire. Okay, you put that fridge there. I'm hungry now, so hurry up. Okay. Look at that bed. Wrong way — too hard too. I'm

	gonna get my grandchild to get good mattress. I see it that river when we drive in. So, river's over there. Now I gotta have my feet face the water when I sleep, see?
BARB	What — how come?
ANNA	Women's gotta do that. You should too, okay? Please, gotta move it round.

BARB moves the bed.

Gee, need more light in here, hey. How am I gonna knit? You knit?

BARB	No.
ANNA	Me, I knit lots. I can even knit them gloves. That's hard work. Just the same, I make it for all my granchilds.
BARB	You got lots of grandchildren?
ANNA	Yes, oh yes. Must be over forty of them. You'll see, they gonna visit me. What about you, you got kids?
BARB	No, I don't have any.
ANNA	Gee, that's gonna be pretty hard to have any grandchilds then, eh? Where's my purse? I wanna have a smoke now.

BARB hands ANNA her purse. ANNA finds what she needs and starts to roll cigarette.

BARB	Anna, you can't smoke in your room.
ANNA	How come? Regulations? Geez!
BARB	Yes, you can go to the coffee room.
ANNA	No, I gotta stay here. Gotta settle in, you know.

ANNA puts her smokes away, brings out Copenhagen.

Okay then, I'm gonna chew it. I need spitcan.

BARB	What kind?

ANNA   You know, you got any old coffee can or something?
                Go get it.

                *She puts snuff in her mouth. BARB exits.
                ANNA hangs up drum, Jesus picture, and starts
                to unpack. BARB enters with a can.*

BARB   Here you go, Anna. Where should I put it?

                ANNA can't talk.

                Right here? What's the matter?

                ANNA nods "no," and points.

                Okay — here.

                *BARB puts the can down, just in time for
                ANNA to spit.*

ANNA   Finally! Gee, hard to talk with snuff in my mouth.

BARB   Okay. Well, you look settled in. I better get to
                work. Anna, you see this string here? It's a call-
                bell. You pull it, and somebody will come, okay?

ANNA   Pull that thing? Gee, I didn't come here to pull
                strings!

                BARB starts to exit.

                Wait, I need help. Wind that clock.

                BARB does.

BARB   There you go. Welcome to your new home, Anna.

                BARB exits.

ANNA   This is not my home. It's just the place I stay. *(she
                goes to the call-bell, yelling)* Barbwire! Barbwire!

                BARB rushes in.

BARB   Is everything okay?

ANNA   Go ahead, pull that string, pull it! I need help.

                BARB pulls it.

BARB   Anna, you're supposed to pull it so you don't have to yell.

ANNA   No, I'm not gonna pull that thing. Thank you, you come. I forgot. You gotta call my grandchild, Mary Rose. She's in Vancouver. Boy, I sure miss her. Why she want to go to school? She's pretty smart already. There's her phone number — go ahead.

BARB dials and hands the phone to ANNA.

BARB   Okay. Goodnight, Anna.

ANNA   See you. Hello, Mary Rose! What you know! *(sing-song)* Boy, I have hard time today, see. Yes, it's today I gotta move. Gee nobody help. Everybody got job, got no time. Except that nurse, I call 'em Barbwire. Yeah. She help me, but she don't do it right. Make me tired. Pretty bad here. I got no friend. That damn Ethel, she trick me. I thought she live here, but no, she move to her daughter's. Gee. How you like it, your school? Oh yeah? Raining down there? You got rubbers? Oh-oh, I better send it. Cold that rain, you got good blanket? I got lots, I better send it to you. You don't forget your gramma. Write me letter, please, sweetheart. I need it. Okay. Good-bye. Do your best, Mary Rose. I love you too.

ANNA hangs up the phone.

Gee, I try it I guess. Nobody come see me, all the time. They say, they busy. Yuh. Then when it's time to go to Potlatch or tell story downtown, then they pick me up, dress me up and take picture. What the hell they gonna do with all those picture? They should come see me instead of look at my pictures. What they think, anyhow? They gonna get old too. Then who's gonna look after them?

Scene Three: Old Folks Home

Time has passed; ANNA has lived there a while.

A feline spirit enters and disturbs ANNA's knitting and pees on her slippers by the bed.

ANNA   Oh, no! Get out, damn cat! *(swatting at it with a
              cane)* Oh, no. He bother every damn thing! Oh, he
              stink up this place. My good moccasins! *(pulling
              the call-bell)* Barbwire! Barbwire! I need help. That
              damn cat! Why he live here anyways? I don't let
              animals live in my house. Gee, look at that! Gotta
              clean it up.

                   BARB goes to take ANNA's slippers.

              No, you leave them. I'm gonna wash it myself. Go
              get it. Dishsoap.

                   BARB exits.

              Gee, they always clean up here — wash everything. I
              only use my nightgown one time, here they gotta
              wash it. My moccasins too. They throw it into
              washing machine, then they throw it into dryer.
              They give it back to me. Just like board — how am
              I gonna wear it? Gee, I get mad. Everytime I go to
              breakfast, I come back and they clean. They move
              everything round, so I can't find anything. I can't
              hardly see, but I know where everything is, see?
              They clean, clean, clean. Clean so much, it stinks!
              Eww! Move my chair here, move my lamp there,
              and my spitcan. If they don't move my spitcan, I
              won't spit on the floor anymore! *(she spits)*

                   BARB enters with soap.

BARB   Here you go, Anna.

ANNA   You watch that Cat. Next time he come in here, he's
              gonna get trouble from me! I see him — he's got
              nice fur. Just like rabbits. He's pretty fat — I could
              make lots of slipper fur trim from him.

BARB   I gotta go, Anna.

ANNA   Never mind; sit down once in a while. I get
              lonesome, you know. I'm out of that chicken. Can
              you get some for me? *(digging around for money)*
              You know that kind — that's the only whiteman I
              know that knows how to cook good! Colonel
              Saunders! Boy, I like em. Is that twenty dollars?

BARB   Yes, it is.

ANNA	Okay. I want five chicken legs. No, six legs. Have one yourself, okay?
BARB	Okay.
ANNA	Yuh, I see that whitelady's face.
BARB	What?
ANNA	You know, what you call him? Queen. Yuh.
BARB	Yeah.
ANNA	Long time ago, she come to Whitehorse. Must be when they give her that fancy hat. My son, Jack, come running home: "Mama, Mama, the town's all bust up!" So I run downtown, see what's going on. Then I see her walking and waves her hand *(imitating the Queen's wave)* like that, see? She look pretty high tune to me, and I like her purse too. So I run up to her and touch her hand. You know, her hand feels just like mine!
BARB	Is that right?
ANNA	Yeah, I don't tell no bullshit story. Oh-oh. Can you help me to the toilet?
BARB	Yeah, here we go.
ANNA	Hurry, pee's gonna start. Oh no, now I wet myself. Make me mad, I told you help me quick!
BARB	Anna, I've put those incontinent pads on your dresser. If you wear them, you won't have that problem any more. *BARB hands ANNA the pads.*
ANNA	Lemme see. Ah you! What you think I am — baby? No, I'm not gonna wear it — diapers! *ANNA throws them down.*
BARB	Just give it a try, okay? *BARB puts them back on the dresser.*

Scene Four: Old Folks Home

> *Scene opens on ANNA, who's knitting. She checks the knitting, then pulls the call bell. BARB enters.*

BARB	Yes, Anna?
ANNA	I don't know. Is that you, Barbwire?
BARB	Yes.
ANNA	Good. I need your help, okay? Look like I skip my stitches. Better check. Count them up.

> *BARB does.*

BARB	Twenty three.
ANNA	Oh, oh. I drop one. I'm not feeling right, Barbwire. Where's my medicine?
BARB	We already gave you your morning medication.
ANNA	Oh, not those damn pills. I get tired of them. Doctor always try give them to me. Just like I'm drunk! Where is it that doctor? I'm gonna tell her take them herself. No, it's in a little jar, my Indian medicine.

> *BARB hands her a jar.*

Oh-oh. Just about finish it. Look it: you know that kind of willows, they look red.

BARB	I think so.
ANNA	That's the kind to use. Gotta peel it, then boil it down. See? Then steep it. I drink it ever'day; it helps with my arthritis.
BARB	Oh yeah? Hmm.
ANNA	Yuh, you should give it to them old people. It'll help them out. I see lots of those willows pretty close by, see . . .
BARB	Yeah, I think I noticed them too.

ANNA   What's happened to that whiteman? I see him walk
              around little while ago. Now I see him that chair
              with wheels.

BARB   Yeah. Well. He's pretty sick. He's got cancer.

ANNA   Oh, that cancer's pretty bad, get lots of my people
              too. Gosh, I feel pretty sad. They say that old David
              die, that's my people. Gosh, feel like everybody's
              leaving camp. They leaving me behind.

BARB   Oh Anna. I'm sorry about old David. That's too
              bad. They — I got some dry meat, from my auntie.
              You want some?

ANNA   Oh, boy! Gee, I teach you good, eh. Gunel cheesh.
              Thank you. Where's it the butter then? Sit down.

BARB   Got any tea?

ANNA   Yes. You know it.

BARB   That cat bother you anymore?

ANNA   You see that uggy thing around? Yuh, I fix him
              good! He try to get my dry meat. I club him good.
              Just the same, he come back. Boy, he must like to
              eat, because he's so fat!

BARB   Yeah, everybody feeds him.

ANNA   Shucks, everybody but Anna! My good dry meat
              from my friend in Old Crow. Gee, I got mad. So,
              I try to set a snare for him. I see him, sure nice fur.
              I was good trapper in my time, see? Lots of traps;
              I could get anything. You ever try it?

BARB   No. But I used to like it at my Grandpa's trapline.

ANNA   Yes, I know it. We used to travel by there, by
              dogteam. We stop by, visit. Your Grandma sure
              treat us good. She used to be busy all the time, wash
              that little girl's clothes.

BARB   Who's that?

ANNA   *(says an Indian name)* You say it.

              BARB tries to say it.

ANNA   (*giggling*) You better practise that one! Gotta know
                your name.

BARB   What? That was me?

ANNA   Sure, used to see your Gramma every spring. You
                too, until you had to go to that church school in
                Carcross.

BARB   I was five years old.

ANNA   Must be when you forget your name. That's okay,
                Barbwire — they give everyone hard time. Me too,
                my kids gotta go there. Boy, I sure get mad. What
                they gonna learn there? I try to sneak them away.
                Shucks, I need help with fishcamp, tan my hides, and
                I even had garden, down in Teslin.

BARB   Really?

ANNA   Yuh, I have fun, grow those vegetables. That's the
                time I like them. Not now, oow, I don't like them
                all the time. I grow carrots, turnips, tomatoes and
                fatatoes. Fatatoes, that's the time I like them. Not
                now! That damn cook here, he cook fatatoe pie,
                fatatoe pancakes, fatatoe soup. Gosh, he crazy. He
                should fry 'em up in oil, with onions. And once in a
                while put salt and pepper on them! Gee, I tell that
                cook, "I can help in the kitchen." He say, "You don't
                know how to cook, Anna." I say, "How you think I
                raise eight kids!" Barbwire, I getting pretty tired this
                place now.

BARB   Well, let's go for a walk, or I could take you to the
                mall, maybe.

ANNA   No, I want to go home. Just about my time to go.
                I can't die here. Gosh, my spirit might get stuck, so
                many around.

BARB   Have you talked to your family?

ANNA   No, never mind them. I want you to take me there.

BARB   Anna . . .

ANNA   What all you got to stay here for? You got no kids,
                            you got no husband. Just look after old people. You
                            come out there, nothing to worry about. Just my
                            light bill is seventeen dollars, and we charge up
                            groceries at the store. You can't say no, hey?

BARB   *(thinking)* What do you want to take?

ANNA   You know, everything. *(giggling)* Thank you, you
                            shoulda be Elder's helper instead. Get good pay, have
                            lots of fun!

                            Final Scene: Anna's Home

ANNA   Oh, hello, home! Boy, finally. Barbwire, you starta
                            that fire, get tea ready. Getting cold out now hey.
                            You go ahead. You know how I figure to come
                            home? I dream it. Couple of nights ago, I was
                            having a good dream about picking berries with my
                            sisters. We were just little girls, that time. We sure
                            have fun, eat lots of cranberries, roll around. Pretty
                            soon, my Momma call us girls. She say, "Liza,
                            Sara, Anna, it's time to go." Then my sisters starta
                            go. They say, "C'mon Anna, come with us. We
                            miss you." Gee, my heart get sore. I say, "No, I
                            still got something to do." So I watch them. Next
                            thing I see your funny face try to wake me up!

BARB   I remember that morning. You been pretty quiet
                            since then.

ANNA   Yes, I try to think of what all I have to do. And you,
                            I get pretty worried about that.

BARB   Why?

ANNA   Because I think your Grandma would want me to help
                            you out. You lost for little while, but pretty soon
                            light's gonna shine in you. Yuh.

BARB   Oh?

ANNA   Yeah. Don't you worry, you get good job after you
              finish here. Now where's that tea? Better get start.
              Where's them ashes? *(BARB gets them)* See, when
              I'm gone, you gotta sprinkle them all over the house;
              door windows and put on your forehead, right there.
              See, that way I won't try to take you to the spirit
              world, eh? You light that candles, put in windows.
              You tell that to my grandchilds too. Cover me up
              with my button blanket. Then after one year
              potlatch, you give it to my son. That drum, you
              keep it. I want you to learn songs. You gotta try it.
              Can't just sing "Old McDonald" all the time!

BARB   What do I do with...

ANNA   Listen good. The night after I pass over, you go
              outside, light a fire. Put some of my snuff in it — I
              gotta have a chew before I leave this place, see. You
              be okay. Gee, I'm not feeling right. Maybe close
              now.

BARB   What can I do, Anna? Do you need anything?

ANNA   Just sit with me. You help out good, now. Lotsa
              time I feel lonesome at that place, but when you
              come visit, I feel better.

              *BARB busies herself. ANNA settles in on her
              bed, she has her drum.*

              I gonna sing little song for you, "Barbara." It's good
              luck song. You young yet. Me, I'm ready to go
              now. *(sings short song)* Good enough. You better
              starta supper. *(BARB does)* No fatatoes!

BARB   Sure, Anna. Gunel cheesh for my "good luck song!"

ANNA   Oh, you speak my language now? Oh good.

              *While BARB starts cooking, ANNA slumps on
              the bed.*

BARB   Anna, you want some more tea? What about pilot
              bread?

              BARB turns to see ANNA.

              Oh! Anna? Anna?

> *BARB checks ANNA's vitals, gets up, walks to window and then starts on ANNA's instructions: ashes, candles, blanket on ANNA, then exits outside to make fire.*

ANNA   Gee, she did pretty good. When I really gonna die, I guess she get it right by then.

END

Colonial Tongues

by

Mansel Robinson

Kent Allen as Butch Barnett.

Mansel Robinson's *Colonial Tongues* is set in a small, single-industry town in northern Ontario. However, Robinson's provincial North is also a metaphor for Canada. The action takes place on June 30th, the day before Canada Day, in 1967 and in 1995, and this choice of our centenary is important. As the character, Butch, argues, Canada is disintegrating: either we acquiesce in this fate and become "a colony of a colony," or we "retrace our steps back to the very point we went wrong and. We. Start. Again." Robinson insists that, in a globalized world of "cyberspace and virtual reality," the "elemental realities of the north (distance, climate, work)" will be increasingly important, and that Canadians must remember "that the vast wealth of this country . . . comes out of the bush, the out-ports, the farms, the Arctic," not Bay Street or New York (qtd from 13 July 1998 letter to Sherrill Grace).

Colonial Tongues is a multi-levelled drama that makes a passionate plea for understanding and celebrating Canada and Canadian identity — before it is too late. On the realistic level, the story portrays the destruction of a family in a dying town, where the railway no longer operates, businesses have moved south, and the members of the Barnett family have been forced to leave their home: the father and elder son to fight in American wars; the daughter to make her fortune in the USA; the mother and younger son to live in poverty in southern Ontario. However, Edna Barnett and Butch try to fight this sell-out; after Edna's death, Butch returns North to rebuild the family home and the town.

On the symbolic level, *Colonial Tongues* is a deeply political play with as much anger and satiric edge as *Esker Mike & His Wife, Agiluk*. And because the story is so deeply rooted in the lives of working-class Canadians and the historical realities of single-resource northern towns, the political allegory works. Simply put, Robinson's lament is for the destruction of the North, which represents Canada and the Canadian way of life, by the South, by US interests, by corporatism and globalization, and, worst of all, by the internalization of a colonial mentality. The disintegration of the family parallels the collapse of the town, which parallels the steady erosion of the nation. "True patriot love" has become little more than a sour joke: "all our sons" are dead, gone South, or mad, and our daughters are traitors. As daughter, Hazel Barnett refuses to mother, nurture, or *become* our "home and native land"; she pursues NAFTA's promises of wealth through exploitation on a scale even larger than Canada's North can afford. The Mother country, our "true north strong and free," is forced to rent herself out, and she dies after losing everything.

At the centre of this domestic tragedy is Butch Barnett, the builder, dreamer, madman, and artist figure. When the play opens in 1967, Canada Day preparations are underway and a teenaged Butch is building a replica of a steam engine to celebrate Confederation. But without a break in the action (a requirement Robinson stresses), it is also 1995; the remnants of the Barnett family have gathered, and Butch is re-building the family home and the entire town. To do this he tries to re-create that June 30th 1967 when, for him, everything started to fall apart, and whether we interpret the co-existence of 1967 with 1995 as his memory play or as a deranged fantasy, we are nonetheless thrust back into the family quarrels and grief that put flesh and bones on the abstract issue of a national sell-out of resources, territory, and identity — "our home and native land."

Colonial Tongues is dense in allusion to history (Canadian and 20th century American), tall tales of the railroad, contemporary television news, with its sound bites and euphemisms ("friendly fire" is one important motif), and Canadian culture. Effective use is made of the national anthem and the Canadian flag, and the themes of the play invoke a host of other cultural icons from Wade Hemsworth's "The Blackfly Song" about northern Ontario survey crews, and Margaret Atwood's *Surfacing*, where Canadians also participate in the annihilation of their country while blaming it all on the Americans, to the cult film *Project Grizzly*, whose obsessive real-life hero recalls Butch.   Although the set must be minimal, even expressionistic, the characters' language is richly textured. Robinson's ear for speech, here the earthy working-class language of small town northern Ontario, is so sure that he carries us with him as he weaves motif and metaphor through the fabric of his text and the story-telling of his characters' lives. "All carpentry is poetry," Butch announces at the climax of his monologue on working language. Like Sam Shepard in *Buried Child* or *A Lie of the Mind*, Robinson roots national mythology in the poetry of everyday language and individual experience.

Completed in 1992 as Robinson's Masters' Thesis at Concordia University, *Colonial Tongues* was first published by Playwrights Canada Press in 1995. In addition to its premier in Saskatoon, the play has been produced by Occasional Arts Productions in Thunder Bay and the Great Canadian Theatre Company in Ottawa. The idea for *Colonial Tongues* grew from Robinson's familiarity with the kind of town represented in the play and from his grief at seeing places, which once were homes, turned into ghost towns. The play draws on his knowledge of mines and railways, and on the oral traditions of men, women, and work in the provincial norths of Canada. In *Slag* (Thistledown, 1997), he captures these voices in a series of prose and poetry meditations on the mines, railways, and cancelled towns of northern Ontario.   Robinson's second stage play, *Collateral Damage* (Blizzard, 1994), won the Saskatchewan Writers Guild award for drama in 1993.   In this play, he moves beyond national boundaries to explore political and personal corruption in a third-world setting.   He has also written radio plays, one of which, *The Education of Annie McBride*, is now the stage play *The Heart as it Lived* (Playwrights Canada Press, 1998). New work scheduled for production in 1998-99 includes a one-hander,

Spitting Slag, adapted from *Slag*, and *Downsizing Democracy*, about debt, deficits, taxes, corporate monopoly, and cut-backs. This play is "pretty funny," says Robinson, "if you can imagine . . . a scene about the Bank of Canada being funny" (qtd from 13 July 1998 letter to Sherrill Grace).

S G

* * *

Colonial Tongues was first produced by 25th Street Theatre in Saskatoon on 28 September 1993.

Butch Barnett	Kent Allen
Edna Barnett	Sharon Bakker
Del Barnett	Richard Hughes
Madison Frayne	Rob Roy
Hazel Barnett	Michelle Wilsdon

Directed by Rod MacIntyre
Set and lighting design by Stancil Campbell
Costume design by Beverley Kobelsky
Sound design by Jack Getzlaf
Stage Managed by Sheila Crampton

To the memory of

Hamel Robinson (1894--1988)
&
Billy Collinson (1925--1992)

Railroaders. Storytellers.

Playwright's Acknowledgements

Colonial Tongues began as an MA thesis for the Department of English, Concordia University, Montreal. A portion of the play, in an earlier version, was published in *32 Degrees*, DC Books, Montreal, 1993.

Many, many thanks to:

Henry Beissel, my thesis advisor, and Robert K. Martin, who was on the examining committee; Ann Lambert and Ray Beauchemin, good friends and good writers in the Concordia English program; the Banff Playwrights Colony, Playwrights Workshop Montreal, Saskatchewan Playwrights Centre and 25th Street Theatre for development assistance; Patti Shedden and Micheline Chevrier for dramaturgy; all the workshop actors, including David James, Kent Allen, Sharon Bakker, Richard Hughes, Rob Roy and Michelle Wilsdon; the Saskatchewan Arts Board for financial support; Don Dunbar, Catherine Cahill and my parents for letting me steal some of their stories; Rod MacIntyre for his own storytelling; Sharon Bakker for getting this thing from the bush to the prairie and beyond.

Mansel Robinson
May, 1995

COLONIAL TONGUES

CHARACTERS

EDNA BARNETT	Early 40's. She wears a house dress, an apron, slippers perhaps.
DEL BARNETT	Mid-20's. Green work pants, denim work coat, bare feet.
BUTCH BARNETT	Early 40's. Sweat pants, T-shirt, running shoes.
HAZEL BARNETT	Early 40's. Casual, monied.
MADISON FRAYNE	Early 40's. Casual, monied.

THE TIME

The scenes between DEL and EDNA take place on the last day of June, 1967. The scenes involving BUTCH, HAZEL and MADISON take place on the last day of June, 1995.

THE PLACE

The remains of a small town in northern Ontario. Some debris, but the look should be stark and lunar. A cyclorama might help. A raked stage is a possibility. Butch has recently begun construction of the house. Some tools and gear are scattered about: a chainsaw; a trunk; a tape deck; beer cases. A table and two chairs are in the "kitchen." Small markers have been placed around the house like grave markers in a potter's field.

MOVEMENT

The action is continuous — no blackouts between scenes.

The essential stage business of the 1995 scenes is Butch framing a small house. Pre-built stud walls can be carried in and pinned into place. This action should not be *realistic*; he might put up a door or window frame instead of a wall, the roof might be in place when the play opens. He works alone.

SOUND

The Saskatoon production employed a simplified and effective version of the sound effects indicated in the script.

Act One

A brief tableau of the five characters. EDNA is standing in her kitchen.

EDNA
Things went well.

DEL and MADISON exit. EDNA lights a cigarette, listening to the sounds of a town coming to life: church bells; baseball game; the shouts of children at recess; beery talk and laughter in the Legion hall; a hockey game; a steam engine, a train whistle; an outboard motor running fine for a moment, then it sputters, coughs, chokes and stalls. Silence.

For a time. *(taking a letter out of her apron pocket)* Can't you goddamn crooks at least throw me out of my house in English? Party of the first part, whereas and wherefore, you can kiss my royal arse.

EDNA sets the letter on fire, smiles, changes her mind, puts it out. She sits at the table; it rocks.

Jesus H. Christ, Del, you said you'd fix this friggin' table.

She folds an empty cigarette packet and uses it as a shim under the table. She calls "upstairs."

Del! Get out of bed!

No response. She walks into the "yard" and speaks as if BUTCH were present in 1967. He neither hears nor answers.

Looking good, Butch. Gonna be ready for the parade? *(pause)* You watch yourself with those power tools. *(pause)* You wanna take a break and go wake your brother up? *(pause)* Then hit him back. *(pause)*

Don't worry what Jesus says, maybe he was wrong.
(pause) Jesus was only human, you know. *(pause)*
Forget it, I'll do it.

> *She fiddles with the chain saw, and drops the*
> *spark plug in her pocket, muttering.*

That's all I need today, Butch bleeding to death in the
back yard. *(walking back into the house)* Del! Get
your drunkard's arse out of bed! Del!

DEL   *(shuffling in)* I'm up. I'm up, Christ what's the
hurry, it isn't Christmas morning is it?

> *His clothes are slept in. He's barefoot. He*
> *crosses to the "window."*

What's that crazy kid doing now?

EDNA   He's building something for the parade tomorrow.

DEL   Noisy little bugger.

> *He pours himself a coffee and sits at the table.*
> *He is painfully hungover.*

EDNA   You look like something caught in a leg-hold trap.
(pause) Worse. *(pause)* I heard you stumble in last
night.

DEL   Somebody musta moved the stairs. Sorry.

EDNA   I wasn't sleeping anyway.

DEL   Your stomach again?

EDNA   It's probably that goddamn television. Should never
have bought one. Like a little box of nightmares.
Another stupid war. Murders. People jumping out
of burning hotels. Radio's bad enough. Who needs
pictures? *(pause)* You were so drunk last night you
were trying to talk Chinese or Korean or something.
Foreign anyway. *(pause)* Were you thinking of your
Dad? *(patting his hand)* I was. All those dead boys
on TV. *(pause, remembers)* But you missed a call
last night. They couldn't find you. First work in
three weeks. You missed it. *(pause)* Did you hear
me?

DEL	Crumbs. *(laying his head on the table)* Nothing but crumbs.
EDNA	*(pause)* You want an aspirin?
DEL	Shot-gun'd work better.
EDNA	*(taking a bottle of aspirin out of her apron)* Here. *(pause)* Where were you this time?
DEL	Out.
EDNA	Don't remember, do you.
DEL	I remember.
EDNA	Liar.
DEL	I was over at Nita's.
EDNA	They tried Nita's.
DEL	I got there around ten.
EDNA	She phoned looking for you at eleven.
DEL	I met up with her later.
EDNA	Liar. You're going to lose that girl treating her that way. And lose the job too.
DEL	Some job.
EDNA	*(pause)* Well, wherever you were, it wasn't jail. *(checking his knuckles)* No fighting either. *(pause)* Course as a rule, it's your face that gets more marked up than your knuckles.

EDNA laughs and DEL pulls his hand away.

Drinking three nights running.

DEL	*(chews some aspirin and chases them with coffee)* Hey Ma.
EDNA	Don't change the subject.
DEL	Do you think you could put a little coffee in the coffee?
EDNA	It tastes just nice to me.

DEL	We're not sitting on the porch of the poorhouse.
EDNA	We'll be right inside the poorhouse you keep pissing your money up against the hotel. You need your arse kicked.
DEL	Hey, sorry, there's not a whole lot to do.
EDNA	Sorry, we should have named you "Sorry." Except for "beer," it's your favourite word.
DEL	Christ, did I kill somebody on my way home last night?
EDNA	I thought you remembered what you were up to last night.
DEL	*(pause)* Don't have a clue.
EDNA	So what is it? Good news or bad?
DEL	What do you mean?
EDNA	You're your father's son. He drank when he was happy and he drank when he was worried. Which is it?
DEL	Nothing. *(looking at her)* Boredom.
EDNA	You could go to work when they call you. And there's plenty of work around the house. You could start with the table.
DEL	*(giving it a shake)* There's nothing wrong with the table.
EDNA	I shimmed it up.
DEL	Oh.
EDNA	*(mimicking)* Oh. *(pause)* I'll ask your cousin to fix it.
DEL	I'll get around to it.
EDNA	Get him to help you.
DEL	*(getting up)* I don't need help. I ain't as good a carpenter as Jesus Christ but I can fix a goddamn table.

EDNA   Piss tank heathen. Are you really my son? *(as DEL
              starts to exit)* Where you going, I want to talk to
              you.

DEL   Excuse me, I gotta puke.

              DEL is gone.

EDNA   *(to herself)* Flush the toilet. Toronto needs the
              water.

              *EDNA goes into the living room and speaks as if
              HAZEL were present in 1967. HAZEL neither
              hears nor answers.*

EDNA   You oughta be outside, Hazel. It's a nice day.
              (pause) Did you get me those potatoes from the
              basement. *(pause)* Take a flashlight. *(pause)* Take
              the dog and the flashlight. *(pause)* You don't need
              Del. *(pause)* You gotta get over that being scared,
              there's nothing down there but potatoes. *(pause)*
              Fine. I'll make rice.

                              * * *

              BUTCH is somewhere in or on the house.

BUTCH   There are stories in this town.

HAZEL   There is no town.

BUTCH   That's because we screwed it up Hazel, we screwed up
              our priorities. You know — like "dying with
              dignity." Question: What happened to living with
              dignity? Why isn't that the priority?

HAZEL   I don't see much dignity here, Butch.

BUTCH   No? You will. Perhaps. I hope.

HAZEL   You hope?

BUTCH   Things were going like stink. Then we let ourselves
              get nailed by friendly fire. We sat on our hands while
              the town got her teeth kicked down her throat. But
              I've put her back together. I mean I've started to put
              her back together. You're standing in the map. The
              blueprint. *(pointing)* The station. The dairy.

Every town north of Superior has a rink and there's
ours, "Home of the Huskies." See it? Anglican
Church. Catholic Church. United Church. Our
street. Our house. Hazel. If you can read a map, we
can start over.

HAZEL   Why are you doing this?

BUTCH   It's obvious, isn't it?

HAZEL   No.

BUTCH   We're on highball train, Hazel, the engineer is dead or
drunk or crazy, there's been a rock slide, a wash out,
someone spiked the switch the wrong way *(HAZEL
knocks over a marker)* but the signals all read clear
approach *(HAZEL knocks over another marker)* we're
doing forty fifty sixty seventy eighty *(HAZEL picks
up another marker)* Stop! Stop.

HAZEL   Why are you doing this?

BUTCH   Because she was right.

HAZEL   Who?

BUTCH   Mom.

HAZEL   Oh Jesus.

BUTCH   She was right.

HAZEL   About what?

BUTCH   All of it.

HAZEL   She never got anything right in her life.

BUTCH   You never liked her did you?

HAZEL   It's simpler than that: I didn't want to become her.

BUTCH   But if she was right, Del was wrong.

HAZEL   What difference does it make. They're dead.

BUTCH   *(walking backwards)* So we retrace our steps back to
the very point we went wrong and. We. Start.
Again. *(tossing a marker at HAZEL)* Remember
Desy's?

HAZEL	Yeah, I shoplifted there every Friday night from the time I was six till I was sixteen. A bag of chips. A pop. Then I sold it to some kid.
BUTCH	Me. You sold the stuff to me.
HAZEL	(smiling) Yeah, I guess it was you. Sorry about that.

> HAZEL tosses the marker back. BUTCH places it. We hear the faint "ker-ching" of a cash register.

BUTCH	A crook even when you were six. Crazy 8's. Every time I won you changed the rules. You and whatsisface live in a mansion now Hazel? I bet you do. Big as a hockey rink. And as cold. Is your big house cold as a hockey rink?
HAZEL	Rinks aren't cold anymore.
BUTCH	That's right. They're not cold anymore. Hockey in Florida. They call that progress. They took our rink and put it in Florida. No wonder so few hockey players come out of Northern Ontario these days. All the rinks are in Florida.
HAZEL	I didn't come here to talk about hockey.
BUTCH	OK. (going to the trunk) You wanna talk about the map? Wedding pictures from 1940. Letters from Korea. Newspapers from '68. Things from the basement. Stories from Mom. You wanna talk about that?

> HAZEL tries to enter the house but the felt presence of EDNA stops her.

HAZEL	No.
BUTCH	How about music then? Maybe you came here to talk about music. "Del's Symphony." (HAZEL turns) Did you play the tape I sent you? You musta played it. Why else would you show up here? You ignored my other invitations. My wedding. Mom's funeral. "Del's Symphony." What did you think?
HAZEL	I think you're a sick man.

BUTCH   "Del's Symphony." *(doing Beethoven's Fifth —
                 opening notes)* Boom boom boom boom.

HAZEL   Have a little respect.

BUTCH   Respect? Well. You still have some old feelings for
                 Del. That's good. *(bitter)* That's something.

HAZEL   *(pause)* Are you going to tell me about it?

BUTCH   About living with dignity?

HAZEL   About the tape.

BUTCH   Del's Symphony.

HAZEL   Yes.

BUTCH   Say it. Del's Symphony.

HAZEL   *(pause)* Del's Symphony.

BUTCH   I'll tell you about it. As soon as you pick up a
                 hammer.

HAZEL   You were screwy as a kid. You've gotten worse.

BUTCH   No. Now I build for real.

HAZEL   *(looking around)* You're really gonna rebuild the
                 house?

BUTCH   Think bigger. *(placing a marker)* Lady Minto
                 Hospital.

                 The sound of a baby crying.

HAZEL   The whole town?

BUTCH   *(pause)* How did you get to be so "successful"
                 thinking so small?

                 *BUTCH picks up one of the markers. He
                 witches the air for sound. We hear a church bell.*

BUTCH   If this marker really were the Anglican Church then
                 perhaps, just perhaps, the steeple would work as an
                 antenna. Then perhaps, just perhaps we could tune in
                 the stories that I know, that both of us know, exist in
                 this town.

> *BUTCH places the church marker and picks up another — we hear talk in the Legion hall. He seems to chase it with his dowsing rod.*

Hear them? Endless arguments over double-draw in the Legion: The railroad will, the railroad will not, abandon the main line. The railroad will, the railroad will not, abandon us. *(another marker — clicking of a telegraph key)* At the telegraph office a message arrives dot dot dash dot, "F," dot dot dash, "U." "FU." Boy, that ain't good news. Stories, Hazel. The things Del taught us, how to whistle, how to play the spoons, how to pick off cans with a .22. *(sound of a .22 repeater)* The stories Mom hung on to, the things Mom hung on to, the basement full of the things she hung on tight to *(HAZEL steps away)* smelling of mildew and railroad creosote but she hung on tight. *(HAZEL exits)* What she hung on to, Hazel, not the commercials for some shiny with all the bells and whistles that we won't ever need, no, the things she hung on to.

> *BUTCH puts a marker carefully in place. We hear a sound fading up — a tinny, small town marching band warming up "O Canada." BUTCH exits.*

> *DEL is in "the living room." He sneaks a shot from a mickey. He talks as if HAZEL were present in 1967.*

DEL
Hi ya, Hazel. How's it going? *(pause)* Yeah, well, I had a rough night. Thanks for asking. *(pause)* Nah. I don't like parades. Especially this year. *(sings)* One little, two little, three little peckerheads. . . . *(pause, smiles)* That's right doll: Expo Sucky Seven. *(pause)* Losers. You got it. *(pause)* Nah. I gotta talk to the old lady. See ya later. *(turns away)* Hey doll. The next time you steal tobacco, close the pouch. It goes stale pretty fast. *(pause)* I ain't gonna tell anybody. You wanna smoke, smoke. You got a mind of your own. See ya.

> *DEL goes back into the kitchen.*

EDNA
Ready?

DEL	I need a cigarette. *(rolling himself a smoke)*
EDNA	*(pause)* Come on Del, you're not rolling for the Queen, I'd like to talk today.
DEL	I can't wake up without a smoke.
EDNA	By the time you wake up you won't have a pot to piss in . . .
DEL	Give me a minute, all right?
EDNA	. . . or a window to throw it out of.
DEL	Jesus, you're crude.
EDNA	Whatever it takes to get your attention.
DEL	What, is the house on fire?
EDNA	*(taking the letter from her apron pocket and putting it in front of DEL)* Yes.

> *DEL reads the letter. He tries to pour a shot of whisky in EDNA's mug. She stops him. He pours himself one.*

Whisky. Is that your answer?

DEL	When did you get this?
EDNA	A week. Two. I didn't say anything. I've been trying to come up with a plan.
DEL	Do the kids know?
EDNA	They'd just get scared.
DEL	*(pause)* You look tired.
EDNA	I am tired. And I'm running out of time.
DEL	You coulda told me sooner.
EDNA	You got enough on your plate.
DEL	I got nothing on my plate.
EDNA	You know what I mean. Goddamnit all. What did we do, Del? What did I do wrong?

DEL	Maybe you shoulda picked yourself richer parents. *(EDNA glares at him)* It's a joke.
EDNA	If you want to cheer me up, tell me how to hang on to my house.
DEL	*(pause)* A house isn't much. Some two by fours, a window to look out of, a roof for the snow and a door to —
EDNA	*(cutting him off)* Slam on a shyster's face.
DEL	A door to close behind you when you leave. You take the family pictures and you find a new wall to hang 'em on.
EDNA	*(pause)* Can't you hear it?
DEL	What?
EDNA	Listen.
DEL	Hear what? The mice in the walls?
EDNA	There's no mice in this house.
DEL	Rats then.
EDNA	Should have drowned you at birth.
DEL	You missed your chance.
EDNA	The house talks, Del.
DEL	Jesus. Lock her up. Talking door-knobs.
EDNA	Don't be so goddamned literal-minded.
DEL	You said the house talks.
EDNA	The day your father went missing, I was sitting here alone. I felt a tap on my shoulder. Then we get a telegram from the army. Two weeks ago, another tap on the shoulder. And a letter from Cyrus at the bank. We've been here so long the house knows bad news is coming before it gets here. It knows.
DEL	Close your mouth, the neighbours will hear.

EDNA   Mrs. Lepage'll tell you. She looked after the house
            one January when we were at Aunt Elsie's. A blowy
            cold night. She was worried about the furnace going
            out and the water freezing up. She stoked the furnace,
            then made herself a cup of tea, you know, just to sit
            for a moment till the kitchen warmed up a little. She
            was hardly finished her cup when the creaking started
            on the stairs, like someone was coming down. The
            creaking stopped about half-way.

DEL   Frost.

EDNA   Someone came down. Looked over the banister and
            saw a friend of the family sitting drinking tea in the
            kitchen. So it went back upstairs.

DEL   Mrs. Lepage makes a lot of dandelion wine for a
            widow.

EDNA   Don't judge other people by your own mirror, boy.
            (pause) Some nights I hear him breathe.

DEL   Who?

EDNA   Your old man.

DEL   Christ.

EDNA   Sometimes he snores. Like he's been drinking
            heavy, maybe poisoned himself. His breath catches
            in the back of his throat, that's what wakes me up,
            that catch. And the sudden quiet. I lie there waiting
            for his breath and his heart to start again. He starts to
            breath. Then I can sleep.

DEL   It's a dream.

EDNA   Sometimes I know, I know, he's still alive.

DEL   Fourteen years.

EDNA   You hear stories of men wandering around with
            amnesia, drifting after a war. Living alone when they
            have a wife and kids, pets even, a house and job
            waiting for them maybe just over in the next town.
            But they don't know. They can't remember.

DEL   I don't think so, Ma. Fourteen years.

EDNA	Not dead. Missing in action. He could be anywhere. The sandy, sunny south. Who knows?
DEL	That's just wishful thinking, Ma.
EDNA	No body.
DEL	He's dead.
EDNA	You haven't heard him snore.

* * *

MADISON is at the extreme edge of the town. No stranger to the bush, he is tying flies, concentrated, happy. HAZEL enters.

MADISON	I've designed a new trout fly. I call it "Nietzche with Plume." Do you like it?
HAZEL	Great. You're going to fish.
MADISON	That was the agreement. I deal with the trout while you deal with your brother. *(pause)* So what happened?
HAZEL	He's a sawed-off little prick is what happened.
MADISON	Don't be vulgar, Hazel. It was a simple question.
HAZEL	I like being vulgar. It relaxes me.
MADISON	You ought to read Samuel Johnson. You would never hear Samuel Johnson say, "My brother is a prick."
HAZEL	Did he have a brother?
MADISON	I'm talking about verbal architecture.
HAZEL	Architecturally speaking, my brother is a sawed-off little prick.
MADISON	*(pause)* Do you need a drink?
HAZEL	I don't think booze is the answer.
MADISON	I brought Scotch and Drambuie. I didn't bring any... booze.

HAZEL	Liquor then, I keep forgetting you were born with a silver pickle up your ass.
MADISON	*(grins)* You know I consider class warfare an aphrodisiac. But let's stay on task, OK?
HAZEL	He's a pack rat. He's got a trunk full of old letters and stuff.
MADISON	A trunkful of memories. Not a very original thinker is he?
HAZEL	He's rebuilding the old house. Can you believe it? *(shaking her head)* Drafty old barn. Icicles hanging off the eaves, four feet long. I used to break them with snow-balls — they'd drop like knives. That's where I put the snowmen — underneath the eaves. Drop those four foot knives right through their skulls. He'd cry when I did that.
MADISON	Still in mourning for long-deceased snowmen. He needs Thorazine. Lithium perhaps. A pharmaceutical lobotomy. Maybe even the actual thing. *(looking at HAZEL)* I hope this... pathological nostalgia doesn't run in your family.
HAZEL	There's nothing wrong with the family tree. Butch fell out and landed on his head. He's so... what... so....
MADISON	Sounds like a hillbilly. Psychotic maybe, but a hillbilly.
HAZEL	Intense, mono-something-or-other.
MADISON	Monomaniacal. Only in your brother's case it's nothing so romantic. He isn't single-minded. He's simple-minded.
HAZEL	He scares me.
MADISON	You can't be afraid of a house.
HAZEL	House my ass. It's an eight-room coffin. *(pause)* And that goddamn tape.

MADISON	Those shoddy sound effects? It's nothing. Butch is trying to manipulate you. Using the oldest family technique — guilt — for the oldest family value — money.
HAZEL	He didn't ask for money.
MADISON	He will.
HAZEL	You have it all figured out, don't you?
MADISON	All I know is that you didn't have a brother till he sent you that tragic little epistle three weeks ago.
HAZEL	Well I have a brother now, don't I?
MADISON	Your choice.
HAZEL	Choice, Christ.
MADISON	Your choice.
HAZEL	I heard you the first time. Epistle? Give me a break. Epistle.
MADISON	An archaic document. An artifact. It complements your ghosts.
HAZEL	I don't have any ghosts.
MADISON	"It's an eight-room coffin." Unquote. *(waiting)* Do you want to go home?
HAZEL	I am home. That's his point.
MADISON	Then show me around.
HAZEL	There's nothing to see but bush.
MADISON	*(referring to the markers)* Public school. Dairy. Main Street.
HAZEL	It's just a bunch of sticks in the ground.
MADISON	Exactly. Shall we?
HAZEL	I need some time.

MADISON   As the man said, our lives are poor, solitary, nasty, brutish and short. We don't have a lot of time for this, we have a business to run. *(gently)* There's nothing here. A mentally-ill man with his plywood and roofing nails, a few memories tossing about in the wind.

HAZEL   My memories.

MADISON   But harmless. You look over Butch's souvenirs, find out what he wants. A little fishing, a little vacation in nostalgialand. And then we get back to work before some trade union cementhead puts our whole operation down the toilet. Love? I'm here to help. *(holding out his hand)*

               Pause. They head into "town."

MADISON   What do you see?

HAZEL   I danced in the gym and learned about the American Civil War in this school. *(she walks)* I see the garbage man. He was old and skinny, gaps in his yellow teeth. But his horses were magical, patient as saints as he dumped the cans into the wagon. Steam from their nostrils in winter. I dreamed they were dragons.

MADISON   Pretty.

HAZEL   *(she walks)* My boyfriend lived here. He must have written me twenty letters asking me not to go away. The last night we went to Lover's Lane. Just for him I didn't wear any underwear.

MADISON   A lucky boy.

HAZEL   *(she walks)* The train station.... We put Del on the train. Me. Butch. Del's girlfriend. My mother wouldn't come. He waved good-bye from the bar car window.

MADISON   How Canadian.

HAZEL   I thought he was some kind of magician.... It was
                        like he whistled up that train and poof.... Gone in a
                        cloud of steam. The last time I see Del he flies off
                        on a magic carpet. And I'm crying. But not because
                        I'm sad, I'm crying because I'm jealous. *(pause)*
                        Then Butch sends me a little package in the mail and
                        I find out Del ended up just another gutless thing
                        bawling for his mother. *(pause)* Harmless, eh
                        Madsion? Just a few harmless memories tossing
                        about in the wind. Unquote.

MADISON   We can pave over the past.

HAZEL   I forget how.

MADISON   Whatever it takes. Ambition. Sex. *(pause)* Sex.

HAZEL   *(smiling)* Will it work?

MADISON   Let's find out.

HAZEL   You wanna play here?

MADISON   *(shaking his head)* Lover's Lane.

HAZEL   *(smiling)* I'm glad you're with me.

MADISON   I want you to be happy again.

                            MADISON holds out his hand. They exit.

                                    * * *

DEL   Maybe it really is time to leave. Just pack it up and
                        go.

EDNA   You're not on the river now. This isn't a camp-site,
                        it's a home. You don't leave a home.

DEL   You don't have any choice, they've taken it from
                        you.

EDNA   If they were coming for that bottle you'd be up on
                        your hind legs. *(as she grabs for the bottle, DEL
                        snatches it away)* See?

DEL   It isn't one house, it isn't just our house. Ten years
        from now, fifteen maybe, Main Street will look like
        somebody kicked her front teeth in. Those goddamn
        diesels don't need firemen. They don't need the
        shops, or the roundhouse either. Ma. The town is
        dying. It might already be dead. It's over. We just
        got our notice a little early.

EDNA   If you were twelve and I said Cyrus was coming for
        our house he'd get a boulder through his front
        window. The bullies never got away without a scrap
        from you. Never.

DEL   You can beat a bully. But you don't argue with a
        bouncer. You don't argue with a banker. They're
        pros.

EDNA   Should have killed all the bankers in the Depression.

DEL   There's nice Christian talk.

EDNA   Christians, Jesus, I share a pew with Cyrus.

DEL   Maybe you should have married him instead.

EDNA   I'd rather kill him.

DEL   Marry him first so you can collect the insurance.

EDNA   He's married to Martha Parker. Use your head.

DEL   Kill her, marry him, kill him, collect, keep the
        house. Problem solved.

EDNA   I like Martha!

DEL   You see? He married a woman you like too much to
        kill. That's a pro.

EDNA   Jesus, what nonsense have you got me talking?

DEL   Go see him.

EDNA   I did. He said it was my own fault, I should have
        done something years ago when things started to turn
        sour. Take in boarders or something. Boarders.
        Jesus. My mother took in boarders. I'll be
        goddamned if I'm going backwards. I told him I
        wasn't raising my children in a two-dollar hotel. It's

bad enough they got a brother who uses this place
like one. That's all we need, some boomtown drifters
feeding their booze to Butch, four or five of 'em
sniffing around Hazel.

DEL   Maybe they'll be more interested in you.

EDNA   What's that supposed to mean?

DEL   Maybe you really ought to get married again.

EDNA   Did you have someone in mind or was I supposed to
                    pick him out at gun-point?

DEL   You aren't... old.

EDNA   You almost broke your face getting that one out.

DEL   Well, you aren't.

EDNA   Thanks, pup, but I've had it with boomers. *(catching
                    herself, getting back on track)* He talked in numbers.
                    Not words. Numbers.

DEL   Cyrus? He's a banker.

EDNA   He's an adding machine.

DEL   It's his job.

EDNA   His job is to serve the community.

DEL   Isn't that in the Bible somewhere? Genesis maybe?

EDNA   Keep your heathen tongue off the Bible.

DEL   No. Sounds more like the New Testament.
                    Matthew, Mark, Larry, Moe and Curly-Joe.

EDNA   Drunken pup. Should've drowned you.

DEL   What kind of offer did you make him?

EDNA   I offered to stay in my house. I work. I pay my bills
                    and give him whatever's left over. That's my plan.
                    It was good enough last year and the year before that.
                    It should be good enough now.

DEL   But it's not good enough. *(waiting)* Is it?

EDNA   It's the best I can do. What have you been doing?

> *DEL pulls some change from his pocket and*
> *spills it onto the table.*

DEL   That's all I got.

EDNA   If you'd go to work . . .

DEL   One trip a month isn't going to buy us five fucking minutes.

EDNA   I can still wash your mouth out with Sunlight soap.

DEL   You wanna see an ancient artifact? That's me — a souvenir from the good old days. I shoulda been a fireman and as good at it as the old man. But there's no firing left to do. So stuff me with feathers, hang a sign on my neck and stick me in the museum with John A's whisky bottles. Zip, zero, fuck all.

EDNA   What the hell's the matter with you?

DEL   You want me to come up with a plan? OK. Bootlegging. No? Um. Sell a little pot to the hippies in Toronto? No, no, no. Beer bottles. Yeah. Collecting beer bottles. As a family. Up and down the lanes, day and night. There's a job for us. Two cents a bottle. We can do that until the pensions come in.

EDNA   I just want my goddamn family to live like a goddamn family.

DEL   It don't look good, Ma. Pack it in. Or open the doors to drunken young men prowling the halls at night. . . .

> *DEL mimics the cretins he describes.*

EDNA   Not in this house.

DEL   Leering, lonely young boomers . . .

EDNA   I want a family.

DEL   . . . horny as goats. . . .

EDNA   Stop it.

DEL   Their pockets jingling with coin. . . .

EDNA	No.
DEL	Then he won, Ma. That prick who shares your pew. He won.
EDNA	*(pause)* Yeah. You look like your father. *(grabbing him by the chin)* But you roll over like you been fixed at the vet.

* * *

> *HAZEL watches as BUTCH puts up the back wall of the house. We hear the voice of DEL SR.*

DEL SR.	*(voice over)* This man gets on the *Canadian* at Nipigon. He's been drinking beer all day.

> *As DEL SR. speaks, EDNA hangs a photograph of him.*

BUTCH	You're standing on Main Street. Facing the river. Turn to your left. What do you see at the end of the street? *(waiting)* I know you remember. *(waiting)* It's summer time. The sidewalk is hot. Maybe you're eating a butterscotch ice-cream. *(waiting)* People then. Who's on the street? Think of the people you liked.
HAZEL	All the people I liked lived somewhere else.
BUTCH	*(pause)* The parade on the First of July. *(waiting)* In '67 I built a little steam engine. Even the smoke stack worked, I had a little smudge pot in it. Big goggles like in the pictures of Dad. I won first prize. It was the Centennial year. A big deal. I made this great little Canadian flag. *(sings)* "It's the hundredth anniversary of Confederation, everybody sing together . . ."
HAZEL	Don't be such a goddamn retard.
BUTCH	Ha! You see? Retard. No one uses that word anymore. Retard. "What are ya, some kinda retard?" That's history. History, Hazel. History! *(waiting)* Remember the year of the big fire? The town was evacuated. Ash was dropping from the sky. But the old lady wouldn't leave. Neither would the cat. It hid

under the house and wouldn't come out. Mom
hooked up the garden hose and soaked down the roof.
A garden hose against a forest fire. You said she was
nuts, like pissing on a volcano you said.

HAZEL   She was nuts — the town was gonna burn to the
ground.

BUTCH   Only if she let it.

HAZEL   What are you saying, the old girl saved the town by
watering her roof?

BUTCH   She stayed. Like the cat. That's all it took. One old
woman and a cat and then the wind shifted and the
town was saved.

HAZEL   *(a serious question)* Are you ill?

BUTCH   You mean does my elevator go all the way to the top
floor?

HAZEL   Does it?

BUTCH   In other words, am I three sandwiches short of a
picnic?

HAZEL   Are you?

> BUTCH *moves to the trunk and removes a stack
> of papers — his documents.*

BUTCH   I'm not sick, but I got a file a mile thick. Wanna see
it? Here's the post-cards you sent Mom. One postcard a year, every Christmas.

HAZEL   Families drift apart.

BUTCH   You got a hole inside of you the size of an INCO
mine shaft. We can fix that.

HAZEL   You don't know anything about me.

BUTCH   You sent her post-cards.

HAZEL   What's your point?

BUTCH   When this town died she was left with nothing.

HAZEL   You looked after her didn't you?

BUTCH	I tried.
HAZEL	A little granny flat in the city. Her junk from the basement. That's all she needed.
BUTCH	She hung on to things. Is that such a crime?
HAZEL	Pack-rats in this family, can't think straight for the crap they got hanging around their necks.
BUTCH	And what do you have?
HAZEL	Lots.
BUTCH	Yeah, you're a big shot.
HAZEL	Look. Maybe squeezing rivets in a St. Catharines auto plant was good enough for you. But not for me.
BUTCH	So you became a big-shot, a boss, hip hip hooray.
HAZEL	I worked for what I got. I'm happy.
BUTCH	Got a lot of people working for you, a few toads to kick around. How many? Ten? Forty? A hundred? You got yourself a whole little town. I salute you. Wanna read Mom's will?
HAZEL	No.
BUTCH	No, there's not much in it. Not enough for a big shot anyway.
HAZEL	I don't need a thing. Not from you. Not from her. Not from this graveyard you call home.
BUTCH	How about my pink slip, my bon voyage from General Motors. Wanna read that? But I guess you know what they say, being a big-shot, must have signed a lot of those in that little town you own. Repossession of a house. Here's Mom's. Here's mine. Wanna see? No? Signed any of those?
HAZEL	Is that why you lured me up here? To feel sorry for you?

BUTCH	*(taking a level and holding it against a stud)* Dead plumb. I don't need pity. *(back to the documents)* See some pictures of my kids? Did you know I named them Del and Hazel? Don't learn do I? *(pause)* I feel sorry for them.
HAZEL	Go back to them. Forget this lunatic crusade and go back to them.
BUTCH	*(flinging a document, like a frisbee at HAZEL)* Separation papers. *(flinging another one)* Divorce papers. *(again)* Visitation rights. What kind of invention is "visitation rights?"
HAZEL	Did your wife leave you before or after you went crazy?
BUTCH	Wasn't her fault, poor woman was born in a shopping mall window. Oh, this town was something, Hazel. And it was ours. Our own power plant.
HAZEL	Yeah, three gerbils and a bicycle wheel.
BUTCH	Our own dairy. Downey baked our bread for us, we didn't have to truck it in.
HAZEL	Any girl, any age, Downey tried to check her "buns" for "freshness."
BUTCH	Two pop plants, two hardware stores, you name it.
HAZEL	We went to school in a condemned building. The dentist was blind. The doctor was a drunk. There were no good old days here.
BUTCH	But we gave it away. This place. The north. We had everything we needed. We could have built a home. But we volunteered to build our own coffins instead. We don't run a thing anymore. It's all run by somebody from somewhere else. We turned this place into a colony of a colony.
HAZEL	That's right Butch. I run things. You weren't smart enough. You weren't fast enough. You weren't butch enough. Don't give me any shit about dignity, about colonies of colonies. You screwed up. But I run my life.

BUTCH	For how long?
HAZEL	For as long as I say.
BUTCH	You're naive.
HAZEL	You're nostalgic.
BUTCH	Where'd you get that word from? That yuppie pirate you come up with? Anything more than five years old we dump it like it was toxic. You know what happened to the graveyard after the town died? After the town was murdered? They moved the gravestones south but they left our dead in the ground like old chicken bones. I've been out there. The stones I guess were worth money so people hung on to those. Probably even had a service when the stones went back in the ground. "Our dollar who art our Heaven, hallowed be thy name." But our people — old chicken bones. You should go out to the graveyard. There's something I want you to see.
HAZEL	What else have you done?
BUTCH	Go see.
HAZEL	Jesus Christ. What is this place anyway? Huh? What is it really?
BUTCH	I told you. We were wrong. Dad left. Del left. You left. I left, like we were pulling the legs off a cat. But Del, Del was the worst.
HAZEL	Del had guts.
BUTCH	How long before you lose everything? Like I did.
HAZEL	I don't lose.
BUTCH	*(pause)* I made myself a copy.

> *BUTCH goes to the tape machine and starts the tape. The sound of a fire fight. He flips the tape off.*

BUTCH   The technical term is friendly fire, recently updated to "fratricidal casualties." Our own bombs landing on our own people. As in we do the bad guys the favour of killing ourselves. As in you can't trust anybody. As in that's Del under all that.

HAZEL   You get sicker by the minute.

BUTCH   I got the tape from Nita. Remember Nita? *(taking a soiled Canadian flag out of the trunk)* And this? The end of June. 1967. We followed Del to Nita's place. She gave him this. She got naked and danced, wearing this. *(wrapping himself in the flag and dancing)* They got drunk and cried. We watched through the window. She went over too. '69 or '70. A nurse, right? I was in Cornwall a while ago, looking for work. That was the last place we had an address for her. So I looked her up.

HAZEL   *(pause)* How's she doing?

BUTCH   She eats out of garbage cans...

HAZEL   Stop it.

BUTCH   . . . jerks off the drunks for sandwich money. . . .

HAZEL   Stop it.

BUTCH   No, you listen. You need to listen. I guess Nita didn't like what she saw over there. All the blood and the lies mixed up with Del and high school and the kids they were going to have. She was cooked, whacko.

HAZEL moves away.

She needed new shoes. I bought some for her. I saw her one time after that, a day or two later. She must've hawked the shoes as soon as I turned the corner. She looked like the wrath of God, though, new shoes or not. But we can fix Nita too. We can fix everyone.

HAZEL   *(pause, looking down the street)* Butch. I do see something down at the end of Main Street. The ice-house.

BUTCH   Thank you. The ice-house.

> BUTCH *picks up a marker and puts it in*
> *position. We hear the short blast of a train*
> *whistle.*

That's right. The ice house. Big blocks of ice to cool the passenger trains — when — '62?

HAZEL   Shit brindle brown.

BUTCH   What?

HAZEL   The colour. CPR shit brindle brown. Whenever I think of home that's the colour I think of. Shit brindle brown. The colour of outhouses.

> *They exit opposite.*

                        * * *

> *During* HAZEL's *"shit" speech,* EDNA *has hung*
> *a brightly-coloured curtain.*

DEL   If I told you you could move anywhere, anywhere at all, where would you go?

EDNA   *(pause)* Are you in trouble with the law?

DEL   Just answer the question. Anywhere at all.

EDNA   You're changing the subject.

DEL   Forget about the house.

EDNA   I can't.

DEL   For a minute.

EDNA   Perth's nice.

DEL   Australia?

EDNA   The Ottawa Valley.

DEL   Jesus.

EDNA   It's nice.

DEL   I said any place. *(pause)* How about the States?

EDNA   What about them?

DEL	Isn't there a place you've thought about?
EDNA	I told you. Perth.
DEL	In the States.
EDNA	You are in trouble with the cops. What did you do?
DEL	Ma.
EDNA	Cheboigan.
DEL	What?
EDNA	Cheboigan. It's in Michigan. I always liked the name. Cheboigan. Cheboigan. This is a stupid conversation.
DEL	Cheboigan. Another dirty little town stuck in the middle of the nowhere bush. C'mon, there's a whole country to choose from. New Orleans. San Francisco. Nashville. Those are magical names. How can you compare Perth to New Orleans?
EDNA	Your grandparents didn't come from New Orleans. They came from Perth.
DEL	So?
EDNA	Nobody in the family ever came from the States What the hell you talking about American cities for?
DEL	There's life there, Ma. People. Jobs.
EDNA	Jobs. Yes, I've heard of those things.
DEL	Decent schools. More than one show. Restaurants. Art galleries.
EDNA	High on your list, I can tell.
DEL	Clubs, the best music in the world.
EDNA	Bars, now you're being honest.
DEL	You see?
EDNA	New Orleans is a long way to go for a beer-parlour.
DEL	You have the imagination of a duck.

EDNA	So who is it?
DEL	Who's what?
EDNA	Maggie Edwards said you've checked the mail every day for the past two weeks. You must be expecting something from someone.
DEL	Maggie talks better than she sorts mail.
EDNA	Who is it?
DEL	What?
EDNA	The girl?
DEL	What girl?
EDNA	This nonsense about New Orleans. You met an American girl, didn't you? Is that why you've been ignoring Nita? 'Cause you met some American tourist?
DEL	No.
EDNA	Don't give me that. If it isn't a girl, how come you were mooning around the post office. Did you join a book club?
DEL	What if I did?
EDNA	It would have to be one for colouring books.
DEL	(*pause*) Sometimes I think you really are as hateful as you talk.
EDNA	Jesus, I've been trying to talk to you for three days, you've been hiding from me, hiding in that goddamn bottle. Now I get this nonsense about New Orleans. (*pause*) You're leaving, aren't you? Leaving town. (*pause*) Your timing stinks.
DEL	One call in three weeks. Even if I was here to take it, I'm barely paying my way. I'd be better off — we'd be better off if I was working somewhere else.
EDNA	What is it with the men in this family?
DEL	Listen.

EDNA   You think women were born to listen.

DEL   Things have a way of working out.

EDNA   But they don't always work out well. *(pause)* What
                  about Butch and Hazel?

DEL   You just said I was a bad influence.

EDNA   In the last little while, yeah, with your boozing and
                  all. But at least you're around.

DEL   Get them another dog.

EDNA   I don't treat you that way. Jesus, can't we have just
                  one conversation, you're as slippery as minnows.
                  (pause) Where are you going?

DEL   Does it matter?

EDNA   *(pause)* I see it every June. The kids graduate and
                  somebody else is going down to Windsor or Oakville.
                  A nice little job. Nice little shopping mall. Come
                  home every third Christmas to keep the old lady
                  happy. *(pause)* What do you think it is about
                  railroad towns that makes everybody want to move?

DEL   It's the new diesels. They make us restless. They
                  idle all night in the yards. Shaking our beds.
                  Shaking our dreams.

EDNA   They don't shake my dreams.

DEL   No, Ma. They shake mine.

                              * * *

                  *MADISON is flyfishing. His actions are
                  elegant, precise, graceful, HAZEL watches.*

HAZEL   Beautiful.

MADISON   I can teach you.

HAZEL   It's OK. Any luck?

MADISON   It's good fishing. And you?

HAZEL   Lover's Lane was fun. But it didn't work.

MADISON	*(casting again)* I got a call on the cell phone about an hour ago. Kentucky has made another offer.
HAZEL	Are you still talking to those guys?
MADISON	Yes.
HAZEL	Give it up.
MADISON	Hazel. We will discuss this.
HAZEL	Madison. We have discussed this.
MADISON	The tax deferrals have been extended ten years. Not a union in sight. It's a dream.
HAZEL	Fuck Kentucky.
MADISON	This is a dynamite package and you know it.
HAZEL	I have other things on my mind.
MADISON	The matter of Butch and his hillbilly madness can be solved with a key-stroke. Delete. Clear screen. New document: Kentucky. The best offer we will ever get.
HAZEL	I'm trying to deal with Butch, OK?
MADISON	Don't try. Do it.
HAZEL	Tell me the truth. You were born thirty years old. Aliens stole your family. What?
MADISON	Yesterday or today. Your choice.
HAZEL	*(pause)* Do you know what he did?
MADISON	Surprise me.
HAZEL	They never found my father's body. But my mother put up a tombstone anyway. Butch dug it up — he stole it and moved it back up here. He's rebuilding the whole goddamn thing, right down to the graveyard. My old man's stone is the first one in it.

MADISON goes to her.

Del. The old man. My mother. They were gone. I was free. As free as you.

MADISON	Kentucky is freedom.

HAZEL	Listen to me. I'm trying to leave. No. I left. Now I got this goddamn anchor around my throat.
MADISON	I've been dancing with Kentucky for months and for months you've been too timid to make the move. You turned back into a fucking hillbilly long before Butch interfered in our lives. Admit it: you don't have the guts for business.
HAZEL	*(pause)* I do have a confession to make. But that isn't it.
	HAZEL pulls a pen from MADISON's pocket and scribbles some numbers on his hand.
MADISON	What's this?
HAZEL	A better offer.
MADISON	What do you mean?
HAZEL	Better. You know. Better.
MADISON	An offer.
HAZEL	What, did you have a stroke this afternoon? An offer to relocate. That's the cash part.
MADISON	Relocate where?
HAZEL	On the Maquiladora.
MADISON	We never approached the Mexicans.
HAZEL	The deal beats Kentucky all to hell.
MADISON	You're serious.
HAZEL	Don't fuck with a Lake Superior hillbilly.
MADISON	How long has this been going on?
HAZEL	A while. I was stalling you with that fuck Kentucky thing while I worked out the details.
MADISON	All behind my back.
HAZEL	I had to prove to myself that I could do it on my own. I'm not going to apologize.
MADISON	I don't expect you to. Unless these are pesos.

HAZEL   You're not mad at me?

MADISON   Are these pesos?

HAZEL   Give me a little credit.

MADISON   Then I'm delighted. Ecstatic. If this is solid — my
                 God — Is this solid?

HAZEL   *(pause)* I didn't close.

MADISON   But you will. *(pause)* This is what we've worked
                 for. They won't wait for us. Hazel?

HAZEL   I'm scared.

MADISON   Of what?

HAZEL   I want this to be the magic carpet.

MADISON   It is.

HAZEL   I don't want to end up on my knees like some gutless
                 little thing.

MADISON   You won't.

HAZEL   You're sure of that?

MADISON   Yes.

HAZEL   You keep reminding me.

MADISON   Daily. Hourly.

HAZEL   Then I have another job for you. You take care of
                 that sawed-off little prick.

                 *HAZEL exits. MADISON makes a final elegant
                 cast.*

MADISON   Bulls-eye.

                        * * *

DEL speaks as if BUTCH were present in 1967.

DEL

Morning, Butch. *(pause)* So how come you're
building an outhouse? *(pause)* Sorry. I haven't seen
a steam engine in a while. *(pause)* Maybe the cab's
a little too tall. *(pause)* A knock down fitting?

Shit, I don't know. I'd just put the boards together
and bang the piss out of them. *(pause, then turning
away, muttering)* Smart-assed little bastard.

EDNA

I had dreams too, you know. So did your dad. Oh,
no place fancy. Here. Home.

DEL

You tried, Ma.

EDNA

I'm still trying. *(beginning to sweep the kitchen
floor)* Do you have good dreams, Del? You gonna
do good things?

DEL

I'm gonna beat the railroad accountants.

EDNA

We can beat them. We can beat them here.

DEL

No.

EDNA

Yes.

DEL

I can save your house. But I gotta leave to do it.

EDNA

Save it with money?

DEL

What else?

EDNA

Then it's just a house. Without the three of you it's
just a house.

DEL

Everyone moves out, Ma.

EDNA

Out, yeah. But you're leaving. You and Nita'll have
kids. But I won't know them. I won't know you.

DEL

(pause) Nita's not coming.

EDNA

Why not? *(waiting)* You're cutting us all loose.
Aren't you?

DEL

No.

EDNA

Just like your old man. "I'll be back, I promise."
Liars, the pair of you.

DEL	Don't call him that.
EDNA	He let us down.
DEL	You were broke so he put his neck on the line.
EDNA	And we're still broke so what was the point?
DEL	He tried.
EDNA	He went for the quickest dollar, the boomtown dollar. That's what you're doing. You'll never have anything but a wallet.
DEL	You want the house, yes or no?
EDNA	I want a family not a ware-house. Is there something wrong with that? Yes, I want my home. And on my terms. It isn't a rock I found on the beach, it isn't a souvenir. I built it. Not with my hands, all right, but I built it with my heart. Yes. Smirk. Laugh. Whatever you like. But I'm trying to teach you kids something besides restlessness. I don't want your money.
DEL	All right. Then I'll give you something else. I wasn't just shooting the breeze about New Orleans. We can go there if you want. Key West. California. Whatever you want. I'm offering the tickets out of this hole. Tickets for everyone.
EDNA	Did you up and join the circus, Del?
DEL	*(pause)* I joined the army.
EDNA	The army.
DEL	Yes.
EDNA	Christ. *(pause)* How is that going to get you to the States? Since when did we send soldiers to the goddamn States? Use your head.
DEL	I joined the American army, Ma.
EDNA	*(puuse)* The American army. *(pause)* Where are they sending you? Key West? New Orleans? Nashville?
DEL	*(quiet)* How about Vietnam?

EDNA	Bullshit.
DEL	I asked to go there.
EDNA	Bullshit.
DEL	They said sure.

EDNA swings the broom at him. He catches it with one hand, disarming her.

Blackout. End of Act One.

Act Two

Lights up on DEL and EDNA, a few moments later.

EDNA   *(quiet)* Vietnam?

DEL   Yes.

EDNA   C'mon, son. This is just a sick joke. Right?

DEL   I wouldn't joke about something like this.

EDNA   Del.

DEL   Sorry, Ma.

EDNA   Don't give me sorry.

DEL   It's the only job I could find.

EDNA goes to DEL. She punches him in the face. She sits down at the table and lights a cigarette. DEL joins her. He hears BUTCH working.

DEL   That friggin' parade nonsense is gonna drive me crazy.

EDNA   *(quiet)* Don't change the subject, son.

They sit at the table. EDNA lights a smoke. DEL rolls one. They watch each other.

* * *

BUTCH enters with a window casement and hangs it around the curtain EDNA has hung earlier. MADISON watches. BUTCH begins to set up another major element of the house.

BUTCH   The second best thing about work is the language. Take footings for example. A footing is the fat part of your foundation — good footing, good foundation. You might have heard the phrase in everyday conversation — "She's on a pretty good footing there."

You probably think it means something about sensible shoes. Not so. The origin of that expression is right here in the ground. Construction is good for the language. And the soul.

MADISON You look at the softness of my hands and you think that I am some kind of social eunuch. Appearances are deceiving.

BUTCH All building has a poetry of its own. Look at cement work: coarse aggregate. Striking off. Bull-floating. Even grout is a good word. There was a man from here whose last name was Grout. Arthur Grout. No one laughed at him though — he half-ran the town. Hard as a chisel that man. Lots to prove, hauling around a name like Grout.

MADISON Wrong verb. A man like that didn't run the town — he built it.

BUTCH When the concrete cures it's time to talk of plumb and level . . .

MADISON What you don't understand is that business men are the craftsmen of the 21st Century.

BUTCH . . . furring, kerfs and nosing . . .

MADISON Business deals have their own aesthetic, the process is similar to sculpture We conceive the idea, make preliminary sketches, select the proper tree, fell it, dry it, shape it, turn it inch by careful inch into a true work of art.

BUTCH . . . all carpentry is poetry . . .

MADISON All very nice except for one thing — the 21st Century. It's here. And it's nasty.

BUTCH . . . timber and joinery . . .

MADISON The aesthetics of this century are the aesthetics of warfare.

BUTCH . . . half-lap and blind dowels . . .

MADISON Warfare without benefit of the Geneva conventions — no prisoners.

BUTCH	. . . bull nose boards . . .
MADISON	Sad I agree, but what are we to do? We can't go backwards.
BUTCH	. . . cheek cuts, twin double tenons with mortise locks . . .
MADISON	So we move forward and engage.
BUTCH	. . . knock-down fittings. Haunched, wedged, pinned and foxed.
MADISON	Remember the French and their trenches? The Poles and their cavalry? Remember what happened? Blitzkrieg, the lightning war. This house. This . . . town. You're digging trenches. You can't win.
BUTCH	Pol Pot emptied the cities of Cambodia, drained half a million people from Phnom Penh. They said he was a psychopath, that he drank blood warm from a baby, they ran out of words for his sins.
MADISON	There are Japanese corporations with 250-year plans. Imagine. A longer lifespan than most countries.
BUTCH	But he let the cities stand. Get it? When Pol Pot was gone, the people had a home to return to.
MADISON	The borders are gone.
BUTCH	But we're the good guys and what do we leave behind?
MADISON	The maps are ancient history.
BUTCH	Not a thing. We knock apart a town and give her back to the blackflies.
MADISON	Somewhere in the world, 24 hours a day, stocks are being traded. Sun-up? Sun-down?
BUTCH	Garbage trains.
MADISON	The sun is irrelevant. The sun is old technology.
BUTCH	They suck us dry and give us garbage trains in return. They turn our trees into skin magazines, they piss the copper into outer space.

MADISON   Time and distance have been liquidated by the new
                 alchemy.

BUTCH   They fill the boxcars with southern PCB's and shit-
                 filled Pampers and they ship the garbage north to us.

MADISON   We're all nomads now.

BUTCH   "You want jobs?" they say. "Become a garbage dump
                 for Toronto, Montreal, for Vancouver and you'll have
                 all the jobs you can handle." They starve us out and
                 then they give us shitty diapers to suck on.

MADISON   Even the rules are fluid.

BUTCH   They're taking apart this country family by family,
                 town by town.

MADISON   Think of it as national euthanasia. Home towns?
                 Provinces? Nation states? Phantoms from the past.
                 (picking up the Canadian flag from the earlier scene)
                 What is this? A piece of textile, made where?
                 (checking the label) Malaysia. Cheaply. Efficiently.
                 (taking a lighter from the kitchen table) Just a piece
                 of textile. Made by ignorant women for silly children
                 who still believe in symbols.

                 MADISON puts the flag to the flame.

BUTCH   Hey. Hey, Hey. Hey,

                 *BUTCH grabs the flag and extinguishes it. He
                 picks up his drill.*

                 This drill. 9.2 Volts. 1100 rpm's. Bores a nice
                 clean hole. A useful tool for building. But if I stuck
                 it into your eye *(laying the drill bit against
                 MADISON's cheekbone)* and squeezed the trigger —
                 I could drain your brains right out. That wouldn't be
                 very constructive. On the other hand... who knows
                 what is constructive when the rules are fluid. Maybe
                 I should do it anyway. Just to check.

MADISON   *(waiting)* Then do it. I'm waiting.

                 BUTCH backs off. MADISON takes a breath.

	OK. Let's talk hockey. Where's your money coming from? *(waiting)* Where is your money coming from?
BUTCH	*(pause)* I run eco-tours. Those garbage trains I was talking about. P.C. yuppies pay big money to come up here, eat bannock and blow up garbage trains. Excitement, squalor and violence. Just like any Third World vacation. Now that this part of the country is the Third World.
MADISON	Are you trying to get it out of Hazel?
BUTCH	Maybe.
MADISON	How much do you want?
BUTCH	Lots.
MADISON	*(digging in his pocket)* Here's lots. Here. *(waiting)* Take it. *(as BUTCH reaches for it, MADISON pulls it away)* Except that's not how union negotiations are carried out. I offer you money — you offer up a concession.
BUTCH	*(pause)* What do you want?
MADISON	I want two days. Just get in your truck and disappear. These are excellent wages for two days of very simple work. After that you can do what you want.
BUTCH	I'm getting to her, aren't I?
MADISON	The details are unimportant.
BUTCH	*(BUTCH goes into the house and stands beside EDNA)* But I don't have the roof shingled yet. What if it rains?
MADISON	*(without looking)* Not a cloud in the sky.
BUTCH	*(wetting his finger, then raising his hand)* Sure feels like rain to me. *(smiling)* Now. Negotiate.
MADISON	*(pause)* Your sister has an important decision to make. If she makes the wrong one she'll be gutted like a fish.
BUTCH	Who does the gutting?

MADISON	Does it matter?
BUTCH	You?
MADISON	No.
BUTCH	Blitzkrieg.
MADISON	Hazel's my partner.
BUTCH	A man like you would gut his mother for bus fare.
MADISON	You live in an extremely simple world, don't you?
BUTCH	I live in the remains of a world.
MADISON	(*pause*) I'll say this once. Get out of our way, let Hazel make her decision. If she's too confused to choose correctly, she will be gutted like a cheap pike. She will live and die poor, and alone. And that will be your fault. And once a year, every year, every anniversary of the disaster you caused, I will send you a post-card from Kentucky. Just to remind you, just in case you forget. Is that clear, brother-in-law? A cheap pike.
BUTCH	Now we're talking hockey, monkey fuck. But I need a little time OK?
MADISON	(*dropping some bills*) Here's a down-payment. In good faith. Try not to think too slowly.
	MADISON exits. BUTCH counts and pockets the cash.
BUTCH	Catch yourself a pan of trout — they're full of mercury.
	BUTCH puts the finishing touch on the element he has been installing. As he sits down at the table between DEL and EDNA we hear the voice of DEL SR.
DEL SR.	This man gets on the *Canadian* at Nipigon. He's been drinking beer all day. He gets on the train and falls asleep. When he wakes up he goes to the conductor.

* * *

EDNA	Why?
DEL	The North Vietnamese are taking over Southeast Asia.
EDNA	Cut the bullshit.
DEL	I need a job.
EDNA	Don't you make fun of me.
DEL	Christ. I'm trying to talk to you. Do you think this is easy? *(pause)* It's no big deal. Dad was out of work when he went to Korea. And Uncle Donald when he joined the air force. Call it family tradition.
EDNA	Look what happened to those fools.
DEL	You used to call them heroes.
EDNA	Hero. Fool. I get the words mixed up, four letters each you know. I never was much of a speller. *(pause)* And where are they now? Say it. Dead. Crazy. Missing. Say it.
DEL	Just a job, Ma. Maybe I'll be driving a tow-truck or cooking soup.
EDNA	Or digging graves.
DEL	And there's a bonus.
EDNA	The pine box they ship you home in?
DEL	I go over there and I become an American citizen almost like that. *(snapping his fingers)* One year and then I come home and I can take you all out of this dying little town. New Orleans, Key West, Nashville. Bonus.
EDNA	Did they send you a letter? Give it to me.
	Stand-off. Then DEL hands it to EDNA. She tears it up.
DEL	*(softly)* That won't change anything.
EDNA	I won't let you go. I'll tell them you're insane.
DEL	But I'm not.

EDNA	I'll tell them you're a queer.
DEL	They already checked.
EDNA	I'll break your legs with a hockey stick.
DEL	Finished?
EDNA	Vietnam. Could you even find it on a map?
DEL	I don't have to fly the plane.
EDNA	Don't smart arse me. We got goddamn Yankees lined up five deep so they don't have to go to that place and you turn around and ask to go. Do you have rocks in your head? Muskeg? What? A job? Jesus H. Christ. People are dying there. Have you forgotten that? Have you forgotten your father?
DEL	I remember.
EDNA	No. You can't remember and hand me that letter.
DEL	I remember the telegram. I remember twenty-one nights running you didn't go to bed. Twenty-one. I counted. I remember twenty-one days of Campbell's canned tomato soup. Twenty-one days of cigarette smoke in the kitchen. Twenty-one days of laundry on the floor.
EDNA	Then what?
DEL	I came home from school on the twenty-second day and Hazel was cleaned up, there was laundry on the line, the floors were scrubbed and supper was on the stove. And we were back to normal.
EDNA	(*turning to him slowly, then quietly*) And that, my blue-eyed child, is where you got it all wrong.
DEL	Not normal but...
EDNA	Not normal, not normal, never again normal, blue-eyed child, eat, sleep, school, play, church, yes, but never ever never again... normal.
DEL	OK.

EDNA   No. It's not OK. Not then. Not now. Not
            tomorrow. Never. Understand me? It's not OK,
            ever. We were never normal again.

            *DEL tries to get out of his chair. EDNA pushes
            him back down.*

                        * * *

            *BUTCH gets up from the table. He flips on the
            "friendly fire" tape. The sound now is mostly a
            man's breath: pained, frightened. BUTCH
            watches for HAZEL.*

BUTCH   C'mon. Take the bait. C'mon. That's it.

            *BUTCH goes back to work, raising the fourth
            element of the house. HAZEL enters. She
            snaps the tape off.*

BUTCH   Hey, where do you think you are? Home?

HAZEL   Do you enjoy his pain?

BUTCH   No.

HAZEL   Then leave it alone.

BUTCH   I've left things alone for too long. So have you.

HAZEL   Didn't Madison have a little chat with you?

BUTCH   Oh, we talked all right.

HAZEL   Then why are you still in my face?

BUTCH   Because he can't train me the way he's trained you.
            You see what Madison sees. Say what Madison says.
            Good trick. He's trained you well. Roll over, Hazel.
            Sit up. Beg, Hazel. Atta girl.

HAZEL   You sawed-off little prick.

BUTCH   But then all the children in our family learned to
            listen well. Who did we get that from? Certainly not
            from Mom. So my analysis . . . *(laughing)* . . .
            analysis . . . Madison's getting to me too . . . my
            analysis is that we got our gullibility genes from
            Dad.

HAZEL	Leave him alone.
BUTCH	He deserves it.
HAZEL	What do you know about Dad? He was gone before you were born.
BUTCH	*(pause)* A nice guy. But blind. And, sadly, in the end... a sucker.
HAZEL	Do you hate him too?
BUTCH	I'm trying not to be nostalgic. The old man, he took the hook right into his guts, swallowing that little minnow about what? Democracy, communism, the American Dream? That little minnow right down into his guts. The only one who wouldn't eat the minnow was Mom. The old man took it. Del took it. You took it. I took it for twenty-some years. That's what they've been feeding us on. Minnows. I'm tired of the diet. Aren't you? You'd leave, Hazel, but I've hooked you too, and you just can't spit that hook out of your mouth. *(jerking his hands as if setting a hook)* You're coming into the boat. May 2, 1953. Dad sends the following post-card from Korea. "Bullshit. Bullshit. Bullshit. Bullshit. Bullshit." "Love, Dad." *(pause)* "Bullshit. Bullshit. Bullshit. Bullshit. Bullshit." What do you think he was talking about?
HAZEL	Leave him alone.
BUTCH	Cut the nostalgic crap, this is the 21st Century. It's the old man's fault Del isn't here. The old man ran away. Listened to the lies and snuck out the window one night when we were all asleep. One last lousy post-card admitting that it was all bullshit — too late. He went missing the next day. They lied to him. He listened. He lied to us — except for that post-card — and we listened to him. Del especially. And then Del lied to us. But it started with Dad.
HAZEL	Leave him alone. He held me. Not you. We don't even know if he was your father.
BUTCH	*(silence)* You're a pro. I'll give you that. *(pause)* He took a wrong turn. I don't think we'll be able to get him back on track.

HAZEL	I swear to Christ I'll do the lobotomy myself.
BUTCH	Back on track. A railroad pun. Get it?
HAZEL	He's dead!
BUTCH	Who's dead?
HAZEL	The old man.
BUTCH	I know that. I'm talking about Del. You know what your problem is? You're gullible. You trust your buddy Madison. You trusted Del. You're going to end up with nothing. Again.
HAZEL	I can't follow your nonsense.
BUTCH	No. But you can see the house going up. Feel it filling up. You can feel the lies the family swallowed like minnows twenty, thirty, forty years ago. And you can feel that I know something about Del. And you're almost certain that I know something about Madison. You think I'm a lunatic. Wrong.
HAZEL	What's next? You beat me to death with a two by four? Do you hate me that much?
BUTCH	I don't hate you. Madison hates you. You're confusing yourself again. He offered me money. A wheelbarrow full.
HAZEL	You should have taken it.
BUTCH	All I have to do is stop reminding you about things like... home. You regret not having kids?
HAZEL	Like a goddamn pin-ball machine, bing, zoom, tilt.
BUTCH	'Course not. If I'da known the cities were gonna turn into spittoons I wouldn't have had them either. I thought I was building a home. I tried too. About twenty years I tried. My wife didn't want a home... she was making... an investment. Investments. That's what we do now. You must have known that. That's why you never had any kids. I shouldn't of had them either. They'd be better off dead. I wish I'd seen that coming. Madison's lying to you though. I don't know how you missed that.

IIAZEL   Madison's on my side.

BUTCH   A wheelbarrow of money. Home: Helping Mom
        around the house. Remember? When she wanted
        something from the basement, home-made pickles or
        potatoes maybe. You wouldn't go alone. You were
        scared. Something scared you skinny. What was it?
        What was it?

         BUTCH turns on the tape machine. A muffled
         voice now, the incoherent sounds of a man who
         believes he is going to die.

HAZEL   Turn it off. Please. *(BUTCH doesn't)* The damp.
        The rot. The smell of a grave.

BUTCH   Deeper.

HAZEL   The coats.

BUTCH   The old coats. Yes. Hanging from the stringers.
        Out of the corner of your eye, in that swaying forty-
        watt light, it was like someone was hanging there.
        Dad's railroad coveralls. And then later on, Del's
        winter parka and his hunting jacket. It was like the
        two of them were hanging in that damp old basement.
        The old man and Del. Night and day.

HAZEL   Please turn that thing off.

BUTCH   We need something from the basement.

HAZEL   You're listening to him die, understand that. Don't
        you care? Are you that far gone? Butch. He's our
        brother. Turn it off.

BUTCH   *(turning the tape off, picking up a flashflight from*
        his tool kit) We're at the basement door now. Smell
        the mildew? Hear the water run down the waste-pipe?
        Remember the bag of potatoes, a thousand eyes
        growing through the burlap? Remember the riddle?
        (singing)

        Cut me up in pieces, bury me alive
        the young ones will live and the old ones will die.

(pause) Just a harmless riddle about potatoes. What are we afraid of? Hear the furnace. Smell the oil. *(pointing the flashlight in her face)* One forty-watt bulb dangles from the stringers in the centre of the room. Turn on the light, Hazel. Flick it on and let's see what's happening in our basement. Make the shadows dance, get those skeletons illuminated, let's see what we can find. Switch it on, Hazel. Switch it on. Do it!

> *HAZEL flicks the flashlight on. The stage lights dim. We catch a glimpse of the photo of DEL SR., of the burnt flag, of the bare bones of the house.*

There's Dad's railroad coveralls. And there. Beside him. There's Del. See him? There's Del.

HAZEL   Del's clothes.

BUTCH   Del! Not his suit, not his parka, not his hunting jacket. Del in the flesh.

HAZEL   Butch, he's dead.

> *MADISON enters.*

BUTCH   And right beside dear brother Del is your buddy Madison. See him? See his $700 suit? A $700 suit looks pretty weird beside a hunting jacket and railroad coveralls. What is Madison doing in our basement? That's a good friggin' question. What the hell is Madison doing in our basement? Look closely now. He's... he's whispering in Del's ear. Whispering. Yes. Can you hear him? No? Sounds like... Kentucky. No. Not like Kentucky. Sounds like... Key... West. That's it. Key West. Madison's saying something about Key West. Hear them now? Kentucky. Key West. Kentucky. Key West. The two of them in our basement. Like termites. Eating away at the post and beams. Like frost, cracking the foundation. Like sewage backing up in the pipe. The whole house collapses.

> *BUTCH holds the light to HAZEL's throat, then flicks it off.*

You wouldn't come for weddings, christenings or funerals. But welcome home, sister dear. Welcome home for Del's rebirthday. Del's alive. Hear me? Del's alive.

Lights begin to restore. MADISON exits.

HAZEL Oh Jesus Christ.

BUTCH He's alive.

HAZEL Don't you.

BUTCH I'm telling you.

HAZEL *(she pops him on the jaw)* You sick freak.

BUTCH He runs a fishing charter out of Key West.

HAZEL I don't want to hear this.

BUTCH Been there since '71.

HAZEL I don't want to hear your nonsense.

BUTCH He's got a nice tan. *(taking some photos out of his pocket)* Here. Look. Go on. They won't bite.

Long pause. HAZEL takes the photos.

HAZEL Del?

BUTCH He says sorry.

HAZEL Sorry?

BUTCH Coupla months ago, just after Mom died, he sent a short letter. About shacking up in Thailand after Tet. A very sad letter. I think our Del took a little too much heat over there. Enough to brown him on one side.

HAZEL Del's Symphony?

BUTCH Oh that's Del. But it has nothing to do with him dying.

They sit together.

* * *

DEL	Even Nita says it's OK.
EDNA	You got a girlfriend who wants you to go to Vietnam? Get rid of her.
DEL	Maybe she likes men in uniform.
EDNA	You ignorant pups. You bring her over for supper tonight.
DEL	We're busy tonight.
EDNA	You bring her. I want to talk to her.
DEL	You stay out of it.
EDNA	I want to read her some of your father's letters.
DEL	She's not coming over.
EDNA	I'll read the parts where he says he puked every morning. How the first time he heard those Chinese bugles he shit himself. I got some interesting little details for miss Nita.
DEL	We've talked it over.
EDNA	What do you know? What the goddamn TV tells you? The TV doesn't come smeared in puke and blood, little Del. Those letters aren't a cartoon, little Del, does she know that?
DEL	She's not stupid. She can read the papers.
EDNA	Not the goddamn lies in the newspapers.

> *EDNA goes to the trunk to retrieve some letters. She holds them out for DEL.*

EDNA	Read the letters, Del. That picture on the wall, the fireman with the big arms and the sparkle in his eye? The man you remember as your Dad? Read the letters, Del. That man evaporated in 8 months. Memorize them. I have.
DEL	I've heard it all in the Legion. The same old thing. Beer and B.S.
EDNA	This is your father talking to us. It isn't beer and it sure isn't b.s. . . . Bullshit.

DEL	With a good story those guys drink all afternoon.
EDNA	Your father isn't sitting in the Legion Hall. You don't have a guarantee on your scrawny little hide. *(grabbing him by the shirt)* Del.

> *Hold. EDNA turns away. Pause, then DEL picks up the flag from the earlier scene.*

DEL	She bought me a flag.
EDNA	A what?
DEL	A shiny new maple leaf. To fly over camp.
EDNA	Red and goddamn white. A target in the jungle. *(pause)* Guess she'll put on a Santa Claus suit for your funeral. *(pause)* Here.

> *EDNA holds out a letter.*

DEL	I've read them.
EDNA	You haven't read this one Del. This one came after the rest.
DEL	Yeah, well, it's probably more of the same.
EDNA	Five years ago.
DEL	*(pause)* What do you mean five years ago?
EDNA	It came five years ago, 1962, can't you do the math?
DEL	What are you saying, Ma?
EDNA	I'm saying I got a letter from your old man nine years after he went missing.
DEL	Bullshit.
EDNA	Look at the postmark. Look at it. It won't bite.

> *DEL reaches for it, EDNA pulls the letter away from him.*

* * *

HAZEL	He got away.
BUTCH	To Key West.

HAZEL	Fishing.
BUTCH	Fishing tuna.
HAZEL	That bastard.
BUTCH	That's right, Hazel. That bastard.
HAZEL	*(looking at the photographs)* He looks like he's done okay for himself.
BUTCH	For himself, yeah. *(holding out his hand head-high)* He looks like this much bullshit.
HAZEL	Happy too. In a Del kind of way.
BUTCH	Shit.
HAZEL	He does. Content.
BUTCH	Mom died thinking he was dead. If he'd of come back maybe she'd still be alive. He faked his own death. But he did hers for real. We helped. But he killed her.
HAZEL	Some things are nobody's fault.
BUTCH	Nothing happens on its own. Somebody decides — somebody pays. Del sold this family out. I'm gonna put it back together.
HAZEL	It's too late.
BUTCH	Nothing's too late. Madison's gonna sell you out. He's got some kind of deal going in Kentucky.
HAZEL	Fuck Kentucky.
BUTCH	He's gonna gut you like a cheap pike.
HAZEL	I can handle Madison.
BUTCH	He's gonna gut you like Del gutted us.
HAZEL	But I'm alive. What happened to you?

MADISON enters, unnoticed.

BUTCH	Commercials. Bells and whistles. All the shinies. They promised us the moon so we went looking. And reading Del's letter you see they really did give us the moon — miles and miles of clear-cut and rubble. His grave opens up and he sits there in his coffin drinking warm Schlitz. Not the first lie. Not even the biggest. But big enough. Now you know. You have no choice but to start again.
HAZEL	OK. *(going to the tape machine)* I'll start like this.

HAZEL unspools the tape.

* * *

DEL	Ma?
EDNA	Don't get your hopes up. The letter got lost in the mail.
DEL	*(pause)* The mail? The fucking mail? Jesus. What the hell are you trying to do to me? You give him back to me for ten seconds then you take him away?
EDNA	I didn't take him away. He left. Like you.
DEL	That was cruel trick, Ma.
EDNA	Two days I stared at that envelope. Two days before I could force myself to open it. The post mark was new. But his words were old. *(pause)* Don't talk to me about cruelty. You got your bags packed, the Yankees call and you go running. Your job is here with us and you go running, don't you dare talk to me about cruelty. Don't you dare. You goddamn mercenary.
DEL	*(pause, then shaking the table)* "Fix the table, Del." "Can't afford a new one." "Go easy on the coffee, Del, save the milk for the kids." Jesus. You've been crying poor mouth for ten friggin' years. About the fucking government...
EDNA	Don't use that gutter language here, this is still my...
DEL	...about the fucking government holding up the pension because he was listed as missing. Christ.

You know what I say when I hear some guy complain about his parents rattling on about the Depression? I tell them they're lucky. The Depression in my family never ended. Baloney and macaroni. Cracked linoleum. Peeling paint. You never shut up about any of it. If you'da laid off with the belly-aching we never would have noticed we were broke.

EDNA   You noticed all right, like you noticed your clothes weren't new. You noticed and you wanted more.

DEL   You wanted more. You. And you're going to get more. The Great Depression, 1953 to 1967 is officially over. I found the war to get the economy going in this house again. The checks'll be in the mail end of every month.

EDNA   There's poison bubbling out of you, boy. Poison. *(pause)* OK then. Help me kill him.

DEL   Kill who?

EDNA   Cyrus.

     DEL laughs, then sees EDNA is serious.

DEL   You want to kill Cyrus.

EDNA   It was your idea. The only good one you've had all day.

DEL   I wasn't serious.

EDNA   I am.

DEL   Have a drink.

     EDNA grabs the bottle from DEL and downs a shot.

EDNA   I'll kill him. You just tell me how. 12-gauge? Thirty-thirty?

DEL   Knock it off.

EDNA   What's best to kill a man? Big hole from a shotgun? *(gesturing)* Small hole from a rifle. *(gesturing)* What's best, Del? Teach me.

Just tell me how and I'll do it. I'll do it tomorrow.
I'll spend the rest of the day cooking so you have
food in the freezer. And, first thing tomorrow
morning, I'll walk uptown to the bank and solve
everything. Rifle. *(gesturing)* Or shotgun.

> *EDNA spews the whisky.*

DEL   Ma.

EDNA   Shot-gun I guess. I won't have to be accurate. But
I'll have to get close to him. Me to you, say. What
do you think? Closer?

DEL   Stop it.

EDNA   Teach me, child. Where do I aim? His face? His
stomach? What if he's standing up? Do I ask him to
sit? Sit down, Cyrus. Sit down, Cyrus. Sit.
Down.

> *DEL sits, pause.*

And then he never gets up again. *(pause)* Will that
work?

DEL   No.

EDNA   Why not?

DEL   They'll just replace him.

EDNA   Who's going to replace you?

DEL   You can't kill a bank.

EDNA   Fuck the bank. Fuck the CPR. I'm talking about
you. You. *(long pause, then quietly)* You don't
remember the silk trains. Number one priority from
Vancouver to Montreal. Pure, raw Chinese silk, the
big dollar, armed guards, the fastest trains in the
country. Even Prince Albert took the siding one
night for a silk train. That was your father's
favourite story: For one night us dumb colonials got
to make the future King of England sit in a Canadian
siding.

DEL   The silk trains...

EDNA	And the men who rode them...
DEL	...are gone.
EDNA	...you never saw anybody walk so tall, so much swagger and stroll after a run like that. They were so pretty.
DEL	The silk trains are gone. Everything is gone.
EDNA	Yeah. Yeah, they're gone. But the men who worked them — they were proud people. Are you going to be proud of yourself? Eh, killer?
DEL	Be careful, old lady. You're on thin ice.
EDNA	I can swim son. But I won't swim in blood.

* * *

MADISON	Is this good news?
HAZEL	Things are fine Maddy. Guess what?
MADISON	Your brother is difficult to predict.
HAZEL	Not him. My other brother.
MADISON	Pardon?
HAZEL	Del. He's alive.
MADISON	Don't start this.
HAZEL	He lives in Key West.
MADISON	He died years ago.
HAZEL	Have a look at the pictures.
MADISON	This has gone far enough.
HAZEL	It's all right.
MADISON	It's not all right. You can't believe in fairy tales.
HAZEL	He's gained a little weight. But it's him. The way he holds his beer, the rollies, everything. Look.
MADISON	He's dead.

BUTCH	I got proof. A letter.
MADISON	*(to HAZEL)* Another "document." Another fantasy.
HAZEL	Maybe we should make him a partner. The boy's a pro. A Lake Superior hillbilly.
MADISON	Stop it. Stop it. Your brother is dead.
HAZEL	I know that. I know I have a dead brother. *(going to BUTCH)* You little brother. You. *(as BUTCH retreats, then to MADISON)*
	But the other one, so alive we oughta salute.
MADISON	Meaning what?
HAZEL	I made up my mind.
MADISON	Spell it out. I had a stroke this afternoon.
HAZEL	I'll close.
MADISON	Mexico?
HAZEL	Yes. I just got the message I needed.
BUTCH	Yeah. Del says "fuck you."
HAZEL	He says the game is called hardball, little sister. You owe nobody nothing.
BUTCH	Mom would string you up for saying that.
HAZEL	*(going into the house)* But Mom isn't around. See Maddy? No more coffins. No more ghosts. It's magic carpet time.
MADISON	Be sure, Hazel.
HAZEL	I'm sure.
MADISON	I won't come back to clean up any messy details.
HAZEL	*(to BUTCH)* The only detail is saying good-bye.
MADISON	Sounds good, Hazel. Sounds very good. I'll meet you at the vehicle.
HAZEL	I won't be long.

MADISON	I promised him money. *(handing HAZEL a wad of cash)* Give it to him. A doctor. Whatever. *(moving off, then stopping)* You're tougher than I thought.
HAZEL	Is that a problem?
MADISON	No. I don't know. It's something to think about.
HAZEL	Yeah. I guess it is. Go.

MADISON exits.

Anything else you got to say? I have to get moving.

BUTCH	What's in Mexico?
HAZEL	Life.
BUTCH	What you do isn't living.
HAZEL	You oughta pay attention to your big brother. He's got lots to say.
BUTCH	*(taking out a letter)* Yeah. He says this: "You take a bead. Squeeze off a round. The little bugger's lights go out. It's kind of neat. Sorry. But I think it's kind of neat."

BUTCH crumples the letter.

* * *

EDNA	You don't give a shit about Vietnam. You're going overseas so you can hunt human beings. The uniform's just a license to poach humans.
DEL	Jesus. H. Christ.
EDNA	I guess you're tired of the four-legged kind.
DEL	Do you know what you're saying?
EDNA	Was I being vague?
DEL	Is that what you said to Dad? That he was killer?
EDNA	I should have taken the butcher knife and cut his trigger finger off at the elbow.

DEL   *(taking out and opening his knife)* Here. *(offering it)* Here. You think I'm a murderer. Stop me. C'mon. Stop me. C'mon. Cut my hand off. C'mon before I go and poach some children.

                               EDNA moves to take the knife. DEL pulls it away.

                The butcher knives are in the drawer. You can get my fingers while I'm sleeping.

EDNA   You think I won't.

DEL   You won't.

EDNA   Why shouldn't I?

DEL   I'm your son.

EDNA   Another license.

DEL   One last time — I need a job, the job's in Asia. I do the job, one year, then I write my own ticket, one year, and then we move anywhere on the continent.

EDNA   *(quietly)* You're making a deal with the devil.

DEL   There's no devil, Ma. Just fat men down south pushing pencils. Between nine a.m. and coffee break — bingo — my life isn't mine anymore. I want to run my own life. Is that such a terrible thing to do?

EDNA   You'll run it all right. But somebody else will pay for it.

DEL   I've been paying. I'm tired of paying. Aren't you tired too? Haven't you paid enough? Haven't Butch and Hazel paid enough. What about them? What are you doing for them? Telling them stories about the silk trains, about the goddamn glory days doesn't cut it when your furniture is parked in the street. *(pause)* With or without your blessing I'm going.

EDNA   *(pause)* My what? My blessing? Is that what you said? *(pause)* You're a clever cruel boy. My blessing. What a hard bargain you drive. I bless your dying and I get to keep my house.

DEL   Not my dying.

EDNA Your killing then. I bless your killing in return for a house. *(pause)* Who made this world, Del?

DEL I don't know. Nobody. It's all one long accident. *(pause, at the window)* Look at Butch out there. His stupid little steam engine, playing at Confederation. You'd think he was the bastard child of John Alcoholic Macdonald.

EDNA He's got faith, Del. Something I guess you never had. I feel sorry for you.

DEL This town and a thousand like it are going down the sewer. And up on Parliament Hill all those school kids will be singing "one little, two little, three little provinces." We've been suckered. There is no country. There never was. It was just a bed-time story they told to shut us up.

EDNA When you say there is no past in this country, you're saying this family never existed. You're saying it will not exist. You're wrong.

EDNA kisses him on the forehead.

* * *

BUTCH He liked it.

HAZEL He made it out of here.

BUTCH He liked it.

HAZEL Whatever it takes.

BUTCH *(pause)* How many people did you say worked for you? Lots, eh? A small town.

BUTCH begins to methodically knock over the markers of the townsite. HAZEL watches impassively.

There goes a job — there goes a family. Job — family. Job — family. The dairy — 4 jobs. The school — 15. Plywood mill — 21. Car-barns — 42. The rink — 6 rink-rats hit the street. There goes a family. And another one. Good-bye. So long.

> *The markers have all been leveled. Perhaps*
> *BUTCH has stacked them at HAZEL's feet.*

Friendly fire. Who needs enemies, Hazel? Who
needs enemies? Colonials for ever and ever amen.
(pause) I am alone.

HAZEL That's right. You are.

BUTCH They've put it in the criminal code — memory has
been outlawed, it's treasonous to keep a past, history
is a crime — like bestiality or sex with an imbecile.
Now. Three lousy letters to sum up our lives.

HAZEL I remember it all, little brother. Decorated bicycles
on the First of July, sunrise on the river. I remember
the smell of Sunday school. But that doesn't mean I
believe in Jesus Christ or Santa Claus.

BUTCH Yeah. There's that other three letter word. God.

> *HAZEL peels some bills off the roll MADISON*
> *gave her and drops them on the ground.*

There's a sign up in God's window. "Under New
Management." If God's still around he's playing for
a farm team, he's with a D-class circus, a side-show
freak, God's on workman's comp, retired without a
pension, panhandling in the subway, bumming
smokes in the tavern. God isn't dead. He just wishes
the rumours were true. Kicked into the street by sons
and daughters, granny-bashed. We toss him out of
his home, we raid the fridge, we crap on the carpets.
And all we've allowed him to keep is a Polaroid snap
from better days — God at the beach with a beer in
his hand, a sunburned nose and a child on his knee.
History, memory, philosophy. Wrong. Wrong.
Wrong. Responsibility. Wrong. Continuity.
Wrong. Sacred trust. Wrong. Free of the past, free
of the future. Guiltless, blameless, free to do as we
please. Right here. Right now. For all time. Until
we end time, too.

> *BUTCH knocks a stud out of a wall. He picks*
> *up the chain-saw. He cranks it once, twice.*
> *HAZEL leaves. He cranks the saw again.*
> *Again. Again. He pauses for breath.*

I. Am. A. Lone.

EDNA   No you're not.

> *BUTCH turns, hearing for the first time.*

And you're not crazy either. Crazy's what they got to offer. Course if you want to knock this place into sawdust and splinters... *(holding up the spark plug)* ...If you want to slit your own throat... *(as BUTCH shakes his head)* ...Then finish what you started.

> *BUTCH puts the saw down. He goes to the house and puts the last piece of the structure in place. The lunar landscape is now habitable.*

EDNA   It's a beautiful piece of work. Not many people bother to build anymore. Thank you. *(the sounds of the town fade up)* You hear it? Listen. There it is. You betcha. Like a church choir. *(they listen together)* Now. Can I borrow your hammer?

BUTCH   You gonna knock some sense into Del?

EDNA   It's too late for that.

> *EDNA goes in the front door of the house. DEL scoots out the back door. He has a stash of beer under the house. He opens one.*

DEL   How ya doin', Butch? *(as BUTCH stares offstage in HAZEL's direction)* Gonna be a clear day for the parade tomorrow, eh? Hey, Butch. C'mon, sunshine. Cat got your tongue? Don't tell me you're mad at me, too.

> *Pause. New tactic. DEL cracks another beer.*

You want a beer?

BUTCH   I'm a kid!

> *He is, but he is also counting the money that HAZEL has dropped for him. It's a tidy sum. He's happy about it.*

DEL   It won't kill you.

BUTCH   I'll go to hell.

DEL   Where do you get that hell stuff from anyway?

BUTCH   Not from you.

DEL   *(sitting with his beer)* The old lady is mad at me.

BUTCH   Mom.

DEL   Mom is mad at me.

BUTCH   You probably deserve it.

DEL   You don't give anybody any slack, do you?

BUTCH   Hazel says I'm a sawed-off little prick.

DEL   *(laughing)* She does, does she? *(pause)* She's just talking. You're a good kid.

BUTCH   Yeah?

DEL   You bet.

BUTCH   *(sitting with DEL)* What's Mom mad about?

DEL   She's having trouble with the bank.

BUTCH   What does that mean?

DEL   It means Jesus needs a hearing aid.

BUTCH   You're going to hell.

DEL   In a hand basket. Here. Drink the damn beer. It's gonna go flat.

BUTCH   Not with you around.

DEL   I'm not gonna be around.

BUTCH   You going down the lake?

DEL   The bush, yeah, sort of.

BUTCH   Can I come?

DEL   You got school.

BUTCH   You taking Hazel?

DEL   No.

BUTCH	*(realizing)* I got no school till September! *(pause)* How long you going for?
DEL	Until I get back. Not a second sooner.
BUTCH	You coming back?
DEL	Sure, Butch. I'll be back. *(pause)* That banker giving Mom a hard time. He needs a rock through his window.
BUTCH	I don't do that kind of thing.
DEL	Jesus kicked the bankers out of the temple.
BUTCH	*(pause)* I'll think about it.

> *EDNA has taken a sign out of the trunk. She climbs the ladder and nails it into place: "rooms for rent." She also hangs the Canadian flag.*

BUTCH	What does that mean?
DEL	Mom'll tell you later.
EDNA	*(coming down off the ladder)* You got that kid drinking beer now?

> *BUTCH tries to hide the beer.*

DEL	It's a holiday tomorrow, Ma.
EDNA	Oh, all right then. Just one though. Don't want to stunt his mental development. Like some people we know. *(pause, then, about the evening)* Quiet.
DEL	Yeah. Too quiet.
EDNA	What's that supposed to mean?
DEL	Nothing. It's a cliché from every war movie I ever saw. Sorry.
EDNA	Shoulda named you "Sorry." *(pause, then looking up at the sign)* Hey Butch. Is it crooked?
BUTCH	*(tilting his head to compensate for the crooked sign)* Mom?
EDNA	It's straight, isn't it?

BUTCH	The house is crooked.

> *EDNA and BUTCH look out into the audience,*
> *tilting their heads from side to side.*

EDNA	Butch.
BUTCH	What?
EDNA	The town is crooked.
BUTCH	Mom?
EDNA	What?
BUTCH	The country is crooked.
EDNA	Butch?
BUTCII	What?
EDNA	The sky is crooked.
BUTCH	Mom?
EDNA	What?
BUTCH	The universe is so crooked God just skidded off. Like he fell off a roof.
EDNA	Where'd he fall off to?
BUTCH	Mom?
EDNA	What?
BUTCH	I don't know.
EDNA	Can you see anything?
BUTCH	Just...
EDNA	Yeah?
BUTCH	Just his army boots. I see him go stomp stomp stomp. Just like he did to Daddy in Korea.
DEL	That was a long time ago, Butch. You don't have to think about it.
BUTCH	I see Daddy walking in the snow with only one boot on. His foot is black and red.

EDNA	What else?
BUTCH	Nothing.
EDNA	Try.
DEL	What are you doing to him, Ma? He's gonna have nightmares as it is.
EDNA	Think about Daddy at home.
BUTCH	I can't.
DEL	Of course he can't.
EDNA	Don't be afraid, Butch. You're not crazy. Listen.
BUTCH	I'm trying.
EDNA	Daddy talked to you through my belly button.
DEL	Jesus, Ma what are you doing?
BUTCH	Yeah. Yeah. I hear him now.
DEL	You don't hear anything.
BUTCH	A story about the guys he works with on the railroad.
DEL	He doesn't remember anything.
BUTCH	I'm not remembering, Del. Daddy's here. I hear him. *(pause)* This man gets on the *Canadian* at Nipigon. He's been drinking beer all day. He gets on the train and falls asleep. When he wakes up he goes to the conductor and asks if he can see his ticket. The conductor goes: "How come you want to see your ticket?" The drunk guy goes: "If I could see my ticket then I'd know where I was going." *(pause)* That's what he says. If I can see my ticket then I'll know where I'm going. *(pause)* Daddy's laughing. *(pause)* True story.

> *Fade on DEL and BUTCH. Fade on the noises of the town. Slow fade on EDNA smiling.*
>
> *END*

Sixty Below

by

Leonard Linklater
and Patti Flather

Lorne Cardinal as Johnny (left), Kennetch Charlette as Henry (centre),
and Gilbert Clements as Big Joe (right).

The title of *Sixty Below* encapsulates at least some of the play's many dimensions. It is the name of the bar where Rosie, a young Gwich'in woman, Henry's "old lady" and Johnnie's sister, works, where the male characters congregate, and where much of the action takes place. "Sixty Below" captures in words the concept of a North where temperatures drop to levels few can survive. In one sense, the name of the bar resonates with the macho image of the stereotypical tough northerner; in another, it suggests the deep cold that, together with drink, is an actual and metaphorical threat to life: the deep cold of displacement, of loss of identity, and of a failure to confront these issues.

The action takes place during the winter solstice, with flashbacks to exactly one year before. The flashbacks reveal the events of the story as they happened both in fact and in the minds of the characters. The time of year succinctly brings together vital elements in the play: North as an unmistakable place, with Northern Lights, forest and river, shading into the small town; North as the locus of spirits; and North as the meeting place of the two cultural traditions that form the background of the people in the play, all of them Native. Christmas is imminent, with its obligatory merrymaking, drinking, and spending and its bleak undertones of being broke, depressed, and out of work. At the same time, we hear of the spirits of the dead, dancing in the Northern Lights, travelling up the river, immanent in the landscape and in the memories of the living.

In this play it is impossible to make a distinction between what is spiritual and what is actual. Just as the past and present are woven together, the spirit world and the landscape are one; the river up which the spirits of the dead travel is the same river that runs through the town with its concrete blocks, bars and bingo; and Johnnie dead continues to influence those whom he influenced when he was alive, and who, in turn, continue to love, admire and fear him. As Johnnie's sister, Rosie, explains while walking home at three in the morning after her shift in the bar: "Lorraine says her people — the Tutchone from around here — have a legend about it. They say some people are trapped in the northern lights because of the way they died. They can't leave the realm of the earth. They have unfinished business" (437) And then later in the same speech: "I don't care what Lorraine says, if Johnnie is dancing in those lights, I'm damn well going to watch him!"

Rosie loves the dance of the Northern Lights for themselves and for Johnnie. She treasures the dolls that Johnnie gave her every Christmas. Henry, her lover, Johnnie's blood brother, was present when he died, and is willing to follow where Johnnie leads, as he was during Johnnie's life; so are the other two friends, Big Joe and Dave, although not to the same extent. Johnnie's wife, Ruth, misses him desperately, with a kind of suppressed rage at his leaving her. Johnnie's spirit intensifies what is in each of them. Under his influence, Ruth incites Rosie to leave Henry, to become as resentful and lonely as she is. Johnnie's spirit sways Henry, against his will, to get drunk, fight, and quarrel with Rosie, and then lures him out to the river to "come with me up the river and meet the old people." It is not until the truth (or part of it) is pieced together that each can be free to rework a new relationship with Johnnie and with one another. Rosie recognizes that his fierce protective love belittled her; Ruth must acknowledge that his friends were not his killers; Henry realizes that he does not want to follow where Johnnie has gone. Before they can move forward, each has to understand an aspect of herself or himself hitherto denied or disregarded. By disengaging themselves from falsehood, they are released, in proportion to their apprehension of the truth, and Johnnie himself is set free, no longer trapped in the Northern Lights.

The inspiration for the play came from the Whitehorse Correctional Centre when, as a journalist, Patti Flather worked on a feature on inmates exploring spirituality. Leonard Linklater joined Patti in developing the text at the Nakai play-writing contest in 1989. It was, according to the playwrights, geared to opening up discussion, especially among those searching for identity and needing to reclaim their own spirituality in order to heal (interview with authors, 5 December 1998). The play reflects its origins and intended audience with its bleakness and humour, downtrodden realism and inner spirituality. When *Sixty Below* first opened in Whitehorse, "a lot of people were on healing journeys and could relate to the situations that were put forward" (qtd from 5 December 1998 interview), and the play received a warm welcome. When it was produced in Toronto, it was greeted with the same kind of recognition. According to Leonard Linklater, "It is not regional, not Canadian, but world wide — you must know who you are and where you've come from to know where you're going."

E.D.

* * *

Sixty Below was premiered at the Native Canadian Centre in Toronto, Ontario by Native Earth Performing Arts Inc. on 3 April 1997. It was nominated for seven Dora Mavor Moore Awards in the small theatre division, including outstanding new play and outstanding production.

Henry	Kennetch Charlette
Rosie	Columpa C. Bobb
Dave	Deak Peltier
Big Joe	Gilbert Clements
Ruth	Carol Greyeyes
Johnnie	Lorne Cardinal

Directed by Vinetta Strombergs
Designed by Stephen Degenstein

Lighting Design by Jim Plaxton
Sound Design and Musical Composition by Jack Nicholsen

An earlier version of the play was produced by Nakai Theatre Ensemble on 31 March 1993 at the Yukon Arts Centre in Whitehorse.

Henry	John Peters Jr
Rosie	Sylvia-anne George
Dave	Evan Tlesla Adams
Big Joe	Joe Migwans
Ruth	Dinah Gaston
Johnnie	Neil E. Smith
Bruiser	Phil Gatensby

Directed by Allen MacInnis
Designed by Donald C. Watt
Lighting Design by Joanne Lantz
Sound Design by Roly Mitton, Doug Smarch, Old Crow Studios

The playwrights acknowledge the contributions of dramaturges Kim McCaw, Judith Rudakoff, Vinetta Strombergs, and Svetlana Zylin.

SIXTY BELOW

CHARACTERS

HENRY	a handsome native man in his mid-thirties
ROSIE	an attractive native woman in her mid-twenties
DAVE	a half-breed man in his mid-thirties
BIG JOE	a native man in his mid-thirties
RUTH	a native woman in her early thirties
JOHNNIE	the ghost of a native man in his mid-thirties
BRUISER	a large native man in his mid-thirties

SETTING

The setting is Whitehorse, capital city of the Yukon Territory, in the present. The action of the play takes place over a period of three nights — December 19th to 21st, the winter solstice.

*Note
The word Jijuu is pronounced with the emphasis on the second syllable.

ACT ONE

Scene One

HENRY alone in spotlight.

HENRY I can't get away from this dream . . .

> *Sounds of fiddle music, musician, children jigging and laughing on stage.*

I'm back home in Old Crow. There's fiddle music. Uncle Albert is tapping away with his foot, the fiddle tucked under his chin. I'm wearing my jigging shoes, the special moccasins my Jijuu made me for my birthday. Mom keeps saying: Dance Henry, dance with the girls! I'm so shy. Mom and my aunties giggle at me. I'm blushing. Mom pushes me out on the dance floor. Dance Henry! So I do. It's the Handkerchief Dance.

> *Sounds of drumming, singing when appropriate. JOHNNIE appears in silhouette, dancing.*

Then the music changes. It's something strange. Fiddle music is what I grew up with . . . that and George Jones. Mom's favourite. But this is from another world. It goes deeper. I've known it before . . . a long time ago. Before I was born, even before the days Jijuu and Jijii tell us about. I'm right beside this guy. He's got this traditional vest, beaded caribou skin with fringes, and then a baseball cap and cowboy boots. And the drum. Jijii says Old Crow people didn't have drums when we danced, but Jijuu, she's from the Delta, she remembers the drums. This guy, can he ever play that drum! He starts off slow, the same drumbeat over and over. Pretty soon I'm nodding my head in time with the rhythm. He starts singing.

HENRY

It's a song about a young man going away and leaving his family and friends. He feels sad, but he has to go. I don't know who the song is about. I can tell it's somebody I know, just because of how I am when I wake up. Otherwise I wouldn't have felt it that strong, you know.

I never remembered my dreams. Until . . . that was the longest night of the year.

> *Drumming/singing down.*

Scene Two

> *ROSIE is alone outside, three in the morning, walking home from work along the river, with her journal. JOHNNIE dances in the northern lights.*

ROSIE

Look at them dance! Wow. Playful. Blue and green. Purple disappearing into black. Like so many people dancing home after a successful hunt. *(beat)* Johnnie was the best dancer. I loved it when he'd drag me out on the dance floor. All the girls were jealous, even though I was just his little sister. We'd have so much fun. Now he's gone to dance in the northern lights.

ROSIE writes in her journal

Lorraine says her people — the Tutchone from around here — have a legend about it. They say some people are trapped in the northern lights because of the way they died. They can't leave the realm of the earth. They have unfinished business. Lorraine says you're not supposed to look at the lights or you'll make their journey harder.

But we're not Tutchone, me and Johnnie are Gwich'in. Bitchin' Gwich'in, our families come from way up north. My Jijuu said the old people believed souls wandered the earth waiting for a child to be born, so they could inhabit a new body. Sometimes they tried to drag the soul of a loved one with them. Creepy, huh? Jijuu said we have a legend about the jealous northern lights. They're in love with a girl on the earth and they won't let anyone near her.

ROSIE I don't care what Lorraine says, if Johnnie is dancing in those lights, I'm damn well going to watch him! Everyone I love dances. Except Henry's really clumsy. Henry . . . I can't believe he's getting out tomorrow! Yee-ha! Nine months I miss him so much. We'll go dancing — the bedspring boogie. Can you hear me, Henry? Get back to the Yukon! I have a surprise for you.

Scene Three

Lights up on ROSIE in sparsely furnished bachelor apartment listening to country music station. There's a knock on the door. ROSIE jumps.

HENRY *(offstage)* Hellooooo! Roseeeeee!

More knocking.

ROSIE	Holy shit! He's early!
HENRY	(*offstage*) Yoooo-hoooo. Anybody in there?!
ROSIE	(*hesitating*) He's gonna think I look like shit.

> *ROSIE turns the radio off, opens the door.*

ROSIE	Hi.
HENRY	Hi? Is that it?
ROSIE	Hi Henry, come in.
HENRY	I was beginning to think I had the wrong place.
ROSIE	I . . . I didn't hear you at first. The radio was on.
HENRY	Oh yeah, your new boyfriend was probably climbing bare-assed out the window . . . Oh, there he goes now!
ROSIE	You're crazy! I don't have another boyfriend!
HENRY	That's what I like to hear . . . Well?
ROSIE	Well what?
HENRY	Do I get a welcome-home kiss?
ROSIE	Yes!
HENRY	Ooooh-eeee!
ROSIE	Finally back home.
HENRY	In all my glory.
ROSIE	I missed you, you dirty bugger.
HENRY	I missed you too.
ROSIE	Yeah?
HENRY	Well of course. Don't think I ever went so long without getting laid! Nine months!
ROSIE	You're not the only one.
HENRY	Come here.
ROSIE	Why?

HENRY   I gotta check something.

ROSIE   What?

HENRY   Oooh.

> *He kisses her ear. She giggles.*

ROSIE   That tickles!

HENRY   Mmmm. I coulda killed a dozen guards for that ear. Wonder if the other one's still there. I better make sure!

ROSIE   Agh! You're giving me goosebumps!

HENRY   Oooh. Goosebumps. Boy, have I got a cure for that.

ROSIE   What?

HENRY   You'll see.

> *HENRY grabs ROSIE and picks her up.*

ROSIE   Agh! Henry! *(she laughs)*

> *Dream music. HENRY and ROSIE do a sensual dream dance as HENRY speaks. JOHNNIE appears with a doll which he treats lovingly as he dances around.*

HENRY   Rosie. Soft. Beautiful. The smell of fresh, washed hair. An angel. An untouchable treasure. Johnnie's baby sister. He watched over her like a hawk.

> *JOHNNIE kisses ROSIE'S forehead and pulls her away from HENRY. JOHNNIE beckons and entices her with the doll. They dance together as HENRY continues.*

HENRY   But, she grew up so fast. One second she was a little girl, and then she had me wrapped around her little finger. She was sixteen and Johnnie couldn't tell her "no." But, he sure as hell told me I had to treat her right.

> *JOHNNIE dangles the doll in front of ROSIE. She grabs for it, seizes it, holds it, then roughly tosses it away. JOHNNIE hides.*

ROSIE	*(looking for him)* Johnnie?
	A ROSIE / HENRY dream sequence which turns into the nightmare.
ROSIE	It was so good when we first got together.
HENRY	Springtime.
ROSIE	A warm clear night.
HENRY	We climbed onto that big cement block.
ROSIE	Behind the White Pass depot.
HENRY	Down by the river.
ROSIE	Watching big chunks of ice float past us.
HENRY	We made up that game about where the ice was going.
HENRY & ROSIE	Wondering.
HENRY	If they'd make it to Alaska.
ROSIE	Or get stuck against each other.
HENRY & ROSIE	Trapped.
HENRY	The current rushing past them.
HENRY & ROSIE	Helpless.
ROSIE	Cutting into each other.
HENRY	Getting real mad.
ROSIE	And you made up that song.
HENRY	Ode to the Lonesome Iceberg.
ROSIE	You sang it at the top of your lungs on that cement block, your arms stretched to the stars.
HENRY	*(singing)* Ode to the Lonesome Iceberg!
ROSIE	That's when I fell in love with you.

*ROSIE goes back to sleep. JOHNNIE returns
and sends HENRY a nightmare.*

*JOHNNIE dances closer and closer. He tries to
steal HENRY'S spirit. He knows the human
spirit can be lost through fright. He pulls
HENRY into the Yukon river for the journey
upriver to the afterworld. The icy water pulls
HENRY deeper and deeper, away from ROSIE.
He sees a beaver and tries to grab its tail.
Suddenly the beaver turns into JOHNNIE.
HENRY's terror is complete.*

HENRY	Get away from me! Don't take me. Nooo!
ROSIE	Henry! Wake up, Henry!
HENRY	Get away from me!
ROSIE	It's me! Rosie!

JOHNNIE exits as HENRY wakes up.

HENRY	Rosie? *(beat)* Where am I?
ROSIE	You're home, with me.
HENRY	Oh. Yeah.
ROSIE	What's wrong?
HENRY	Oh jeez . . . scary. Whoa.
ROSIE	You're shaking.
HENRY	All sweaty too.
ROSIE	Bad dream?
HENRY	Yeah.
ROSIE	About what?
HENRY	Uh. Nothing.
ROSIE	That wasn't nothing.
HENRY	I don't remember.
ROSIE	You were fighting someone.

HENRY	Oh. Um. What was it. I know. Going back to jail. Yeah. They were taking me back.
ROSIE	What?!
HENRY	Yeah, funny huh? Just get out and already dreamin' about going back.
ROSIE	That's not funny.
HENRY	Don't worry, I ain't planning on a return visit.
ROSIE	You better not.

> *HENRY is really convincing himself as much as ROSIE. He keeps interrupting what ROSIE is trying to say.*

HENRY	I'm not going to screw up. This time it's gonna be different, Rosie. You'll see. I'll get a job. Get my grade twelve . . .
ROSIE	That would be great! And guess what, Henry, I got my . . .
HENRY	*(continuing)* Yeah! I'll go easy on the booze, really take care of you Rosie. Maybe I can play in a band.
ROSIE	Well, I've got some great news too. I went and . . .
HENRY	*(continuing)* You and me can do anything together! I know it!
ROSIE	It's just that . . .
HENRY	*(continuing)* I got so many plans! I can't wait, Rosie!
ROSIE	Henry, listen! *(she finally gets HENRY's attention)* It was hard when you were gone. I'd lie awake at night, my legs aching after a long shift, and pretend you were there beside me. But you weren't. Henry, I don't want to be a barmaid for the rest of my life. I've been doing a lot of thinking.
HENRY	Yeah. I've been thinking too. Every day I thought about you and how it was gonna be for us. I'd think how happy we'd be with a cabin in the bush. And we could have some kids. Little Henry Junior.

ROSIE	Henry, you're dreaming. What you want takes a lot of work.
HENRY	Yeah, and we can do it Rosie! I can do it. You gotta believe in me.
ROSIE	I do. I've always stuck by you.
HENRY	Sometimes I don't know why.
ROSIE	*(joking)* Yeah, Ruth says I'm crazy to give you another chance.
HENRY	I wish she'd just butt out.
ROSIE	She just worries about me. She's like my own sister. She'll come around . . . You know I love you.
HENRY	I love you too. Ever since I can remember.
ROSIE	Ever since you can remember, huh?
HENRY	Uh-huh.
ROSIE	Sure took you long enough to show it.
HENRY	You can thank Johnnie for that. Any guy that danced with you too many times, Johnnie'd take the poor little shit aside, crack the knuckles on his hands and tell that quivering kid, You lay one finger on my baby sister and I'll have your balls.
ROSIE	You weren't scared of Johnnie?
HENRY	Nah . . . Of course not . . . You were worth it.
ROSIE	I'm so glad you're home.

HENRY starts caressing ROSIE, they kiss.

HENRY	Oh you're so beautiful.

They snuggle and go back to sleep.

Scene Four

The next day. HENRY is dressing and getting familiar with the apartment again.

HENRY   God, I ain't seen that shirt in a long time. Hellooo
again! Well, Henry ole boy, what are we gonna do
with ourself today? Get to do whatever *we* want for a
change! *(HENRY grabs the paper)* Well let's look
for a job, keep me outta them there bars . . . *(reading
the want ads)* You know, there ain't too much here
for an ex-con. Chambermaids and waitresses . . . Ah
this looks interesting. Government job. Starting at
sixty grand. I can handle that. Yeah lots of coffee
breaks, a secretary to do all the work, and a coupla
free trips Outside every year. Your so-called northern
allowance. Yep. No Indian gonna get that job, that's
fer sure . . . Hey look at this, a band worker needed
in Carcross. Grade twelve required. Ooooh . . .
Indian pay too. Twenty-five thousand dollars . . .
vehicle required . . . Fuck this is depressing.

> *HENRY throws down the paper, picks up the
> phone and calls BRUISER.*

Hello, Bruiser? It's Henry . . . Yeah, I just got
out . . . Thanks. Listen, are you doing a smudge
today? . . . Great! I'll be right there.

> *HENRY grabs his jacket and leaves the
> apartment.*

> *HENRY in a spotlight, talking to the audience.
> He is doing a smudge with BRUISER /
> JOHNNIE.*

HENRY   *(referring to BRUISER)* I always thought of them as
flakes . . . These born-again Indians, walking around
in their buckskins, with their silver and turquoise
jewellery. Their hair all of a sudden in braids.
Maybe it was so they didn't get it in their ever-
present cup of coffee. But, there was always
something about guys like Bruiser, a peacefulness
that made you want to know more. So when they
locked me up I got to talking with this inmate. He
tells me about the sweatlodge. He said it really
helped him deal with some of the bad things that
happened to him. So I tried it out.

This ex-con led the ceremony. Tattoes all over his
arms. He didn't preach at all. I felt comfortable with
him. I told him stuff I could never say to Dave or

Big Joe, or even Rosie. I felt naked in the
sweatlodge . . . Well, I was naked pretty well! But
naked inside too, like the guy could see inside of me
and I couldn't hide anything. It gave me the willies.
But I kept going. I couldn't turn back.

> *HENRY walks back into the apartment, as he*
> *continues talking.*

HENRY Well maybe these smudges and sweats will help keep
me on the straight and narrow. I'm not going back to
jail, that's for sure. If Rosie and me are gonna have
some kids, the last thing they need is to spend their
weekends visiting their old man in jail. I want
people to look up to me now. I'm ready. I know I
am.

Scene Five

DAVE (*offstage*) Ow! Watch it you fat goof!

BIG JOE (*offstage*) Bug off, Dave!

HENRY Oh-boy. Here comes Test Number One.

DAVE (*offstage*) Move over! Christ, you're blockin' the
whole fuckin' doorway! You and that big fuckin'
beer gut!

BIG JOE (*offstage*) Aw, c'mon, Dave! My head still hurts!

DAVE (*offstage*) You still can't handle your booze, ya big
oaf!

BIG JOE (*offstage*) Can so.

HENRY Yup. Those voices sound pretty familiar. (*HENRY*
opens the door) Hi Dave.

DAVE Henry you old fuck you're out. Fuckin eh!

HENRY Hey Big Joe.

BIG JOE Henry, I meant to write you down there. I started this
letter this one time but I couldn't think of nothing to
say . . .

DAVE	Yeah, cuz, I was all set there too, I was gonna call you one morning after this all-nighter, I got some operator broad on directory assistance and couldn't remember what the fuck the place was called . . .
HENRY	Matsqui, B.C.
DAVE	Yeah yeah, but you know when you're having fun, all I could think of was Moosehide!
BIG JOE	Up by Dawson? There's no jail up there.
DAVE	No kidding, Joe.
HENRY	Forget it, guys. Good to see you again!
BIG JOE	So you check out the bars yet?
DAVE	There's an idea! Let's go celebrate!
HENRY	You two don't waste any time, eh?
DAVE	Hey Buddy, life's too short! Gotta show my cousin a good time again! Do you know what that is anymore?
HENRY	Naw I think I forgot. Why don't you tell me?
DAVE	Later. Now about that Brewski. Come on!
HENRY	No can do, guys.
DAVE	Henry! Your first day out! You can't stay all cooped up in here! Let's have a drink!
BIG JOE	Yeah, I need something for this hangover.
HENRY	Hair of the dog that bit you, eh, Joe?
BIG JOE	Whaddyou mean, Henry?
DAVE	Big Joe said he's buying!
BIG JOE	I did? *(beat)* Wait a sec.
HENRY	Hey, you guys working?
BIG JOE	Sometimes . . .
DAVE	*(interrupting)* No way man. UIC drinking team all the way! Chug-a-lug!

BIG JOE   Yeah, but didn't your UI run out, Dave?

DAVE   No kidding, Joe, you just had to remind me.

BIG JOE   Well you told me you was gonna get some money off
                your mom to pay me back all that money you owe
                me . . .

DAVE   What's the big hurry all of a sudden? I ain't goin'
                nowhere. Let's go buy Henry a cold one.

HENRY   Naw, I been doing a lot of thinking . . . You know
                the only time I get in trouble is when I'm pissed.

DAVE   We're not asking you to get drunk.

HENRY   I promised Rosie I'd take it easy on the booze.

DAVE   What, you goin' soft on us there Henry ole boy?

HENRY   Well I just did this smudge with Bruiser . . .

DAVE   You're not going religious on us, are you?

BIG JOE   I don't see no smudges on you.

HENRY   It's not like that other church stuff. It's a whole
                different way of looking at the world. It's like, you
                know how we felt back at fish camp . . . like there's
                nothing but you and the world. It felt so good to be
                part of nature.

BIG JOE   Hey isn't that like the sweatlodge or something?
                This one time Bruiser was trying to explain it
                to me . . .

DAVE   *(interrupting)* We don't need to hear about that shit.
                You're coming with us. You gotta get caught up on
                the latest!

BIG JOE   That Bruiser don't drink, eh? Not even beer. Jeez!

HENRY   Hey, what is everybody up to these days? Joe, how's
                Lorraine?

BIG JOE   Aw . . . she's gone.

HENRY   Gone?

BIG JOE   Off to Vancouver. Took the kids.

HENRY	Hey, I'm sorry.
BIG JOE	Yeah, well I knew she was a little fed up . . .
DAVE	(*interrupting*) Come on, Joe, Henry don't wanna hear that right now . . .
BIG JOE	Yeah, but . . .
DAVE	But it's time for a beer! Gotta come with us to get all the news.
HENRY	Well, maybe . . . But I'm only drinking coffee.
DAVE	Good enough. To the Capital!
BIG JOE	I wanna go to the Sixty Below. Beer's cheaper there.
DAVE	Yeah but there's no peelers.
BIG JOE	Them barmaids are nicer at the Sixty.
HENRY	Yeah, Rosie's working.
DAVE	How 'bout the Roadhouse? Shoot some pool at the Stretchmark Hotel.
BIG JOE	I like the Sixty.
HENRY	Me too.
DAVE	Alright, ya big babies. To the Sixty.

They exit.

Scene Six

The Sixty Below bar. There's canned Christmas country music. ROSIE is setting up or clearing off a table to sit down for her break.

ROSIE	(*grumbling to herself*) I'm so sick of that Christmas tape I could rip it to shreds.

Just as ROSIE sits down to write in her journal . . .

VOICE OFFSTAGE	Hey you workin' or what? My beer's empty!

HENRY	*(sarcastic)* Hi Ruth! Oh hi Henry, welcome home! Thanks Ruth, good to see you again!
RUTH	Hi Henry. Haven't seen you guys in a while.
BIG JOE	I don't get up that way much, I never know when my truck is gonna break down.
RUTH	You boys used to stop by every other weekend at least.
ROSIE	Crash is more like it.
RUTH	Drinking our beer, smoking our cigarettes, sleeping on our couch, begging me to do your beer runs.
DAVE	Ha! And you never would neither!
ROSIE	Putting up with these guys . . . I don't know how you did it, Ruth.
RUTH	Ah, they made me laugh sometimes.
BIG JOE	It was fun coming over to see you and Johnnie.
DAVE	Yeah, well, enough reminiscing. I'm thirsty.
RUTH	So, have one for Johnnie, eh? Here Rosie, get the boys a round. Even Henry.
DAVE	Hot damn! Bring on the beer!
HENRY	Just coffee, Rosie.
RUTH	*(sarcastic)* Oh right, we wouldn't want to do anything we might regret later, would we?
HENRY	No Ruth, we certainly wouldn't.

> *As ROSIE walks away to get the drinks, RUTH catches her.*

RUTH	Come on Rosie, bingo or bust.
ROSIE	I don't get off till seven.
RUTH	Perfect! Bingo starts at eight.
ROSIE	Maybe for a little while . . .
RUTH	Great! See ya later.

ROSIE	I'm on a break. Get it yourself.
VOICE OFFSTAGE	Jesus, man!
ROSIE	Oh quit your griping. *(beat)* December the 20th. Me and my bright ideas — why did I think it was such a good idea to surprise him with my diploma? I should have told him this morning, I know I should have, but he was so excited about his dreams. When he said he wanted to get his grade twelve my stomach just double-flipped over and over. I feel so guilty. It's like I've already done what he's only dreaming about. How can I tell him how great it was being back in school, how happy I was, while he was locked up down South? I have to tell him today.

> *RUTH enters.*

RUTH	Hey! How much does the Sixty pay you to write in that thing?
ROSIE	Not enough. Hey, aren't you working today?
RUTH	Had a meeting downtown. Besides, I'm on my lunch break.
ROSIE	Oh sure, I know what kind of lunch breaks everybody at the band office takes.
RUTH	Well?
ROSIE	Well what?
RUTH	Did you get it?
ROSIE	What are you talking about?
RUTH	That piece of tail you waited nine months for. Was it worth it?
ROSIE	As a matter of fact, yeah, it was.
RUTH	Well he couldn't have kept you up all night. You're still walking straight!

> *ROSIE replies with a physical reaction rather than a word.*

RUTH	Honeymoon time again. Enjoy it while it lasts.
ROSIE	Don't start . . .
RUTH	*(RUTH starts stroking her shirt)* All right . . . but when Henry starts drinking again . . . poof! He'll be on a tear and the next thing you know . . .
ROSIE	Ruth . . .
RUTH	Yeah yeah . . .
ROSIE	Is that Johnnie's shirt you're wearing?
	RUTH shrugs.
RUTH	It's one year tomorrow.
ROSIE	I know.
RUTH	*(beat)* Hey, your exams are over, right? Have you heard anything?
ROSIE	Yeah . . .
RUTH	Yeah . . . so . . . ?
ROSIE	So I finished top of my class!
RUTH	Awright! We have to celebrate!
ROSIE	Sure!
RUTH	How about tonight, just the girls, we can order pizza and pick up some cider, you can play radio bingo with me . . .
ROSIE	I don't know if I should . . .
RUTH	Eight thousand dollar jackpot tonight! It's on me. And the kids are sleeping over at my Mom's.
ROSIE	Henry just got back . . .
RUTH	Oh right, Henry's back and I won't see you anymore.
ROSIE	I won't abandon my best friend.
DAVE	*(entering)* Hey is this a desert or what? We're dying of thirst over here!

ROSIE	Go outside and suck on an icicle!
	DAVE enters, followed by HENRY and BIG JOE.
ROSIE	Henry! What are you doing here?
RUTH	*(to ROSIE)* Honeymoon's over.
ROSIE	*(ignoring RUTH)* And what are you doing with these things?
DAVE	Come on, he just got out, don't go nagging him right away. *(to RUTH)* Ain't you supposed to be working?
RUTH	What would you know about work?
BIG JOE	*(to DAVE)* Did she just call us things?
HENRY	Just came in for a coffee. I was talking to Bruiser about a job.
ROSIE	Oh. That's good. Doing what?
HENRY	Woodcutting. I gotta see the guy tonight.
	As the guys sit down at a table, RUTH nudges ROSIE.
RUTH	*(mouthing the word)* Bingo!
DAVE	Fuck the coffee, I'll have a beer, Rosie. Blue.
RUTH	Good to see you haven't changed.
DAVE	Never knew you to turn down a drink.
RUTH	It's happened, Dave, it's happened.
DAVE	My beer, Rosie?
ROSIE	Listen, you little asshole. You want anything you ask for it nice, you hear? Otherwise you can get you scrawny ass outta here.
BIG JOE	I'll have a Canadian, Rosie. Please.
DAVE	Come on, just get us a beer.
ROSIE	Maybe.

> *RUTH exits. ROSIE gets the guys' drinks.*

DAVE   Do you ever miss things?

HENRY   Like what?

DAVE   Like we used to take that old skidoo out. 'Member Grandpa's skidoo?

HENRY   Yeah. That sucker could fly.

DAVE   You're tellin' me!

BIG JOE   Fucking fly away. Oh man.

DAVE   Remember back in Old Crow, that Easter break? We were all piled on, going down by the river just cruising along. We hit a bump. I fall off first, grabbing Henry and he grabs Johnnie. But the throttle sticks and that fucker keeps flying! We start running after it, I'm in front. I wipe out in some deep snow. Face down. Henry and Johnnie just keep running right over me with their boots! Choong, choong, choong, just like that! I'm eating snow, man! I pick myself up and chase after them. We finally catch that skidoo parked in a snowbank. Fuck, that was funny! I don't even know where Joe was, his old skidoo broke down and he had to walk back!

HENRY   I miss being out in the bush.

DAVE   One o' these days, man, we gotta go back up there . . . Yeah. Do some hunting . . . get some nice fat caribou . . .

BIG JOE   I'll go with ya.

DAVE   Man, I haven't gone hunting in ages.

HENRY   Me neither . . . Not since . . .

> *Long silence. Lighting change for flashback to one year ago.*
>
> *Flashback. One year ago. JOHNNIE brings beer and joins the three men at the table. They are all drunk.*

JOHNNIE	*(plonking down the beers)* Merry fucking Christmas!
ALL	Ho, fucking, ho!
BIG JOE	It's not Christmas yet, is it? I ain't even got the kids' presents yet.
DAVE	Don't piss yourself, you got three more shopping days.
HENRY	What did you buy the boys, Johnnie?
JOHNNIE	Who's got money for presents?
BIG JOE	I thought Ruth was working, Johnnie.
JOHNNIE	Guess she's buying for the lot of us. What a joke.
HENRY	Don't worry about it. Rosie's gonna spoil your boys.
JOHNNIE	When are you and Rosie gonna have kids?
HENRY	Says she ain't ready. She sure loves kids though — especially yours. That little Charles, Rosie says he'll be a real lady killer.
DAVE	Kid don't even look like him.
BIG JOE	I think he does. That Charles is real cute.
DAVE	*(to HENRY)* Gotta watch them broads, eh?
HENRY	. . .Yeah.
JOHNNIE	. . .Yeah. December 21st. Darkest day of the year. Everyone in this bar looks like they just opened up their VISA bill and they're two-thousand bucks over their limit.
HENRY	What's your problem?
BIG JOE	Johnnie don't have any problems.
JOHNNIE	Yeah. Johnnie don't have any problems.
DAVE	He's got you around, don't he?
BIG JOE	I'm a better friend than you are.

DAVE	Shee-ee-it! Johnnie yanks your sorry butt out of the river once and you're kissing his boots for life.
JOHNNIE	I would've done the same for you.
HENRY	You're a better man than I am, Johnnie.
BIG JOE	Better than all of us.
DAVE	Spare me please.
JOHNNIE	I'm no different than anybody.
BIG JOE	No way.
HENRY	You're a lot better dancer than I'll ever be. Them girls go nuts over you.
JOHNNIE	Then you get an old lady and that stuff just gets you in trouble.
BIG JOE	I'd give anything to dance like you.
DAVE	Just gotta wiggle your hips is all. Practice that pelvic action. *(he illustrates)*
HENRY	I think you need lessons.
DAVE	*(pretending to threaten HENRY with his fist)* Maybe I should give you a lesson.
HENRY	You! That I'd like to see.
BIG JOE	And not only that, Johnnie. You're a good carpenter too.
JOHNNIE	No work for carpenters now. Nothing happening on the hospital job. And our first Indian hotel project? New government cancels it. I guess them old rednecks don't like seeing Indians with money in their pockets.
HENRY	Once that land claim comes through, they'll be knocking at our doors!
DAVE	That'll be worth seeing!
BIG JOE	Yeah, it'll pick up Johnnie.
JOHNNIE	Doesn't help me right now.

DAVE	Let's go somewheres else. You guys are fuckin' depressing me.
HENRY	Isn't the solstice feast on?
DAVE	*(sarcastic)* Oh yeah, let's check that out.
JOHNNIE	You're a spiritual kind of guy.
DAVE	You got it, Pontiac.
HENRY	His hand-made drum never leaves his side.
DAVE	Next to my medicine pouch.
BIG JOE	What have they got at that feast? I'm kinda hungry.
DAVE	Go shoot a moose.
BIG JOE	I never got a moose.
DAVE	You told us already.
BIG JOE	Went out three times this fall and didn't see one moose.
DAVE	You're supposed to drive out of town first.
JOHNNIE	*(singing)* Deck the halls with moose and money,
ALL	Fa la la la la la la la la . . .
HENRY	'Tis the season to get loaded,
ALL	Fa la la la la la la la la . . .
JOHNNIE	That's about it. No money for Christmas so might as well get loaded.
HENRY	No sense being poor and sober. Bring on the beer!
JOHNNIE	Beer and good cheer!
DAVE	Let's go for a spin.
HENRY	What about beer?
DAVE	Get off-sales.
HENRY	Who's got money?

They all look at JOE.

BIG JOE	I saw your truck out there Johnnie. You left it running, huh?
JOHNNIE	Yup. Cold out there.
DAVE	It's sixty below out there . . .
ALL	And it's Sixty Below in here.
BIG JOE	Where are we gonna go?
JOHNNIE	Let's go hunting. It's like a morgue in here.

As JOHNNIE leaves the table, lights switch back to the present, and ROSIE pours HENRY another coffee. Silence.

DAVE	It's like a morgue in here. Hey, Rosie, another Blue!
ROSIE	Please.
DAVE	Fuck! . . . Please, Rosie.
ROSIE	You sound so cute when you talk like that.
DAVE	Fuck off . . . Hey, Henry, have a beer, man.
ROSIE	Quit hounding him.
DAVE	Why don't you go clear them bottles off those tables over there.
ROSIE	No that's okay, Dave, I'll save them for you.
BIG JOE	'Nother round for everybody. Dave said he's buying.
HENRY	Just coffee for me, Rosie.

ROSIE gets coffee.

DAVE	They really did a number on you up there.
HENRY	It wasn't like that.
DAVE	Well, I ain't never seen you like this. Drinking coffee and talking about the sweatlodge . . .
HENRY	You see things different when you're in the can . . .
DAVE	Fuckin' go to jail to get born again! You and Bruiser gonna be best buddies now or what?

HENRY   I just went to a few sweats. They got a little lodge
                 outside. Nothing better to do, it's boring as hell in
                 there.

DAVE   Fuck, my cousin sitting in some Indian sauna
                 praying his ass off. Never thought I'd see it.

HENRY   You just don't understand.

DAVE   You got that right.

HENRY   If you were there, you'd know. You'd know how
                 good it feels to get away from the screws for even a
                 little while, and forget about those walls all around
                 you. It's like you're not in jail. You're free, man.

DAVE   This sweatlodge don't even come from around here.
                 It's not our ways. It's some southern Indian thing.

HENRY   I remember Jijii talking about sweatlodges for people
                 who·were sick.

DAVE   Sick people maybe. Not for prayin' with some
                 medicine man.

HENRY   It's better than going to the white man's church.

                 ROSIE brings beer.

DAVE   White or Indian — church is all the same to me.
                 You know what I believe? I believe I'll have another
                 beer. Amen.

                 ROSIE exits.

HENRY   Why don't you come to a sweat with me? See for
                 yourself.

DAVE   Yeah right. I get enough religion from Mom.

HENRY   Like I said, white man's church. Come on, what are
                 you afraid of?

DAVE   I'm not afraid.

HENRY   No? All we learned in school is how to be white . . .
                 get down on our knees to bless Columbus and
                 Mackenzie and all those other goofs that "discovered"
                 our land. And you're too chicken to check out a real
                 native ceremony.

DAVE   Just fucking drop it.

> *Lighting change. DAVE and JOE drink and freeze. HENRY'S internal point of view. HENRY observes DAVE and BIG JOE and speaks to the audience.*

HENRY   I don't know what to say. Dave and Big Joe, they're my good friends, we stick together, in for a penny, in for a pound. But they just don't get it. Them cons told me, "Getting out is the easy part." I didn't listen to them. But it's like watching a television program, you never believe it till you're in the middle of it. Now I can sit here and say, "What do you see in this life?" There's no rewards. Look at Dave. An obvious alcoholic. And Big Joe . . . well, he's drowning in misery. I got more to live for than that. I got my dreams. I got my old lady, and tomorrow I'll likely have a job. What more do I need? *(beat)* I can feel good without the booze.

> *Lighting change back to the present, hours later. Bad bar music. DAVE and BIG JOE are very drunk by now.*

DAVE   *(noticing HENRY staring at the beer)* Henry . . . Henry . . . Them beers calling your name again, Henry?

HENRY   *(coming out of his thoughts)* Yeah. Sort of.

DAVE   They're pretty tempting, aren't they?

HENRY   Funny how when you're drinking, no one will give you a nickel. Soon as you sober up, everyone's happy to hand you a bottle.

BIG JOE   Lorraine?

DAVE   She's gone, fuckhead. Get it through your thick skull.

HENRY   Leave him alone.

DAVE   Making fools out of all of us, the way he's blubbering away.

BIG JOE   Lorraine? Is that you?

HENRY   I think you're the one with the problem. You just don't know it.

BIG JOE   Go get me a beer. Be a friend.

DAVE   You're cut off, buddy.

BIG JOE   Aaaaw. I always get the beer. You get me a beer. Dave! Go get that money off your Mom.

DAVE   *(to JOE)* Go to sleep.

> *BIG JOE puts his head down and starts sobbing. HENRY shakes BIG JOE.*

HENRY   Hey, Big Joe, what's the matter?

DAVE   He's just drunk. I keep telling him he can't handle his booze.

> *ROSIE enters.*

ROSIE   Is he crying again?

DAVE   Yeah.

ROSIE   Shit.

BIG JOE   I tried . . . I got a job . . . didn't drink so much . . . helped her out with the baby . . . bitch! She took my kids! She took my little babies.

HENRY   Come on, time to go, Joe.

BIG JOE   I did my best . . . what more did you expect? Lorraine! Come back! I want my kids!

HENRY   Hey, take it easy, Joe. Let's go. *(to ROSIE)* I'll see you at home later.

> *HENRY helps JOE exit.*

DAVE   Wish he'd get over that bitch.

ROSIE   You pig! Lorraine just had enough. Joe was out with you more than he was home. What was she supposed to do?

DAVE   I don't know.

ROSIE	No one knows. But it's pretty sad when your old man can't save enough money to buy diapers.
DAVE	Fuck, get off my back. Why don't you do your job and bring me a beer.
ROSIE	You're cut off.

ROSIE walks away.

DAVE	(*shouting after her*) Yeah, well you don't deserve my company anyway. Guess I'll just take myself over to the Capital. Check out the peelers.

DAVE exits.

Scene Seven

HENRY enters helping drunken BIG JOE into ROSIE'S apartment. JOHNNIE is waiting in the shadows.

HENRY	Come on Joe, one foot in front of the other, we're almost there.
BIG JOE	Henry, you're a real pal.
HENRY	It's nothing, Joe. Here we are.
BIG JOE	Not like Dave.
HENRY	What would you two do without each other?
BIG JOE	I wanna tell him where to go! Henry, I just about had it up to here with Dave. One more joke about how stupid I am . . . how fat I am . . . how slow I am . . . I may take my time to think things over before I say something, but I ain't stupid. I'm thoughtful. Dave just puts me down because it makes him feel better. Just 'cause he can't even remember the last time he got laid — let alone had a girlfriend! Still hung up on his mother.
HENRY	Tell you what, you can crash here awhile.

HENRY struggles to get BIG JOE onto the couch. JOHNNIE arranges it so that they knock the phone off the hook.

BIG JOE	Henry, you're my best friend now that Johnnie's gone.
HENRY	Aw Joe . . .
BIG JOE	Really! I missed you when you were down South in that Moosehide place.
HENRY	Thanks Joe.

JOHNNIE appears to JOE, but not HENRY.

BIG JOE	*(to JOHNNIE)* I miss you too, Johnnie.
HENRY	Yeah. So do I.
BIG JOE	You know it's one year almost. I looked on the calendar. I figured it out . . . tomorrow is the day. Did you remember that, Henry?
HENRY	Yeah. Kinda hard to forget.
BIG JOE	'Course you remembered. You and Johnnie were blood brothers.
HENRY	Yeah.
BIG JOE	Wish I was Johnnie's blood brother.
HENRY	Christ, it was just a kid thing.
BIG JOE	I keep goin' over it, Henry. I shoulda been there for Johnnie that night, like he was there for me. Remember how he was there for me? We were all in High School. Remember?
HENRY	I remember.
BIG JOE	Johnnie saved my life. I owe my life to Johnnie.
HENRY	I know.
BIG JOE	He was there for everyone. You needed to talk about something, Johnnie would listen to you. I shoulda saved him, Henry. We shoulda saved him.
HENRY	It's just one of those things, Joe. I feel bad too, but it's not our fault.
BIG JOE	I wasn't paying attention.

HENRY	It was an acccident! An accident, Joe! Can't you get it through your thick skull!
BIG JOE	Henry, you never talked to me like that before.
HENRY	I'm sorry . . . I just don't see why you're dwelling on this.
BIG JOE	I am not dwelling.
HENRY	Yeah, you are. He's gone and we ain't bringing him back! Now let's get you sobered up. I'll make some coffee.

HENRY goes to the cupboard. As he opens the door, JOHNNIE makes ROSIE's diploma fall out. HENRY catches it.

Bingo voice-over kicks in as we switch to the scene at RUTH's place.

BINGO VOICE-OVER	Thanks to all of you who played radio bingo with us tonight. And now back to regular programming.

Scene Eight

RUTH'S apartment. Bingo voice-over. The women are drinking cider and eating pizza. RUTH is getting quite drunk. She's still wearing JOHNNIE'S shirt. JOHNNIE is present, somehow affecting the action, and particularly affecting RUTH, who seems to become more and more unbalanced.

ROSIE	B-fifteen! Why couldn't it have been B-fifteen!
RUTH	Shut up and have another cider.
ROSIE	I'm always one number off.
RUTH	Kiss another thirty bucks goodbye. Do you think we'll ever win that jackpot?
ROSIE	One number! That's all I needed, B-fifteen!
RUTH	Eight thousand beautiful dollars! That would buy us a night on the town!

ROSIE	You and me . . . we'd be crazy!
RUTH	We don't need a jackpot for that!
ROSIE	Like this summer . . . we were bad! Remember those guys? What did they call you?
RUTH	*(acting sexy)* Hello I'm raunchy Ruth!
ROSIE	They really thought they were gonna get lucky! *(putting on an American/Texan accent, imitating the guys that tried to pick them up)* "How's about another peach cider, my little Yukon Rose?"
RUTH	"We'll have two more peach ciders, please. And don't forget the Tequila shooters. And bring extra limes for my little sister here." And what about the way you were slow-dancing with that, what's his face . . . ?
ROSIE	*(laughing at the name)* Arnold!
RUTH	Arnold and Mervyn!
ROSIE	From Alaska.
RUTH	God I'd never get it on with an army boy.
ROSIE	Yeah. Little crewcuts . . .
ROSIE & **RUTH**	. . . Little hard-ons!

> *They crack up together. ROSIE dials phone.*

ROSIE	If Henry found out, he'd flip!
RUTH	My lips are sealed.
ROSIE	They better be. Or I'm up shit creek.
RUTH	I know how to keep a secret.
ROSIE	Speaking of secrets . . . How should I tell Henry about the diploma? I want to do something special.
RUTH	Hmmmm . . . I know! Give him a blow job! He'll be so happy you can tell him anything!
ROSIE	*(laughing)* No! Something romantic!

RUTH	How much more romantic can you get for a guy than a blow job!
ROSIE	You know how on our anniversary we always climb up on that cement block by the river. Some wine, a vase of flowers . . . the flowers usually freeze and die by the time the wine is finished . . . The river. It's perfect! *(ROSIE hangs up phone)* I'll bring the diploma, hide it in my purse. Nighttime, when no one's around. Do you have a flashlight? He has to be able to read my name on that beautiful diploma!
RUTH	He ain't worth all that trouble.
ROSIE	I have to do something special. I feel like I cheated on him.
RUTH	That's not cheating. Believe me.
ROSIE	I told Henry everything before this.
RUTH	You're not embarrassed, are you?
ROSIE	About what?
RUTH	About finishing top of your class. You know how guys are, they get weird about stuff like that. If you do anything better than them, they feel insecure or something.
ROSIE	Henry wants to go back to school too.
RUTH	Henry! No way!
ROSIE	That's what he told me. He did a lot of thinking in jail. He went to sweatlodges and everything.
RUTH	Oh that means a lot. Everyone knows that's where you go to smoke dope. They have a few tokes and use the sage and sweetgrass to hide the smell.
ROSIE	Really?
RUTH	It's common knowledge. *(beat)* You know, I'm so proud of you. I wish I had my grade twelve.
ROSIE	I thought you did.
RUTH	I was so close. Only two more courses, that's all I needed. I would have been the first in my family to

466 / Patti Flather & Leonard Linklater

graduate. Then I got pregnant. Johnnie wanted me to stay home with the baby. Yeah, I put my life on hold for that guy. And now I'm stuck with three kids, trying to make ends meet. Never enough money . . . Johnnie didn't leave me anything. Now, I don't have a life and I don't have Johnnie.

ROSIE   Do you ever think about seeing other guys? It might be good for the boys to have a father again.

RUTH   (*suddenly angry*) Johnnie is their father!

ROSIE   Sorry.

> *Uncomfortable silence. RUTH gets cider.*

RUTH   Besides, when do I have time for guys? Work and kids and meetings and laundry . . . And I have to leave time for the occasional girls night out, don't I?

ROSIE   I know it's been hard for you.

RUTH   Yeah. So.

ROSIE   Last night I dreamed about Johnnie again. He was trying to give me another doll.

RUTH   Him and his dolls.

ROSIE   I wouldn't take it. I threw it away . . . I hurt his feelings.

RUTH   It was just a dream.

ROSIE   I wonder . . . I found this old book at the college library. Some anthropologist who talked to our people a long time ago.

RUTH   What does some friggin' anthropologist know about us?

ROSIE   Souls travel south to the afterworld.

RUTH   Really. Maybe Johnnie got a free trip to Vancouver.

ROSIE   Some people believed the souls travel up the Yukon River.

RUTH

Do they stop at the fish ladder for a lunch break? Wave at all the tourists? Look out salmon, here comes a ghost!

ROSIE

I remember now. Jijuu told me some souls get stuck. *(JOHNNIE appears)* They hang around the living. Or try and grab someone to take with them to the Land of the Dead.

RUTH

For crying out loud, Rosie!

ROSIE

There's special places where souls wait to be reincarnated. They can send dreams. I know they can. What if Johnnie is sending us dreams? His spirit is still around us. I think he needs our help.

RUTH

You're freaking me out. *(beat)* I keep seeing him down the Long Lake Road. I'm on top of the ridge looking down. I see the river and the clay cliffs. I can make out the truck and little stick men. I can't tell who's who. Someone gets something out of the back of the truck. I'm running down the path to the road. I'm in the trees, there's willows in my way but the branches are like claws scraping my skin, they scratch my eyes and I can't see anymore, and I trip on a root and it's too late.

> *RUTH breaks down in tears. ROSIE comforts her.*

RUTH

Big finale to girls' night out.

ROSIE

Yeah. *(beat)* I should go . . . Henry's waiting.

RUTH

Look, I know you're real happy 'cause you got your man back. But if it weren't for those guys, Johnnie would be sitting here with me now. It's their fault.

ROSIE

You don't really mean that.

RUTH

I do. I hate them for that night. Those guys know something they're not telling. What were they doing out at Long Lake, in the middle of the night, pissed to the gills, hunting?! Did one of them think Johnnie was a moose? Did one of them trip on a log and blow Johnnie's head off? Maybe there was a fight. You know how Henry gets when he's drunk . . . he'll pick a fight with anybody.

ROSIE   Henry loved Johnnie! They all did. None of those guys would ever hurt Johnnie.

RUTH   They were all jealous of him.

ROSIE   You're not thinking straight. You've had too much too drink and you don't really mean that.

RUTH   Yes I do. They killed Johnnie, and they're gonna pay! And you better watch out or Henry will hurt you too.

ROSIE   You're wrong!

RUTH   You gotta stay away from Henry. Get rid of him.

ROSIE   No! I love him!

RUTH   There's a lot of stuff you don't know about Henry. You don't know how many times he's lied to you. How many times he's played around on you.

ROSIE   I don't believe you. Why are you saying these things?!

RUTH   Because I know! Everyone thinks Johnnie was a saint! But I know the other side. Half the time he didn't come home at all. Out screwing around . . . and Henry too! The two of them out fucking around . . .

ROSIE   No! Henry wouldn't do that to me!

RUTH   The sooner you get away from that guy the better!

ROSIE   I can't listen to you! I gotta go!

ROSIE runs out. RUTH is in tears. She strokes and tries to smell JOHNNIE'S shirt, then angrily starts ripping the shirt off. JOHNNIE appears to her, gently comforting and caressing her. He carries her off.

Scene Nine

ROSIE returns to her apartment. She is still upset about her fight with RUTH.

*JOE is passed out on the couch. HENRY is
sitting at the table, fuming about finding the
diploma. JOHNNIE is perched overhead, casting
a dark shadow on HENRY.*

ROSIE   *(kissing HENRY on the cheek)* Hi!

HENRY   *(smells booze)* Smells like you've been having fun.

ROSIE   Is that against the law?

HENRY   No.

ROSIE   Ruth and I had a few ciders while we were playing
radio bingo.

HENRY   Glad *you* had fun.

ROSIE   You're in a fine mood.

HENRY   Is that against the law?

ROSIE   Guess not.

HENRY   Just how much fun did you have?

ROSIE   What's your problem?

HENRY   You know I'm trying not to drink. One day back and
you can't even hold off on the party with Ruth.

      *ROSIE notices the phone off the hook and
replaces it. JOHNNIE now starts to affect
ROSIE, inflaming her.*

ROSIE   I tried to call you. And it wasn't a party!

HENRY   I just get out and already my old lady is getting
tanked. Thanks for the support.

ROSIE   Wait a minute. I'm not the one that put you in jail.
You've got to take some responsibility for that.

HENRY   I am! But . . . it'd be nice if you'd spend some time
with me.

ROSIE   What, you don't want me to go out? You expect me
to put my life on hold for you, just because *you*
screwed up!

HENRY	I guess I'm supposed to jump through all these hoops for everyone, while all my friends, and my old lady are getting pissed right under my nose.
ROSIE	I'm not the one who drinks so much I fight every guy in sight, and gets sent back to jail for assault . . . again!
HENRY	I told you, I'm laying off the booze!
ROSIE	And what about the dope? Those sweatlodges you told me about . . . smoking drugs wasn't one of the attractions, was it?
HENRY	Who gave you that idea?
ROSIE	Well it's pretty common knowledge the guys in jail like to get stoned in the sweatlodge.
HENRY	So a few guys got high. Sure. I never did. I wanted to respect the ceremony . . . Fuck! You don't have a clue what it's like in Matsqui.
ROSIE	Seems I don't have a clue about a lot of things. If you really want to know, it wasn't much of a party at Ruth's. She says you and Johnnie did more than dance with all the girls. Like all those nights you never came home and said you crashed at Dave's place.
HENRY	That bitch! She's lying!
ROSIE	Did you, Henry? Did you cheat on me?
HENRY	No!
ROSIE	You sure you wouldn't hide something like that from me?
HENRY	I should be asking you about hiding stuff. *(he shows her the diploma)* Just a little something I found tucked away in a cupboard.
ROSIE	I guess it's not a surprise anymore.
HENRY	I guess not.
ROSIE	I'm sorry. You know, you haven't been home very long . . .

HENRY	Takes a real long time to say, Guess what Henry, I got my grade twelve. Must be all of three seconds.
ROSIE	I tried to tell you this morning . . .
HENRY	All those months in jail, you couldn't slip it in during a phone call, or write it down in a letter. And what else have you been up to?
ROSIE	I've been going to school and working, that's what I've been up to. When are you gonna get a job?
HENRY	I told you, I'm going out woodcutting. It's almost for sure.
ROSIE	Good. 'Cause the rent's due next week, and I want to take a writing course up at the college.
HENRY	Was that going to be my next surprise?
ROSIE	You make it sound like some kind of conspiracy.
HENRY	That's what it feels like.
ROSIE	It was hard working and going to school. I'm sick of doing it all by myself, trying to pay the rent every month, and my tuition . . . You gotta help me.
HENRY	*(sarcastic)* Oh help me Henry, the rent's due and I gotta pay my tuition, it's real important to me even though I didn't tell you about my diploma.
ROSIE	You asshole! I waited nine months for you!
HENRY	Why? So you could hide things from me?
ROSIE	I wasn't hiding anything!
HENRY	*(sarcastic)* Oh no, I wouldn't hide anything from you Henry. Especially not in a fucking Kraft dinner cupboard.
ROSIE	You are so immature!
HENRY	*(angry)* You don't want to tell me anything so you stuff your precious diploma way the fuck up in a Kraft dinner cupboard!
ROSIE	You say you want to have kids . . . You're not ready to have kids!

HENRY	Fuck you!

HENRY gets his coat on.

ROSIE	Where are you going?
HENRY	Out.

HENRY storms out.

ROSIE	Well fuck you too!

ROSIE throws JOE out of the apartment. She picks up a doll and hugs it.

Scene Ten

Late at night. HENRY is down by the river, in a dark place. The northern lights are active. JOHNNIE appears, dancing in the lights.

JOHNNIE moves towards HENRY, who can see him now. HENRY is terrified. As HENRY speaks, JOHNNIE drums and dances a frightening dance, reaching out for him and beckoning him to follow. HENRY is reliving his nightmare.

HENRY Johnnie! I . . . I'm scared Johnnie! Nobody understands. Do you, Johnnie? I hope you do. I did so much praying in that sweatlodge. I tried to do what they said and look inside myself. And to the Creator, and the grandmother and grandfather spirits. It was like I could never come clean. I need help!

JOHNNIE So you want some help?

HENRY I don't know. I'm scared.

JOHNNIE Our people have forgotten the old ways, Henry. Now I'm here to show you the way. Just give me your hands and let me help you along, my brother. Come with me up the river and meet the old people. You can get rid of all your fears and be happy in the land of the old bones. See the beaver. The beaver's tail is right in front of you. The beaver is strong and sleek, Henry. You can see its fur glistening just ahead of you. Grab onto the tail Henry and let it pull you home.

HENRY

Slow down! Wait! My boots are dragging me down. It's getting colder. The ice is cutting into me! I'll never make it.

JOHNNIE

You're not far from shore Henry. You can always yell for help, or you can try to claw your way through the ice. You're strong, my blood brother. Remember how we helped each other through thick and thin. Just give me your hand and I'll help you.

HENRY

No! I'm little and weak.

JOHNNIE

So what does your life mean, Henry? It's time to face the truth, Henry. It's time to face yourself . . . You'll be so proud to be yourself again.

HENRY

How can I be proud of myself with my boots stuck at the bottom of this goddamned river!

JOHNNIE

Okay, Henry, die on that river bottom. Say goodbye to Rosie. And your mother and father. And goodbye to yourself too.

HENRY

I don't deserve them anyways!

JOHNNIE

Come with me up the river, Henry. You can come clean. The river washes your soul clean, good as new, Henry. Your soul will be clean and new.

HENRY

Will it really, Johnnie?

JOHNNIE

I wouldn't lie to you, would I?

ACT TWO

Scene One

December 21ˢᵗ. Early morning. Sound of knocking and arctic wind in darkness. HENRY shows up at DAVE's place, needs a place to crash.

HENRY knocks persistently on DAVE's door, huddling himself to get warm. Finally DAVE answers.

DAVE   *(groggy)* Hey man, what happened to you? Did Rosie kick you out again?

HENRY   I walked out on her.

DAVE   You look like shit.

HENRY   I need a place to crash.

DAVE   Get in here. Come on, we don't want to heat the whole fuckin' Yukon.

HENRY enters, looking very freaked out.

DAVE   You want a drink? I got some J.D. stashed.

HENRY   No.

DAVE   You wanna talk or something?

HENRY   I don't know.

DAVE   Hey your old bed's still here. You want your favourite blanket? I think it's still in the closet.

HENRY   Thanks.

DAVE   Mom'll be glad to see you. You gotta stay for breakfast, eh Henry?

DAVE exits.

HENRY   *(suddenly explaining)* After waiting so long to touch her again and hold her, really hold her, I walk out on her. I felt like I was gonna explode. I wanted to hit someone, anyone. It scared me. I ran out the door and down the hall and outside and I just started to cry.

And I couldn't stop. It was like I was five years old again. All alone in the dark. No friends in the world. Five years old. *(beat)* I think I'm going crazy.

> *DAVE returns with blanket as HENRY speaks. DAVE doesn't know what to say or do. He awkwardly tries patting HENRY and puts the blanket over him.*

DAVE   It's all right Henry, you're with Dave again. You can stay here as long as you want.

Scene Two

> *ROSIE'S apartment. December 21st. RUTH knocks on door. ROSIE opens door.*

RUTH   Rosie, I'm really sorry about last night.

ROSIE   Whatever.

RUTH   I was really drunk.

ROSIE   Sure.

RUTH   You have to hear me out. Please.

ROSIE   Okay, I'm listening.

RUTH   I just lost it . . . the anniversary of Johnnie and everything . . .

ROSIE   Well you got what you wanted. I walk out on you, and Henry walks out on me.

RUTH   When was this?

ROSIE   Right after I got home last night. You gave me lots of ammunition for my fight with Henry. I had such big dreams and now everything's a mess.

RUTH   Rosie! Look at yourself. You don't need Henry. I'm so proud of you.

ROSIE   For what?

RUTH   Oh, don't give me that! So you had a fight with Henry. It's not the end of the world.

ROSIE	Things were going to be different. Now it's all fallen apart.
RUTH	He's the one who walked out on you, right?
ROSIE	Yeah, but I was out drinking with you.
RUTH	I hope you're not blaming yourself for Henry's problems. Forget about what Henry's feeling.
ROSIE	How can you say that . . . ?
RUTH	Just wait. I don't mean it like that. I mean think about yourself. What are *you* feeling? You have to think about yourself first and what makes you happy.
ROSIE	I thought that me and Henry could make each other happy.
RUTH	Henry can't make you happy. Henry's never made you happy. You have to do that for yourself. Look, what kind of things make you feel good?
ROSIE	Being with Henry.
RUTH	Besides that.
ROSIE	Dancing, I guess.
RUTH	Yeah.
ROSIE	Writing in my journal.
RUTH	What else?
ROSIE	Graduating top of my class.
RUTH	See! Jeez, girl, not everyone could do that! I couldn't.
ROSIE	Look at you raising your kids all by yourself and working too.
RUTH	You know what? We're both pretty damn smart women! And you're gonna be okay whether Henry walks back in that door or not. Right?
ROSIE	What if he doesn't come back? He was so mad when he left. What if he's drinking again? What if . . . Maybe I should've gone after him.

RUTH	*(angry)* Henry's fine! Stop babysitting him. So what if he's drunk, you can't chase after guys all the time!
ROSIE	It's freezing outside.
RUTH	Quit wasting your time worrying about him and worry about your own life!
ROSIE	How can you talk like that? You were the same with Johnnie . . .
RUTH	You don't know . . . Forget it.
ROSIE	*(beat)* Maybe we should do something special tonight. Something for Johnnie. Let's light a candle for him.
RUTH	Yeah. Sure, okay.
ROSIE	Here, you light it.
RUTH	No, that's okay. You do it.

The ritual proceeds.

Scene Four

December 21st. DAVE, BIG JOE and HENRY entering a bar.

DAVE	I always said ya' can't trust women.
BIG JOE	All he said was she didn't tell him about it. Doesn't mean she wasn't going to.
DAVE	Listen, Henry. If she was going to tell you don't you think she would have by now?
BIG JOE	Hey, you gonna get your grade twelve, Dave? I remember you talking about it.
DAVE	No and shut up. I got better things to do.
BIG JOE	Hey, I was just checking.
HENRY	Maybe she was waiting for a special time.

BIG JOE	Yeah, Rosie's kind of romantic. 'Member she got you all them roses that time? A girl sending a guy roses! Pretty funny!
DAVE	What do you know about romance? Your old lady just took a hike.
BIG JOE	Least I had an old lady. Better than you . . .
DAVE	Why would I want some broad? Look at you guys whining and snivelling over them. I don't need complications.
HENRY	Don't you ever get lonely?
DAVE	You kidding?! I got you and Big Joe. The three of us, that's something you can always count on. Listen we got to stick together boys. Even the girls know that. I mean look at Rosie and fucking Lorraine.
BIG JOE	So what about Rosie and Lorraine?
HENRY	Yeah, what about them?
DAVE	Come on, you guys . . . Lorraine had no money to take off to Vancouver. Where do you think she got it? Her good friend Rosie, that's who. You're not that fucking stupid are you?
HENRY	Rosie never told me that.
BIG JOE	Rosie did that?
DAVE	Yup. And if I was you Henry, I'd be asking myself what else that bitch has been hiding from you. What was she doing all them long lonely nights you were in jail?

Pause. HENRY thinks about this.

DAVE	You can't trust her now, can ya? Her or Lorraine. That means we got to stick together. Right?
BIG JOE	Right.
DAVE	*(to JOE)* Hey, Joe, our buddy looks ex-treeeem-ley dehydrated here. He's had a rough ride . . . his old lady hiding stuff on him and all.

BIG JOE	You don't look so good, Henry. A beer might help.
DAVE	Just one eentsy teentsy weentsy little sip. Yum yum!
BIG JOE	Yeah, that coffee's gonna kill you, man.
HENRY	Drop it.
DAVE	Drop a beer? That's sacrilege! No, stupid, I said drink it!
HENRY	I ain't got no money anyways.
DAVE	I'll buy my cousin a beer.
HENRY	Okay.
DAVE	What?!
HENRY	I said okay. You can buy me a beer.
DAVE	Whoa! Do I need my hearing aid checked or what?
HENRY	I just said I'll have one bloody beer, don't piss your pants over it.
DAVE	Yeeha! He's ba-a-ack!
BIG JOE	I'll buy you one Henry. But I ain't buying one for this fuckhead.
DAVE	Ooooh, tough words. I'm gonna go home and cry.
BIG JOE	To your mommy . . .
DAVE	You fat fuck . . .
HENRY	(*interrupting*) For chrissakes! Can we just have some fun? For a change?
DAVE	All right! Beers and cheers!
BIG JOE	Beers and cheers!
HENRY	Fuckin' eh!

JOHNNIE does a beer dance, bringing more and more beer as the guys get drunker and drunker. Fast speed, silent movie style to indicate passage of time. After JOHNNIE delivers each round, he physically taunts HENRY, a little more each time.

HENRY goes into party mode, then becomes belligerent, picking a fight with JOHNNIE. DAVE and JOE have to drag him out of the bar, kicking and screaming.

Scene Five

Outside a local bar. It's night and dark. DAVE and BIG JOE enter nervously, each grabbing tightly onto one of HENRY's arms and dragging him as quickly as they can. HENRY is actively resisting. His knuckles are raw and he has blood on his face.

DAVE   Fuck, Henry, take it easy, man!

HENRY   I'm gonna kill that fucker! Kick his head in! Where is he?

HENRY breaks free, DAVE and BIG JOE regain control.

BIG JOE   Ouch! Henry, it's me! Big Joe.

HENRY   Where the fuck is he?!

DAVE   Shit, we gotta get outta here. Before someone in the bar calls the cops. We need a cab.

BIG JOE   I don't see none around. Ow! Henry! I'm your buddy!

HENRY   Let go of me you assholes! You pale-faced pigs!

BIG JOE   Fuck! I never been called no white guy. I sure ain't ever been called a cop.

DAVE   He's drunk, dummy. Drunker than drunk.

HENRY   Bloody cops!

DAVE	Henry! Look at me! I said, look at me! It's Dave. I'm not a goddamned cop! But you're gonna see one pretty damn fast if you keep fighting me like that!
HENRY	I'm gonna get you! Put you in jail this time! See how you fucking like it.
BIG JOE	I'm getting cold.
HENRY	That guy's asking for it! Goddamned screw! Your face is gonna kiss this boot!
BIG JOE	I think we should get him home.
DAVE	Would you just stop thinking and get us a cab!

> *HENRY bites BIG JOE'S hand. BIG JOE lets out a huge wail.*

BIG JOE	Oh fuck! He bit me! He bit me! Henry bit me!
DAVE	Shut the fuck up.
HENRY	How'd you like that you asshole!
BIG JOE	Ow! I think it's bleeding!
DAVE	Jesus Christ!
BIG JOE	Ow, I need a Band-Aid!
DAVE	Quit your wailing and find a fucking taxi!
BIG JOE	I'm trying . . . Ow, Jeez!
DAVE	Hurry up!
HENRY	Fucking double-crossing Dave . . .
DAVE	What the . . . ?
HENRY	And Big Joe.
BIG JOE	What about me?
DAVE	Keep looking!
HENRY	And Rosie. Fuck all of you!
DAVE	I see one. Wave him over.
BIG JOE	I'm doing it as good as I can.

HENRY	Get off my back! Just leave me alone!
DAVE	Wave harder!
BIG JOE	*(yelling)* Over here! Hey! Over here!
HENRY	And Bruiser . . .
DAVE	*(yelling)* It's an emergency!
BIG JOE	I think he's coming.
HENRY	Just 'cause you done it you think anybody else can. Just go to a few sweatlodges, say a few prayers and that's it . . .
BIG JOE	Henry's really acting wierd.
DAVE	Is this something you just noticed?
HENRY	Well fuck your religion and your fucking feelings and fuck you too!

HENRY spits in DAVE's face.

DAVE	Henry, you're pushing this too far.
HENRY	Did you hear that? I said fuck you too!

HENRY spits again. DAVE hits HENRY.

BIG JOE	Come on Dave, don't. He don't know what he's saying.

The two of them are down fighting.

DAVE	Henry, you've been nothing but a pain in the ass ever since you got out.
BIG JOE	Dave . . .
DAVE	I don't know what they did to you in there . . .
BIG JOE	Dave! The cab's here! Break it up!
DAVE	Fuckin' born-again Indian . . . worse than . . . I don't know what . . .

BIG JOE pulls them apart.

BIG JOE	Dave! Snap out of it!

DAVE	Okay. Okay. Let's get the hell out of here!
HENRY	I'm gonna kill you!

DAVE and BIG JOE pull HENRY offstage.

Scene Six

RUTH and ROSIE are at ROSIE's apartment later that night, December 21ˢᵗ. ROSIE is pulling out some of her dolls from JOHNNIE.

ROSIE	There's this one . . . Oh I remember this one . . .
RUTH	I can't believe how many dolls he gave you.
ROSIE	I always knew what Johnnie would give me for Christmas.
RUTH	When did he start that?
ROSIE	I was ten years old. The puppy chewed up my favourite doll. I cried and cried. Mom and Dad told me to grow up. They said I was too big for dolls anyways. That year there was a doll under the Christmas tree . . . the tag said it was from Santa. The next year the same thing happened, and every year after that. I never knew who Santa was. Until I was sixteen. I caught Johnnie swearing away, trying to cover this huge doll in wrapping paper.
RUTH	Every Christmas he talked about what kind of doll he was going to get you. Each doll had to be different. *(beat)* Wish he spent as much time shopping for me.
ROSIE	He loved you, Ruth.
RUTH	. . . Sure.
ROSIE	That beautiful kitchen table, he made that for you.
RUTH	For me and the boys. More the boys, I think. Explaining it every step of the way, trying to teach them.
ROSIE	He never made me anything like that.

RUTH   Yeah well. He *usually* grabbed a bottle of perfume for me at the mall and paid for the wrapping job.

JOHNNIE enters.

ROSIE   *(beat)* What do the boys want for Christmas? I haven't got them anything yet.

RUTH   I can't think about it.

ROSIE   Let me shop for them. *(beat)* Come on, Ruth.

RUTH   No!

ROSIE   Please. I want to.

Sound of gunshot.

RUTH   *(beat)* Rosie, there's something I never told you.

Flashback to December 21ˢᵗ one year earlier, RUTH and JOHNNIE.

JOHNNIE   You're the one with the job. Band manager trainee. You might as well buy all the presents this year. It's not like I have anything to contribute.

RUTH   I told you not to buy that snowmachine.

JOHNNIE   How was I supposed to know the government would cancel the contract? It was all signed and sealed.

RUTH   I don't like buying more than we can pay for. You know that.

JOHNNIE   First time in years I did that. I go crazy stuck in town all winter. Besides, the boys really like it.

RUTH   They like Christmas presents too.

JOHNNIE   Get them some then. Your old man's broke.

RUTH   We'll go shopping together.

JOHNNIE   *(laughs)* Just like the old man.

RUTH   What are you talking about?

JOHNNIE	Mom busy cooking at Yukon Hall, me making Kraft Dinner and fried meat for little Rosie, Dad out pinching bums and babysitting the bottle. Go Dad go.
RUTH	You're not like that anymore.
JOHNNIE	Aren't I?
RUTH	You don't fool around like you used to. I'd know if you were, I could tell.
JOHNNIE	Could I tell?
RUTH	What's gotten into you?
JOHNNIE	Nothing.
RUTH	You're coming shopping with me. They're your kids too.
JOHNNIE	Are they?
RUTH	Not this again!
JOHNNIE	How come Charles don't look like me?
RUTH	Johnnie!
JOHNNIE	*(holding her)* One week gone, lots of time for you . . . While the cat's away . . . that's what they say, isn't it. Ruth got one up on her old man. She sure showed him two can play the game, knew how to shame him in front of everybody, just give him a son that doesn't belong to him, that don't look like him, and let everybody talk. And boy do they talk!
RUTH	Stop it!
JOHNNIE	All those meetings you have . . . no other wife in the village has so many meetings and conferences as you . . .
RUTH	You know what the problem is? You cheated on me all the time! You think because you can't resist, everyone else is just like you!
JOHNNIE	Lots of nice handsome young men at those meetings, those college guys. And poor old Johnnie back at home mixing formula for someone else's baby . . .

RUTH	You and Henry! Always whoring around on Rosie and me . . .
JOHNNIE	Yeah, I stop and what do I get? My old lady starts screwing around.
RUTH	*(sarcastic)* Yeah. Maybe I should. Maybe I should screw one of your friends.
JOHNNIE	See! I knew it!
RUTH	Which one should I choose? They're always crashed here, it would be so easy. Let's see, Dave? Naw, he's too inexperienced. Prob'ly wouldn't even know what to do! Big Joe's kinda nice, I bet he'd be good in the sack.
JOHNNIE	Henry. That's who it is.
RUTH	Yeah. Henry's as handsome as you but he doesn't know it like you do, that's what a girl likes, a good-looking guy who's a little bit shy . . .
JOHNNIE	You and Henry, right under my nose . . .
RUTH	*(sarcastic)* You're right! All these years I've been doing it with Henry!
JOHNNIE	I fuckin' knew it!

       JOHNNIE storms out, RUTH yells after him.

RUTH	Johnnie!

       RUTH / JOHNNIE flashback ends. ROSIE and RUTH still at ROSIE's place, RUTH is crying and ROSIE is also emotional.

RUTH	He just slammed the door and took off! I didn't know where he was going.
ROSIE	Why didn't you tell me?
RUTH	I don't know . . . I felt guilty. I should have gone after him.
ROSIE	You went and told Johnnie flat-out that you were doing it with Henry.
RUTH	I never said that, Johnnie did.

ROSIE His best friend. Henry. I can't believe you said that to Johnnie.

RUTH He was acting crazy! He was making me crazy! That's what I'm trying to tell you but nobody believes me 'cause Johnnie was so perfect!

DAVE and BIG JOE enter loudly, supporting HENRY, who's been fighting.

ROSIE Oh my God! Henry! *(to DAVE and BIG JOE)* What happened?

DAVE He got in a fight.

ROSIE No kidding.

BIG JOE We tried to stop him. He just flipped out on us.

HENRY The guy picked a fight with me.

DAVE What do you expect when you call his girlfriend ugly!

BIG JOE He was even fighting us. He bit me too. Look! It was bleeding!

RUTH You guys never change.

DAVE We got him out of there fast.

HENRY You shoulda let me finish him off.

RUTH Yeah. Then they can lock you up for good.

HENRY You stay out of this.

ROSIE Stop it! Both of you! *(to HENRY, mad)* I thought you didn't want to go back to jail. Guess I was wrong.

HENRY You all expect me to go back. I don't want to disappoint you.

ROSIE That's a real great attitude.

HENRY You don't want my kids. I got the message all right.

ROSIE Oh, you're mad at me. So you go and do this again.

RUTH Go for it, Henry. Get that return ticket to jail.

HENRY	Matsqui, B.C. and me!
BIG JOE	Henry I don't want you to go back there.
RUTH	Henry misses those sweatlodges so much he can't wait to get back.
HENRY	No wonder Johnnie wanted to screw around. It was all he could do to get away from you!
RUTH	What?!
HENRY	One thing I don't understand . . . why Johnnie gave a shit about you cheating on him!
RUTH	I never cheated on him!
HENRY	I don't know about that. Johnnie sure thought you were playing around.
RUTH	Yeah right. And who did he think I was having a big affair with, Henry? Maybe it was the same friend who was with him when he died!
BIG JOE	Ruth and Henry . . . did they really?
DAVE	Sssssh! Shut the fuck up.
RUTH	That was the night Johnnie decided I was fooling around with you, Henry. *(to ROSIE)* Pretty funny, huh? Pretty funny that you're the only one with him when he dies. Pretty funny you tell us it was an accident.
HENRY	I'm sick of you spreading lies about me.
RUTH	The truth hurts, Henry.
HENRY	Don't listen to her, Rosie, she's poison.
ROSIE	Henry, did you get in a fight with Johnnie?
HENRY	It wasn't my fault! You treat me like I'm a criminal! You all think I'm some kind of murderer! I'm not! It wasn't like that!

Lighting change. Final flashback to one year ago. The guys have just arrived at Long Lake and they've gotten out of the truck drinking beer. The Northern Lights are active and JOHNNIE is standing with two guns.

JOHNNIE   Yee-hoo!

DAVE   Johnnie, you fuckin' pulled her out at the last second! That was great! I was staring at the tree, I was figuring my face was gonna be wearing it! Coming round that curve and starting to hit the ditch but you pulled her out, the last second, hah! One second it's a tree saying Hello Dave and then we're back on the road! Joe, crack me another beer there.

HENRY   I thought we'd be pushing the truck out for sure. You musta been pushing eighty there.

JOHNNIE   Could have gone eighty-five.

BIG JOE   You're the best drunk driver I know.

DAVE   Joe, where's my beer?

BIG JOE   Get your own damn beer. I'm freezing.

DAVE   Have fun rolling around back there?

BIG JOE   I ain't riding back there on the way back.

JOHNNIE   Anyone for rabbit?

HENRY   Hunting! All right! I haven't been out in ages!

HENRY takes one of the guns

BIG JOE   It must be forty below, Johnnie.

HENRY   Start trekking around in the bush. You'll warm right up!

DAVE   Pretty skinny rabbits this time of year.

HENRY   Hey you're the one who wanted to go for a spin. Don't quit the party now, cuz.

JOHNNIE   Rabbit stew for Christmas! That's what I'm gonna give everybody! See what Ruth thinks of that!

HENRY   Oh I miss Mom's rabbit stew.

BIG JOE   Let's make some snares, Johnnie, like we used to, when we were kids. We'll get some wire and come back tomorrow.

JOHNNIE   I want rabbit stew now.

DAVE   You drove us all the way out here on the longest night of the year for target practice on Bugs Bunny in the dark?

HENRY   Yeah! A Long Lake rabbit! Don't listen to them, Johnnie, they couldn't shoot their way out of a paper bag.

JOHNNIE   Northern lights'll help us. Look at them dancing now! Yee-hoo!

>*JOHNNIE starts a wild dance with his gun. HENRY joins in. They dance around BIG JOE.*

BIG JOE   Johnnie, you're acting like some wild man.

JOHNNIE   Don't you know the rabbit dance? Every good Indian does!

HENRY   Try it Joe. Put your cute little bunny ears up like this and hop around. Come on Dave. Call those little rabbit spirits.

>*BIG JOE joins in reluctantly.*

DAVE   You guys are wasted.

HENRY   Dave's sober! Omigod! Those rabbits won't believe their ears!

DAVE   Okay you guys, you had your fun. Let's have a beer and head back to town.

JOHNNIE   You have your beer. I want fresh meat.

DAVE   Come on, we'll go to the Capital.

>*JOHNNIE heads into the bush and HENRY follows.*

BIG JOE   Don't go too far in, Johnnie.

HENRY	*(calling back)* Don't worry, he knows what he's doing!
DAVE	You sound worried about your big idol. That's so touching it makes me want to cry.
BIG JOE	Shut up Dave.
DAVE	*(loud fake crying)* Waaaaaaaaaa!
BIG JOE	I think we should check on them.
DAVE	I'm getting in the truck.

> *DAVE exits. BIG JOE doesn't know which way to go. There is a gunshot off-stage.*

BIG JOE	*(yelling)* Johnnie! Did you get one?
HENRY	*(offstage)* Johnnie! Where are you?

> *BIG JOE exits in the direction JOHNNIE went. JOHNNIE appears, dancing with his gun. HENRY watches behind.*

JOHNNIE	I used to have the power. Dancing made people so happy. Dancing for Mom. *(beat)* I feel so alone . . . so scared . . . like I'm gonna explode. All alone in the dark.

> *JOHNNIE shoots twice more. HENRY approaches and JOHNNIE aims at him. Freeze.*

HENRY	Be careful, you're gonna hit one of us!
JOHNNIE	You think I don't know how to fire a gun?
HENRY	Joe or Dave might be taking a whizz behind some tree.
JOHNNIE	They're back in the truck, cuddling up and getting pissed. You and me are getting rabbits.
HENRY	Cut it out Johnnie, you're acting crazy.
JOHNNIE	Don't you think I can get a rabbit?
HENRY	I never said that.
JOHNNIE	Don't you think I'm gonna get my Ruth some rabbit stew?

HENRY	I didn't say that.

> *JOHNNIE motions HENRY to join him.*

JOHNNIE	*(looking at Northern lights)* Nice and quiet out here . . . I been thinking . . . You remember the story about Man Without Fire?
HENRY	Sure Johnnie, my Jijii's favourite. It's been a long time since I heard it.
JOHNNIE	He's this great chief. Everybody loves him. Then this enemy tribe comes and kills all his people. But Man Without Fire escapes. And his wife — they don't kill her — they keep her 'cause she's real smart. Her name is Back and Forth Between Tribes, because she's been caught other times before this, eh? Man Without Fire wanders around for a real long time, looking for his wife. It's winter. He just lives on rabbits, until he gets to this other camp of people. He tells them all about the enemy and they get ready to fight them.
HENRY	It's damn cold out here Johnnie.
JOHNNIE	*(stopping him)* Just wait . . . I'm not finished.
HENRY	Okay Johnnie . . .
JOHNNIE	Put your gun down.
HENRY	Sure Johnnie.

> *HENRY carefully puts the gun down. JOHNNIE sits and HENRY joins him.*

JOHNNIE	See all this time Man Without Fire is looking for his wife, she never gives up either. She marks the trail by making scratches on the trees. And she puts Indian paint on the bottom of her moccasins. Man Without Fire finds that enemy tribe. His wife is waiting. His wife has been waiting years for that day. The warriors kill all the enemy, all because of his wife. Then they rescue her.
HENRY	Great story Johnnie. Now let's get back to the truck.

JOHNNIE	*(stopping HENRY and circling him)* That's love, Henry. A wife that does that for her man. I wanted my wife to be like that, Henry. Loyal to the end.
HENRY	She is. Ruth would do anything for you.
JOHNNIE	I used to think that, Henry. But Ruth's not like that. I know for sure now.
HENRY	What are you talking about?
JOHNNIE	She's cheating on me.
HENRY	No way, Johnnie.
JOHNNIE	You know what they say about Charles — they say he doesn't look like me. You think I don't hear it?
HENRY	People have to talk. They can't find something, they make it up.
JOHNNIE	I know who she slept with.
HENRY	Johnnie it's getting cold, let's go talk about this over a beer in the truck, come on . . .
JOHNNIE	She came right out and told me it was you.

JOHNNIE aims the gun at HENRY.

HENRY	It's not true, Johnnie! I wouldn't do that to you . . .
JOHNNIE	You and me had some hot times there . . . lots of girls . . . never thought you'd steal my own wife.
HENRY	*(as HENRY speaks he gets closer to JOHNNIE so that by the end of the speech, JOHNNIE'S gun is right against his chest)* Hey Johnnie, I didn't . . . Johnnie no! You forgot something about that story, Johnnie . . . You forgot about the chief's friend. He had a friend, remember? Big Stone. Big Stone went to live with the enemy tribe. When Man Without Fire escaped, his friend gave him his mitts, to help him survive the winter. And when Man Without Fire came back for revenge, he didn't kill Big Stone . . . He made sure his friend was out hunting caribou. Man Without Fire didn't want to kill Big Stone. They were friends.

JOHNNIE	Big Stone never fooled around with his friend's wife.
HENRY	Neither did I!
JOHNNIE	*(pushing HENRY away with the gun)* Are you the real daddy?
HENRY	Johnnie, you're gonna hurt someone . . .
JOHNNIE	No fucking kidding.

JOHNNIE sits and turns the gun on himself.

HENRY	*(screaming and lunging to stop JOHNNIE)* Holy fuck Johnnie! Don't!

Flash of light and gunshot. Blackout.

Lighting change back to the present in ROSIE's apartment. ROSIE is hugging her first doll from JOHNNIE. RUTH is in shock.

HENRY	I tried to stop him! Don't you see? I couldn't talk any sense into him.
ROSIE	No! That's not what happened! That's not it at all!
HENRY	He wouldn't listen to me, Rosie.
ROSIE	No! Johnnie did not . . . he would never kill himself . . .
HENRY	Johnnie committed suicide.
ROSIE	I can't listen.
HENRY	I'm telling you the truth.
ROSIE	You're drunk. Why should I believe you?
HENRY	You have to.
ROSIE	I don't have to do anything! He was strong. He gave me dolls.
HENRY	He was depressed. I know he was.
ROSIE	Now you tell me my brother was depressed! Why didn't you tell me sooner?! Why didn't you come to me?! Why did you lie to me?!

RUTH	I didn't know what to do! I couldn't tell you. I wanted to protect you. He was so important to you, to all of us. I don't know. I'm sorry, Rosie.
RUTH	You losers. About the only thing you guys are good at is fucking up. You just aren't happy until everything is totally fucked up, are you?
BIG JOE	I didn't know what happened . . .
RUTH	Of course you didn't. You and your so-called buddies are so clued out you wouldn't even realize if you saw the whole thing. You don't even realize what you've done. My kids. My kids don't have a father anymore. Rosie, they took your brother away.

RUTH exits.

HENRY	Rosie, I didn't mean to hurt you. I love you so much.
ROSIE	All these months I'm on my own waiting for you to get out, reading your letters about healing yourself and you couldn't even tell me what happened to my own brother! Get out! All of you, get out of here!
BIG JOE	I'm just leaving, Rosie.
DAVE	Come on, let's go.

DAVE grabs HENRY, who struggles to stay.

HENRY	You're an angel and I'm not an angel, and neither are you Johnnie. He tried to take me up the river with him It's fucking cold in there.
DAVE	Henry you are making no sense at all. I'm taking you home, man.
HENRY	It's hard to be an angel. We can't all be angels.

The guys exit, dragging HENRY out.

ROSIE is left alone, with JOHNNIE and her dolls.

ROSIE

No. We can't all be angels. Did you hear that, Johnnie? Tell me it isn't true. I guess you can't, can you? What am I going to do, Johnnie? You were always there to catch me, to cushion the fall. Was I the only one who didn't know you? No big deal, right? You didn't have to tell me. A man and wife thing, sure, I understand. Little Rosie wouldn't know anything about that. Best to keep it to yourself, you're a big hero, wouldn't want to spoil your image. But I'm your sister, Johnnie . . . ! The keeper of the dolls, remember. You gave them to me and I took care of them. I was there to help you too, Johnnie. Couldn't you just let me catch you for once? I would've done it. You would've been so proud of me. I'm strong, you know. But you never gave me the chance. Well guess what, Johnnie . . . I know what I'm going to do!

> *ROSIE grabs a garbage bag and stuffs all of her dolls into it. Then she gets her coat and exits with the bag.*

Scene Seven

> *By the bridge over the river. JOHNNIE dances in the Northern lights.*
>
> *RUTH appears carrying JOHNNIE'S shirt. She sits by the river clutching it and rocking to herself, coming to grips with what she has heard.*
>
> *HENRY appears, distraught. He doesn't see RUTH. He is walking out on the river ice, repeating his nightmare. JOHNNIE is leading him on.*

HENRY

Johnnie! Damn I miss you. I wish you were still here beside me. God it was fun, your laugh, and watching you dance . . . Maybe you know something I don't, brother. It can't be any colder in that river than it is out here. It's warmer, ain't it? That's what you been trying to tell me all this time.

> *HENRY starts taking off his boots and jacket. RUTH notices HENRY.*

RUTH	*(panicking)* Henry, what the hell are you doing?
HENRY	Nice and warm. Now I understand why, Johnnie.
RUTH	Henry! Stay where you are!

> *RUTH tries to reach HENRY, but he's too far out. She keeps trying to reach him.*

HENRY	Leave me alone!
RUTH	I want to talk to you!
HENRY	You think you got it all figured out. You been knocked down so many times but you pull yourself up and you're on your feet again feeling pretty damn cocky 'cause this time you're gonna stay standing, man. And then wham, it's like a Don Cherry Rock'em Sock'em video. Splat, you're back on your ass trying to get the licence plate of the bus that ran you over. I know why he did it. Because it's warm.
RUTH	You're going to freeze. I don't want you to freeze.
HENRY	Don't get any closer.
RUTH	I don't want anything to happen to you Henry. If anything happened . . . I could never forgive myself.
HENRY	I'm going to see him. He's right here with us. Hey, blood brother.
RUTH	I'm sorry, Henry.
HENRY	Ah hell what for? We're all sorry.
RUTH	It was my fault. I thought you took Johnnie away from me, you were the last one to see him, not me. I said the wrong things and he ran out the door. I wish I never said those things to him that night, I wish I could take it back, you don't know how many times I wished I could take it back . . . If only I went after him when he walked out that door . . .
HENRY	It's not your fault, Ruth.
RUTH	Yeah well . . .
HENRY	It's my fault. I should have stopped him.

RUTH   Look at us. Now you and me are in a contest about whose fault it was. No point jumping in some frigging cold river over it, right? Henry?

HENRY   I tried to stop him.

RUTH   I believe you, Henry.

HENRY   You do?

RUTH   Yeah.

> *HENRY walks toward RUTH and safety.*

HENRY   He loved you.

> *RUTH helps HENRY back into his jacket and boots. ROSIE appears on the bridge with the first doll JOHNNIE gave her.*

ROSIE   *(she holds the doll out as she speaks)* It's really hard to say good-bye to you. I had you ever since I was ten and we had a lot of fun times together but you have to go back to Johnnie now and help him on his way . . . out of the Northern lights and up the river to the Land of the Dead. You tell him it's always summer there and the animals are fat and nobody gets sick and the only work he has to do is cut up the meat from the animals he hunts. Well, maybe it's different now. Maybe he'll find some snow and ride his snowmachine, or make some tables or something . . . But he can't stay here . . . trapped . . . dancing around me. He has to be set free . . . and so do I.

> *RUTH and HENRY see ROSIE drop the doll in the river. JOHNNIE catches it and dances off.*

ROSIE   See you 'round sometime.

> *ROSIE exits.*

HENRY   Seems like we should do something.

RUTH   Like what?

HENRY   I don't know. *(beat)* One year after someone died, our people would sing songs praising the person.

RUTH

A potlatch song? You want to sing a happy song after just about jumping in the river?

HENRY

Yes.

RUTH

You're serious?

HENRY

Yes.

RUTH

Well . . . sing it Henry. Sing it!

HENRY

(singing) Johnnie, you're a crazy guy
But I love you, that's no lie
Hottest dancer in the town
Wild women all around

> *RUTH smacks HENRY.*

HENRY

I was singing about you and Rosie! Come on, sing with me.

RUTH

If that doesn't scare him off, nothing will.

> *They laugh together and sing the song again*

Scene Eight

ROSIE in a spotlight with her journal.

ROSIE

I had to push everyone off before I could pull anyone back. I want to get back with Henry with every bone in my body. I want him I want him I want him. Even more than all those months he was in Matsqui. It's agony keeping him away but he needs time to be with himself.

I quit the Sixty today! Yes! No more slinging beer! I'm registered at college now and my band funding should come through next week. They said there might be a job up for a heritage assistant up in Old Crow this summer. Hey it could be my big chance to ask the elders some questions. Where would I start? Reincarnation . . . ? I'll always see Johnnie in those boys of his.

I still walk down by the river and look at the
Northern lights, even though I know Johnnie's not
there anymore, or hanging around like some shadow.
That all seems like a dream from another world now.

Scene Nine

HENRY in the spotlight.

HENRY   It's strange being back in Old Crow after all this
time. I'm learning to jig a lot better. My aunties
stopped giggling at me. Now they just laugh out
loud. But, I'm not blushing . . . I'm proud. After
all, this is me.

I needed to hang out in Old Crow. Spend some time
with the old people, in the old country. They gotta
know how to deal with all this. They've only had a
few millennia to figure it all out. *(beat)* I think a
little time away from Rosie may help us out in the
end. I know most guys are not much different than
me. If I can improve myself a bit then hell, I'll be
the pick of the litter for her, right?

Dave's nose was a little out of joint when I told him
where I was going. I think he was jealous. Here's
one. He said he'll get a job so he can buy a ticket
and come visit me. Think I'll ever see that day? Big
Joe went to Vancouver to try to make up with
Lorraine. I have a feeling he'll be all right.

They say the longest journey is the one you take
inside. They don't tell you it's the scariest. I've just
taken the first few steps, but being back on the land
is a big help. Every time I stand on Caribou
Lookout, watching for the herd crossing the
Porcupine River, I feel alive, something I never felt
all those nights in the Sixty. My nightmares are
gone. But I still remember my dreams. And my
family is there when I wake up. I'm glad, because
life is a long journey.

END

Bibliography

Laguna, Frederica de , ed. *Tales from the Dena: Indian Stories from the Tanana, Koyokuk, & Yukon Rivers.* Seattle and London: University of Washington Press, 1995.

Osgood, Cornelius. *Contributions to the Ethnography of the Kutchin.* New Haven: Human Relations Area Files Press, Reprint from 1933, Yale University Publications in Anthropology, 1970

NOTES ON THE EDITORS

Sherrill Grace is a professor of English at The University of British Columbia, where she teaches 20th century literature and drama. Her publications include books on Malcolm Lowry, Margaret Atwood, and Expressionism, the two-volume edition of Lowry letters, *Sursum Corda! The Collected Letters of Malcolm Lowry*, and articles on Sharon Pollock, Wendy Lill, Judith Thompson, Robert Gurik, Herman Voaden, and Sam Shepard. She is currently writing *Canada and the Idea of North*, to be published by McGill-Queen's University Press.

Eve D'Acth teaches English literature at Yukon College, Whitehorse. Prior to coming to Canada, she taught English at the University of Cape town and the University of Natal (Durban). She has a personal and professional interest in literary representations of the North and teaches a course on the representation of the North in Canadian literature. In addition to her activity with theatre as both the instrument and reflection of the development of community, she has published various works of short fiction and, with Linda Costain, she co-authored a book on teaching Shakespeare in 1989.

Lisa Chalykoff is completing her doctoral dissertation, "Space and Identity Formation in Canadian Narratives," at The University of British Columbia. She has published articles and notes in *Studies in Canadian Literature* and *Canadian Literature*, and a chapter in *Painting the Maple: Essays on Race, Gender, and the Construction of Canada* (1998). Her scholarly interests include interdisciplinarity, theories of identity formation, literary regionalism and nationalism, the politics and poetics of spatial practice, cultural geography, and critical social theory.